THE ACTS OF JOHN:
a two-stage initiation
into Johannine Gnosticism

STUDIES ON THE APOCRYPHAL ACTS OF THE APOSTLES

Edited by T. Adamik, J. Bolyki, J.N. Bremmer (editor in chief), P. Herczeg, A. Hilhorst, G.P. Luttikhuizen and J. Roldanus

In recent years the Apocryphal Acts of the Apostles have increasingly drawn the attention of scholars interested in early Christianity and/or the history of the ancient novel. New editions of the most important Acts have appeared or are being prepared. The series *Studies on the Apocryphal Acts of the Apostles* contains studies of the individual aspects of the main Acts: those of John, Paul, Peter, Andrew and Thomas. So far, six volumes are scheduled.

1. *The Apocryphal Acts of John*, J.N. Bremmer (ed.), Kampen 1995
2. *The Apocryphal Acts of Paul and Thecla*, J.N. Bremmer (ed.), Kampen 1996
3. *The Apocryphal Acts of Peter: Magic, Miracles and Gnosticism*, J.N. Bremmer (ed.), Leuven 1998
4. *The Acts of John: a two-stage initiation into Johannine Gnosticism*, P.J. Lalleman, Leuven 1998
5. *The Apocryphal Acts of Andrew*, J.N. Bremmer (ed.), Leuven 1998
6. *The Apocryphal Acts of Thomas*

Gedrukt met steun van
de Stichting Het Scholten-Cordes Fonds te Rotterdam

# The Acts of John

PIETER J. LALLEMAN

## A Two-Stage Initiation into Johannine Gnosticism

PEETERS

© 1998, Uitgeverij Peeters, Bondgenotenlaan 153, B-3000 Leuven (Belgium)
ISBN 90-429-0573-5
D. 1998/0602/256

CONTENTS

# LIST OF ABBREVIATIONS

| | |
|---|---|
| AAA | Acta Apocrypha Apostolorum |
| AAn | Acts of Andrew |
| AJ | Acts of John |
| APe | Acts of Peter |
| APl | Acts of Paul |
| ATh | Acts of Thomas |
| *FS* | *Festschrift* |
| *IEph* | *Inschriften von Ephesos*, eds. H. Vetters, D. Knibbe *et al.*, 8 vols. (Die Inschriften der griechischen Städten Kleinasiens 11-17), Bonn 1979-1984 |
| *JECS* | *Journal of Early Christian Studies* |
| JK | E. Junod and J.-D. Kaestli (eds.), *Acta Iohannis*, Turnhout 1983 |
| *NA*$^3$ | *Neutestamentliche Apokryphen* II, eds. E. Hennecke and W. Schneemelcher, Tübingen $^3$1964 |
| *NA*$^5$ | *Neutestamentliche Apokryphen* II, ed. W. Schneemelcher, Tübingen $^5$1989 |
| *TynB* | *Tyndale Bulletin* |
| *VigChr* | *Vigiliae Christianae* |
| *ZNW* | *Zeitschrift für die neutestamentliche Wissenschaft* |
| *ZPE* | *Zeitschrift für Papyrologie und Epigraphik* |

Titles of other journals which are abbreviated in the notes are given in full in the bibliography at the end of the book.

I follow the division of the AJ into chapters as introduced in the edition of Bonnet and taken over by JK, who slightly change the points of division between cc.36 and 37, 88 and 89, and 110 and 111 (JK, 66-67). The position of cc.87-105 will be discussed in chapter 2. Numbers after a full stop refer to the lines in the edition of JK (19.2 means c.19, line 2).

Biblical quotations are from the Revised Standard Version unless otherwise stated. Quotations from the AAA usually follow J.K. Elliott (ed.), *The Apocryphal New Testament*, Oxford 1993.

Surveys of earlier research of the AAA in general can be found in G. Poupon, 'Les actes apocryphes des apôtres de Lefèvre à Fabricius', in F. Bovon *et al.*, *Les actes apocryphes des apôtres*, Genève 1981, 25-47, and in J.-C. Picard, 'L'apocryphe à l'étroit: notes historiographiques sur les corpus d'apocryphes bibliques', *Apocrypha - Le champ des apocryphes* 1 (1990) 69-117.

# PREFACE

The present book was written as a dissertation for the Faculty of Theology and Religious Studies of the Rijksuniversiteit Groningen. Most of the work was done from 1993 until 1997, when I was a graduate under the direction of Prof.dr. G.P. Luttikhuizen, Prof.dr. J. Roldanus and Dr. A. Hilhorst. Prof.dr. J.N. Bremmer also assisted in various ways, and he kindly accepted the book for publication as the first monograph in the series Studies on the Apocryphal Acts of the Apostles. Each in their own way, these four persons played a considerable part in my work; I am immensely grateful to them.

My first contact with the Apocryphal Acts of the Apostles came only after I had finished my studies in the Department of Theology of the University of Utrecht, when I was asked to write a review of Lieuwe van Kampen's Utrecht dissertation *Apostelverhalen*. When "Groningen" looked for a graduate to study the Apocryphal Acts, Van Kampen's book greatly helped me to write an application and to have the subsequent interview.

My work on the Acts of John was much stimulated by the annual exchanges with Budapest, which are documented in the other volumes of the series Studies on the Apocryphal Acts of the Apostles.

# INTRODUCTION

The second century is probably the least known period in the history of Christianity. It is the era before the canonisation of the books of the New Testament and before the formulation of the creeds. As a result, it confronts us with a bewildering variety of forms of faith and of religious practice. Next to what is variously called 'emerging mainstream Christianity', 'emerging Catholicism' or 'proto-orthodoxy', there were many other groups, one of which was the Gnostic movement. The Nag Hammadi findings have greatly increased our knowledge about the teachings of this important current; but many factual questions remain unanswered, such as those about its origins, its geographical spread and its relative strength.

The second century is also the period in which the leadership structure of Christianity was still far from uniform. This is one of the reasons why the writings of individuals had a relatively great influence. However, we have only scant information regarding most second-century theologians because their works are completely or nearly completely lost. More than a few of those who were then influential were later branded as heretics. Many important texts are also anonymous or pseudepigraphical.

The proto-orthodox movement came to argue that its adversaries misinterpreted the Scriptures and, towards 200, that the adversaries' origins were too long after Christ's life. In contemporary research judgment in matters of right and wrong is suspended and all voices that reach us from the period receive an equal treatment. Only in this way can the variety of responses to the revelation in Jesus Christ be appreciated. As a result of this approach, there is an ever increasing interest in the full spectrum of the second century's literary works.

Part of this inheritance is formed by the five anonymous Apocryphal Acts of Apostles: the Acts of Paul, Peter, Andrew, Thomas and John. In their present form some of these books probably date from the third or fourth rather than from the second century, but each of them reflects aspects of second-century Christianity. It is generally assumed that they go back to popular Christian beliefs in the Eastern part of the Roman Empire. In later times, the Church rejected these writings, although all five were not equally condemned. The official condemnation could not prevent the considerable influence that the Acts exercised on later popular hagiographical writings. With the possible exception of the Acts of Thomas, however, it did result in the loss of the original textforms.

Recent attention given to the aspects of second-century Christianity that would seem to be peripheral from the point of view of later centuries has also focused more attention on the Apocryphal Acts. Since 1981, a group of French speaking scholars, the AELAC (Association pour l'étude de la littérature apocryphe chrétienne), has undertaken the fundamental task of re-editing the texts and incorporating material discovered since the appearance of the Lipsius and Bonnet standard edition (1890). So far, the Acts of John (Junod and Kaestli, 1983) and those of Andrew (Prieur, 1989) have been published in the Corpus Christianorum, series Apocryphorum, whereas the Acts of Peter (Poupon) and Paul (Rordorf) are still eagerly anticipated.

The research which resulted in the present book takes advantage of the recently published editions. The specific question from which I departed was that of the marginality of the Apocryphal Acts. Were these Acts marginal from the very beginning or were they marginalised in the course of time? What was the position of these texts and their respective authors in their second-century contexts? And as for their afterlife, was it the theological differences between them and the (later) orthodox church, or was it their popularity among groups considered heretic, that led to their being banned?

Thanks to studies such as Lieuwe van Kampen's *Apostelverhalen*, the first Dutch dissertation on the Apocryphal Acts, it soon became evident that the five texts cannot be considered together: they must be treated as individual works with their own specific origins, concepts and interests. Consequently, the Acts of John (AJ) has been selected for further study on account of its fascinating and extraordinary Christology. As the reception of the AJ has already been discussed by Eric Junod and Jean-Daniel Kaestli in their *L'Histoire des actes apocryphes des apôtres du IIIe au IXe siècle: le cas des actes de Jean*, this feature receives only minimal attention in the present work.

In order to form an adequate conception of the AJ, several topics need to be considered. Next to the text's view of the person and work of Christ, there is its attitude towards (sexual) asceticism. Until now, it has generally been assumed that on this subject all five Apocryphal Acts speak with one voice. Likewise, the position of the AJ in relation to Gnosticism, a matter about which contradictory opinions exist, must be carefully examined. In this respect, previous views of the AJ as a two-part text, one non-Gnostic and the other Gnostic, need to be investigated. If correct, such a division of the text is bound to have important methodological consequences for the present research as well as for all future readings of it. And in order to study the AJ in context, the present study is also the first one to survey the text's intertextual relations. From the books of the New Testament, the Johannine writings and Acts of the Apostles most certainly qualify as possible sources of information and inspiration for the author of our text.

The above plan results in the following outline. Chapter 1 will deal with some preliminary questions regarding the constitution of the AJ. Although we have testimonies from Antiquity that it existed, the text has not been preserved in its entirety nor does it exist under its original title. Before it can be studied, the reconstruction suggested by previous scholars must be presented and evaluated. The most vital question in this respect is that of the extension of the original book. I will discuss the textual witnesses and reach a conclusion about which fragments should be included and which not.

After this introductory chapter, chapter 2 will deal with the structure of the AJ. I will suggest that cc.87-105, preserved in only one manuscript, should be located in a different place in the text than the one that is commonly suggested. This chapter will deal with the alleged Gnosticism of this part of the AJ, especially with the hypothesis of Junod and Kaestli that the text consists of two parts, each with different theological viewpoints. Subsequently, the genre of the separate parts and that of the text as a whole must be established. We will also investigate whether the two main parts of the AJ were put together just because they both deal with John or if the text in its final form has a meaningful structure. As a result, the types of thought in the two main parts of our text will be discussed separately. At the end of the chapter, attention will be paid to the readership, circumstances of writing and authorship of these two distinct parts.

These two preliminary chapters open the way for the study of the intertextual relationships and the teachings of the constituent parts of the text. Hence, chapter 3 will deal in detail with the structural and lexical relations that the AJ has with other texts. The survey is preceded by a discussion of the concept of intertextuality and a number of methodological remarks. With regard to the relationship with the Gospel of John and, especially, with the Acts of the Apostles, I will draw conclusions that differ considerably from what has been generally assumed. A consideration of the links with the other Apocryphal Acts will situate the AJ among the Apocryphal Acts. Possible Classical and Nag Hammadi parallels will also be given attention.

In chapter 4 I will focus on the text's concepts, among which, as I said, Christology is the most important. Here again, it will be vital to distinguish carefully between the two main parts that together form the AJ. The polymorphy of the Lord, the mysterious cross of light, the text's concept of salvation, and the applicability of the term docetism will be important points addressed in this discussion.

Chapter 5 will then discuss the text's views on the Christian life, including asceticism. In this respect, many common assumptions about the Apocryphal Acts and about the AJ in particular will be criticised. The importance of looking at each of the Apocryphal Acts individually will once more become clear.

Chapter 6 tries to apply the results of the previous chapters to the study of some particular aspects of the AJ. I will first consider the position of our text among the Johannine writings, especially the conceptual relations to the First Epistle of John. Second, I will try to draw new conclusions regarding the date and place of origin of the text. The book will be rounded off by an epilogue in which the main results are brought together and a few suggestions for future investigations both of the AJ and of the second century as a whole are formulated.

# CHAPTER 1: THE ORIGINAL TEXT OF THE ACTS OF JOHN

## 1 The textual witnesses

We do not have a complete manuscript of the Acts of John and not even a manuscript that contains the title 'Acts of John'.[1] The text that we are going to study has been reconstructed by modern scholars, but nowadays the essential elements of this reconstruction are generally accepted as accurate. I will present an outline of the facts and discuss some marginal matters. The present chapter will provide an introduction to the textual witnesses to the AJ, consider the lacunae in the text and discuss both the original length of the text and the authenticity of disputed fragments.

Many ancient and medieval sources inform us about the existence of the AJ, but the text itself disappeared because the church condemned it several times and prohibited the making and possession of copies.[2] Until far into the last century, episodes from the AJ were only preserved because they had been incorporated into manuscripts of a more recent story about John. This later account, the so-called *Acts of John by Prochorus*, dates from the fifth century and was popular in the Byzantine church.[3] In several medieval copies of this text, there appear episodes that are considerably older than the fifth century and which, taken together, form a rather homogeneous text, the early AJ. The recovery of the AJ from the *Prochorus Acts* was mainly the work of Theodor Zahn and Richard Lipsius.[4]

Nowadays the division of the episodes belonging to the AJ and those

[1] The title Πράξεις 'Ιωάννου first occurs in Eusebius *HE* III.25.6.

[2] E. Junod and J.-D. Kaestli, *L'histoire des Actes apocryphes des apôtres du IIIe au IXe siècle: le cas des Actes de Jean*, Genève/Lausanne/Neuchâtel 1982, deal with the ancient testimonies and the censorship.

[3] The full title is Πράξεις τοῦ ἁγίου ἀποστόλου καὶ εὐαγγελιστοῦ 'Ιωάννου τοῦ θεολόγου, συγγράφοντος τοῦ αὐτοῦ μαθητοῦ Προχόρου, ed. Th. Zahn, *Acta Joannis*, Erlangen 1880, repr. Hildesheim 1975, 1-165. Zahn dates the text between 400 and 600 AD (*ibid.*, lix), JK, 749, prefer the fifth century. Regarding its popularity, see JK, 3 (to my knowledge the study about its manuscript tradition, which Junod and Kaestli promise, has not yet appeared).

[4] Zahn, *Acta Joannis*, esp. the justification of his selection lxxxi-cxlii; R.A. Lipsius, *Die apokryphen Apostelgeschichten und Apostellegenden. Ein Beitrag zur altchristlichen Literaturgeschichte* I, Braunschweig 1883, esp. 44-117 and 348-542. The distinction is not yet made in J.A. Fabricius, *Codex apocryphus Novi Testamenti* II, Hamburg 1703 ($^2$1719). J.C. Thilo, *Colliguntur et commentariis illustrantur fragmenta actuum S. Ioannis a Leucio Charino conscriptorum, particula I*, Halle 1847, made a start with this work.

belonging to the *Acts of John by Prochorus* is beyond dispute. The differences in doctrinal stance between the post-Nicene Prochorus-text and the heterodox AJ are clear to everyone who reads the texts; besides, most of the action in Prochorus is concentrated on the Isle of Patmos, which is never mentioned in the early AJ.

To establish a reliable text for some parts of the AJ we must not only use the Greek manuscripts but also the ancient translations of the text and the Acts of the second Council of Nicea. Since these materials, as well as other later stories about John, will be frequently mentioned in the discussions below, I will now briefly introduce them.

### *1.1 Manuscripts*[5]

The Prochorus-text and the stories from the AJ are frequently found in so-called menologies, books used for daily liturgical readings. In nearly all cases complete episodes from the AJ have been handed down as appendices to the Prochorus-text. My survey of the relevant manuscripts begins with the trio **R**, **Z** and **K**, which contain the longest pieces of text, viz. AJ 18-55, 58-86, 106-115.[6] The text of the AJ preserved in these three manuscripts goes back on a common source, probably from the Isle of Patmos.[7]

**R** (Patmos 188), 16th century.

**Z** (Mezzojuso 2), 16th century, which remarkably resembles **R**.

**K** (Lesbos 82), 1575. Junod and Kaestli have shown that this manuscript is a direct copy of **R**, so that there is no reason to use it.[8]

**H** (Halki 102), a palimpsest which contains parts of the AJ together with other stories about John and other saints. These texts, copied in the 11th century, have been erased and the leaves have been rearranged for the writing (in 1435) of another text. Many leaves have disappeared and much of the erased script is illegible. Where it can be used, this manuscript often provides a longer and better text than all other ones.[9] What we have is a partly legible text of AJ 21-35, 47-52, 59-64, 70-84, 106-115.

**M** (Venice gr. 363), 12th-13th century; this manuscript is an exception to the rule that complete episodes have been transmitted. It contains the full text of AJ 58-76 and a summary of cc.77-80; at the end of the

[5] This survey is heavily indebted to JK, esp. 12-22.

[6] The chapters numbered 1-17 are not part of the original text, see section 2 below.

[7] JK, 22.

[8] JK, 18.

[9] JK, 14, cf. 19-20: '... le texte de H était d'une qualité et d'une fidélité très supérieures à celles du texte RZK.'

episode, which in **R** and **Z** occupies cc.63-86, cc.81-86 are omitted. The scribe has also made changes to the text with the apparent aim of improving its literary qualities.[10]

**O** (Ochrida 4), 10th century, AJ 58-81.20 and 106-115. The leaves of the manuscript that probably contained the complete text of the episode cc.63-86 are lost from 81.20. **M** and **O** have better texts than **R** and **Z**, and Junod and Kaestli generally follow **O**.[11]

Recently a newly found manuscript has been published which contains parts of the episodes AJ 63-86 and 106-115 (viz. cc.84, 85, 106 and 109 in a much abbreviated form; cc.86, 107 and 108 are missing altogether). This manuscript was not yet available to Junod and Kaestli. It was found among the remains of a Manichaean library at Kellis, Egypt, and called Papyrus Kellis 1.[12] It is a fragmentary leaf from a codex that dates from the first half of the fourth century.[13] The opinion of the first editor, G. Jenkins, that this papyrus is a primary witness to the text of the AJ must, however, be doubted.[14] Jenkins assumes that the version of the text in the papyrus and the AJ as we now have it are both dependent on a common ancestor text.[15] However, two things must be said against this assumption. Jenkins overlooks the fact that the text of the Kellis papyrus is theologically more developed than the text of the early AJ and that liturgical formulas have

[10] JK, 21; Zahn, *Acta Joannis*, x-xi.

[11] JK, 24.

[12] First edition by G. Jenkins, 'Papyrus 1 from Kellis. A Greek text with affinities to the Acts of John', in J.N. Bremmer (ed.), *The Apocryphal Acts of John*, Kampen 1995, 197-216; second edition I. Gardner and K. Worp, 'Leaves from a Manichaean Codex', *ZPE* 117 (1997) 139-155, who label the papyrus **A**.I and are rather critical of Jenkins. They suggest (142, 145) that the papyrus also reflects AJ 112 and 114 as well as AJ 75, but the latter case is based on one word only. I. Gardner, 'The Manichaean Community at Kellis', in P. Mirecki and J. BeDuhn (eds.), *Emerging from Darkness. Studies in the Recovery of Manichaean Sources*, Leiden 1997, 161-175, provides an overview of the Kellis findings without mentioning (166) the publication by Jenkins.

[13] Jenkins, 'Papyrus 1', 197; Gardner and Worp, 'Leaves', 141.

[14] Gardner and Worp, 'Leaves', 140, are more cautious: 'It appears that the section ... is not in itself a version of the *Acts of John*, but rather it draws upon a textual tradition also accessed (perhaps at a different stage of development) by the compiler of the known apocryphal work.'

[15] Jenkins, 'Papyrus 1', 215 n.30, thinks of the common source as a kind of eucharistic liturgy and makes the unfounded claim that 'the use of such a document by the compiler of the *AJ* has long been recognised'. There are no reasons to assume that the text of the early AJ that we have is based on a still earlier version.

been added.[16] Secondly, the text in the papyrus is, as a whole, much shorter than the text provided by **R**, **Z**, **H** and **O** because most narrative elements have been eliminated. Though the fragmentary state of the papyrus precludes certain judgment, it appears to consist of the AJ reduced to a set of prayers. It is most probable that the Manichaeans, the original owners of the papyrus, were responsible for this editing.[17] The conclusion that the text provided by Papyrus Kellis 1 derives from the early text cannot be avoided. The value of the papyrus for the study of the ancient AJ is that it preserves original readings of passages where the text has not been abbreviated and where the other manuscripts of the AJ present an obviously corrupt version (e.g. 85.9).

So much for the list of witnesses to cc.18-55, 58-86 and 106-115. The last episode, cc.106-115, has not only been preserved in **H**, **R**, **Z** and **O**, but in fifteen other manuscripts in three different recensions.[18] As I will not deal with this episode very much, there is no need to discuss the manuscripts here. We now come to manuscripts that contain other episodes.

**C** (Vienna hist. gr. 63), 1319, contains cc.87-105. It was first published and studied by M.R. James.[19] This hagiographical manuscript is unique for several reasons. Its Greek is of a very poor quality. It is the only manuscript not to contain later stories about John. Also, it is the only witness to the important cc.87-105 in their entirety, whereas it contains no other parts of the AJ. Junod and Kaestli express doubt if the scribe knew that what he copied was a part of the ancient AJ.[20]

**Q** (Paris gr. 1468), 11th century. This manuscript contains no Prochorus-

[16] In what parallels AJ 84, the papyrus has the phrase 'in the holy church and in the holy ...' (ἐν τῇ ἁγίᾳ ἐκκλησίᾳ καὶ ἐν τῷ ἁγ[ίῳ). Jenkins completes the phrase by adding 'Spirit' (πνεύματι), although references to a Holy Spirit are conspicuously missing in the early AJ. Gardner and Worp, 'Leaves', 155, speak of a liturgical use of the codex to which our fragments belong.

[17] *Pace* Jenkins, 'Papyrus 1', 214-215.

[18] JK, 317-343, have not only printed a reconstruction of the best text, but also separate editions of these recensions.

[19] M.R. James, *Apocrypha Anecdota. Second Series*, Cambridge 1897, ix-xxviii, 1-25, 144-154; details about the manuscript and the circumstances of James' *editio princeps* on ix-xv. The text is also edited by A. Hilgenfeld, 'Der gnostische und der kanonische Johannes über das Leben Jesu', *Zeitschrift für wissenschaftliche Theologie* 43 (1900) 1-61, esp. 6-18; cf. JK, 28 n.1. James, xv, dates the manuscript as a work written in 1324, followed by M. Bonnet, *Acta Apostolorum Apocrypha* II.1, Leipzig 1898, repr. Hildesheim 1959, xxx; Th. Zahn, 'Die Wanderungen des Apostels Johannes', *NKZ* 10 (1899) 191-218, esp. 192; E. Plümacher, 'Apokryphe Apostelakten', in *RE*, Supplementband XV, 1978, 11-70, esp. 15.

[20] JK, 27.

text. It offers the story of John and the partridge, which forms cc.56-57 in the edition of Bonnet. Junod and Kaestli think that this story does not belong to the early text.[21]

Junod and Kaestli discovered a Smyrnean story which they inserted between cc.55 and 58 instead of the partridge-story, with the result that there are now two pieces of text bearing the numbers 56-57.[22] The manuscripts in which Junod and Kaestli found this story are nearly identical and were both written in Constantinople. They distinguish themselves because they contain the *Acts of John by Prochorus* in a different recension than appears in the other manuscripts:

**L** (Athos, Laura Δ 50), 1039.

**S** (Sinai, monastery gr. 497), 10th-11th century.

I will come back on the 'rivalry' for the numbers 56-57 below.

*1.2 Acts of the second Council of Nicea*

In 787, the participants of the second Council of Nicea, the seventh oecumenical Council, debated (and disapproved of) the theological correctness of two episodes from the AJ. As part of the discussions, fragments of these episodes were read aloud to them and consequently became included in the Acts of the Council. These fragments are parts of cc.27-28, 93-95 and 97-98. The Acts are available in several manuscripts, all of which have been edited by Junod and Kaestli.[23] One of the two Latin translations of the Acts is important because it has been preserved in manuscripts from the ninth century, which are much older than the Greek manuscripts of the Acts.[24] For cc.93-95, 97-98 the text in the Acts is to be preferred over that of **C**, the only other witness to that episode. Because the Fathers of the Council quote the AJ by name, the Acts are the certain proof that cc.87-105 indeed belong to the AJ.

*1.3 Hagiographical stories about John*

As stated above, the episodes that form the early AJ, with the exception of cc.87-105, have mainly been preserved in copies of a later story concerning John, the *Acts of John by Prochorus*.[25] There also exist other ancient stories about John. Contrary to earlier scholars, Junod and Kaestli hold that with only one exception, the texts of these stories cannot be used in recon-

[21] JK, 145-153; edition JK, 369-375.

[22] J.K. Elliott, *The Apocryphal New Testament*, Oxford 1993, translates both stories as A and B.

[23] JK, 361-365; cf. Junod and Kaestli, *Histoire*, 123-126.

[24] JK, 344-360, esp. 352, for details about the manuscripts.

[25] On which cf. A. de Santos Otero, 'Jüngere Apostelakten', in *NA*[5], 385-391.

structing the text of the AJ because they were written without direct knowledge of the early AJ.[26] Therefore the *Acts of John by Prochorus*, the *Acts of John in Rome*, the Latin *Passio Johannis* that goes under the name of (Pseudo-) Melito (fifth-sixth century) and the Syriac *History of John* (fourth century) are not used by Junod and Kaestli; I conform to their example.[27]

An example will show that the character of these later stories indeed differs from that of the early AJ. The example is taken from the earliest of them, the *History of John* in Syriac. In this narrative John travels from Jerusalem to Ephesos on foot. On the third day he kneels down and prays:

> Lord Jesus, now that Thy promise is fulfilled, and we have all received of Thy fulness, grant to the garland of Thy disciples, that wherever, Lord, they make mention of Thy birth from the Virgin, and Thy abiding among men, and Thy passion on the Cross, and Thy death and Thy entering within the grave, and Thy resurrection on the third day, and Thy ascension unto Thy Father in Heaven, the feeble race of mankind may be strengthened, ...[28]

It is clear that the theology of this text is completely different from that of the AJ. Examples from the other later stories about John would yield the same conclusion.

The one exception is the *Virtutes Johannis* in Latin, a story that is part of the *Virtutes Apostolorum* (sixth-seventh century) attributed to Pseudo-Abdias.[29] This narrative is important for the establishment of the text of AJ 62-86 and 106-115 because it closely, often literally, follows the Greek version of these chapters.[30] Other parts of the *Virtutes* are much further removed from the early AJ.

[26] JK, 705-710, 715-716, 720.

[27] Junod and Kaestli nevertheless present us with several of these texts, so that their late and independent character can be verified. For the text of the *Prochorus Acts*, see note 3 above, for comments JK, 718-749. The *Acts of John in Rome*, introduction and edition JK, 835-886. Within their treatment of the *Virtutes Johannis*, JK, 750-834, also discuss the *Passio Johannis*, see esp. 764-771. First edition of the *Passio* J.A. Fabricius, *Codex Apocryphus Novi Testamenti* III, Hamburg 1719, 604-623. The Syriac text was edited and translated by W. Wright, *Apocryphal Acts of the Apostles*, 2 vols., London 1871, repr. Amsterdam 1968; cf. JK, 705-717, and De Santos Otero, *NA*$^5$, 391.

[28] Wright, *Apocryphal Acts*, II.5.

[29] Fabricius, *Codex Apocryphus* II, 531-590; in order to replace this edition, Bonnet prepared an edition that was never published; now JK, 750-834, include an introduction and edition. For the stories about the other apostles, Fabricius provides the most recent (!) edition.

[30] JK, 11.

*1.4 Ancient translations*

There are ancient translations of the final episode of the AJ (cc.106-115) into Old-Slavonic, Syriac, Coptic, Armenian, Georgian, Arabic and Ethiopian, and these have some value in establishing a reliable text.[31] Because, as I have said, this episode receives relatively little attention in my research, it is not necessary to discuss these translations in any detail. More importantly, a part of the *Virtutes Johannis* can be considered to be a Latin translation of AJ 62-86 and 106-115.

## 2 The early Acts of John

The first edition of the AJ proper was published by Zahn in 1880. It appears in one volume along with the *Acts of John by Prochorus* for which he used papers from the estate of Constantin Tischendorf.[32] The actual value of Zahn's work lies in his views about several introductory matters; his edition of the text was soon surpassed by the appearance of Max Bonnet's much more complete edition.[33] This latter rendition remained the standard text until the appearance of the edition by Eric Junod and Jean-Daniel Kaestli which provides the basis for the present study.

Most of the important manuscripts were not yet known to nineteenth-century scholars. Zahn could only use the Acts of the Council of Nicea, the *Virtutes Johannis*, manuscript **M** and several witnesses for the final episode (cc.106-115). Bonnet had, in addition, **R** and **C**; **H**, **O** and **Z** are first used by Junod and Kaestli. Nevertheless, their text has not been generally accepted. Both Paul Schneider and Keith Elliott prefer the Bonnet edition;[34] Knut Schäferdiek and his pupil Gerlinde Sirker-Wicklaus use Junod and

[31] Cf. JK, 30, 40-44; they only include an edition of the Coptic version, 376-397. Schäferdiek, *NA*[5], 151, holds that the Slavonic is not a translation of the AJ but of the *Prochorus Acts*. It is unclear why in *NA*[5] the clearly secondary Irish story *Beatha Eoin Bruinne* immediately follows the AJ (191-193) instead of being included with the younger Apocryphal Acts (381ff.).

[32] Zahn, *Acta Joannis*, 219-252. Tischendorf first edited cc.106-115 together with cc.1-14 (on which see below) in *Acta Apostolorum apocrypha*, Leipzig 1851 ([2]1876). For earlier publications see Zahn, *Acta Joannis*, iii-ix; Lipsius, *Apostelgeschichten* I, 34-43.

[33] Bonnet, *Acta Apostolorum Apocrypha* II.1 (1898). Vol. I of *AAA* was published in 1891 by Lipsius, who died in 1892. The three volumes *AAA* are often ascribed to 'Lipsius-Bonnet'.

[34] P.G. Schneider, *The Mystery of the Acts of John. An Interpretation of the Hymn and the Dance in the Light of the Acts' Theology*, San Francisco 1991, 7 n.1 (thinks JK are too free in their alterations); Elliott, *Apocryphal NT*, 307 (no reason given).

Kaestli's work.[35]

The remarkable agreement regarding the authenticity of most of the material now ascribed to the early AJ (cc.18-115, with the exception of cc.56-57)[36] can largely be explained by the homogeneous style of the long narrative parts cc.18-86 and 106-115. The AJ contains stories about John's activities, sermons and prayers. John raises several people from the dead and converts many Ephesians. In the end, he dies peacefully in the grave that has been dug at his request. With the exception of cc.94-102 and c.109, the text also displays great theological coherence.[37]

Junod and Kaestli argue that cc.94-102 and 109 come from another source than the rest of the text does. This hypothesis is based on the observation that cc.94-102 and 109 are strongly influenced by Gnostic theology, while the rest of the text is not clearly Gnostic. The consequences of this hypothesis have not yet been fully explored and a major part of my study will be devoted to investigating them.

Within cc.94-102, the poetic hymn and dance parts (cc.94-96) distinguish themselves from the rest of the section which is in prose. The poetic passage proper (94.7-95.50) is preceded by a few introductory words (94.1-6) and followed by an explanation (c.96) The poetic text addresses all the disciples, whereas John alone is addressed in the framing text. The fact that, in the last part of the dance section (95.43-50), the plural gives way to the singular suggests that this part, addressed to John, has a separate origin.[38] These observations lead to the conclusion that 94.7-95.42 differ from their context in that they are a poetic address to more than one person.[39]

So far nothing has been said about cc.1-17. This silence, however, is caused by the fact that the authentic beginning of the AJ has been lost. The story about John in Rome, edited by Bonnet as cc.1-14 of the AJ, as well as Bonnet's cc.15-17, are generally considered to be later (fourth-fifth cen-

[35] Schäferdiek, *NA*[5]; G. Sirker-Wicklaus, *Untersuchungen zu den Johannes-Akten. Untersuchungen zur Struktur, zur theologischen Tendenz und zum kirchengeschichtlichen Hintergrund der Acta Johannis* (Diss. Bonn), Witterschlick/Bonn 1988.

[36] For cc.1-17, see below.

[37] See chapter 2.

[38] A.J. Dewey, 'The Hymn in the *Acts of John*: Dance as Hermeneutic', *Semeia* 38 (1986) 67-80, 69-74; J.-D. Kaestli, 'Response [to Dewey]', *ibid.*, 81-88, 83; G.P. Luttikhuizen, 'A Gnostic Reading of the Acts of John', in Bremmer, *Acts of John*, 119-152, 129.

[39] Dewey, 'Hymn', 73-74, and Kaestli, 'Response', 86-88, agree that c.94 and some phrases in c.95 are the work of 'a redactor' and that only c.95 consists of older material, which in their opinion originally had the form of a revelation discourse and was turned into a hymn by the redactor.

tury) texts than the early AJ.[40] These stories are colored by a trinitarian theology and are much more 'Catholic' than the early AJ.[41] No other text has been found that can have been the beginning of the early AJ, which means that this beginning has likely been lost. The missing part constitutes the first lacuna in the text.

Another issue concerning the reconstruction of the text has already been mentioned above. There are two mutually independent stories which bear the chapter numbers 56 and 57. Bonnet gave these numbers to the story about John and the partridge found in manuscript **Q**, whereas Junod and Kaestli gave them to the story of the healing of the demon-possessed sons of Antipatros in manuscripts **L** and **S**. As a result we have, on the one hand, too much, but on the other hand too little. By 'too little' I mean that both stories are not connected with what precedes (c.55) and what follows (c.58) them. This disjuncture means that whichever of the two stories we consider original, there is a lacuna of unknown length between cc.55 and 58. An unknown amount of information about John's Asiatic tour, which started and ended in Ephesos, has disappeared.[42]

To return to the two rival stories, neither mentions individuals who figure elsewhere in the preserved text, so that they cannot on that basis be considered parts of the original AJ. We must examine them independently. The partridge story has been preserved as part of a more complete narrative about John which, in its present form, postdates the *Acts of John by Prochorus* and is found only in manuscript **Q**.[43] The story fits loosely into this context and may well be older than the surrounding text. The passage contains no indications of time and place. Besides, Junod and Kaestli observe that it lacks the supernatural elements as well as the prayers and the speeches that are found in all authentic parts of the AJ.[44] As an argument from silence, this reasoning is strong but inconclusive. I want to leave open the questions regarding the authenticity and the original place of the partridge episode. Instead, I will only cautiously use it in my research.

[40] JK, 840-842, 857; text and translation *ibid.*, 862-880. Regarding Bonnet's cc.14-17 see JK, 836 n.2. Bonnet himself doubted the authenticity of what he printed as cc.1-17 (*Acta Apostolorum Apocrypha* II.1, xxviii) though it was defended by Lipsius, *Apostelgeschichten*, 483-484. According to Zahn, 'Wanderungen', 193-194, Bonnet included them because he wanted to use everything that had been contained in Tischendorf's edition, which he meant to replace.

[41] F. Siegert, 'Analyses rhétoriques et stylistiques portant sur les *Actes de Jean* et les *Actes de Thomas*', *Apocrypha* 8 (1997) 231-250, esp. 234-237, argues that the style is also different.

[42] More on lacunae in the next section.

[43] JK, 145-158, 369-375.

[44] JK, 151.

If the story about Antipatros and his sons has to be accepted as authentic,[45] its reference to baptism in the name of the Father, Son and Holy Spirit (57.8-9) must be recognised as a later addition.[46] As it is situated in Smyrna, the geographical information in this episode fits well into the lacuna between cc.55 and 58. The expression 'first of the Smyrnaeans' (56.3)[47] is typical of the AJ and can serve as an important indication that this episode is authentic. I conclude that this episode is probably original.

It is possible that both stories originally belonged to the AJ. In that case one of them is probably out of place and should be placed before c.18. If not, the piece of text which connected them is lost.

## 3 The original length of the Acts of John

So far it is clear that the text of the AJ has at least two lacunae. We must now ask if enough of the original text has come down to us to enable us to make convincing statements about its structure and theology. There is one ancient source which informs us about the length of the AJ. A list of canonical and apocryphal writings, the so-called Stichometry (attributed to Nikephoros, the early ninth-century patriarch of Constantinople), states that the AJ contains around 2500 stichoi.[48] The same number is given for the Gospel of Matthew. The present text has about 1700 stichoi,[49] which means that, if the stichometry is correct, about one third of the text has been lost. Nobody doubts that the list refers to the early AJ, but the numbers given in it cannot always be trusted.[50] I will nevertheless show that what we have of the AJ gives us no occasion to doubt the suggested

[45] It is also preserved in Armenian, see JK, 238 note, and *NA*[5], 144.

[46] In chapter 4, I will demonstrate that the AJ knows neither a divine Son nor a Holy Spirit.

[47] On this expression J.N. Bremmer, 'Magic, martyrdom and women's liberation in the Acts of Paul and Thecla', in *idem* (ed.), *The Apocryphal Acts of Paul and Thecla*, Kampen 1996, 36-59, 41, and *idem*, 'The Novel and the Apocryphal Acts: place, time and readership', forthcoming in H. Hofmann and M. Zimmerman (eds.), *Groningen Colloquia on the Novel* 9, Groningen 1998.

[48] Ed. Th. Zahn, *Geschichte des Neutestamentlichen Kanons* II, Erlangen/Leipzig 1890-1892, 295-301, cf. 384-408, and I, Erlangen 1888, 76; Junod and Kaestli, *Histoire*, 126-127; JK, 71. P.J. Alexander, *The Patriarch Nicephorus of Constantinople*, Oxford 1958, 187, supports Zahn's opinion that the Stichometry is not from Nikephoros. A στίχος, the prose equivalent of a hexameter, is about 16 syllables or 36 letters. Some inferior manuscripts give 2600 or 3600 for the AJ.

[49] JK, 71.

[50] Zahn, *Kanon* II, 403-404; JK, 71 note.

length. Where then are the gaps in the AJ and what stories have disappeared?

*3.1 The lost beginning*

Scholars have put forward several proposals about the lost beginning of the AJ. One possibility is that it resembled the beginning of the ATh, viz. that in the opening scene the apostles were together in Jerusalem and divided the world among them soon after Pentecost. In that episode, John was appointed to go to Asia, and he arrived there, possibly after surviving a shipwreck.[51] Such a scene indeed exists in the *Acts of John by Prochorus* and in the *Acts of John* in Syriac, so that it seems logical to suppose that the authors of these books had found a shipwreck episode in the AJ.[52] But it is now known that these later books were written without direct knowledge of the AJ.[53] There is another reason why it is unlikely that this reconstructed opening is correct. The author of the AJ knew the NT book of Acts quite well.[54] On the narrative level the AJ was a kind of sequel to Acts, though its theology is much different. Consequently, the lost beginning of the AJ must have been in line with what the Lukan Acts tell us. In Acts, the apostles do not leave Jerusalem soon after Pentecost and after casting lots. Instead, they remain in the city for a prolonged period (8:1; 11:1; 15:23; 16:4). The proposal of a division scene at the beginning of the AJ must consequently be rejected because it does not take into account Acts' influence on the AJ.[55]

The second suggestion is based on what the AJ itself narrates in c.113. It says that the text began with John being instructed by Jesus (in Palestine) to remain a virgin and to follow him.[56] Recently, a slightly different form of this hypothesis was put forward, for which there is some evidence in medieval illustrations; in the opening scene, John says farewell to his

[51] JK, 81-82.

[52] So Lipsius, *Apostelgeschichten*, 12-13. The beginning of the *Acts of John by Prochorus* narrates the casting of lots and John's shipwreck, see Zahn, *Acta Joannis*, 3-13: ἔβαλον οὖν κλήρους, καὶ ἔπεσεν ὁ κλῆρος τῆς 'Ασίας ἐπὶ 'Ιωάννην (5); καὶ διεγερθεὶς λαῖλαψ μέγας, ἐκινδύνευε συντριβῆναι τὸ πλοῖον. (...) καὶ δὴ κυρτωθέντων τριῶν κυμάτων καὶ ἀπαφρισάντων δεινῶς καὶ ὑφ' ἓν ἐλθόντων, διερράγη τὸ πλοῖον (8-9).

[53] See above n.26.

[54] I will show this in chapter 3, despite the fact that clear influence of the Lukan Acts on the individual AAA is often denied.

[55] Other valid arguments against this hypothesis in J.-D. Kaestli, 'Les scènes d'attribution des champs de mission et de départ de l'apôtre dans les actes apocryphes', in F. Bovon *et al.*, *Les Actes apocryphes des apôtres*, Genève 1981, 249-264, esp. 261-262.

[56] JK, 83-85; Schneider, *Mystery*, 21 n.1, 22 n.1.

wife and follows Christ.[57] But it is unlikely that a scene about John's decision to become celibate was part of the early AJ because, as it stands, c.113 is a complete episode that tells its own story without looking back on any earlier episode.[58] A story that enlarges on John's celibacy can only be an addition based on this chapter.[59]

Both suggestions discussed so far presuppose that the AJ covered the whole 'apostolic career' of John, but it is not likely that this was the case. At the beginning of John's first stay in Ephesos, there is a scene in which a portrait is made of him showing him as an older man (πρεσβύτης, 27.9). Consequently, unless the lost beginning was very long, John cannot have been a young man at the start of the narrative.[60] It is therefore likely that the AJ only contained stories about the later part of John's career. This observation leads me to venture a third hypothesis: the AJ began with a scene describing the end of John's exile on the isle of Patmos (cf. Rev 1).[61] Such a beginning would fit with the fact that in the first preserved chapter of the text John is in Miletus, which is the natural place to go after leaving Patmos.[62] Against this hypothesis, it could, however, be argued that nothing in the AJ suggests that the author knew Rev.[63] Although it cannot be excluded that traditions about the exile of the prophet John cir-

[57] D.R. Cartlidge, 'Evangelist Leaves Wife, Clings to Christ: An Illustration in the Admont 'Anselm' and Its Relevance to a Reconstruction of the *Acta Ioannis*', in Lovering, *SBL 1994 Seminar Papers*, 376-389.

[58] Cf. JK, 84-85; L. van Kampen, *Apostelverhalen. Doel en compositie van de oudste apokriefe Handelingen der apostelen*, Dissertation Utrecht 1990, 116: 'De beschrijving in c.113 is te gestructureerd en gedetailleerd om aan te nemen dat dit een toespeling op een eerder *verhaalde* episode moet zijn' (italics his).

[59] The majority of the other stories for which Cartlidge found pictorial evidence are also secondary to the AJ. In 'Evangelist', 386, he lists twelve scenes of which only one, 'John realizes that his time is up; he says his last mass while his grave is dug for him', could have belonged to (a Catholicised version of!) the AJ.

[60] Words of the root πρεσβ- denote senior persons in the AJ (30.2, 4; 32.2; 51.2, 10; 52.12). Although the designation of John does not imply that he was older than all others, it, at least, implies a person of advanced age. Note that John is addressed as 'father' and addresses others as 'children'.

[61] I may find some support in Zahn, *Acta Joannis*, cxxiv; *idem*, 'Wanderungen', 198.

[62] W.M. Ramsay, *The Letters to the Seven Churches of Asia*, London $^{2}$1906, 227-228, argues that, in normal sea travel, Ephesos was the natural 'main port' in Western Asia. From Patmos, however, Miletus is much nearer than Ephesos.

[63] See chapter 3. K. Schäferdiek, 'Herkunft und Interesse der alten Johannesakten', *ZNW* 74 (1983) 247-267, esp. 257, 261, seems to argue first that the author of the AJ must have known Rev as part of the Johannine tradition because the AJ was written in the third century, and second that he did not acknowledge it.

culated orally, my suggestion, which implies that the amount of text lost at the beginning of the AJ was not very large, admittedly lacks evidence.

The first scene that has been preserved, which narrates John's travel from Miletus to Ephesos (c.18), also poses several questions. We do not know how long John stayed in Miletus and how much was told about this stay before c.18, for the text begins with his departure and contains no summary. It is probable that Miletus is the first city in Asia that John visited, but even this suggestion is beyond proof. Only new textual finds can reveal what the beginning of the AJ contained. In the meantime, nothing forces us to suppose that the missing beginning of the AJ was very long.[64]

*3.2 Other real lacunae*

It is evident that the miracle story cc.30-36 has been broken off.[65] The start of this story creates the expectation that John is going to make a great impression on the public by healing many Ephesian women. But after John's long address, the healing is only briefly mentioned and nothing is said about the reactions of the people. The final sentence of c.36, 'Having spoken thus, John healed all their diseases by the power of God', seems like a half-hearted attempt to round off the story.[66] What we now have in cc.30-36 is a story with heavy emphasis placed on words (cc.33-36) at the expense of actions.

It is likely that not only the end of the miracle story is lost, but also an episode about the conversion of Andronicus in which his wife Drusiana was introduced. In c.31 Andronicus appears as an unbeliever, but in c.46 he is a Christian who allows John to receive people into his house, a change not explained in the text that we have.[67]

As we have seen above, some material between cc.55 and 58 has disappeared. One of the episodes that could be placed in cc.56-57 describes John's arrival and first acts in Smyrna, while c.58 narrates how he returns from Laodicea to Ephesos. It is likely that, between these scenes, the author described a tour of John in Asia Minor, but we do not know in how much detail. We need to say more about the role of travel in the AJ in order to throw some light on this question.

The idea, held by several scholars, that travel played an important role

[64] When Schneider, *Mystery*, 22 n.1, speaks about 'the missing eighteen chapters at the beginning of the acts', he forgets that this number is a nineteenth-century artefact.
[65] So already Zahn, 'Wanderungen', 197 n.1.
[66] I will suggest below what caused this abbreviation.
[67] Zahn, 'Wanderungen', 197, and many others.

in the AJ,[68] is at least in part based on the supposition that the AJ was heavily influenced by ancient novels and their many travel stories. Now the influence of ancient novels is real (see below) but need not have dictated all elements of the AJ. It certainly is not important enough to force me to suppose that more than one travelogue has been lost from the AJ.

In the present form of the text most of the action is concentrated in Ephesos, where John arrives from Miletus and where the events in cc.18-55 take place. When leaving this city, John goes to Smyrna. At the end of a lengthy trip (62.2), John's last stop before returning to Ephesos is Laodicea (58.1 = heading to cc.58-86). On his way from Laodicea, John sleeps in a way-side inn (60-61)[69] before arriving in Ephesos (62.1) where the action in cc.62-115 is set and where he dies. As a certain amount of information between cc.57 and 58 is missing, the reference to the passage of time leads us to suppose that John did not go immediately from Smyrna to Laodicea, but that he visited other cities en route. This is quite likely since we are told in 55.4-7 that envoys from Smyrna ask John to come to their city and to 'the other cities'.[70] 'The other cities' may have been dealt with in the part of the text that is now lost, but major events did not necessarily take place in all of them,[71] as the narrator may have written a summary sentence like, 'Having preached in several places, the apostle arrived in A where he ...' From this survey we see that travel is not a very important element in the AJ, which, with some justification, can be described as the story of John in and around Ephesos.[72] Based in this city, he makes one round trip which starts and ends there.

Another question connected with the element of travel in the AJ involves the influence of Rev 2-3. Ephesos, Smyrna and Laodicea happen to be the first, second and last cities mentioned in Rev 2-3, which led to the suggestion that John in the early AJ visited all seven cities of Rev. This idea is old and not unattractive because it explains the fact that Smyrna

[68] R. Söder, *Die apokryphen Apostelgeschichten und die romanhafte Literatur der Antike*, Stuttgart 1932, 29-50; Ph. Vielhauer, *Geschichte der urchristlichen Literatur. Einleitung in das Neue Testament, die Apokryphen und die Apostolischen Väter*, Berlin/New York 1975, 693-695; Schäferdiek, *NA*$^5$, 177 n.62.

[69] The short episode in the inn is not geographically located but is only situated in a lonely place, one day's travel from Laodicea (60.1-2).

[70] ἐλθὲ εἰς τὴν Σμύρναν καὶ εἰς τὰς λοιπὰς πόλεις.

[71] Cf. JK, 94.

[72] Van Kampen, *Apostelverhalen*, 99-101, 272-273, who states that *mutatis mutandis* the same is true of the other AAA as well: travel is unimportant as a means of structuring the narrative.

and Laodicea are mentioned as stations on John's tour,[73] but there are two reasons to doubt its validity. First, as I said above, the present research has not rendered a single indication that the author of the AJ knew Rev. In the second place, an alternative model for John's route is the assize tour of the Roman governor of Asia.[74] A new reading of cc.37, 45 and 55 suggests that our author was familiar with the governor's annual visits to cities that competed with each other in order to be his host for as long as possible.[75]

To conclude, the contents of what was lost between cc.55 and 58 still remain uncertain. We saw that parts of the text have been lost at the beginning, between cc.36 and 37, and between cc.57 and 58. This means that there are no grounds to doubt that there around 2500 stichoi in the early text.[76]

### *3.3 Hypothetical lacunae. Abbreviation and censorship*

The above suggestion, that the AJ originally comprised about 2500 stichoi and that we have about 70 percent of that text, must now be defended against hypotheses that estimate the AJ to have been originally much longer. One such hypothesis is advanced by Junod and Kaestli, who argue that there were other gaps than the three considered so far. They hold that before and after cc.87-105 major pieces of text are absent. Now it is clear that these chapters - available only in manuscript **C** - are not closely con-

[73] Zahn, 'Wanderungen', 197-198; *idem, Apostel und Apostelschüler in der Provinz Asien* (Forschungen zur Geschichte des neutestamentlichen Kanons und der altkirchlichen Literatur VI.i), Leipzig 1900, 197-199; C. Schmidt, *Die alten Petrusakten im Zusammenhang der apokryphen Apostellitteratur untersucht. Nebst einem neuentdeckten Fragment*, Leipzig 1903, 123; *idem*, Gespräche Jesu mit seinen Jüngern nach der Auferstehung, Leipzig 1919, 366-367; M. Blumenthal, *Formen und Motive in den apokryphen Apostelgeschichten*, Leipzig 1933, 25, 155; *NA*[5], 151, 177 with n.62; Sirker-Wicklaus, *Untersuchungen*, 228, cf. 21; M. Hengel, *Die johanneische Frage*, Tübingen 1993, 53.

[74] An assize tour is the tour during which the governor, in his quality of highest judge, visits cities to administer justice.

[75] E. Plümacher, 'Apostolische Missionsreise und statthalterliche Assisetour', *ZNW* 85 (1994) 259-278, whose thesis implies that the route of John's Asiatic tour spanned the same cities as the governor's, which probably covered 13 or 14 cities, among which Miletus, Pergamon, Apameia, Laodicea, Smyrna and Ephesos, in a random order. Among these cities, Ephesos and Smyrna were most important for our author, as we will demonstrate later.

[76] Van Kampen, *Apostelverhalen*, notes 199 and 226, accepts the number 2500 with some reservation.

nected with their context,[77] but nothing forces us to think that much of the text was lost on either side of this episode when it was separated from its context.[78] Before and after it, John is in Ephesos in the presence of more or less the same persons. One or two simple connecting sentences may well suffice to reconstruct the original text.[79]

Junod and Kaestli are convinced that the AJ was originally much longer than the text that we now have. They think that the AJ once contained a veritable, important Drusiana cycle which followed c.36.[80] Now the fourth century Manichaean Psalms indeed refer to Drusiana, a main character in the AJ, in a way that suggests that in the version of the AJ that circulated among the Manichaeans there were more elaborate stories about her than we have. These references suggest that such stories were not only known by the Manichaeans, but that they were also part of the early AJ.[81]

Moreover, Junod and Kaestli suggest that each of the persons mentioned in the lists of names in 18.2-4 and 59 (Aristobula and Tertullus, Aristippe and Xenophon, the chaste prostitute, Aristodemus, Damonicus, Cleobius, Marcellus and his wife) belongs to the main characters of a separate story once part of the early AJ.[82] If both these hypotheses are correct, the AJ was originally much longer than our present text.[83] This view implies that, in a later period, the AJ was subjected to a rigorous editing process in which many episodes were lost.[84]

[77] This supports Schäferdiek's hypothesis, accepted by Junod and Kaestli, that the original context of these passages is not between cc.86 and 106 but between cc.36 and 37, a position which will be discussed at lenght in chapter 2. What I argue here is valid both if the hypothesis is correct and if it is not.

[78] *Contra* JK, 91.

[79] Cf. Van Kampen, *Apostelverhalen*, 119-120.

[80] JK, 90-91: 'Le récit perdu qui précédait *AJ* 87-105 représentait certainement un cycle romanesque d'une certaine ampleur.' '... une des composantes les plus typiques et littérairement les plus intéressantes de notre texte.' Cf. 86-91.

[81] C.R.C. Allberry (ed.), *A Manichaean Psalm-Book* II, Stuttgart 1938, 142-143, 192-193. Cf. *NA*[5], 83-86, 177; P. Nagel, 'Die apokryphen Apostelakten des 2. und 3. Jahrhunderts in der manichäischen Literatur', in K.W. Tröger (ed.), *Gnosis und Neues Testament*, Gütersloh 1973, 149-182.

[82] JK, 77-80, 94-96.

[83] JK, 101, speak about an excessive length. The hypothesis was prepared by Nagel, 'Apokryphe Apostelakten', 165-171, whose own words however imply that the Manichaeans' copy of the AJ was different from the early AJ: the Manichaean Psalm (142.20-24) mentions a martyrium of John, 166.

[84] JK, 101-107; on page 104, they call this process a 'cure d'amaigrissement'. Cf. Van Kampen, *Apostelverhalen*, 121.

Although the AJ is, and probably always was, a chain of rather loosely connected episodes with the apostle as the central link,[85] the possibility that there were many more episodes and that the text was 'thinned down' is unlikely given the weak evidence supporting such a view. With the exception of the brief references to Drusiana in the Manichaean Psalms, absolutely no traces of these hypothetical stories exist. In addition, it is unlikely that the Manichaeans preserved the AJ in its earliest form;[86] as we have seen in section 1, the Manichaean papyrus from Kellis that was recently published contains a fragment from the AJ that has both been theologically altered and, in comparison with the original text, abbreviated. If this papyrus is in any way representative of Manichaean practice, the Manichaean Psalms have no direct value as evidence for the contents of the early AJ.

C.82 is also mentioned as proof that the text once contained much more information about Drusiana and her husband.[87] But the recapitulation of her life that is given in that chapter is in no way a summary of any (now lost) preceding episodes. Instead, it is just a hint by the author at God's many great deeds which were not necessarily given a fuller account in the text; as such, it resembles Acts 4:30; 5:12; 14:3.

Having seen that the evidence from the Manichaean Psalms contradicts rather than supports the possibility that there may have been a complete Drusiana cycle, we are left with the alleged evidence of the lists of names in cc.18 and 59. I think that the names are not references to other once extant stories,[88] but that they are comparable to the flashbacks in cc.19.7-13, 63.6-13, 82 and 113. These pieces of text function as summaries which inform us about events that were never told in the text but which are either essential for the story or an illustration of its message. In the case of the lists of names, the author wants to illustrate the effectiveness of John's missionary work and the progress of the faith in Asia by telling that he had

[85] This literary characteristic does not diminish the text's *theological* coherence.

[86] Cf. note 83 above. Nagel, 'Apokryphe Apostelakten', 170-171, shows that these Psalms impose an explicitly Trinitarian theology on AJ 94-96, which is at most implicitly Trinitarian, cf. chapter 4.

[87] JK, 73-75.

[88] We cannot exclude the possibility that some names indeed refer to persons about whom oral stories circulated. This admission has little bearing on the establishment of the text of the AJ. Generally speaking, the hypothetical oral background of the episodes that we have in the AJ is beyond our reach because of the uniform style and theology of the text. Moreover, the AJ does not follow such laws of folk literature as the 'Law of Two to a scene' and the 'Importance of the Final Position', which are discussed by A. Olrik, 'Epic Laws of Folk Narrative' in A. Dundes, *The Study of Folklore*, Englewood Cliffs, N.J. 1965, 131-137.

many famous followers.

Junod and Kaestli's defence of their hypothesis also fails to be convincing. First, they discuss references in the AJ to hypothetical lacunae together with a number of textual fragments that are sometimes said to belong to the AJ.[89] In the second place, they suggest reasons for a hypothetical secondary abbreviation of the text which cannot be proved. I will outline their argument and provide a few comments on their main points.

1. Junod and Kaestli state that a later redactor was especially interested in Ephesos and left out stories that were situated in other cities.[90] In itself, it is probable that the AJ was particularly popular in Ephesos and that the lacuna between cc.57 and 58 is due to a rather deliberate omission of the narrative of John's travel. But several facts speak against a *deliberate* Ephesian redaction, attractive as the hypothesis might be, such as the preservation of the heading 'From Laodicea for the second time to Ephesos' (58.1) in both manuscripts **M** and **O**, which a redactor would have had to omit. On the other hand, he would have preserved a Drusiana cycle had there been any, since, she and her husband Andronicus being Ephesian aristocrats, the cycle would likely be situated in Ephesos. This hypothesis also fails to explain the lacuna between cc.36 and 37 discussed above. Moreover, a self-conscious Ephesian redactor would have deleted the 'references' to otherwise unknown persons from other cities (cc.18, 59); the fact that these people are named is a strong argument against the very existence of this redactor.

2. Junod and Kaestli suggest that doctrinal censorship especially affected John's narrative about Christ (cc.87-105), and episodes with a very strong encratite tendency.[91] Against this view it can be argued that the ideological tendencies of the existing parts of the text make speculations about such doctrinal censorship rather unlikely. Besides, ecclesiastical texts that condemn the AJ contain no references to parts of the text that no longer exist.[92]

If, nevertheless, we suppose for a moment that ecclesiastical censorship caused the omission of complete stories, it becomes virtually impossible to explain the preservation of two particular sections; cc.87-105, which have survived Christological censorship, and cc.63-86, a horrifying story in the

[89] JK, 91-98.

[90] JK, 104.

[91] JK, 104-106; Van Kampen, *Apostelverhalen*, 120-121.

[92] E.g. Leo the Great, *Ep.* 15, PL 54.677-692; *Decretum Gelasianum*, ed. E. von Dobschütz, Leipzig 1912.

opinions of several modern readers,[93] were preserved in spite of the alleged cutting out of encratite tendencies. It is certainly not enough to say that the latter story is situated in Ephesos and therefore of interest to the censor. The same question comes up for the no less appalling story in cc.48-54: If so much of the narrative suffered censorship, why not this scene? A form of censorship that opposed encraticism is purely hypothetical.[94]

3. It is also Junod and Kaestli's view that several long and tedious prayers and speeches were abbreviated. In contrast with the previous hypotheses, there is some evidence for this one. It does not, however, apply to complete stories, but only to a few parts. The omission of words and sentences is visible in the differences between the manuscripts. The most reliable manuscript **H** offers in many places a longer text from which whole sentences have been left out in the (later) manuscripts **R** and **Z**.[95] **M** also frequently has a longer text than **R** and **Z**.

4. According to Junod and Kaestli, the shortening of the text was facilitated by the presence of sub-titles at the beginning of various constituent episodes. One such sub-title has been preserved (58.1).[96] But the original number of sub-titles is unknown, so that the one remaining sub-title does not really support hypotheses of abbreviation.

I conclude that there is insufficient evidence that the AJ was to any extent condensed in its later history. There are probably no more than three gaps in the text. We are therefore entitled to accept the present text as a good approximation of the original AJ. About 70 percent of the original is present, and the loss of material is largely limited to the three instances (before c.18, between cc.36 and 37 and between cc.55 and 58). Apart from the beginning, there are no indications that any vital information about John and his work or about the theology of the text has disappeared.

[93] E.g. Schmidt, *Petrusakten*, 60; A.F. Findlay, *Byways in Early Christian Literature. Studies in the Uncanonical Gospels and Acts. The Kerr Lectures ... 1920-21*, Edinburgh 1923, 215; Schäferdiek, 'Herkunft', 266; R.I. Pervo, 'Johannine Trajectories in the *Acts of John*', *Apocrypha - le champ des Apocryphes* 3 (1992) 47-68, 55; Vielhauer, *Literatur*, 707; R.A. Culpepper, *John, the Son of Zebedee. The Life of a Legend*, Columbia SC 1994, 205 ('bizarre').

[94] Van Kampen, *Apostelverhalen*, 116. Although JK, 105 n.1, find parallels in the fate of other AAA, these cases of lost material may well have other causes, such as lack of coherence in a long narrative.

[95] See the apparatus and JK's notes, e.g. at 23.15, 25.3, 29.19, 33.13, 76.10 and JK 15, 20.

[96] JK, 101-104, 104, 105.

*3.4 Stories that might belong to the AJ*

The reconstruction of the early AJ does not only confront us with missing passages, but also with several short pieces of ancient text that have John as their main character and that may have been part of the early AJ. These fragments include small texts that deal with a couple about to marry, with a demon-soldier, with Zeuxis, and with a miracle in which hay was changed into gold.[97] They have one remarkable characteristic in common: they do not fit into one of the aforementioned lacunae. They are not mentioned in the text that we have nor do they provide a better understanding of the present text's meaning. Furthermore, unlike most episodes in the authorized text, they contain no geographical place names. Therefore it is impossible to argue with reasonable certainty that any one of those fragments was part of the early AJ.[98]

[97] JK, 98-99, 109-136. These stories are preserved in Papyrus Oxyrhynchus 850 and in the Irish Life of John. On the *Epistula Titi* which may also preserve parts of the AJ, see chapter 5.

[98] It is surprising that JK, 145-153, 369-375, admit that the stories preserved in fragments in other languages and in a badly preserved Greek text may belong to the AJ, but at the same time exclude the story of John and the partridge (cc.56-57 Bonnet), for which we do have a complete Greek version.

# CHAPTER 2: THE STRUCTURE OF THE TEXT

In this chapter I will expound my hypothesis about the composite structure of the finished text of the early AJ. This final text consists of a small section with a distinct theology (cc.94-102) inserted in an older text. I will argue that, although the AJ harbours more than one editorial intention and theological viewpoint, the resulting text nevertheless forms a unity.

The structure of the text becomes visible when we change the order of the sections from the one given them by recent scholars. It will become clear that the sequence indicated by the chapter numbering introduced by Bonnet (and still current) is to be preferred over the later innovation (par.1). Arguments will also be adduced for the hypothesis that cc.94-102 are indeed an addition (par.2) and the particular genre of the constituent parts will be discussed (par.3). Having demonstrated that the intentions of these parts of the text differ from each other (par.4), I outline the main thesis in par.5. The final paragraph discusses the circumstances in which the text was composed.

In order to facilitate references to the text, I have subdivided it into three sections: section A (cc.18-86, 106-108 and 110-115), B (cc.87-93 and 103-105), and C (94-102 and 109). This specific division is partly based on the internal tensions signalled in chapter 1. Section A comprises the episodes that deal with the activities of John in Asia. Sections B and C are the parts of the text in which John talks about Christ. Of these, C is the segment which Junod and Kaestli describe as a Gnostic interpolation into the otherwise non-Gnostic AJ. The rest of this chapter will make the reason for this division obvious by showing how it provides a valuable tool of reference.

## 1 The position of chapters 87-105 (sections B and C)

### *1.1 The problem of the separate transmission*

As we learned in the first chapter, the text of the AJ has been reconstructed from various manuscripts, of which many contain the *Acts of John by Prochorus* as main text. The order of most episodes is firmly established by the order in which they appear in the manuscripts **R** and **Z**, both of which contain cc.18-55, 58-86 and 106-115.[1] But the placement of cc.87-105 must be determined by modern editors since this passage occurs only in manuscript **C**, which contains no other parts of the text.[2] The text

[1] For the sake of clarity, I notice that the position of c.109 within 106-115 is not under discussion.

[2] The Acta of the Council of Nicea quote cc. 93.1-95.22 and 97.1-98.12, out of context.

offered by **C** must be inserted somewhere in the story. The problem is that **R** and **Z** show no sign that there is a lacuna at either of the two most likely places (between cc.36 and 37 or between cc.86 and 106, see below); the same holds true for **H** and the new papyrus Kellis 1, in as far as the parts they contain are concerned.[3]

Here the new papyrus must be mentioned. We saw in chapter 1 that, although Papyrus Kellis 1 is by far the earliest of all manuscripts of the AJ, it testifies to an early abbreviation of the text. Other evidence for this abbreviation is provided by the version of the AJ on which the *Virtutes Johannis* draws[4] and by the testimony of Augustine. Augustine quotes from a Latin version of the hymn (cc.94-95) but is unaware that it belongs to the AJ. He also shows ample knowledge about the episode of John's death (cc.106-115), but does not mention the AJ or refer to other parts of the text.[5] This fact illustrates that there was some early abbreviation of the AJ which led to a separation of sections B and C as well as cc.106-115 from section A. These sections probably came in separate circulation. The fact that it postdates this development, disqualifies Papyrus Kellis 1 as a witness to the original place of sections B and C.

Thus the other manuscripts do not help us to locate the material of manuscript **C**. The testimony of the Byzantine church is equally unhelpful, although this church preserved the complete AJ well into the Middle Ages. The Councils of Hiereia (754) and Nicea II (787) had versions of the AJ which still contained sections B and C,[6] and the ninth-century patriarch Photius had a volume of AAA which also included them.[7] Despite their

[3] **H** cannot inform us concerning a lacuna between cc.86 and 106; for the possibility of a lacuna between cc.36 and 37, what JK, 15, say is relevant: 'Le nombre de folios manquants entre [35.4] et [47.1] pourrait être de deux. Le texte de **RZ** pour *AJ* 35,4 - 47,1 tient en effet en 137 lignes de l'édition Bonnet; or deux folios de **H** donnent environ 152 lignes imprimées, donc un texte légèrement plus long.'

[4] K. Schäferdiek, 'Die "Passio Iohannis" des Melito von Laodikeia und die "Virtutes Iohannis"', *AnBoll* 103 (1985) 367-382, esp. 374-377; cf. *NA*$^5$, 140-141. Kaestli's reply, 'Le rapport entre les deux Vies latines de l'apôtre Jean. A propos d'un récent article de K. Schäferdiek', *Apocrypha* 3 (1992) 111-123, recognises Schäferdiek's essential correctness.

[5] Augustine, *Tractatus cxxiv in Iohannis Evangelium* (*CCL* 36, 680-688, esp. 681-682); see Junod and Kaestli, *Histoire*, 81-86. Note the fact that in dealing with Jn 20:27 (*noli esse incredulus, sed fidelis, Tractatus cxxi*) Augustine shows no knowledge of AJ 90. Likewise the available evidence for the Priscillianists, a fourth/fifth-century Spanish sect which used the AJ and other apocrypha, only indicates that they knew the hymn and dance and the episode about John's death, see Junod and Kaestli, *Histoire*, 92-93, 99-100; *NA*$^5$, 141 n.32.

[6] JK, 344-360; Junod and Kaestli, *Histoire*, 119-126.

[7] Evident from reading Photius, *Bibliotheca*, cod. 114, ed. R. Henry, Paris 1960. Cf. Junod and Kaestli, *Histoire*, 133-137, esp. 136.

references to the text, it is still impossible to be certain regarding the position of cc.87-105. The order in which the fragments were read at the Council of 787 demonstrates that these sections come somewhere after cc.27-28, but does not help us to situate them with any great precision.

Two possible locations for sections B and C have been suggested. The older suggestion is reflected in the still current chapter numbering and was not questioned until Schäferdiek proposed an alternative. According to this older alternative, these sections form the penultimate episode of the AJ, and should be inserted in section A between cc.86 and 106. This place was chosen because Drusiana, the heroine of cc.63-86, is mentioned at the beginning of section B (c.87).[8] Schäferdiek's alternative places the problematic segment between cc.36 and 37, although for practical reasons he preserves the familiar chapter numbers. Schäferdiek is followed by Junod and Kaestli, by the translations of Elliott and Klijn, and by all recent scholars except one.[9]

*1.2 The original position of sections B and C*

There are several reasons to maintain the earlier location of cc.87-105 of the AJ, and to reject Schäferdiek's alternative. First of all, let us look at the opening words of section B: 'Those who were present sought the meaning (of what had happened)[10] and were especially perplexed because Drusiana had said,[11] "The Lord appeared to me in the tomb in the form of John and of a youth"' (87.1-3). These words imply that the believers seek the meaning of a recent event. This event can hardly be any other than the unconvertibility and the subsequent death of Fortunatus, told in cc.83-86. This is by far the most shocking element in the adventures of Drusiana because it has no happy end. It is this event that makes John aware of the need to strengthen the faith of the believers by telling them about his experiences with the Lord (87.3-5). Therefore, sections B and C seem to be the natural continuation of cc.83-86.

[8] James, *Apocrypha anecdota*, xv: 'As to its place in the complete book a word only need be said. It follows immediately upon the long episode of the raising of Drusiana, ...' He is followed by Bonnet, *Acta* II.1, Zahn, 'Wanderungen', Hilgenfeld, 'Johannes', and by G. Schimmelpfeng, 'Johannesakten', in E. Hennecke (ed.), *Handbuch zu den Neutestamentlichen Apokryphen*, Tübingen 1904, 492-543, 520-521.

[9] Schäferdiek, *NA*$^3$, 132-134 (fuller than *NA*$^5$, 162-163); A.F.J. Klijn (ed.), *Apokriefen van het Nieuwe Testament II*, Kampen 1985. The exception is F. Corsaro, *Le* ΠΡΑΞΕΙΣ *di Giovanni*, Università di Catania 1968. Van Kampen, *Apostelverhalen,* 117-119, hesitates.

[10] 'Εξήτασαν οὖν οἱ παρόντες τὴν αἰτίαν; Elliott's 'about the cause' is less fitting.

[11] The Greek has a perfect form here (ἠπόρουν εἰρηκυίας τῆς Δρουσιανῆς ὅτι ..., 87.2). That 'Drusiane *vient de* rapporter aux frères que...' (JK, 72, my italics) is incorrect; in their formal translation JK, 190, have, 'Drusiane avait dit'.

Other considerations support this view. It is easy to imagine that John's gospel has the character of a memoir told at the end of his life. From a structural point of view, it closely parallels c.113, a flashback in which John narrates what took place in his early life. In both cases the author provides important information not in chronological order but near the end of the text, so that he creates a climax in his story and tells the story in a manner that is more than just an enumeration of facts.[12]

A third argument is based on an exegesis of cc.71-76. These chapters describe how both a snake and a beautiful young lad appeared in the tomb of Drusiana. The snake and the boy have parallel functions in the story and, in fact, one of them seems to be somewhat superfluous. At first the narrator says that the apparition of the snake caused Callimachus to become unconscious (71). Then Andronicus suggests that it was a beautiful youth who was responsible for the situation (74.11-12). In Callimachus' own account (c.76), both the horrible beast (76.7-11) and the shining boy (76.11-20) appear in order to intervene on behalf of Drusiana. The story could well have been written with only one of these characters. The introduction of the boy, who is Christ-in-metamorphosis, is a device that anticipates Christ's appearances to his disciples.[13] The shining boy makes the readers familiar with the idea that Christ can appear on earth in different forms, that not everybody recognises him (c.76), and that sometimes a mere voice may articulate his revelation (c.73, cf. c.98). Consequently, the appearance of the radiant boy somewhat artificially paves the way for the Christophanies that are described in cc.87-105, and that must follow rather than precede this episode. I conclude that cc.71-76 are meant to prepare the reader for cc.87-93.

The resulting order of the episodes gives a better story-line than the order suggested by Schäferdiek, as the suggested sequence creates a tension and delays the revelation of John's most important message to the end. The same procedure recurs in the APe. In the 41 chapters of this text, Peter tells his mysteries in cc.37-39. This structural parallel between the AJ and the APe is very interesting.[14] In both texts miracle stories attract the atten-

[12] Schneider, *Mystery*, 9-11, agrees that cc.87-105 should follow c.36, but his whole approach deals with them as if they were the final part of the AJ.

[13] C.L. Sturhahn, *Die Christologie der ältesten apokryphen Apostelakten*, typescript Dissertation Göttingen 1952, 45-46. The view that the boy is a manifestation of Christ and not an angel will be discussed in chapter 4.

[14] Zahn, 'Wanderungen', 210, 215; Van Kampen, *Apostelverhalen*, 63-64; cf. Schmidt, *Petrusakten*, 113, who is convinced that the APe was written with prior knowledge of the AJ and talks about 'Das angebliche Fortschreiten von geheimchristlicher Redeweise zu immer tiefer in die Geheimlehre einführendem Vortrag ...'

tion of the reader and sermons call him to conversion. In both cases, the revelation of the texts' main messages comes near the end.

*1.3 Discussion of counterarguments*

Since my view deviates from the almost unanimous opinion of present-day scholars, I must respond to some of their arguments. These arguments for placing sections B and C between cc.36 and 37 all come from Schäferdiek, the progenitor of the whole idea.[15] He takes his point of departure from c.82 in which Drusiana thanks the Lord for the many things that he did in her life. In order to discuss Schäferdiek's view, we will first quote the relevant words of Drusiana with the numbers Schäferdiek gave to the events mentioned:

> (1) You allowed me to see signs and wonders and (2) granted me to partake of your name. (3) You breathed into me your spirit with your polymorphous face, and showed much compassion. (4) With your rich goodness, you protected me when my former husband, Andronicus, did violence to me, and (5) gave me your servant Andronicus as a brother. (6) Until now you have kept me, your maiden, pure. (7) You raised me when I was dead through your servant John. (8) To me, risen and free from offence, you showed me him who was offended at me. (9) You gave me perfect rest in you, and delivered me from secret madness.[16]

We see that the third event mentioned by Drusiana is a polymorphous revelation of Christ,[17] that the fifth is the conversion of her husband Andronicus, and that the last three events are narrated in cc.63-81 of the present text. This order of events leads Schäferdiek to the conclusion that some stories are lost from the AJ. In his opinion, before cc.63-81 not only a Christophany to Drusiana and a story about the conversion of Andronicus were narrated, but also John's gospel-like sermon. These elements must have been placed in the lacuna between cc.36 and 37. Now it can readily be granted that the Christophany (3) and the conversion story (5) once were part of the text, and occurred somewhere before c.82, in which case the lacuna between cc.36 and 37 is indeed their most logical location. But this admission does not necessarily imply that John's gospel-like sermon (sections B and C) was also located there. There is no clear reason to assume that the telling of the sermon about Christ, occasioned by the

[15] JK, 73-75, and Schneider, *Mystery*, 9-11, follow Schäferdiek without adding to his arguments.

[16] NA[3], 132. In Greek all nine phrases begin with ὁ plus participle.

[17] More on polymorphy in chapter 4.

Christophany, took place in the same setting as that Christophany itself.[18] On the contrary, it is remarkable that in c.82 (quoted above) Drusiana does not refer to the revelations contained in cc.87-102 at all! This fact may imply nothing else than the fact that the gospel of polymorphy was not provided before c.82, so that this chapter must indeed precede cc.87-105.

To be sure, it cannot be excluded that John pronounced the gospel sermon immediately after the Christophany, but its natural location is near the end of the text. Before the interpolation took place in the AJ, cc.87-93 may have been situated between cc.36 and 37 as a mere speech of the apostle. But when the final redactor added cc.94-102, he made the gospel into a flashback which forms the culmination of the whole text and which could only be spoken just before the death of John.

It is clear that c.82, which is most important in Schäferdiek's theory, in fact opposes his very suggestion. The evidence indicates that sections B and C should be placed between cc.86 and 106.

## 2 Gnostic and non-Gnostic sections

### *2.1 The theological orientation of the AJ*

The theological orientation of the AJ has been a major subject of discussion ever since the text began to be studied. Scholars know that the text has repeatedly suffered ecclesiastical condemnation and that the judgment of Photius about its heretical character is sharp.[19] But often the question of the theology of the text was reduced to a discussion of its alleged Gnostic character, and this research has long been handicapped by the lack of a clear definition of gnosis and of a middle term between gnosis and 'orthodoxy' to denote the plurality of early Christianity.[20]

Lipsius is convinced of the Gnostic character of the early AJ, which has partly been removed by catholic editors. As a result, the Gnosticism does not resound with equal force in all parts of the text. He also works without a good definition of gnosis, as can be seen from the fact that he

[18] Once again I refer to the perfect tense of the verb in 87.2, which does not suggest that Drusiana had recently given her account.

[19] Junod and Kaestli, *Histoire*, 102-103, 121-126; E. Junod, 'Actes apocryphes et hérésie: le jugement de Photius', in Bovon, *Actes apocryphes*, 11-24.

[20] This is e.g. apparent in Sturhahn, *Christologie*, esp. 21-50, 51, and in A. Ehrhardt, 'Christianity Before the Apostles' Creed', *HTR* 55 (1962) 73-119, who just know two poles that they call Catholicity and Gnosticism, so that everything that does not fit into emerging mainstream Christianity is labelled Gnostic. Findlay, *Byways*, 223-237, is better because he regards the AJ as neither 'Catholic' nor fully Gnostic.

mentions asceticism, docetism, belief in supernatural powers and respect for the souls of animals among its features.[21] Along similar lines, Dobschütz even presupposes that all the AAA are Gnostic, witness his words, 'das Christenthum der Enthaltsamkeit, des Vegetarianismus, mit einem Wort die Gnosis.'[22] Popular literature and lexicon entries often just label the AJ as Gnostic.[23]

For the sake of completeness only, I mention that there are several scholars for whom the AJ and the AAA in general are not far removed from Jewish Christianity.[24] Whatever may be true about the other AAA, it must be stressed that this suggestion is not at all supported by the text of the AJ. Later chapters will give evidence that the AJ does not recognise the Old Testament as Scripture and has none of the characteristic traits of Jewish Christianity.

*2.2 Attempts at a solution*

In order to solve the disputes, Junod and Kaestli argue that the AJ is an originally non-Gnostic text in which a Gnostic section has been interpolated. According to them, the second half of the gospel flashback (cc.94-102) is an early Gnostic addition, of which c.109 is also a part.[25] But this thesis is not totally without precedents. Zahn notes that the author of the AJ is a prototype of the Valentinians described by Irenaeus (*AdvHaer* 3.15.2) because, in the first part of his work, he hides his true ideas behind a veil of ecclesiastical language and he reveals them towards the end.[26] In a more or less similar vein, Carl Schmidt denies the Gnostic character of

[21] Lipsius, *Apostelgeschichten*, 4-9, 520-542, who holds that the speeches and prayers in manuscript **M** have undergone catholic censorship (465), says regarding the original texts '... dass sie einem bereits sehr ausgebildeten Gnosticismus angehören ...' (515). Cf. E. von Dobschütz, 'Der Roman in der altchristlichen Literatur', *Deutsche Rundschau* 111 (1902), 87-106, esp. 105.

[22] Dobschütz, 'Roman', 104.

[23] E.g. B. Altaner and A. Stuiber, *Patrologie*, Freiburg/Basel/Wien [8]1978, 138.

[24] E. Peterson, 'Einige Bemerkungen zum Hamburger Papyrusfragment der Acta Pauli', in his *Frühkirche, Judentum und Gnosis. Studien und Untersuchungen*, Rom/Freiburg/Wien 1959, 183-208, esp. 185 n.8, 212; A. Hamman, '"Sitz im Leben" des actes apocryphes du Nouveau Testament', *Studia Patristica* Vol.VIII, Berlin 1966, 62-69, esp. 66; K. Niederwimmer, *Askese und Mysterium. Über Ehe, Ehescheidung und Eheverzicht in den Anfängen des christlichen Glaubens*, Göttingen 1975, 166 n.19; W.C. van Unnik, 'A Note on the Dance of Jesus in the "Acts of John"', *VigChr* 18 (1964) 1-5, repr. in *Sparsa Collecta* III, Leiden 1983, 144-147. Jewish wisdom is suggested by W. Bousset, 'Platons Weltseele und das Kreuz Christi', *ZNW* 14 (1913) 280.

[25] JK, 425, 581-632.

[26] Zahn, 'Wanderungen', 215.

the AJ with the exception of the hymn cc.94-95.[27] Schäferdiek goes a step further and tries to solve the dilemma Gnostic - non-Gnostic by attributing the contents of the AJ to two sources, one Gnostic (cc.87-105, which he calls a gospel) and one not (the rest of the text).[28] Junod and Kaestli's view that cc.94-102 and 109 are Gnostic additions, is in fact based on this suggestion. The difference is that their opinion of section B differs: they include it with the non-Gnostic segment of the text.

I adopt Junod and Kaestli's thesis as a basis for the present study.[29] In order to justify my position, a more exact definition of 'Gnostic' is necessary. This study will demonstrate how the old dilemma 'Gnostic or not' is indeed resolved by following the lead of Zahn, Schäferdiek and Junod and Kaestli.

*2.3 Gnosis*

The hypothesis that only cc.94-102 have a Gnostic character must be discussed from two perspectives, for it says something about these chapters as well as about the rest of the text. The first part of our task is fairly simple because, regardless of the definition of Gnosis with which one works, the Gnostic character of cc.94-102 is so generally accepted that it is no longer necessary to argue for this position.[30] To mention just one of the arguments, it is clear that humanity as portrayed in cc.94-102 is alienated from its divine origin and, through the revelation of Christ, receives the knowledge that enables it to return to its origin.[31]

But the counterpart of Junod and Kaestli's thesis is that sections A and B of the AJ are not a specifically Gnostic text. This part of their thesis has so far not been generally recognised. Indeed, the non-Gnostic character of sections A and B is rejected by Sirker-Wicklaus and probably also by Schneider.[32] It is therefore necessary to demonstrate the absence of Gnos-

[27] Schmidt, *Petrusakten*, 127-129.

[28] *NA*[3], 142-143; cf. Plümacher, 'Apostelakten', 49-51; Klijn, *Apokriefen II*, 13.

[29] The hypothesis has been rejected by Sirker-Wicklaus, *Untersuchungen*, 1-2, cf. 242-245, and Schneider, *Mystery*, 209-214, who both take the whole text to be Gnostic but do not give a definition of Gnosis. In his 'Transformation of a Christian Community', in W.E. Helleman (ed.), *Hellenization Revisited: Shaping a Christian Response within the Greco-Roman World*, Lanham MD 1994, 241-269, esp. 241 with n.4, Schneider seems to have changed his mind.

[30] See JK, 589-632; now also Luttikhuizen, 'Gnostic Reading'.

[31] Alienation: 96.5; 100.1-4; revelation: 96.6,13-16; 100.4-7. More on this in chapter 4.

[32] Sirker-Wicklaus, *Untersuchungen*, 203-221, already sees the Gospel of John as a Gnostic text, of which the theology is only radicalised in the AJ. Schneider, *Mystery*, 77, admits that the Gnostic character of section A is not very clear but nevertheless maintains that the section is Gnostic. In 'Gnostic Transformation' he argues that the original text leant itself

tic elements and the presence of non-Gnostic ideas in those two sections. The Gnostic form of Christianity is notoriously difficult to describe because of its 'parasitic' character.[33] It differs according to the form of Christianity to which it is attached, but it is always characterised by a negative attitude towards the world and its creator.[34] If we nevertheless try to be more specific, we can say that Gnostic Christianity can be distinguished from other forms of Christianity by the following characteristics:

1. dualism between an absolutely transcendent God and a cosmos that is not his creation, but the work of an imperfect and evil demiurg (identified with the God of the Old Testament). The result is a strong anticosmism;[35]
2. the essential divinity of the inner man, a spark of light which is alien to the material world;[36]
3. salvation by revelation (originating in the world of light) of knowledge about the provenance of the self which is at the same time knowledge of God.

very well to Gnostic use.

[33] The hypothesis (!) of a pre-Christian Gnosis has been criticised by E. Yamauchi, *Pre-Christian Gnosticism. A Survey of the Proposed Evidences*, Grand Rapids 1973; *idem*, 'Pre-Christian Gnosticism in the Nag Hammadi Texts?', *Church History* 48 (1979) 129-141; *idem*, 'Pre-Christian Gnosticism, the New Testament and Nag Hammadi in recent debate', *Themelios* 10 (1984) 22-27; *idem*, 'Gnosticism and Early Christianity', in Helleman (ed.), *Hellenization Revisited*, 29-61 (with a Response by M. Desjardins, 63-67); S. Pétrement, *Le Dieu séparé. Les origines du gnosticisme*, Paris 1984 (ET *A Separate God. The Christian Origins of Gnosticism*, London 1991); A.H.B. Logan, 'John and the Gnostics: The Significance of the Apocryphon of John for the Debate about the Origins of the Johannine Literature', *JSNT* 43 (1991) 41-69; *idem*, *Gnostic Truth and Christian Heresy. A Study in the History of Gnosticism*, Edinburgh 1996; C. Markschies, *Valentinus Gnosticus?*, Tübingen 1992; J. Holzhausen, *Der 'Mythos vom Menschen' im hellenistischen Ägypten. Eine Studie zum 'Poimandres' (= CH I), zu Valentin und dem gnostischen Mythos*, Bodenheim 1994. See the balanced survey by R.McL. Wilson, 'Half a Century of Gnosisforschung - in Retrospect', in H. Preissler and H. Seiwert (eds.), *Gnosisforschung und Religionsgeschichte. FS Rudolph*, Marburg 1994, 343-353.

[34] K. Koschorke, *Die Polemik der Gnostiker gegen das kirchliche Christentum*, Leiden 1978, 211-219, esp. 217 ('Entweltlichungstendenz').

[35] The anticosmism is stressed by e.g. J.-M. Sevrin, 'Le quatrième évangile et le gnosticisme: questions de méthode', in J.-D. Kaestli *et al.* (eds.), *La communauté johannique et son histoire. La trajectoire de l'évangile de Jean aux deux premiers siècles*, Genève 1990, 251-268, esp. 256-260.

[36] Because the Gnostic religion holds that the inner man is divine, it must be distinguished from Jewish mysticism and from Hermetism, which is essentially a mystery religion that teaches deification through initiation. Not all forms of Hermetism have a negative view of the cosmos.

4. the expression of the above tenets in the form of myths which deal with the many hypostases within the universe; even when the myths are not expressly stated they are presupposed.
Such other features of the Gnostic religion as asceticism, docetism and the allegorization of both OT and NT are accidental. In cc.94-102 and 109, the first characteristic is less clearly present than the others. Docetism and the allegorization of the NT Gospels are prominent, while traces of myths and hypostases also appear.[37]

We are now going to compare this description of Gnostic Christianity to sections A and B of the AJ. This text proclaims that there is only one God who is all powerful. This one God has just one important adversary, the devil (cc.21.20-22; 49.4; 54.2-12; 66; 86.10).[38] The world is called God's creation (79.13) and it is said that God reveals himself through nature (112.4-5). The conditions for becoming a Christian are not clearly defined. Sometimes faith seems to be the most important prerequisite for salvation (cc.40-45), faith which must persevere in order to be effective (cc.67-69; 104.6-7); but in most of John's sermons (cc.29; 35-36; 69.20-70.3; 107) and in the short story cc.60-61 good behaviour is stressed; in other cases love of God is all-important (58.10-12). Not all persons who are converted are also said to have been resurrected (e.g. c.54); the AJ is just not that systematic. The AJ truly displays a variety of ways that lead to salvation. It is especially significant that, amid this variety, insight and knowledge are absent and that there is no fixed pattern of higher knowledge in John's teaching. In cases when faith and knowledge appear together (26.11; 29.5-6; 76.39-40; 113.19), it is faith that is mentioned first while knowledge has just the God Christ as its object. So far we have found nothing that is specifically Gnostic in the AJ.

For the present research it is especially noteworthy that the part of the text which follows after section C, viz. cc.106-115, can in no way be described as Gnostic. These chapters do not continue the esoteric revelations of section C but resemble the rest of section A. This state of affairs is most visible in the person of John, who is still a normal human being awaiting redemption, not somebody who has been redeemed through the knowledge that he has received. His final words to the Lord give no evidence of confidence in anything that he has nor in his participation in

[37] Cf. chapter 4.

[38] Cf. E. Junod and J.-D. Kaestli, 'Les traits caractéristiques de la théologie des "Actes de Jean"', *Revue de Théologie et de Philosophie* 26 (1976) 125-145, 136-138.

the divine nature,[39] but just the fear and trembling of a weak man who hopes that on balance God will accept him (cc.112, 114). It can finally be observed that the AJ gives a remarkably large place to miracle stories,[40] which are very rare in Gnostic texts.[41] (It is possible that it was the Gnostic final editor who left out the part of the text which followed c.36 because of the description of healing miracles.) The AJ is not anti-cosmic, humanity is not seen as essentially divine and the text does not emphasize (the revelation of) knowledge but rather aims at great clarity for a wide public. I conclude that sections A and B of the AJ do not contain clear Gnostic features.

*2.4 Spiritualism*

It must be emphasized that, despite the fact that the main part of the AJ is not Gnostic, Gnostic readers were undoubtedly attracted to the spiritual character of its theology,[42] John's character and many other elements in various individual episodes.

Generally speaking, the AJ represents a form of Christianity that breaks completely with Judaism and with the authority of sacred texts. We will discuss this fact in more detail in the next chapter. Again, references to historical facts and creeds are altogether absent, a quality that gives the spirituality of this text a sense of timelessness. The AJ contains no reflection on incarnation and no explanation of the meaning of the sacraments. The eucharist also has a spiritual form and functions as a rite for the worthy members of the community.[43] The ceremony is simply designated as 'breaking the bread' (cc.85-86, 109-110). The reference to the sacra-

[39] Similarly E. Junod, 'Les vies de philosophes et les actes apocryphes des apôtres poursuivent-ils un dessein similaire?', in Bovon, *Actes apocryphes*, 209-219, 215-216. Contra Schneider, *Mystery*, 23-24, 70-71, 76, 122-123, 161.

[40] Besides raising dead or unconscious people in cc. 23-24; 47; 51-52; 75; 80; 83, there are other miracles in cc.30-36; 42; 56-57; 60-61; 73.1-2; 113.7-10; cf. John's own summaries in 39.6-8; 106.5-7. I think that the Christophanies belong to a different category.

[41] So L. Schottroff, *Der Glaubende und die feindliche Welt*, Neukirchen-Vluyn 1970, 267-268, who has difficulties explaining the presence of miracles in the Fourth Gospel, which she sees as Gnostic; U. Schnelle, *Antidoketische Christologie im Johannesevangelium*, Göttingen 1987, 255. The fact that there are miracles in the AJ accords with the essential humanity of the apostle John. The docetic tendency behind the AJ, which has led to the spiritualisation of the person of Christ, has not yet affected John and his deeds.

[42] Esp. Schneider, 'Gnostic Transformation', 251-252, 255-256; Schäferdiek, 'Herkunft', 265, states that section A is 'vorgnostisch' or 'gnostisierend', 'und insofern steht er natürlich auch (...) gnostischer Deutung offen'; cf. Junod and Kaestli, 'Théologie', 143; Luttikhuizen, 'Gnostic Reading', 150.

[43] J. Roldanus, 'Die Eucharistie in den Johannesakten', in Bremmer, *Acts of John*, 72-96.

ments in c.84 gives the impression that the author is talking about the practices of others rather than about things that are dear to both himself and his community. There is furthermore no mention of the church or of ecclesiastical institutions. The Christian community in Ephesos is a group of individuals gathered around John and designated as 'the brothers'.[44] It cannot be said who will lead them after his death and break the bread for them. The text is not interested in the future of the individual or the community at all.

A particular feature of the AJ is that the Christian God is completely identified with Christ Jesus.[45] It also lays particular stress on the fact that God is a very high and perfect Being. There is a battle going on between this God and his fierce opponent, satan, but its outcome is not in doubt. Thus we read this prayer in c.41: 'God, who are God above all so-called gods (...), you have abrogated every form of worship through conversion to you. In your name every idol, every demon, and every unclean spirit is banished.' And in c.79 John prays: 'You who alone are God, I call upon you, the immense, the unspeakable, the incomprehensible, to whom all wordly power is subject, before whom every authority bows, before whom every pride falls down and is silent, before whose voice the demons are confounded, at whose contemplation the whole creation surrenders in quiet meditation.'

The word resurrection occurs rather frequently, but it denotes a completely spiritual concept. There is an important role for women, and contempt of the body is also stressed. As we have just seen, there is a multiplicity of ways that lead to salvation. These characteristics make the AJ an ideal point of departure for an individualistic faith with a spiritualising interpretation of the death and resurrection of Christ.

Another feature of the AJ attractive to Gnostics is the person of John, the main character. He may have appealed to Gnostics, first of all because of the Gospel that bore his name and because of his alleged role in it.[46] We know that the Fourth Gospel was popular with second-century Christians who did not belong to the developing Main Church. One of these groups, the Gnostics, apparently found this Gospel a congenial work.[47] 'The disciple whom Jesus loved' is the principle witness to Christ

[44] 62.1-2; 63.2; 66.4; 70.2; 72.2; 86.2, 3; 88.1; 93.1, 14; 103.1; 105.1, 3; 106.1, 2-3.

[45] See chapter 4.

[46] Hengel, *Johanneische Frage*, 204-209, has convinced me that the Gospel of John bore this name from the beginning.

[47] The thought that the Gospel of John was read *mainly* by Gnostics is found in W. von Loewenich, *Das Johannes-Verständnis im zweiten Jahrhundert*, Giessen 1932, 60-61, and R.E. Brown, *The Community of the Beloved Disciple*, New York 1979, 147-155. It is denied

in the Gospel. This disciple was an attractive choice for the role of the main initiate of Christ and to serve as an example of true spiritual life.[48]

When we look at the spiritual aspects of the individual episodes, we see that in the story about Cleopatra and Lycomedes John says that Christ is above all the powers of the universe (23.2-6). At the end of the text we find an even longer catalogue of powers in c.114. The terminology in both passages is not Gnostic, but the world-view approaches the Gnostic one with its belief in the existence and importance of many aeons and cosmic powers in the spheres between the high God and mankind.

Next to John, Cleopatra and Drusiana are very important characters in the text. Both women are attractive examples of individuals with a firm faith who are even granted the power to raise others from the dead.[49] The story in which a friend of Lycomedes paints a colourful portrait of the apostle John is highly spiritual. John rejects the portrait as 'the dead picture of what is dead' (29.19). True painting, according to him, takes place in the spiritual realm and strengthens the soul because the soul is the true man. The text suggests that a true 'picture' of a person is a spiritual image in which the colours represent virtues. Again, these ideas are not specifically Gnostic,[50] but they coincide with the Gnostic stress on the spiritual life.

In the next episode John's sermon to the Ephesians stresses that the true life is not here below and not in the body (c.34). The same spiritualising tendency is again clearly audible in the central message of cc.46-47: 'Take care of your soul!' The stories in cc.48-54 and 63-86 have asceticism as a theme, an important topic for all second-century Christians.[51] Besides, the value of corporeal resurrection is again strongly relativised in these episodes, e.g. by John's words, 'If you rise up to the same life, you would be better to remain dead. But rise up to a better' (52.9-10). The description of the conversion of Callimachus has a Gnostic ring because this character says that after his physical resurrection he will come to *know* the truth.[52] The command that a heavenly voice gave to this person, 'Die,

by W.G. Röhl, *Die Rezeption des Johannesevangeliums in christlich-gnostischen Schriften aus Nag Hammadi*, Frankfurt usw. 1991, esp. 206-210, Hengel, *Johanneische Frage*, 30-31, 45-46, and J.-M. Poffet, 'Indices de réception de l'Évangile de Jean au IIe siècle, avant Irénée', in Kaestli *et al.*, *Communauté johannique*, 305-321.

[48] Luttikhuizen, 'Gnostic reading', 150. John is also the eponym of the *Apocryphon of John*.

[49] Cf. Luttikhuizen, 'Gnostic reading', 151.

[50] Inferiority of the body is part of Greek dualism. JK, 448-452, refer to philosophers like Plotin; Sirker-Wicklaus, *Untersuchungen*, 175, to the Stoa.

[51] See chapter 5.

[52] ὁ ἀλήθειαν γνωρίζων, ἣν παρακαλῶ ὑπὸ σοῦ γνωρισθῆναί μοι (76.40).

that you may live',[53] is also open to a gnosticising interpretation.[54] A more difficult element is the determinism in c.84. Most scholars now think that gnosis does not imply determinism, but the motif may have appealed to individual Gnostics.[55]

What is true about section A applies even more to B. This section is a spiritual treatment of the NT gospels and of the person of Christ. Its introduction (88.1-9) speaks of mysteries that cannot be understood by everybody, a concept well known in Gnostic thinking. In actual fact this section implies that the polymorphous Jesus is a transcendent divine being who needs not be associated with this world below. His doubling (there are two 'Christ's' in 91 and 92) gives ample room for Christological speculations. It is well known that many Gnostics distinguished between Jesus, the one capable of suffering, and Christ, the impassible.

Again, it is attractive to think that the dimensions of Christ depend on the 'dimensions' of the faith in the person who beholds him (88.9-89.6, 9-10; 90.13-22). In the eyes of the reader, John and the other disciples in the text, James and Peter, can easily become types, if this was not yet part of the author's intention; John represents the true believers, the Gnostics; the others represent the members of the church who still lack the real knowledge of the Lord, who only know him 'after the flesh'. At least one of his qualities occurs again in section C: The light seen in (or on) Christ (90.1-4) has become an element of the cross of light in cc.98-101. That Christ does not eat (93.4-10) may be an indication of how the true Gnostic finds earthly things to be unimportant, but it may be used to support ascetic views as well. In the final episode (cc.106-115) married life and 'earth's vain pleasures' are again strongly depreciated. Special stress falls on John's exemplary asceticism, although he is an ascetic only in the broad sense of the term (c.113).

This survey suggests that the earliest text of the AJ was not in itself Gnostic, but as a result of its spiritual theology readily lent itself to use by a Gnostic editor.

[53] 76.19-20, 37: ἀπόθανε ἵνα ζήσῃς. Elliott shortens the second occurrence to 'Die to live'.

[54] So B. Gärtner, *The Theology of the Gospel of Thomas*, London 1961, 243-244, who also refers to 1 Cor 7:31; 1 Jn 2:8; cf. T. Baarda, 'Jesus said: Be Passers-by. On the meaning and origin of logion 42 in the Gospel of Thomas', in his *Early transmission of words of Jesus*, Amsterdam 1983, 179-205, esp. 180-181.

[55] J.A. Trumbower, *Born from Above. The Anthropology of the Gospel of John*, Tübingen 1992, holds that the Valentinian gnosis is deterministic; W.A. Löhr, 'Gnostic Determinism Reconsidered', *VigChr* 46 (1992) 381-390, denies it.

*2.5 Other differences*

Our attention to the theological characteristics can easily blind us to the fact that there are more arguments for arguing that section C comes from a different source than the rest of the early AJ. To forget these arguments would be an unnecessary limitation of the evidence.[56] In chapter 4 a detailed study of the Christology of the AJ will reveal major tensions between sections A and B on the one hand, and section C on the other. The different uses of the NT writings discussed in chapter 3 are also an indication that the AJ is a composite work.[57]

## 3 The genre of the text

The main thesis of the present chapter turns on the special function that cc.87-105 have in the AJ. In order to explicate these chapters in full, it must be noted that they belong to a different genre than the rest of the text does.

*3.1 The genre of section A*

A brief survey of previous opinions might be enlightening. In what is probably the first discussion of the genre of the AAA,[58] Dobschütz identifies them as novels.[59] He notices that the main element of the ancient novel,

[56] 'Cette différence de continu doctrinal constitue l'argument majeur en faveur de notre thèse sur l'origine indépendante de ces chapitres. Mais des arguments d'ordre littéraire viennent également l'étayer', JK, 581, cf. 582-589, where they refer to differences in genre, themes and vocabulary between cc.94-102 and 109 and the rest of the text.

[57] An additional (though admittedly not compelling) lexicographical argument in favour of the idea that section C was written by another hand than section A is based on the fact that the word κάτοπτρον in 28.4, 5 is used to denote a mirror whereas the word ἔσοπτρον occurs in 95.45. This variation is not likely to be explained by the difference in context, for although κάτοπτρον is used in its literal meaning and ἔσοπτρον is a metaphor, Liddell-Scott-Jones, *A Greek-English Lexicon, with a Supplement*, Oxford 1968, s.v., indicates that κάτοπτρον could evidently be used metaphorically as well as literally.

[58] Despite the differences between them, the AAA have common generic marks; see chapter 3.

[59] Dobschütz, 'Roman'. For recent research on the ancient novel see T. Hägg, *The Novel in Antiquity*, Oxford 1983; J.R. Morgan and R. Stoneman (eds.), *Greek Fiction. The Greek novel in context*, London/New York 1994; G. Schmeling (ed.), *The novel in the ancient world*, Leiden/New York/Köln 1996; English translations are available in B.P. Reardon (ed.), *Collected ancient Greek novels*, Berkeley/Los Angeles/London 1989.

erotic love, has its equivalent in the asceticism of the AAA.[60] Schmidt rather sees the AAA as forming a genre of their own, that of novels about apostles, inaugurated by the AJ and related to Acts of the Apostles rather than to the ancient novel.[61] He is more sceptical about the presence of historical reminiscences than Zahn, the scholar who basically sees the AJ as historiography, although he is far from uncritical of their historical value.[62] In the three early scholars mentioned so far, the basic positions are already represented: the AJ and the other AAA are seen as novels, historical accounts, or as representatives of a new genre.[63]

One's view regarding the genre seems to a great extent to be determined by one's conviction about the genre of the canonical Acts and about the extent of its influence on the AAA. The genre of Acts in itself is still a subject of debate,[64] but the majority of scholars have traditionally seen

[60] Dobschütz, 'Roman', esp. 101. Vielhauer, *Literatur*, 707, calls the ascetism of the AJ 'Erotik mit negativem Vorzeichen'. D.E. Aune, *The New Testament in Its Literary Environment*, Philadelphia 1987, 153, rightly states that the AAA cannot be novels because they lack a plot and are, as a result, a loose collection of episodes.

[61] Schmidt, *Petrusakten*, 99, 154-155.

[62] Zahn, *Acta Joannis,* clii, believes that most characters in the story, e.g. Drusiana and Andronicus, are historical persons, and that the AJ informs us about the historical John, cliv; but cf. cxlvii-cliv. I found, however, no extra-canonical information about the historical John in the AJ, except perhaps his city of residence (Ephesos), and his identification as the beloved disciple. In chapter 3 we will see that the following elements were probably collected from the canonical Gospels: the idea that John was a rather old man when he worked and died in Ephesos (cf. chapter 1 section 3.1); the description of his death as peaceful; his implicit designation as the author of the Johannine Gospel (88.3-5), and his identification as the brother of James, one of the three main disciples of the Lord (88.10-89.6).

[63] Söder's influential book, *Apostelgeschichten*, esp. 3-4, 183-186, 216, holds that the AAA are popular novelistic texts. Her opinion about the AJ is marred by the fact that she often quotes from the later stories about John (e.g. 48, 58-59, 92, 95, 153). Her followers include Blumenthal, *Formen und Motive*, 158-159, 165, and Pervo, 'Early Christian Fiction', in Morgan and Stoneman, *Greek fiction*, 246-247; *idem*, 'The ancient novel becomes Christian', in Schmeling, *Novel*, 685-711, esp. 694. Van Kampen, *Apostelverhalen*, 25, sees the AAA as a new genre of fictional 'stories about apostles' that contains no references to historical persons or situations; see his criticisms of Söder, 17-18.

[64] The following words by S.M. Sheeley, *Narrative Asides in Luke-Acts*, Sheffield 1992, 29, aptly describe the situation: 'Ancient narratives can be classified into three genres: romance (or novel), history and biography. Attempts have been made to classify Luke-Acts within all three genres.' See also R.S. Ascough, 'Narrative Technique and Generic Designation: Crowd Scenes in Luke-Acts and in Chariton', *CBQ* 58 (1996) 69-81.

Acts as a kind of history.[65] I support the case that is made to call it a short historical monograph, a type of work for which antiquity had no technical term.[66] The next chapter deals with the great influence of Acts on the AJ.

The most recent and most specific suggestion about the genre of the AAA takes the influence of Acts fully into account. Its proponent, Richard Bauckham, holds that the AAA form a subgenre of the novelistic biography.[67] He observes,

> The genre of the acts of an apostle is defined as a narrative of the missionary activity of an apostle subsequent to the ministry, death and resurrection of Jesus. ... the genre has been determined by the literary division of salvation-history represented by Luke's two volumes and reinforced by the second-century classification of Luke's Gospel with other Gospels and consequent treatment of Acts as a fully separate work.
>
> The apocryphal Acts are neither as different from Acts as the mainstream of scholarship has supposed nor as similar to Acts as Pervo has argued. The new genre to which they belong has been decisively influenced by Acts, but is both more biographical and more fictional. Their differences from Acts have much to do with the popular literary currents of the late second and early third centuries in which they originated.[68]

Bauckham states that this particular type of biography, dealing with a specific kind of historical figure, the Christian apostle, was also influenced

[65] So M. Hengel, *Zur urchristlichen Geschichtsschreibung*, Stuttgart 1979, 18; Aune, *Literary Environment*, 77-141; G.E. Sterling, *Historiography and Self-definition. Josephos, Luke-Acts and Apologetic Historiography*, Leiden 1992; F.F. Bruce, 'The Acts of the Apostles: Historical Record or Theological Reconstruction?', in *ANRW* II.25.3 (1988) 2569-2603; C.K. Barrett, 'The First New Testament?', *NT* 38 (1996) 94-104.

[66] E. Plümacher, 'Die Apostelgeschichte als historische Monographie', in J. Kremer (ed.), *Les Actes des Apôtres. Traditions, rédaction, théologie*, Gembloux/Leuven 1979, 457-466; Hengel, *Geschichtsschreibung*, 37; D.W. Palmer, 'Acts and the Historical Monograph', *TynB* 43 (1992) 373-388, esp. 387-388; *idem*, 'Acts and the Ancient Historical Monograph', in B.W. Winter and A.D. Clarke (eds.), *The Book of Acts in Its Ancient Literary Setting*, Grand Rapids/Carlisle 1993, 1-29.

[67] R.J. Bauckham, 'The *Acts of Paul* as a Sequel to Acts', in Winter and Clarke, *Book of Acts*, 105-152, 150.

[68] Bauckham, 'Sequel', 151, 152. He refers to R.I. Pervo, who argues in *Profit with delight. The Literary Genre of the Acts of the Apostles*, Philadelphia 1987, that Luke's Acts are a novel and in 'Early Christian Fiction' that the same holds for the AAA. J.K. Elliott, 'The Apocryphal Acts', *Expository Times* 105 (1993-'94) 71-77, esp. 77, points out that the miracle stories in Acts may have influenced the AAA.

by the novels.[69] In my opinion, this description can certainly be applied to section A of the AJ, which narrates John's career in Ephesos and the rest of Asia, provided we keep in mind the fact that the term biography should not be taken in its modern meaning.[70] The AJ does not represent John as a round character. The first part of his life is only of interest insofar as it shows how he became an ascetic for the Lord and as he is able to report several meetings with the Lord and to indicate their theological relevance (cc.112-113). But the John of the AJ, for all his human traits, does not undergo any development and is not much more than his message.[71] In fact the author uses an apparently personal form, a story about a specific character, to convey a religious message that could also have been clothed in the form of a tract or a letter. This choice cannot be seen apart from his acquaintance with the canonical Acts as well as with popular novels.

### *3.2 The genre of sections B and C*

It is clear that the genre of sections B and C (cc.87-105) needs to be considered separately. They do not deal with John and his activities in Asia Minor, but reflect John's experiences with the Lord Christ. The label 'gospel' has been used by several scholars, and rightly so, as we will see.[72]

If there was no hypothesis that section C is an addition, the genre of section B (cc.87-93 and 103-105) would not have become the subject of a separate discussion. These sections together form a single sermon delivered

[69] Bauckham, 'Sequel', 147-150, who also mentions the lives of philosophers and novelistic biographies as influences, cf. Aune, *Literary Environment*, 153. But the lives of the philosophers are from the third century and later, see Van Kampen, *Apostelverhalen*, 268-269, whereas the best examples of novelistic biographies date from the third century: the Alexander Romance (end of the third century AD, according to H. van Thiel, *Leben und Taten Alexanders von Makedonien*, Darmstadt 1974, xii) and the *Life of Apollonius* by Philostratus (shortly after 217 AD). Hägg, *Novel*, 160-161, also holds that the AAA form a new genre that was open to elements from other genres.

[70] A. Cameron, *Christianity and the Rhetoric of Empire. The Development of Christian Discourse*, Berkeley 1991, 117-118, argues that the AAA differ from the novels in that they belong to the realm of intended truth, not to that of fiction.

[71] As Van Kampen, *Apostelverhalen*, 267-268, 273-274, shows for all the apostles in the AAA.

[72] First by Zahn, 'Wanderungen', 192; Schimmelpfeng, 'Johannesakten', 492; Sturhahn, *Christologie*, 17; Pervo, 'Trajectories', 49, 57, 59, 66-67; *idem*, 'Ancient novel', 698. Schäferdiek, *NA*[3], 142, describes these chapters as a revelation discourse which *qua* genre resembles the Gospel of John; *idem*, 'Herkunft', 255, 261; JK, 583-586. There is an elaborate discussion of cc.87-105 as a gospel in K. Beyschlag, *Die verborgene Überlieferung von Christus*, München/Hamburg 1969, 97-116.

by John, which resembles the many other sermons in the text insofar as John addresses his hearers in the same way in all of them.[73] Admittedly, the specific subject of this sermon lies in the past: it deals with the 'life of Christ' or rather his brief appearances to the disciples. In this respect the sermon resembles c.113 (section A), which also deals with past events, in this case John's early years. Within the whole of the text, both sermons can be seen as flashbacks.

We begin our inquiry by observing that in the present text section B has been joined with section C (cc.94-102) to form a remarkable new unity. The focus of this unity differs from that of section A, for while the latter deals with John and his activities in Asia, the former has the identity of the Lord and the true meaning of his suffering as its subject matter.[74] As a sermon of the apostle John who now lives and works in Asia, this section forms as much a flashback within the whole of the text as a section formed on its own.[75]

Its contents can be outlined as follows: in cc.88-93 John narrates twelve brief encounters with the Lord, most of which resemble stories about the life of Jesus in the canonical gospels. The first of these narratives mentions the calling of disciples, and the sixth, seventh and eighth are related to the transfiguration. Cc.94-96 tell what happens immediately before the arrest of Jesus: Jesus sings a hymn and performs a dance, after which he explains the meaning of the latter. The theme of the hymn is the suffering of the Lord. The canonical gospels tell that Jesus and his followers sang a hymn after their last meal (Mk 14:26 par.). Cc.97-102 tell us about events that occur at the moment of the crucifixion. John is in a cave on the Mount of Olives, where he has a vision and hears the voice of the Lord, who explains its meaning. At one and the same time, the Lord[76] is hanging on the cross in Jerusalem, while a(nother) Lord meets John at the Mount of Olives in order to reveal his true identity and the meaning of his apparent suffering. The sequence of vision and consequent explanation

[73] 'brothers', 86.3-4; *88.1; 90.18; 93.1, 14; 103.1, 10;* 106.3, 14; 107.10; 115.4; 'beloved', *104.1*; 110.5; cf. 97.1.

[74] Cf. Luttikhuizen, 'Gnostic reading', 130. Schneider argues that cc.87-105 focus on the position and divinisation of John and the other believers. He sees the dance (cc.94-95) as an initiation rite for all disciples (*Mystery*, 113-127, 166-200), but this does not fit with the fact that cc.97-102 narrate a revelation that is granted to John *alone*. I would maintain that both a *prima facie* reading and a careful study of the text show that the focus of attention in cc.87-105 is on Christ alone, whereas neither John nor the other believers are given much attention.

[75] The term flashback first in Corsaro, ΠΡΑΞΕΙΣ, xxiv.

[76] One would rather expect 'Jesus' as subject of the sentence, but the verb 'was hang' (97.6) has no specified subject; the subject in 97.1 and 97.7 is 'the Lord'.

also occurs in the Book of Revelation and other prophetic and apocalyptic books.[77] In this case not an angel but the Lord himself interprets what John has seen (cf. the *Apocalypse of Peter*), even without his asking for this interpretation. Taken on its own, the long revelatory speech (98.7-101.16)[78] resembles the speeches of the Lord in the Fourth Gospel. It deals with the meaning of the cross (98-99) and its implications for the believers (100), while it rejects conflicting views about the suffering of the Lord (101). Since the speech is not interrupted by questions, it is a true discourse and not a dialogue, although this generic distinction should not be overstated.[79] John is the perfect believer who has no need to ask about anything.[80] After his discourse, the Lord 'was taken up without any of the multitude having seen him' (102.2-3). His disappearance marks the end of his presence on earth.[81] This conclusion implies that, for the AJ, the revelation discourse belongs to what we may call the period of Jesus' appearances on earth, and that it is not a later event.[82]

If we define a gospel as a mainly narrative text which deals with the words, deeds, death and resurrection of Jesus of Nazareth allegedly written down by or in the commission of one or more eyewitnesses,[83] we come to the tentative conclusion that *qua* contents, sections B and C constitute a single gospel.[84] Like the other gospels, it consists of different elements,

[77] The analogy with *Hermas* goes even further: in a vision there appears somebody in the likeness of a tower, who later appears as an older woman and declares that she is the 'Ἐκκλησία (11.3).

[78] Vielhauer, *Literatur*, 709; Schäferdiek, *NA*[5], 152.

[79] On Gnostic dialogues, see P. Perkins, *The Gnostic Dialogue. The Early Church and the Crisis of Gnosticism*, New York 1980; G.P. Luttikhuizen, 'The evaluation of the teaching of Jesus in Christian Gnostic revelation dialogues', *NT* 30 (1988) 158-168. A further resemblance is the luminous appearance of the Lord (Perkins, *Dialogue*, 45, 50-51).

[80] Questions are asked by the community of believers in c.87. In response their leader John, not a heavenly Revealer, pronounces his gospel, which was not originally Gnostic, as we have seen above.

[81] The verb ἀνελήμφθη (the spelling variant μ is negligible) also occurs in Mk 16:19, Acts 1:2, cf. Acts 1:11.

[82] In contrast, the revelation dialogues generally have a post-resurrection setting.

[83] Surprisingly enough, a suitable definition of 'gospel' cannot be found in such monographs as D. Dormeyer, *Evangelium als literarische und theologische Gattung*, Darmstadt 1989, and R.A. Burridge, *What are the Gospels?*, Cambridge 1992, nor in Introductions to the NT. A text such as the *Gospel of Thomas* or the reconstruction of Q, I would label as 'Collection of sayings of Christ'.

[84] The major difference between the genres of gospel and acts does not involve the form but the period described in each (before resp. after Easter/Pentecost) and the main speaker (Jesus resp. apostles). In a gospel, Christ is permanently present on earth (in this respect

such as short stories and pronouncement stories. A difference is that the canonical gospels have miracle stories, while the AJ only has the account of a vision and its explication by the Lord.

Now let us see if the structure of the section confirms our tentative conclusion that we are dealing with a gospel. First of all it is evident that sections B and C follow a chronological order, just as the canonical gospels do. They start with the calling of followers (88.9-11), give most attention to what, according to the canonical gospels, is the last week of Jesus' life (a designation not applicable here because of the docetic Christology of the text) and end with Christ's departure (102.1-2). Moreover, the outline of these sections remarkably resembles the canonical gospels, and the Fourth Gospel in particular, as is illustrated in the following table:

| | Gospel of John | Acts of John |
|---|---|---|
| introduction | 1:1-18 | 87.1 - 88.8 |
| public ministry | 1:19 - 12:50 | 88.9 - 93.17 |
| private teaching | 13 - 17 | 94 - 96 |
| ceremony | 13:1-30 | 94 - 95 |
| teaching proper | 13:31 - 17:36 | 96 |
| the glorious cross | 18 - 20 | 97 - 102 |
| epilogue | 21 | 103 - 105 |

The table enables us to surmise that sections B and C have the same general form as the NT gospels; we will come back to this point in the next chapter. Thus the structure of the material supports the use of the designation gospel for these chapters.

The gospel is presented in the form of a sermon of John in Ephesos. The sermon-form is a frame that encompasses the whole and is consistently maintained until the end.[85] A direct consequence of this formal choice is that the present story is in the first person (John is the narrator), a fact that distinguishes this gospel-like text from the canonical gospels.

The fact that both cc.88-93 and 98-101 have a highly visionary character and that there is no report of a resurrection complies with the theology

cc.87-93 contradict a feature of the genre) and presented as the main speaker. In acts he appears from time to time while an apostle carries the action and seldom quotes words of the Lord.

Only in APl scene 10 one of Paul's speeches (of which large parts are lost) quotes Jesus at length; see further Acts 10:38-41. There are no words of Jesus in the AAn and the APe; the ATh over forty times quotes the four gospels but has no independent logia.

[85] Cf. the passages mentioned in italics in note 73 above.

of the text. According to its viewpoint, the Lord never was a human being whose 'biography' could be written, but he was seen now and then as a divine messenger in a more or less human appearance which should not be confused with a real body. Thus the impression that the Christ who is presented here resembles more the Christ of Rev 1 than the Jesus of the gospels does not alter our conclusion that the text is a gospel text.

It is worth mentioning that the above implies that cc.87-93 and 103-105 (section B) occupy a very remarkable position in the AJ. They belong to the earliest stage of the text, but have now been integrated into the addition to the text and given a new function within the gospel flashback.[86]

*3.3 The genre of the final text*

What can we say about the genre of the complete text in its final form? Does the addition of section C, which created the gospel flashback, imply a decisive change in the genre of the text as a whole? I would argue that, unlike the work's theological orientation, the genre of the text was not notably affected by the editor. The narrative frame of the original AJ already contained such various textforms as travelogues, prayers, sermons and an animal tale.[87] To this list, one must now add short stories about the Lord, hymn and dance, and a revelatory discourse.[88] Within this conglomerate the gospel flashback (sections B and C) is the most notable segment because of its length and its remarkable contents. At the same time, its presence does not prevent us from viewing the final version of the text as a novelistic biography of an apostle, especially because the gospel flashback is presented as a sermon delivered by John, the protagonist of the book.[89]

[86] Note that the distinction between novelistic biography (cc.18-86, 103-115) and gospel (87-102) does not coincide with that between non-Gnostic (18-93, 103-108, 110-115) and Gnostic (94-102, 109).

[87] Cc.60-61; see E. Plümacher, 'Paignion und Biberfabel', *Apocrypha - le champ des Apocryphes* 3 (1992) 69-109. J. Bolyki, 'Miracle stories in the Acts of John', in Bremmer, *Acts of John*, 15-35, discusses the genre of each miracle story separately.

[88] Cf. the fact that a prophetic book in the OT like Jeremiah contains pieces as diverse as history, laments, prophecies against other nations, words of hope and words of doom. Cf. also the observation of B. Layton, *The Gnostic Scriptures. A New Translation with Annotations and Introductions*, Garden City NY 1987, 24, that the *Apocryphon of John* has a novelistic framework, within which pieces that belong to other genres have found a place.

[89] Barrett, 'First NT', 102-103, suggests that in their times both Luke-Acts and Marcion's canon were in fact complete New Testaments, and that Marcion's influence determined the form of the New Testament to be 'Gospel and Apostle'. If we follow this idea, the AJ can be seen as a New Testament 'two volumes in one' or 'two stages in one volume'. (But

## 4 The aim and the intended readers

Who were the intended readers of the AJ and what is the message that the author wants to convey to them? These two questions must be taken together because our answer to the one (e.g., unbelievers or believers) influences our answer to the other (conversion resp. instruction).

Scholarship has so far been unable to reach agreement on these crucial matters. Some people take the fact, demonstrated by the oldest extant papyri, that the AAA were copied on codices, as 'an indication of popularity', and they suggest that the AAA were intended to offer both edification and entertainment.[90] Others even claim that entertainment was the primary aim of the AAA.[91] But there are also theories about a more serious intention. Many scholars detect a more or less polemical tone in the AJ and consequently see it as propaganda for a specific form of Christianity, directed at other Christians with the intention of winning their allegiance.[92] More specifically, analogous to the ancient novels which are supposed to contain moral messages, the AAA are considered to be propaganda for an ascetic type of Christianity directed at a Christian public.[93] A different suggestion is that the author of the AJ wants to keep believers from seeking martyrdom, which he considers inappropriate for Gnostics who know that Christ did not really suffer; in this view the AJ attempts to win converts from the non-Gnostic church.[94]

Junod and Kaestli deny that the original AJ played a part in inner-Christian polemics; the work was rather intended for a non-Christian audience.[95] In their opinion sections A and B are directed both at the conversion of heathens and at the edification of open minded believers; the propaganda for the faith is most important. The simplicity of the text and

notice that neither Marcion nor the AJ recognise the Old Testament.)

[90] Aune, *Environment*, 141-142, 149. The newly discovered papyrus fragment of the AJ is indeed part of a codex; see Jenkins, 'Papyrus 1', 197.

[91] Blumenthal, *Formen und Motive*, 107; Altaner and Stuiber, *Patrologie*, 132.

[92] Hilgenfeld, 'Johannes'; Zahn, 'Wanderungen'; Schäferdiek, 'Herkunft'; H. Koester, *An Introduction to the New Testament*, Berlin/New York, 636 (esp. regarding cc.94-102!); Sirker-Wicklaus, *Untersuchungen*, 232-234; Pervo, 'Trajectories'.

[93] Dobschütz, 'Roman', 104; for the novel cf. *ibid.*, 91, and Söder, *Apostelgeschichten*, 116. S.L. Davies, *The Revolt of the Widows. The Social World of the Apocryphal Acts*, Ph.D. Dissertation Temple University 1978, particularly thinks that by means of the AAA female Christians want to edify other Christian women. Note again the collective treatment of all AAA and see J.N. Bremmer, 'Women in the Apocryphal Acts of John', in his *Acts of John*, 37-56, for a balanced treatment of the role of women.

[94] Schneider, *Mystery*, 15-16, 72, 76, 79 n.1, 127, 130-131, 220.

[95] Junod and Kaestli, 'Théologie', 144; JK, 685.

the inclusion of amusing scenes in it indicate that it was aimed at a large audience. Consequently, anything that might be scandalous in Christianity has been left out.[96] Eugene Gallagher argues that the explicit aim of the miracle stories that make up much of the AJ is conversion. However, the text indicates that the witnessing of miracles is insufficient to cause conversion, if commitment does not follow. He seems to think that both unbelievers and Christians were intended readers.[97]

Disagreement about the intended readership and the principle message of the AJ is so great that it seems as if scholars were not talking about the same text. In fact, such is exactly the case, for what is seen as the aim and intended readers of the work depends on which part of the composite text receives most attention. Exclusive attention to section A leads to a denial of polemics and to an insistence on the propagandistic goals of the AJ; one-sided attention to section C leads to the opinion that the text is, for the most part, polemic directed at other Christians. Once it is recognised that the AJ is a composite text and that both parts deserve due attention, it can be seen that these two parts have their own separate aims and intended readers.

### *4.1 Sections A and B*

Section A calls on people to live a life of faith, to love God and others, and especially to practice good behaviour. The text often deals with conversion and obedience, and its rather simple and repetitive language can be understood by a large audience.[98] Previous knowledge of the Jewish scriptures or of any part of the Christian tradition is not necessary. John's words in c.33 are typical of this text:

> I am no merchant who buys or exchanges goods; but Jesus Christ, of whom I preach, will, in his mercy and goodness, convert you all through me and deliver you from your error, who are domineered by

[96] JK, 685: 'Ils passent sous silence l'incarnation et la passion, ainsi que l'Ancien Testament avec ses représentations anthropomorphiques de Dieu et son thème de l'élection d'un peuple.' Van Kampen, *Apostelverhalen*, 113-114, is critical but nevertheless agrees in principle. See also Junod, 'Connaissance du christianisme', 22-23.

[97] E.V. Gallagher, 'Conversion and Salvation in the Apocryphal Acts of the Apostles', *The Second Century* 8 (1991) 13-29, 17-21, who says, 'Conversion stories portray what conversion *already means* to those who have accomplished it and what it *can mean* to those who might consider it.' 'In that sense conversion stories serve both as *models of* and *models for* the process of conversion' (29 with n.39, italics his).

[98] N. Holzberg, 'The genre: novels proper and the fringe', in Schmeling, *Novel*, 11-28, esp. 25 n.32, follows Hägg in thinking that repetitiveness points to the fact that texts were read aloud to an illiterate audience, but in the same volume E. Bowie, 'The ancient readers of the Greek novels', 87-106, esp. 95-100, 106, denies this.

unbelief and are sold into ignominious lusts.

This text does not polemise against other groups of Christians or their ideas. It has been claimed that cc.53-54 contain references to an inner-Christian polemics over asceticism and self-castration,[99] but self-castration was well known outside Christianity.[100] Moreover, the text neither specifically addresses Christians nor uses specifically Christian arguments. Section A is critical of a form of hedonism (cc.34-36) and of the heathen reliance on Dike, the goddess of justice (20.14-19). Among the cults under criticism are those of Artemis (cc.39-44) and of Asclepius (22.5-6; 56.18-20)[101] and the worship of images of deities in general (c.27).

It is likely that this text is intended as propaganda in favour of a spiritual form of Christianity aimed at non-Christians.[102] In this respect, the women Cleopatra and Drusiana are important examples for readers. They have a very firm faith, great self-restraint and the power to raise others from the dead. The author presents them as persons with whom the reader can identify.

We also briefly look at another aspect of the readership, viz. its social status. The main characters in the AJ are all from the higher classes (see cc.19, 31, 56, 73) but that does not necessarily imply that the readers must also have belonged to this group.[103] The fact that popular stories in all ages tend to deal with kings and other noblemen is no indication of their intended audiences. More important is the observation that the AJ lacks the references to classical Greek literature that are common in educated authors who write for their own group and of whom Clement of Alexandria is the most prominent example.[104] The text contains two slightly contradictory elements with regard to money. On the one hand John is severely critical about richness and even about 'the rich' in general (cc.34-36). The author does not see himself as a member of the upper class and deliberately addresses this class with an eye to readers from other social classes. When, on the other hand, we read that John possesses much money, which he

[99] Plümacher, 'Paignion', 106-108. The allegedly parallel texts all have uncertain dates and Alexandria almost certainly was not the place of origin of the AJ (see chapter 6).

[100] A.D. Nock, 'Eunuchs in ancient religion', *ARW* 23 (1925) 25-33, repr. in *idem, Essays on Relgion and the Ancient World* I, Oxford 1972, 7-15; H. Strathmann, 'Attis', *RAC* I, 889-899; R. Lane Fox, *Pagans and Christians*, New York 1987, 348.

[101] Plümacher, 'Missionsreise', 278 n.67.

[102] Cf. Bremmer, 'Women', 46-47.

[103] *Pace* Bolyki, 'Miracle stories', 35, and Bremmer, 'Women', 52.

[104] See A. Méhat, *Études sur les 'Stromates' de Clément d'Alexandrie*, Paris 1966, 178-195; H. Steneker, ΠΕΙΘΟΥΣ ΔΗΜΙΟΥΡΓΙΑ. *Observations sur la fonction du style dans le Protreptique de Clément d'Alexandrie*, Nijmegen 1967, 77-118, 141-174; A. van den Hoek, *Clement of Alexandria and his Use of Philo in the Stromateis*, Leiden 1988.

wants to be given to the poor (c.59), John himself seems to be among the rich.

*4.2 The Gnostic addition*

It is important to notice that the insertion of section C changed the character of the whole text. The addition of section C to the already existent section B resulted in the carefully composed gospel flashback which, because of its complicated message, is not suited for propagandistic purposes. It is rather meant to strengthen the faith of believers. On the textual level only a small group of believers is present when John delivers his message about the Lord (87; 88.1; 93.14-17; 104.6-7; 105). In section C the editor repeatedly stresses the fact that John is the only person whom the Lord entrusts with the secret revelation.[105] As a result John becomes a provider of inside information for those already believing, and he intimates that he must still withhold several things. The fact that John laughs at all those who remain ignorant of his teaching (102.1-4) implies that the author has little regard for those who do not believe his message. Thus the easy and accessible text of section A is followed by the more esoteric section B and the secret teaching of section C.[106] Propaganda has made way for esoteric teaching.

Can our knowledge of Gnostic practice shed light on the intended readers of the final text? Most probably Gnostic Christians directed their missionary efforts not at heathens but at ordinary Christians. That is what made them such a threat to emerging mainstream Christianity. And alternatively, when they addressed non-Christians, they first of all tried to make them 'ecclesiastical Christians' and only in a second stage did they try to convert them to the deeper, that is the Gnostic, form of Christianity.[107] Irenaeus and his predecessors, as well as Tertullian, had great difficulty in distinguishing the Gnostics from other Christians and in describing the exact ideas of the Gnostics, because in the initial stages their teaching hardly differed from that of the proto-orthodox church and because they presented themselves as just 'Christians'.[108] It is noteworthy that both

[105] 96.2, 5-6, 11-13; 97.10-12; 98.7-8; 101.1-4. I would suggest that 88.3-8 and 93.14-17 with their stress on secrecy stem wholly or in part from the author of section C.

[106] On the secrecy of mystery texts see now C. Riedweg, *Jüdisch-hellenistische Imitation eines orphischen Hieros Logos*, Tübingen 1993, 53.

[107] Tertullian, *De Praescr haer* 42.1-3 ('They make it their business not to convert the heathen, but to subvert our people'), cf. *ibid.* 41.1, and Origen, *Comm Prov* II.16; see Koschorke, *Polemik*, 222-224.

[108] E.g. *AdvHaer* 1 praef., 3.15.2; 3.17.4, 5.26.2, and Koschorke, *Polemik*, 175-179, 207, 224, 244, 246.

Irenaeus and Tertullian see the discovery of what the Gnostics really thought as their greatest task, undertaken in order to distinguish Gnosticism from the apostolic tradition.[109] Tertullian writes:

> The Valentinians ... care for nothing so much as to obscure what they preach. (...) If you ask them in good faith, they answer you with stern look and contracted brow, 'It is impenetrable.' If you try them with subtle questions, with the ambiguities of their double tongues they affirm the common faith. If you intimate to them that you understand (it), they deny everything of which they recognise (that you know it). If you come to a close engagement with them, they destroy your simplicity by their death.[110]

It thus appears very likely that the intended readers of the Gnostic part of the AJ are non-Gnostic Christians. The text indeed presupposes a working knowledge of the canonical gospels. People who already know about the Lord are now drawn into a revelation regarding the mysteries of his person, the interpretation of his suffering, and about the true meaning of the Gospel. These are matters which Gnostics often discussed with others Christians in order to win them to their version of the Christian faith.[111]

When we notice that the preliminary teachings of the Gnostics hardly differed from that of the rest of the church, it becomes inevitable to ask again whether all of the AJ was written by a Gnostic Christian? Is not even section A the work of a Gnostic who writes like a non-Gnostic Christian? Has it not been observed that Gnostic writings can be remarkably inconsistent and even self-contradictory,[112] so that the whole AJ could have had just one author? Can section A have been an attempt to adapt Gnostic views to non-Gnostic readers? The problem with this question is that the very fact that Gnostics behave as chameleons and that their texts can include almost anything, deprives us of the usual criteria for evaluating the issue. Nevertheless it seems wise to maintain the thesis that we are dealing with two different texts, the first of which is not Gnostic; we should not forget the other arguments presented above (section 2.2) which also

[109] Irenaeus, *AdvHaer* 1 praef.; 1.31.3-4; Tertullian, *Adv Valent* 3.1,5.

[110] *Adversus Valentinianos*, ed. J.-C. Fredouille (SC 280), Paris 1980, I.1, 4, translated with the aid of the only available English translation, P. Holmes in *The Writings of Q.S.F. Tertullianus* II (Ante-Nicene Christian Library 15), Edinburgh 1884, which is based on an antiquated Latin text. The last line is textually uncertain.

[111] See Koschorke, *Polemik*, 212-214, and the next section.

[112] Koschorke, *Polemik*, 44-45, 186, 197-198, 216.

indicate that section C was an addition.[113] The later chapters of this study will accumulate further evidence in support of this view of the AJ as a composite text.[114]

## 5 Initiation in two stages

### *5.1 The AJ as a two-stage initiation*

As we saw, the final editor has interpolated his material into the existing AJ, joining the already extant section B with the added section C. Together these sections form a gospel flashback that initiates the reader into the mysteries surrounding the Lord and his suffering. What is then the function of section A, which the editor left more or less unaltered, in the final text?

János Bolyki states that the purpose of the first part of the AJ (i.e., our section A) resembles that of a modern billboard that invites passers-by to the show inside the building. The fact that the stories in section A arouse a reader's curiosity is more important than the reaction of the crowds who witness the miracles. In effect, the different miracle stories serve as colourful invitations for the readers to what follows: the final revelation (cc.87-102).[115] Expanding on this point, I would argue that, in the final version of the text, the long narrative about John's activities in and around Ephesos functions as an introduction to the first principles of a spiritual form of Christianity. The miracles demonstrate the power of God, the sermons announce his ethical standards and the prayers illustrate his qualities. Section A aims to attract as many readers as possible and promises them spiritual rebirth (cc.47, 52, 82).

The final editor refrains from making changes in section A and deliberately withholds his Gnostic insights until the second stage of the text's didactic program, which deals with such topics as the real identity of Christ, the question whether he suffered, and the true meaning of the cross. Thus the narrative is also a kind of façade, which inspires trust in the

[113] In his latest contribution, 'Johannes-Akten', *RAC* Lief. 139-140 (1997) 564-595, esp. 573, K. Schäferdiek argues for a two-part structure that differs from mine: his first part ends with the (lost) story of the conversion of Drusiana and Andronicus and culminates in the gospel; the second ends with the Drusiana and Andronicus story and culminates in John's death.

[114] Section C contains insufficient information for a separate discussion of the social status of its readership.

[115] Bolyki, 'Miracle stories', 15-16, 34-35, who shows that of the miracle stories in the AJ, just two refer to a large crowd. Only these two, the second (cc.30-36) and third (cc.37-45), are grand displays of power that lead to the conversion of many. Bolyki does not discuss the order of the chapters.

genuineness of the Christianity of the text as a whole. The reader first comes to know John as the authoritative, powerful and trustworthy messenger of the Lord and his worship. In the second stage of the text, this authoritative messenger can initiate interested readers into the mystery of the person of Christ. Readers who have read the first stage and have been spiritually resurrected, have come into the sphere of influence of the Lord to such an extent that they are well prepared to be introduced to Gnostic Christology.

The first stage surely arouses curiosity in the reader. It contains an appearance of the Lord as a young man (cc.73, 76) that is not openly recognised as a Christophany.[116] In a part of the text that is now lost, it was also revealed that the Lord appeared to Drusiana in the form of John (cf. c.87). Towards the end of the section it becomes clear that not everybody is able to be converted (cc.84, 86). The resulting questions posed by the believers cause John to elucidate the mystery of the identity and the suffering of the Lord.

But the reader is not automatically drawn into the second stage. The transit is clearly marked by the stress on secrecy in the first half of c.88:

> I, indeed, am able neither to set forth to you nor to write the things which I saw and heard. Now I must adapt them to your hearing; and in accordance with everyone's capabilities I will communicate to you those things whereof you are able to become hearers, that you may see the glory that surrounds him who was and is both now and forever.

Thus the earliest text is now the first stage in a two-stage structure. The older section A is intended to arouse the interest of readers for the second stage which conveys the redemptive knowledge about the Lord himself and the mystery of salvation through him. A century ago Zahn already noticed the contours of this two-stage structure in the AJ:

> Während dieser Johannes in den auf Bekehrung der Heiden berechneten Missionspredigten sich im allgemeinen in den Formen der gemeinkirchlichen Verkündigung hält und nur hier und da seine Sondermeinung durchblicken lässt, enthüllt er im Kreise der längst Bekehrten und nur noch nicht zur ganzen Höhe gnostischen Glaubens und gläubiger Gnosis Entwickelten die Geheimnisse seiner Schule, die er aber auf eigene Erlebnisse des Johannes im Verkehr mit Jesus, die zu diesem Zweck erdichtet werden, gründet.[117]

That the two-stage structure is not original can be seen from the fact - already signalled above - that cc.106-115 in no way contain the same

[116] In chapter 4 I will prove that the person is indeed Christ himself.

[117] Zahn, 'Wanderungen', 199-200. The suggestion that cc.94-102 are an interpolation is much more recent.

theological accents as the second stage, but again display the non-Gnostic theology of the first stage.[118] If the AJ would have been the work of just one author, this move would be inexplicable because, after the gospel flashback, the author and his main character no longer need to hide their insights. As if he nevertheless wished to put his seal on these final chapters, the editor has interpolated them with the Gnosticising prayer c.109.

*5.2 Two-stage initiation in other texts*

It may be interesting to compare the AJ with texts that have a similar form of two-stage structure. In this section we will also compare the second stage of the AJ with another initiatory text, the *Rebirth Tract*. It must be stressed that these parallels are just illustrations of what we find in the AJ.

The communicative strategy behind the two-stage structure is discussed in other Gnostic texts. It is expressed in an allegory in the *Gospel of Philip*, which states that every kind of animal must receive its own proper food:[119]

> The owner of an estate acquired all sorts of things - children, slaves, cattle, dogs, hogs, wheat, barley, chaff, fodder [...], meat, and acorns. [Now], he was wise, and knew the food of each sort. He fed the children bread [...], but he fed [the] slaves [... and] grain. [He fed] the cattle [barley], chaff, fodder; he fed [the] dogs bones; he fed [the hogs] acorns and slops. Just so are the disciples of God: if they are wise they are perceptive about discipleship. Bodily forms will not deceive them: rather, what they consider is the condition of each person's soul, and they speak with that person accordingly. In the world there are many animals that have a human form. If the disciples of God recognise that they are hogs, they feed them acorns: if cattle, barley, chaff, and fodder; if dogs, bones; if slaves, a first course (that is, a single dish); if children, a complete meal.

The animals stand for several categories of human beings, more exactly, several humans are in fact beasts in a human shape (*Gospel of Philip* 81.7-8).[120] The passage describes how Gnostic preachers should adapt their sermons to the understanding of their hearers. They must taylor their

[118] For this reason we include them in section A.

[119] p.80.23-81.14 = Layton, *Gnostic Scriptures*, nr. 100.

[120] Like so much in the *Gospel of Philip*, this allegory is an extension of a short saying from a canonical writing, in this case Mt 7:6, 'Do not give the dogs what is holy; and do not throw your pearls before the swine'; see J.-É. Ménard, *L'Évangile selon Philippe*, Dissertation Strasbourg 1967, 32. In the *Gospel* animals usually stand for the psychic and the hylic classes of men; see Ménard, *ibid.*, 174, 236, 240.

discourse to suit each individual group.[121] If we apply this advice to the written word, the AJ suits the description of Gnostic preaching: it contains several different levels of teaching. The simple and more spectacular stories are for those who have just started on the way (the multitude), whereas the best teaching is for the Gnostics. What the first group gets is called *nsorp*, the first elements; the pneumatikoi receive *nteleion*, the complete and perfect teaching.[122]

In a much shorter form the Gnostic exegete Heracleon also alludes to different classes, when he comments on John 4:48: '"Unless you see signs and wonders you will not believe" was properly spoken to such a person as had the nature to be persuaded through works and through sense-perception, not to believe a word.'[123] Of this Heracleon, it is said that he 'could present a clear, consistent, and intentionally *exoteric* or publicly oriented exposition of his theology for non-initiates (like Flora), while reserving his *esoteric* theology (including the pleromatic myth) for initiates.'[124] Such a division closely parallels what we find in the AJ. Similarly, the Gnostic Theodotus claimed that the apostle Paul delivered his teaching on two levels, one for those on the left - the ordinary Christians - and one for those on the right - the Gnostics.[125]

The merger of Gnostic and non-Gnostic sections in one writing has several parallels in other Nag Hammadi texts, one of which is relevant for our purposes. The *Letter of Peter to Philip* (NHC VIII.2) quotes a non-Gnostic confessional formula about which Peter subsequently makes Gnostic comments. In this commentary, the simple faith of the church members is not rejected but transposed to a higher level.[126] The confession serves as a point of departure for the more mature teaching of the Gnostics.[127] H.-G. Bethge concludes that the Gnostic dialogue and the Gnostic preaching of Peter, which deviates from the confessional formula, have

[121] K. Koschorke, 'Eine gnostische Pfingstpredigt', *ZTK* 74 (1977) 342. Earlier W. Till, cited in R.McL. Wilson, *The Gospel of Philip*, London 1962, 179, stated that the slaves are given the first elements of doctrine, the children the complete and perfect instruction. The anthropological ideas of Ménard, *Philippe*, 236-237, miss the core because the point of comparison is in the food, not in the eaters.

[122] Wilson, *Philip*, 179; Y. Janssens, 'L'Évangile selon Philippe', *Le Muséon* 81 (1968) 79-133, 123-124.

[123] Herakleon frg. 40, quoted in R.M. Grant, *Gnosticism*, New York 1961, 205.

[124] E. Pagels, *The Johannine Gospel in Gnostic Exegesis: Heracleons' Commentary on John*, Nashville/New York 1973, 18, cf. 19.

[125] Clément d'Alexandrie, *Extraits de Théodote* (ed. F. Sagnard; SC 23), Paris 1948, repr. 1970, § 23.3.

[126] p.139.6 - 140.1.

[127] Koschorke, 'Pfingstpredigt', 333.

been interpolated into an originally non-Gnostic text. The original *Letter of Peter to Philip* belongs to the same genre as do the Acts of the Apostles. Yet Bethge's conclusion, that the final text is not Gnostic, fails to be convincing. Just as in the AJ, the Gnostic material excercises a profound influence over the whole text.[128]

The so-called *Rebirth Tract* from the Corpus Hermeticum (CH xiii, probably from the second half of the second century) describes the initiation of Tat into the mysteries of Hermes Trismegistos.[129] Does a comparison of this text with the second stage of the AJ enable us to say that in the case of John we are faced with an initiation? Common to both texts are the passive role of the recipient of the revelation (John, Tat), the reticence in communicating the mystical experience (AJ 102; xiii.13) and the singing of hymns, though in CH xiii the hymn is placed at the end of the text.[130] But the differences exceed the similarities: CH xiii vividly describes the inner experiences of Tat, who notices that twelve spirits leave him and that ten others return (7, 10), becomes extatic (4, 6), is changed and is made divine in the process (2, 14). Such features are absent from the AJ, in which John is just a silent listener and little attention is given to him as a character. The AJ speaks, in very general terms, of the members of the Lord who are now dispersed but will be reassembled (100.1-7); the most concrete words tell how John would become like the Lord (100.8-10; the phrase is conditional). It is the Christological revelation that forms the central content of the second stage in the AJ, not the inner experiences of John (cf. c.96). In this respect, the AJ resembles other Christian revelations that focus on what is being heard and seen rather than on anthropocentric

[128] H.-G. Bethge, *Der Brief des Petrus an Philippus. Ein neutestamentliches Apokryphon aus dem Funde von Nag Hammadi (NHC VIII.2)*, Berlin 1997, 55, 75-76, 123-125; *contra* e.g. G.P. Luttikhuizen, *Gnostische geschriften* I, Kampen 1986, 126-131.

[129] *Hermes Trismegistos to his son Tat, a secret discourse on a mountain, about regeneration and the rule of silence*, ed. A.D. Nock and A.-J. Festugière, *Corpus Hermeticum* II, Paris 1960; recent trans. B.P. Copenhaver, *Hermetica. The Greek* Corpus Hermeticum *and the Latin* Asclepius *in a new English translation, with notes and introduction*, Cambridge 1992. For the date cf. Pétrement, *Dieu séparé*, 14 n.14, 636, and K.W. Tröger, *Mysterienglaube und Gnosis in Corpus Hermeticum XIII*, Berlin 1971, 8, who opts for about 200. A comparison of this tract and the AJ from the point of view of docetism occurs in A.-J. Festugière, *La révélation d'Hermès Trismégiste IV. Le dieu inconnu et la gnose*, Paris 1954, 233-238.

[130] G. Zuntz, 'On the hymns in Corpus Hermeticum xiii', *Hermes* 83 (1955) 68-92, repr. in his *Opuscula Selecta*, Manchester 1972, 150-177, 164-165, suggests that the hymns included in CH xiii were originally sung in a community and were adopted by the author of this individualistic prose text, so that 'The relation then between prose-text and hymn in CH xiii would appear to be (...) as in the Acts of Thomas and of John.'

mystical experiences like those contained in CH xiii.[131] The AJ is primarily an initiation into the mystery of the person of Christ, not an account of the divinisation of John. The proper insight into the mystery of suffering that transforms the Gnostic receives less attention.

We finally turn to a totally different text, one which has a structure parallel to the AJ: the novel *The Golden Ass* (or *Metamorphoses*) by Apuleius (mid second century AD). After ten books of adventures, the eleventh and last book of *The Golden Ass* has a more serious character. It describes the redemptive initiation of the main character Lucius into the mysteries of Isis.[132] Much debate has been focused on whether or not book 11 was part of the original composition, but it is now widely thought that it was.[133] The (present) structure of *The Golden Ass* resembles that of the AJ insofar as it has two stages. The first stage is primarily amusing, although its pessimistic outlook must not be overlooked; the second is evidently meant to convey a serious message.[134]

The parallels adduced illustrate the function of the two-stage structure of the AJ, which stands in service of the Gnostic ideal of first converting people to Christianity and consequently initiating them into the deeper teachings of their group. For both purposes, the AJ makes use of contemporary literary forms.

[131] Another difference is that the revelation in the AJ is theocentric (Christocentric) in that Christ takes the initiative, whereas in CH xiii the initiate Tat by his questions pushes Hermes to reveal ever more.

[132] G.N. Sandy, 'Book 11: Ballast or anchor?', in B.L. Hijmans Jr and R.Th. van der Paardt (eds.), *Aspects of Apuleius' Golden Ass*, Groningen 1978, 123-140.

[133] R. Heine, 'Picaresque novel versus allegory', in Hijmans and Van der Paardt, *Aspects*, 25-42, 34-37, is one of those who deny the originality, even stating that book 11 was not originally planned by the author. But Hägg, *Novel*, 182-183, and S.J. Harrison, 'Apuleius' *Metamorphoses*', in Schmeling, *Novel*, 506-507, hold that this apotheosis is duly prepared in what came before; G. Anderson, *Ancient fiction. The novel in the Graeco-Roman world*, London 1984, 198-210, states that the story is modelled on folklore predecessors from Arabia, Sumeria and India in which the conversion is integral; but see the cautious review by K. Dowden, *Classical Review* 36 (1986) 59-61.

[134] One of the best-known speeches of Dio Chrysostom, *Euboicus* (*Or.* VII), also consists of two parts, the first mainly entertaining and the second serious in tone; see S. Swain, 'Dio and Lucian', in Morgan and Stoneman, *Greek Fiction*, 166-180, 168-172; D.A. Russell (ed.), *Dio Chrysostom Orations VII, XII, XXXVI*, Cambridge 1992, 8-13. V. Schmidt, 'Reaktionen auf das Christentum in den *Metamorphosen* des Apuleius', *VigChr* 51 (1997) 51-71, argues that Book 11 is not serious at all.

## 6 The circumstances in which the parts of the text originated

Now that we have sketched the structure and the purpose of the AJ, we turn to the origin of its two constituent parts. Place and date of origin will be dealt with in chapter 6; suffice it to say here that, as the activity of John in the AJ takes place in Asia Minor, scholars used to believe that it was written there. Nowadays Schäferdiek thinks that it was composed in Syria, Junod and Kaestli in Egypt, and other recent authors tend to agree with this latter view without reviewing the matter themselves.[135]

### *6.1 The background of sections A and B*

Sections A and B are first of all characterised by a lack of references to the Scriptures (see the next chapter). We also look in vain for allusions to any communal elements of religious life aside from the eucharist, such as baptism or another initiatory rite.[136] The text is silent about church leadership and about a successor for John.[137] The brief mention of ecclesiastical practices in c.84 does not give the impression that these were important for the author.[138] Junod and Kaestli suggest that there is a correlation between the absence of baptism and the fact that there is no real community.[139] It is remarkable that the author gives the impression of not knowing that the apostle Paul had already founded a Christian church in Ephesos.

But other observations create a sense of community, such as the repeated references to the crowds who witness John's words and miracles (cc.30-36, 37-45) and to the people who follow him on his tours (cc.18.1-4, 59). The community of believers seems to travel with John rather than to reside in Ephesos. Eucharistic bread is broken by the group of believers, and this celebration creates a clear bond (cc.85-86, 106-110). Especially during his last days, John has a circle of followers around him (63.1-2; 105; 106.1-3; 111.1-2), though they do not constitute an organised church.

These observations do not enable us to draw clear and firm conclusions about the external circumstances in which the text originated.

[135] Bremmer, 'The Novel', is an exception.

[136] Cf. Schneider, 'Gnostic Transformation', 254 n.5, 255 n.9; Roldanus, 'Eucharistie', 92, suggests that an initiatory rite was unnecessary because the members of the community became worthy either by conversion to asceticism or by divine election.

[137] Cf. Schäferdiek, 'Herkunft', 264.

[138] Cf. Schäferdiek, 'Herkunft', 264.

[139] Junod and Kaestli, 'Théologie', 133: 'Que les *Actes de Jean* (...) ne soient pas soucieux de recourir à un rite d'agrégation, cela peut s'expliquer par le fait qu'il n'y a pas à proprement parler de communauté, mais seulement des frères réunis autour de Jean et recevant l'eucharistie de ses mains.'

It may have its origin in a small community without officers and firm structures, or with an author who is just not interested in such matters. This state of affairs suggests an association with the Johannine community, for the Johannine epistles reflect a similar, apparently loose communal structure. The spiritual character of the faith (section 2.4 above) strengthens the value of this suggestion, to which we will return in chapter 6.

It can also be said that in section B the apostles James and Peter appear to be inferior to John (c.91). John is extremely curious, a trait that is sometimes criticised (90.7-17; 92) and sometimes not (89.7-8). It is clear that those among whom the text originated had a special interest in the person of John.

*6.2 The background and integration of section C*

*6.2.1 The composition and integration of section C*

As can already be deduced from the above discussions, it is likely that the author of section C (i.e., the end of c.95, cc.96-102 and c.109) is the same person who incorporated this section into the AJ. In my opinion, this author knew the older text (sections A and B) while he was at work; his own text is best understood when read in connection with the older text.[140] In several respects there is a remarkable continuity between sections A and B on the one hand, and section C on the other. With regard to the concepts there is the use of the theme of polymorphy, which is the idea that Christ can be seen in different form by different persons at the same moment. This theme is an important motif in the earliest text, especially in section B; besides, as I have argued elsewhere, the AJ is the earliest extant text in which it occurs.[141] The fact that this theme is taken up by the author of cc.96-102 makes it almost certain that he knew the older sections well.

An equally important datum in this respect is the form of the final text. The gospel flashback is a narrative unity whose form, as we saw above (section 3.2), closely parallels that of the Fourth Gospel. This composition can therefore hardly be the result of an accidental merger of two texts (sections A and B, resp. C); it probably originated because section C was written as an extension of section B.[142]

[140] Cf. Schneider, 'Gnostic Transformation', 247-249.

[141] P.J. Lalleman, 'Polymorphy of Christ', in Bremmer, *Acts of John*, 97-118, esp. 107-108, 117; more on polymorphy in chapter 4.

[142] JK, 581, argue that cc.94-102 have been interpolated so roughly between c.93 and 103 that this proves that the interpolation was not the work of the author of cc.94-102; they specially refer to 93.14-17. Schäferdiek, *NA*$^5$, 152, disagrees. I would rather see 93.14-17, a command to the listeners to keep silent about the revelation, as the editor's amendment, see

I suggest that the integration of section C occurred not long after the first version of the AJ had been written, probably still in the second century. The AJ has rather close links with the APl and the APe, which are both dated in the second century. The APe already seems to know the AJ in its final form,[143] so that this form must have originated well before the year 200. The Manichaean Psalms also show sign of knowledge of the AJ in its final form.[144] Secondly, the gospel flashback in the AJ represents the narrative type of gospel that constitutes a kind of biography of the Lord. All other examples of this type of gospel (the four canonical gospels, the *Gospel of Peter* and *Papyrus Egerton 2*) date from the first and second centuries.[145] Again, the lists of predicates used for cc.98 and 109 have parallels in texts from the second century (see chapter 4). And finally, in the first section of this chapter we saw that the complete gospel flashback disappeared from the AJ at a rather early moment, and we must allow time for that to happen.

I would argue that my hypothesis of a two-stage structure does more justice to the text in its final form than both other theories which have been proposed since the discovery of the heterogenity of section C. Junod and Kaestli, who first suggested that section C is an addition, hold that it originated independently of the rest of the AJ. In their view it was integrated into the text at some later moment by an otherwise unknown person, so that two authors and an interpolator contributed to the AJ.[146] They spend relatively few words on the merger of the two parts,[147]

note 105 above. Notice also that this phrase is in the present tense so that it forms a bridge to cc.94ff. rather than just an end to cc.87-93.

[143] See now P.J. Lalleman, 'The relationship between the Acts of John and the Acts of Peter', in J.N. Bremmer (ed.), *The Apocryphal Acts of Peter: Magic, Miracles and Gnosticism*, Leuven 1998, 161-177. Junod and Kaestli, *Histoire*, 36-40, seek to prove that the ATh, written in the first decades of the third century, depends on the final form of the AJ.

[144] JK, 700.

[145] The non-canonical narrative gospels (*Peter*, *Papyrus Egerton 2*) are from the second century; J.D. Crossan, *Four Other Gospels. Shadows on the Contours of the Canon*, Minneapolis 1985, even tries to date them in the first century. Other types of gospels are the collection of sayings (*Thomas*, *Philip*) and the revelation of the risen Lord to one or more of his disciples (*Gospel of Mary*, *Apocryphon of John*); these two forms also appear in combination. The collections of sayings are from different periods, the revelations are all relatively late.

[146] In 'Théologie', 144-145, they hold that the original text is earlier than the added material. But in JK, 700, they think that the two parts are 'à peu près contemporaine'; cf. *Histoire*, 4.

[147] JK, 700-702.

suggesting that it may have been Syrian Manichaeans who were responsible for it, 'à moins que cet assemblage n'ait été effectué plus tôt encore par une communauté gnostique attachée à la personne et à l'enseignement de Jean.'[148] Thus they see the AJ in its final form as an incidental fusion of two originally independent texts.

Now Junod and Kaestli are right insofar as the background of section C differs from that of sections A and B in two respects. The author of C condemns a group that adheres to some form of belief in the physical suffering and death of Christ. In opposition to them, he polemically marks his position in cc.99-102. In the other sections the suffering and death of Christ are, however, not referred to at all. Again, the canonical gospels seem to play a very minor role in sections A and B, whereas in section C the gospels are amply though critically used, as we will see in the next chapter. Moreover, because sections A and B contain no Gnostic ideology, they probably originated outside the sphere of influence or before the rise of Christian Gnosticism. But Junod and Kaestli do not notice the clear relations between the constituent parts which are uncovered in the present study. Consequently, they unnecessarily create the impression that the AJ is a rather disparate text.

Schäferdiek pays more attention to the unity of the final text than Junod and Kaestli, but he is no more convincing. He proposes that the AJ originated in a Johannine community, which was open to Gnostic ideas. Section A incorporates sections B and C which originated before 200, in such a way that the final text is a balanced whole.[149] But this idea meets with two objections, the first of which is that Schäferdiek's dating of section A is unduly late.[150] Secondly, he disparages the differences between the Christologies of the constituent sections to such an extent that he states that they are in agreement.[151] But the Christologies of sections A and C are indeed different, as chapter 4 will make evident.

[148] E. Junod and J.-D. Kaestli, 'Le dossier des "Actes de Jean"', in *ANRW* II.25.6, Berlin/New York 1988, 4293-4362, esp. 4342-4343, probably think of a moment in the third century as the date of integration; cf. *iidem*, *Histoire*, 4: 'L'intégration de ces deux textes à l'intérieur des *AJ* a pu se produire dès la fin du IIe siècle et elle est sans doute imputable à un cercle gnostique, à moins qu'elle n'ait été faite au IIIe siècle par les Manichéens.'

[149] Schäferdiek, 'Herkunft', 255, 258, 267; *idem*, *NA*$^5$, 152, 155. The priority of cc.97-102 was already argued by Plümacher, 'Apostelakten', 19.

[150] See chapter 6, and Bremmer, 'Women', 55.

[151] Schäferdiek, 'Herkunft', 266-267.

### 6.2.2 Is the final text a cultic text?

In what kind of environment did the final text originate and function? Is it a literary creation, meant to be read in private, or does it reflect the ideology of a Gnostic cult or an initiatory sacrament?[152] Does it represent the beliefs and practices of a community or is it just the result of an individual's creativity? Here we touch upon the formidable question of the social forms and cults of Gnostic Christianity. Very little is known about the situations in which Gnostic texts, such as those found in Nag Hammadi, originated, and about the social aspects of Gnostic Christianity.[153] In the present context, I can only discuss a few conflicting opinions.

Some scholars are convinced that Gnostic Christians formed real communities.[154] The idea that Gnostics, like adherents of mystery-cults, formed brotherhoods (φρατρίαι, θίασοι) is in itself not unlikely, but is not supported by much evidence from the sources.[155] Other scholars therefore hold that, due to the individualism of the Gnostics, their organisation was very loose, a view that goes back to Tertullian.[156]

A well-known explanation of the organisational structure within Gnosticism holds that these people formed the upper class or - in Koschorke's words - the inner circle within the Christian churches. They

[152] So Schneider, *Mystery*, 80-81, who says little about its life setting except that the community was persecuted, and adduces as evidence for the sacramental character the presence of dance in the *First Book of Jeu* and in Methodius of Olympus, rather remote parallels in my view. Concerning persecution see *ibid*., 16, 72, 76, 127, 220.

[153] In 1965, before the publication of most Nag Hammadi texts, Van Unnik stated that the Gnostics maintained total silence about the church and about their own social groups, if indeed any of the latter existed; see W.C. van Unnik, 'Les idées des gnostiques concernant l'église', in *Sparsa collecta* III, Leiden 1983, 285-296.

[154] K. Rudolph, *Die Gnosis*, Göttingen [3]1990, 228-258, 223. Hendrix and Segal, in Schneider, *Mystery*, i, affirm Rudolph's opinion but admit that 'very few Gnostic liturgical or cultic texts have been discovered.'

[155] B. Malich, 'Die Stellung der Liturgen in den koptisch-gnostischen Schriften', in P. Nagel (ed.), *Carl-Schmidt-Kolloquium 1988*, Halle 1990, 213-220, merely illustrates the absence of cultic materials in the texts by showing that 'Liturg' has a different meaning from the one we are seeking. The *Gospel of Thomas* shows a high degree of individualism and often calls the Gnostic believer μοναχός.

[156] Tertullian, *De praescr. haer.*42: 'The majority of them have not even churches'; see also E. Pagels, *The Gnostic Gospels*, Harmondsworth 1990 (1979), 149, 151 and *passim*; Layton, *Gnostic Scriptures*, 270-272; F. Wisse, 'Stalking those elusive Sethians' (563-576) and 'Discussion' (578-587), in B. Layton (ed.), *The Rediscovery of Gnosticism*, Vol. 2, Leiden 1981.

remained part of the church as long as possible.[157] But a recent study states that many Gnostic texts are purely literary products, that are not identifiable with the beliefs of any group. It stresses the fact that the ancient heresiologists and even the open-minded, widely-travelled Origen had only documentary evidence about many Gnostic sects. Only the Valentinians really formed separate groups, whereas other forms of Gnosis are best described as 'audience cults', loose groups which disseminate their ideas not through personal contact but through their writings.[158]

Both theories, that the Gnostics constituted an upper class and that they were a group of audience cults, are able to explain the lack of evidence for the existence of separate Gnostic communities and their initiatory rites. Probably the theories can even supplement each other. Gnostic Christians normally stayed within the church but those who left it did not form communities; instead they but remained solitary.

There is one text which gives us more relevant information: the *Apocalypse of Peter* (NHC VII.2). The community reflected in this text probably comprised one or more Gnostic sub-groups within a proto-orthodox majority. Henriëtte Havelaar argues convincingly that the larger community underwent a process of disintegration and that the Apocalypse was written as a program for a separate Gnostic group that was in search of an identity.[159]

When we compared the AJ explicitly with Corpus Hermeticum xiii, it appeared that the actual existence of Hermetic cults was as much disputed as we now see that is the case with the reality of Gnostic communities.[160] The evidence for Hermetic cults is scant and allows only the existence of small cult groups.[161] Scholars who deny the existence of Hermetic communities[162] are opposed by many who affirm it.[163] The former group

[157] Koschorke, *Polemik*, 220-224, 227-232, 246-249.

[158] A.B. Scott, 'Churches of Books? Sethian Social Organization', *JECS* 3 (1995) 109-122, 116-119. Irenaeus tells us much about the ideas of the Gnostics, but *AdvHaer* book 1 gives no indication of their organisation other than that it consisted of 'the teacher and those who follow him'. He mentions initiation (1.21.3-4) without explaining the details.

[159] H.W. Havelaar, *The Coptic Apocalypse of Peter (Nag Hammadi Codex VII,3). A Study of Generic, Intertextual and Christological Questions*, typescript Dissertation Groningen 1993, 182-189.

[160] For Reitzenstein's change of mind from 'Gemeinde' to 'Lesemysterium', see Copenhaver, *Hermetica*, li-liii.

[161] See the survey of opinions in W.C. Grese, *Corpus Hermeticum XIII and Early Christian Literature*, Leiden 1979, 40-43; and now G. Fowden, *The Egyptian Hermes*, second ed. Princeton 1993, esp. 160, 173, 186, 193.

[162] E.g. Festugière, *Hermès Trismégiste* IV.

can now refer to the analysis of the Nag Hammadi text that forms a close parallel to CH xiii, *The discourse on the eighth and ninth* (NHC VI.6). This *Discourse* frequently refers to books, but it contains no positive indications for the existence of a group. In view of this lack of evidence, it has been suggested that CH xiii is a mystery text meant for private reading.[164]

6.2.3 Basis for a new group

From our discussion so far, there emerge three possible sets of external circumstances in which Gnostic texts in general and the AJ in its final form in particular originated: they were either written and read in private or in a very small group, or by the Gnostic inner circle of a larger church,[165] or as a definition of identity for a new group. On the basis of the internal evidence, I will argue that the latter option is the most likely.

The AJ includes cc.94-95, which narrate the recital of a hymn and the performance of a dance by the Lord and his disciples and do not mention John by name. This piece gives the impression that it is associated with communal practice.[166] If that were indeed the case, we would be greatly interested in knowing more about this community and the editor's relationship with it. But the very existence of such a community must be doubted for at least two reasons. First, Junod and Kaestli point out that of the whole of cc.94-96, only 95.2-17, 37-50 existed as a hymn previous to the composition of the AJ, while the rest of these chapters is an editorial addition.[167] More recently it has even been argued that c.95 is not originally a hymn at all, but that the hymnic form of the material was imposed on it by the editor of the AJ.[168] This recognition implies that the hymn does not testify to the existence of a real sacrament; instead it is a literary creation. Again, the editor supplements the hymnic material with

[163] R. van den Broek, 'Hermes en zijn gemeente te Alexandrië', in G. Quispel (ed.), *De Hermetische Gnosis in de loop der eeuwen*, Baarn 1992, 9-26, 15, states that the Hermetic texts indicate the existence of small communities without priests or offerings, but with hymns, prayers and a holy kiss. Cf. S. Giversen, 'Hermetic Communities', in J.P. Sorensen (ed.), *Rethinking Religion. Studies in the Hellenistic Process*, Copenhagen 1989, 49-53.

[164] 'Lesemysterium'. So Grese, *CH XIII*, 201-202; cf. H. Köster, *Einführung in das Neue Testament*, Berlin/New York 1980, 401.

[165] Sirker-Wicklaus, *Untersuchungen*, 199, states that the minority group behind the AJ is a self-professed elite.

[166] So e.g. Plümacher, 'Apostelakten', 17; JK, 624-627, and Schneider, *Mystery*, 158 and *passim*.

[167] JK, 638-642.

[168] Dewey, 'Hymn', 70, 73-74; Kaestli, 'Response', 82, 86, agrees to abandon the term 'primitive hymn' for c.95. Schneider, *Mystery*, 158, 168, does not reply to these arguments.

explanatory pieces in which Jesus addresses John in the singular (95.43-96.23).[169] The added individualistic interpretation makes it unlikely that the hymn and dance were part of the cultic practice of the community to which the editor belonged.[170] In that case we would expect the additions to be in the plural.

Now we saw above that the structure of the gospel flashback is remarkably similar to that of the Fourth Gospel. My next chapter gathers the evidence that the text also betrays some knowledge of the Synoptic tradition, a fact that also implies a familiarity with the story of the Last Supper. I would therefore suggest that the editor consciously introduced his artificial alternative sacrament at the place where the Synoptics narrate the institution of the Last Supper.[171] The strained construction - plural form in the dance proper and singular in its explanation - suggests that the editor intended to write an alternative gospel, in which the disciples are addressed in the plural, but that he does not describe an existing sacrament. We conclude that cc.94-95 are a program for cultic innovation in a community that does not recognise the canonical gospels as authoritative, and that they do not mirror an existing practice. The idea of a dance may have been suggested by Jewish Passover practices and/or by Mt 11:17 (Lk 7:32).[172]

It is unlikely that the new sacrament is meant to replace the eucharist. It has a different function, as it it is initiatory, whereas the breaking of the bread in the first stage of the text has a confirming function;[173] second, the redactor has left the narratives about the eucharist in his final text and even extended one of the eucharistic prayers (cc.108-109).

The reader of section C is struck by its very sharp tone. 'The multitude down below in Jerusalem' no doubt stands for the ignorant majority of Christian believers, in contrast with the initiate John (97.8-10).[174] These people are explicitly criticised for having a totally wrong Christology and saying unworthy things about the suffering of the Lord (99.5-7). The author argues that unlike what 'they' say, the Lord's suffering was not physical, though it was real (101.1-3, 8-11). The true body of the divine saviour Christ is celestial, and composed of the believers (c.100). But these

[169] Cf. chapter 1, section 2 above.

[170] *Pace* Kaestli, 'Response', 84-86, and Roldanus, 'Eucharistie'.

[171] Cf. section 3.2 above.

[172] JK, 598, 623. Evidence for the Passover practice is provided in Van Unnik, 'Dance'.

[173] Roldanus, 'Eucharistie', 95, emphasises the similarities between the eucharists in cc.85-86 and 106-110 on the one hand and the present sacrament on the other hand: both primarily praise Christ and stress the brotherhood. I doubt the latter element.

[174] 'Ιωάννη, τῷ κάτω ὄχλῳ ἐν 'Ιεροσολύμοις - σοὶ δὲ. Here κάτω has primarily a local, but also a cognitive meaning.

ordinary Christians are not just described as ignorant. It is said that they are 'outside the mystery' and that therefore John should ignore and even despise them.[175] John laughs about them because they allegedly take the Gospel stories literally (c.102). These facts imply that the author is not just conscious of being in a minority position and of the fact that his text would probably not be accepted by all Christians. They also demonstrate that he actively widened the divide between himself and these others.

*6.3 Conclusion*

To sum up, section C's sharp criticism of the majority church makes it unlikely that the author had been for a long time an isolated individual, but rather that until recently he had been part of a larger group of Christians whom he left in order to seek a new position. The author probably belongs to, or even is the sole initiator of, a small minority group involved in a process of defining its identity and communal practice by distinguishing itself from the majority.

As we will later see, the majority and minority groups are both strongly influenced by Johannine theology. There are no indications that the majority knows or acknowledges the AJ. On the other hand, the editor had already come into contact with sections A and B of the AJ and with Gnostic ideas. As a result he sets out to compose his own version of the AJ as a program for the new Johannine community. At about the same time the larger group is giving its own answers to the problem of the Lord's suffering.

The two-stage structure makes the text a suitable introduction to the new group. It can be presented to the majority church, to interested outsiders and to new members. For the actual initiation the text supplies the group with a self-created sacrament.

Previous research did not reach agreement about the main objective of the AJ: is it a missionary text or a polemical piece of advanced Christian teaching? The road to an answer is open when cc.94-102 are recognised as an addition and the hypothesis of the two-stage structure is adopted. We are now in a position which enables us to see that the early text, now the first stage in the composite text, aims at the conversion of outsiders, who are to be attracted by the miracle stories and the missionary speeches. The final editor made the gospel flashback, more specifically cc.97-102, the climax of the text, thus turning it into an initiation into the mysteries of the person and mission of Christ that individual readers can undergo. In the two-stage structure of the final form of the text, both aims are visible.

[175] τῶν οὖν πολλῶν ἀμέλει καὶ τῶν ἔξω τοῦ μυστηρίου καταφρόνει (100.10-11) - a clear synonymous parallelism.

*6.4 Authorship*

The AJ has come to us as an anonymous text, but when the ninth-century patriarch Photius read the AAA in a one-volume edition, his copy of that text probably referred to the author by name. He writes: 'These are written by Leukios Charinos, as the same book makes clear' (γράφει δὲ αὐτάς, ὡς δηλοῖ τὸ αὐτὸ βιβλίον, Λεύκιος Χαρῖνος). The words δηλοῖ τὸ αὐτὸ βιβλίον make unmistakably clear that the name was in the text of the book itself.[176] Since Photius' writing, the name Leukios became associated especially with the AJ. Many scholars indeed believe that the name Leukios occurred in the original text of the AJ; yet Zahn became convinced that the name was a pseudonym,[177] obviously devised in order to be associated with the author of Acts, Luke.[178] Junod and Kaestli have demonstrated that Photius is the very first to connect Leukios specifically with the AJ and that this attribution is not supported by earlier attestations, so that it is highly unlikely that this name was in the text of the early AJ.[179] The assumption that the author of the AJ also wrote the APe has no advocates in our time.[180]

[176] Photius, *Bibliotheca* cod. 114 (cf. p. 26 above); his first sentence is: Ἀνεγνώσθη βιβλίον, αἱ λεγόμεναι τῶν ἀποστόλων περίοδοι, ἐν αἷς περιείχοντο πράξεις Πέτρου, Ἰωάννου, Ἀνδρέου, Θωμᾶ, Παύλου. Note the singular βιβλίον which suggests redaction into one volume with possibly a preface or colophon. When Photius discusses a work that consists of more parts ('books'), he indicates this with the word λόγοι (e.g., codd. 4, 8, 13), βιβλία (codd. 10-12) or τόμοι (codd. 15, 21). On Photius and the AAA see Junod, 'Actes apocryphes et hérésie'.

[177] Schäferdiek, 'Herkunft', 261-263; *idem*, 'Die Leukios Charinos zugeschriebene manichäische Sammlung apokrypher Apostelgeschichten', in *NA*$^5$, 91-93; *idem*, 'Johannesakten', in *NA*$^5$, 151, 156; 'Johannes-Akten' (*RAC*) 592; Culpepper, *John*, 189; C.-J. Thornton, *Der Zeuge des Zeugen. Lukas als Historiker der Paulusreisen*, Tübingen 1991, 129 n.105; Zahn, *Apostel und Apostelschüler*, 14-18; *idem*, *Geschichte des Kanons* II, 856-859; cf. Dobschütz, 'Roman', 104.

[178] Zahn, *Acta Joannis*, lxx; James, *Apocrypha Anecdota*, xi-xii, followed this suggestion, like Zahn presupposing that the AJ knows Acts: '(...) it will be allowed that the choice of the name Leucius by a writer of Acts of the Apostles, is exceedingly likely to be an intentional suggestion of the name Lucas, which belonged to the author of Acts already accepted.' Zahn also uses the name Leucius in order to distinguish the original AJ from later stories about John which are linked with the authors Prochorus, (Pseudo-) Melito and (Pseudo-)Abdias.

[179] Junod and Kaestli, *Histoire*, 133-145. Leukios is a pupil of John in Epiphanius, *Panarion* 51.6.

[180] For this view see Zahn, *Geschichte des Kanons* II, 839-841, 860-861; *idem*, 'Wanderungen', 210-211; James, *Apocrypha anecdota*, x, xxiv-xxix, 151-153; rejected by Schmidt, *Petrusakten*, 76-77, 95-99, 125; cf. James's review of Schmidt's book in *JTS* 5

The opinion that a woman was the author and/or that the AJ originated in circles of Christian women was first ventured a generation ago.[181] It suffers from the fact that it treats the AAA as a corpus, arguing that 'the AAA' were written by women and therefore the AJ as well. No specific study of the AJ has been made on this basis. The main proponent of the hypothesis of female authorship, Stevan Davies, treats AJ 1-17 and the Acts of Xanthippe as part of the AJ.[182] He also assumes that the AJ and the other AAA advocate an absolute rejection of sexual intercourse, a feature that, in his opinion, indicates composition by women in strictly celibatarian conventicles, who considered themselves brides of Christ.[183] In chapter 5 we will see that this opinion has no textual base. Similar weaknesses are found in Virginia Burrus' suggestions that the AAA were women's literature. Burrus tends to overlook the fact that many episodes in the AJ are not related to women's - as opposed to men's - interests at all.[184] But rejection of female authorship should not blind us to the importance of a female readership and the liberating effects of these texts on Christian women.[185]

The present study has demonstrated that we are dealing with two authors. Of course, this conclusion only complicates the question of the authorship. There are no suggestions regarding their identity and I can only conclude that the names of both authors must remain unknown since the internal evidence of the text renders insufficient information.

(1904) 293-296, and my 'Acts of John and Acts of Peter', 161-162.

181 Hamman, 'Sitz im Leben', 64; cf. now Davies, *Social World*; V. Burrus, *Chastity as Autonomy. Women in the Stories of Apocryphal Acts*, Lewiston/Queenston 1987.

182 Davies, *Social World*, 7-10, 34, 47.

183 Davies, *Social World*, 73-75, 121-122.

184 Kaestli, 'Fiction littéraire', 281-283, shows that Davies and Burrus differ in their view of the literary status of the AAA: Davies treats them as original creations, whereas Burrus thinks that they have an oral prehistory as legends. Kaestli thinks that just the APlTh, later incorporated into the APl, was composed by a woman, 291-294.

185 Bremmer, 'Women', 50-54; *idem*, 'Magic', 57-58; *idem*, 'The novel'.

# CHAPTER 3: INTERTEXTUAL RELATIONS

## 1 Introduction

### *1.1 Intertextuality*

This chapter deals with the allusions in the AJ[1] to earlier and contemporary writings with the object of discovering which writings were known to the authors of the AJ and how these earlier texts function within the later text. Special stress will fall on the influence of the genres of the 'gospel' and of 'acts' on the AJ. No new theory of intertextuality is offered because previous studies of intertextual relations, such as those of Paulien, Hays and Bastiaens, provide a suitable frame of reference.[2] I opt for what Jean Bastiaens calls a limited theory of intertextuality, that is, the question how the younger writing (the phenotext, in our case the AJ) takes up and 'transforms' older writings (architexts: mainly early Christian texts) and how new meanings are created in this process.[3]

There are three kinds of intertextual relationships, which we will label generic, structural and lexical. Of these three, the generic influences on the AJ have already been discussed earlier in this study (chapter 2.3) and they determine the structure of the present chapter (see below). Structural and lexical intertextuality is well defined and distinguished by Daniel Patte.[4] Works are said to be structurally related when the structure of (part of) the phenotext has wholly or in part been influenced by the architext. Thus an episode may have been modelled on an episode in an earlier text, or a

[1] As above, I refer to sections which are studied separately:
cc.18-86, 106-108, 110-115 (A)
cc.87-93 + 103-105 (B)
cc.94-102 + 109 (C)
It should be noted that, as far as genre is concerned, section B is associated with C, but that its origin and authorship are shared by A.

[2] J. Paulien, *Allusions, Exegetical Method, and the Interpretation of Revelation 8:7-12*, Dissertation Andrews University 1987; R.B. Hays, *Echoes of Scripture in the Letters of Paul*, New Haven/London 1989, 15; J.C. Bastiaens, *Interpretaties van Jesaja 53. Een intertextueel onderzoek naar de lijdende Knecht in Jes 53 (MT/LXX) en in Lk 22:14-38, Hand 3:12-26, Hand 4:23-31 en Hand 8:26-40*, Tilburg 1993, 10. What I state in the main text implies that I leave out the so-called intertextuality of present day readers. The present research studies intertextuality as it contributed to the text's composition. The influence that the AJ had on texts dated after 300 also falls outside the scope of the present book; see Junod and Kaestli, *Histoire*, passim.

[3] Bastiaens, *Interpretaties*, 10, 24.

[4] D. Patte, *Early Jewish Hermeneutics in Palestine*, Missoula 1975, 171-172, 184; cf. Havelaar, *Apocalypse of Peter*, 118-119. Lexical relations are also called anthological; see A. Robert, *Dictionnaire de la Bible. Supplément* V, Paris 1957, 411.

permanent trait of a text can be traced back to another text. In the case of such structural affinities, the phenotext is often engaged in a kind of dialogue with the architext.[5] A lexical form of intertextuality, on the other hand, is a more atomistic type of relationship, in which the wording of (part of) a phrase has been chosen from the words of a writing known to the author of the phenotext. Such lexical kinship can consist of anything from an explicit citation to a mere echo. When the author of a text explicitly quotes an earlier text, the task of the modern scholar is relatively easy. But when the author is less explicit, we are faced with considerable questions of verification. Studies in intertextuality have not developed a clear method of determining if there is an intertextual relationship at all. This problem frequently occurs in connection with the AJ because explicit quotations are rare, if not entirely absent.[6]

The Belgian literary critic Paul Claes has developed a further classification of intertextual relationships on the basis of their ideological qualities. He distinguishes four ways in which the phenotext can be related to the architext: it can repeat it, add to it, subtract from it, or substitute one thing for another. On the level of meaning these respective transformations correspond to the notions of allusion, deepening, fading or distortion. All three types of intertextual relationships (generic, structural and lexical) may involve any of the four transformations; the nature of the transformation(s) shows the attitude (e.g., approval or criticism) of the phenotext towards the architext.[7]

Within lexical intertextuality I follow Jon Paulien in distinguishing citation from quotation and allusion. A citation is thus stipulated as a repetition of words from an architext, which is explicitly identified by the author of the phenotext. A quotation selects enough words from an architext to make certain that the author had that writing in mind, although he leaves it to the reader to detect his borrowings.[8] An allusion is the intentional use of elements from a previous work in such a way that the context of the idea alluded to resounds in the later writing. To speak of an allusion requires that at least two words of more than minor significance are parallel. But in my opinion a name alone (such as Andrew, AJ 88) is

[5] P. Claes, *De mot zit in de mythe*, Leuven 1981, 57, 162 calls this relationship 'textual'.

[6] In this respect, the AJ can be compared to Rev, which has many allusions to the OT, but hardly any explicit quotations from it. I will come back to this point in the section on method.

[7] Claes, *Mot*; *idem*, *Echo's echo's. De kunst van de allusie*, Amsterdam 1988; cf. Bastiaens, *Interpretaties*, 15-18.

[8] Cf. Paulien, *Allusions*, 170-171.

sufficient for an allusion.[9] An echo, on the other hand, is the use of a key word, symbol or theme apart from its context and without needing authorial intention.[10] As such, it is the 'weakest' form of intertextual relationship.

In addition to such textual links, texts can have ideological associations: they can agree on the level of ideas and can share concepts. Such relationships may or may not go hand in hand with other forms of intertextuality. A well-known example of an ideological relationship is that between the Gospel of John and Ignatius of Antioch. It is questionable if the writings of Ignatius are textually related to the Fourth Gospel,[11] since there are only three passages that can be used to support such a hypothesis. There is, however, no doubt that John and Ignatius have rather close theological connections.[12] We will deal with the theological or ideological affinities of the AJ (or, the notable absence of such affinities) with some early Christian writings, especially with the Johannine literature.

*1.2 The structure and method of the present investigation*

In chapter 2 we saw that the AJ consists of two main parts, each of which had its own audience. It also became evident that the addressees of the first part (sections A and B) were non-Christians, who could not be supposed to know any Christian writing. This fact makes it a priori unlikely that the text of the first part has intricate relations with earlier Christian writings. The second author of the AJ, on the other hand, envisages 'competent' readers with at least some knowledge of other Christian texts. In the part

[9] P. Soemers, who studied and classified the references to Scripture in Athanasius' *Vita Antonii*, considers references to certain persons or events as a separate category next to explicit quotations and references which are not indicated in the text but are signaled by the reader. See his *Athanasius, die Vita Antonii und die Bibel* (2 vols.), Vaals/Frankfurt am Main 1989, vol.2, xxiii, cf. v-xvii.

[10] Paulien, *Allusions*, 171-173; cf. 305 n.1: 'An echo is where the author uses the symbol itself in its general meaning, while a direct allusion uses a symbol in context, i.e. as a reference to the surrounding language in an earlier text.' Notice that Hays generally uses the term 'echo' for Paul's use of Scripture.

[11] Von Loewenich, *Johannes-Verständnis*, 33-38, is uncertain about this issue; V. Corwin, *St.Ignatius and Christianity in Antioch*, New Haven 1960, 69-79, 76-77, is more negative; Hengel, *Johanneische Frage*, 69, calls a textual relation 'not unlikely'. The most straightforwardly positive view is held by C. Maurer, *Ignatius von Antiochien und das Johannesevangelium*, Zürich 1949. W.R. Schoedel, 'Polycarp of Smyrna and Ignatius of Antioch', *ANRW* II.27.1 (1993), 272-358, esp. 306-307, leaves the matter open, while C. Munier, 'Où en est la question d'Ignace d'Antioche? Bilan d'un siècle de recherches 1870-1988', *ibid.*, 359-484, is more negative.

[12] Von Loewenich, *Johannes-Verständnis*, 26-32; Hengel, *Johanneische Frage*, 68-71.

that he contributed to the AJ (section C), we may find more interesting intertextual exchanges. Remarkably, we will see that it is this part which is marked by a negative attitude towards other Christian writings.

Another conclusion from chapter 2 which must be repeated here is that *qua* genre section A of the AJ resembles the book of Acts and the other Apocryphal Acts, while sections B and C form a gospel-like text. This observation determines the approach in the present chapter, which begins with the relationship between section A on the one hand and the canonical book of Acts and the other AAA on the other. The second area of investigation will deal with the ways in which the other sections of the AJ relate to the gospels, especially that one which bears the name of John. Convergences in the areas of lexical and especially structural matters will serve to confirm the generic congruencies. Some of the treatment of the theological and historical position of the AJ within the Johannine sphere of influence will anticipate the treatment of the Christology in the next chapter.

The present research aims at attaining several objectives. First, we need a more extensive knowledge of the background of the AJ than we now have, in order to illuminate its realm of thought and to aid in future interpretations. Secondly, we want to know what view of Scripture and what phase in the history of the canon of the NT is reflected in the AJ. Are the Christian writings in any way seen as Scripture?[13] The conclusions from my research may inform us about the second-century vicissitudes of the NT writings, a subject about which our knowledge is still insufficient.[14] Thirdly, the discovery of the influence of specific texts or traditions may help us to characterise the environment in which the AJ originated.

As yet a full length study of the intertextual relations involving the AJ does not exist.[15] In gathering the material, all texts listed in the bibliogra-

[13] As the AJ was probably written in the second century, it is not *a priori* unlikely that it also interacts with words of Christ that still circulated orally. To find traces of these will, however, be a difficult matter.

[14] See the symposium *The New Testament in Early Christianity*, ed. J.-M. Sevrin, Leuven 1989.

[15] There is of course the *Biblia Patristica*, ed. A. Benoît *et al.*, which refers to the AJ a total of 190 times. However, the reference is to cc.1-17 in 47 cases; this section no is longer considered part of the original text; 23 more references are to secondary texts printed by Bonnet, which leaves 120 real references. Of these, one is to Sap, the others are all to the NT. They can be arranged as follows:

phy were collected and critically filtered. I also found a number of additional possible relationships by reading numerous Hellenistic, Jewish and early Christian texts. This chapter presents the results of this research, viz. those cases in which there is sufficient certainty about a meaningful intertextual relationship. From the New Testament writings only the gospels and Acts need to be fully considered.[16] Some cases which readers may find more convincing than I find them, have found a place in the footnotes, but their number has been kept to the absolute minimum.

The evaluation of possible intertextual relationships will always contain a measure of uncertainty,[17] but the seven criteria for the evaluation of supposed echoes of Scripture in Paul formulated by Richard B.Hays can profitably be applied to any intertextual research and thus diminish the degree of subjectivity.[18] Of these seven, in the case of the AJ, history of interpretation is of little help because of the limited amount of work that has been done on our text. The criterion of historical plausibility ('Could the author intend this and would the readers understand it?') has become more useful, since the lack of information about the authors and the addressees of the AJ is being remedied in present day studies. As far as availability is concerned, many Christians in the second century would know the Scriptures only from hearing them being read in their communi-

| | Section A (18-86, 106-115) | Section B (87-93, 103-105) | Section C (94-102, 109) |
|---|---|---|---|
| Mt | 3 | 5 | 14 |
| Mk | 2 | 5 | 10 |
| Lk | 2 | 7 | 11 |
| Jn | 1 | 7 | 27 |
| Acts | 4 | - | 3 |
| 1 Jn | - | 4 | 1 |
| Rev | - | - | 2 |
| other | 9 | 1 | 2 |
| total | 21 | 29 | 70 |

The long section A has fewer references than the shorter sections B and C. The Gospel of John occurs very often in relation to section C. 86 out of the 120 references link the four gospels with sections B and C. Acts appears relatively infrequently. Note that the edition of Bonnet lists 11 references that do not occur in the *Biblia Patristica*, a fact that illustrates the methodological problem of the question what constitutes a reference or an allusion.

[16] The other New Testament writings are discussed in par. 7.2 below.

[17] Whereas Paul is relatively well-known and most of his Letters offer some amount of explicit information about their addressees, reconstructions of authors and readers of the AJ are more hypothetical.

[18] Hays, *Echoes*, 29-32.

ties, while only few people would have copies of the writings.[19] If the AJ appears to interact with one of these books, the question whether it depends on oral traditions rather than on written texts should therefore be given some attention. But when there are one or more clear indications that refer to the actual text of one and the same book, we may conclude that the author of the phenotext indeed knew that writing well enough to justify our stating that he 'used' it.

## 2 The Acts of John and the canonical Book of Acts

### *2.1 Introduction*

Until now, a thorough comparison of the AJ with Acts has never been undertaken. What we have are general pronouncements about the relation between the AAA and Acts. Carl Schmidt and several subsequent scholars argue that the form of the AAA depends on that of the canonical Acts.[20] Elliott and A.F.J. Klijn even hold that Acts is the main source of inspiration for the AAA.[21] But other scholars, such as W. Schneemelcher and E. Plümacher, deny that Acts had more than just casual influence on the AAA,[22] while L. van Kampen stresses the differences between Acts and AAA on the basis of the fact that Acts is primarily history while the AAA are purely fictional.[23] In this respect, essays have appeared which compare other AAA, viz. the APl and the APe, with Acts,[24] whereas no such study

[19] See e.g. R.E. Brown, 'The *Gospel of Peter* and Canonical Gospel Priority', *NTS* 33 (1987) 321-343, esp. 335-336, and the volume referred to in n.14 above.

[20] Schmidt, *Petrusakten*, 154, cf. Blumenthal, *Formen*, 78-79; Aune, *Literary Environment*, 152-153; Pervo, *Profit*, 122-131; Siegert, 'Analyses rhétoriques', 233 n.5.

[21] Elliott, 'Apocryphal Acts' (few of his examples are from the AJ); A.F.J. Klijn, *The Acts of Thomas*, Leiden 1962, 18, 22.

[22] W. Schneemelcher, 'Apostelgeschichten des 2. und 3. Jahrhunderts. Einleitung', in *idem* (ed.), *Neutestamentliche Apokryphen* II, Tübingen [5]1989, 71-81, 74, 78; Plümacher, 'Apostelakten', 12-13.

[23] Van Kampen, *Apostelverhalen*, 230. The difference in the amount of detail indeed points to the fact that Luke is primarily writing history, whereas the AJ is primarily fictional. But note the remark of C.K. Barrett, 'The first New Testament?', *NT* 38 (1996) 94-104, 98: 'There is no necessary formal difference between a fictional and a historical biography.' See also P.J. Lalleman, 'The canonical and the apocryphal Acts of the Apostles', in H. Hofmann and M. Zimmerman (eds.), *Groningen Colloquia on the Novel 9*, Groningen 1998.

[24] Bauckham, 'Sequel', and J.V. Hills, 'The Acts of the Apostles in the *Acts of Paul*', in E.H. Lovering (ed.), *Society of Biblical Literature 1994 Seminar Papers*, Atlanta 1994, 24-54, independently argue that the APl markedly depends on Acts; cf. now R.J. Pervo, 'A Hard Act to Follow: The *Acts of Paul* and the Canonical Acts', *Journal of Higher Criticism*

involving the AJ exists. The specialists on the AJ, Junod and Kaestli, spend few words on the matter and intimate that there is no meaningful relation between Acts and the AJ.[25] It is clear that a more thorough-going investigation is required.

*2.2 Section A*

*2.2.1 Structural intertextuality*

Several typical features of the first section of the AJ especially invite comparison with Acts. The most promising of these is the incidental use of the we-form outside the *oratio recta*. The occurrence of 'we-episodes' is a well-known characteristic of Acts, although there is no real agreement about its explanation. The only study of the we-phrases in the AJ so far is by Van Kampen. Furthermore, the AJ is a narrative of travel, which makes John visit places that according to Acts were also visited by Paul. Both the descriptions of the actual travels and of the stays in the diverse cities, especially Ephesos, will be discussed, but let us begin with the we-form.

*2.2.2 The we-form*

2.2.2.1 The we-form in the Acts of John

It is remarkable that the first person plural occurs several times in the AJ, whereas the main part of the story is told by an anonymous narrator. In addition to this use of 'we', which at first sight is haphazard, the text of Junod and Kaestli has one occurrence of 'I' (ἐγώ, 61.1). Both the 'we' and the 'I' remain anonymous, at least in the surviving part of the text. The presentation of all relevant material will be followed by an effort to evaluate it.

The first preserved episode (cc.18-25) starts in the third person plural. The reader is led to think that he is dealing with a text told by a narrator who is not part of the action. This voice tells how John and his company set out for Ephesos. But suddenly a sentence that had commenced in the third person plural reports that *we* all heard a voice from heaven (18.6-

2 (1995) 3-32, and D. Marguerat, '*Actes de Paul* et *Actes canoniques*: un phénomène de relecture', *Apocrypha* 8 (1997) 207-224. On Acts and APe see R.F. Stoops, Jr, 'Departing to Another Place: The *Acts of Peter* and the Canonical Acts of the Apostles', in Lovering, *SBL 1994 Seminar Papers*, 390-404; W.J. Stroud, 'Models for Petrine Speeches in the *Acts of Peter*', in *ibid.*, 405-414.

[25] JK, 684, admit that the author of sections A and B knows Acts, 'mais sans pouvoir apporter de preuve décisive.' This implies that the influence of Acts was minimal.

8).[26] This first person plural form continues in c.19, but after some direct speech in 19.15-17 it disappears just as suddenly as it appeared. According to the story the party splits, but neither those who leave nor those who remain are designated as 'we'. In the rest of the episode, which is situated in Ephesos, the we-form does not return. It seems as if the text needed this form to describe John's arrival in Ephesos, but its use is against all literary conventions, as it starts and stops very suddenly, while the narrator is not introduced.

The we-form is absent from the episodes cc.26-29, 30-36, 37-45 and 46-55. Its use reappears at the moment John wants to leave Ephesos in cc.56-57 but is again inconsistent: the opening sentence of the scene tells that 'we' left the city and arrived in Smyrna, but thereafter 'we' is no longer used. It is absent again from the farewell scene cc.58-59.

The only *consistent* use of the first person in the AJ is in the two short pieces cc.60-61 and c.62. Within cc.60-61, an episode situated on John's way back to Ephesos, the first sentence in c.61 even has an unidentified 'I', after which the use of 'we' resumes. C.62 also forms an independent episode which has 'we' in the first sentence; the absence of it in the remainder of this short narrative is only natural, so that we can say that both episodes are first person narratives.

Yet the episode cc.63-86, which follows on c.62 without a gap in the narrative, begins in the third person. There is also no reason to think that a future narrator is among the company described. But the beginning of c.72 is a transition like the one in c.18: 'On the following day John and Andronicus and the brethren went at the break of day to the tomb in which Drusiana had been for three days, so that *we* might break bread there.'[27] After more first person sentences in cc.72 and 73, the form disappears again in the rest of the episode. Contrary to its earlier occurrences, this time the phenomenon is not connected with travel so that we cannot assume that the we-passages exclusively belong to a travelogue.

It is within this long episode that Van Kampen's study of the we-form recovers two hitherto unnoticed instances of the use of 'I'. The first of these is in 73.2, where Van Kampen translates εἶδόν not as 'they saw' but

[26] 'Ως δὲ ὑπὸ βαθὺν ὄρθρον ἐξῄεσαν καὶ ἤδη τῆς ὁδοῦ ἤνυστο ὡσεὶ μίλια τέσσαρα, φωνὴ ἠνέχθη ἀπ' οὐρανοῦ πάντων ἡμῶν ἀκουόντων... Elliott, *Apocryphal NT*, leaves the 'we' out!

[27] Τῇ δὲ ἑξῆς ἡμέρᾳ ὁ 'Ιωάννης ἅμα τῷ 'Ανδρονίκῳ καὶ τοῖς ἀδελφοῖς ἐξ ἑωθινῆς παραγίνεται εἰς τὸ μνῆμα - ... - ὅπως ἄρτον κλάσωμεν ἐκεῖ.

as 'I saw'.[28] This translation fits very well within the context that mainly uses first person forms. On the other hand, Van Kampen's second case is less convincing. In 86.7 the printed editions have the form εὗρεν in stead of εὗρον, which occurs in the only two manuscripts that contain the text, **R** and **Z**. Although this emendation renders a grammatically better construction, Van Kampen objects to it and thus retains one more case of 'I'.[29] However, the absence of the we-form in the rest of c.86 makes it likely that the conjecture of the editors is to be preferred as a valid correction of a scribal mistake.

Cc.106-110 are again inconsistent in the use of the we-form. John talks to people designated by third person forms (αὐτοῖς, 106.3; πρὸς αὐτοὺς, 108.1), after which he gives '*us*' (ἡμῖν) the Eucharistic bread (110.1). Insofar as the we-form is concerned, cc.110-111 are the most interesting part of the AJ because here it occurs at a moment when only a limited number of people are involved. The narrator tells us that John and Byrrhus, the companion of John who was mentioned earlier in the text, leave Ephesos together with two unnamed young persons (110.5-8) and arrive at the tomb of 'a brother of ours' (111.3). John commands 'the young persons' to dig a grave, which they (not we!) do (111.3-4). Then there is once more a transition to the first person plural: 'And as they dug, he preached to them the word of God, and exhorted those who had come out of the house with him, building them up and preparing them for the majesty of God, and praying for each of *us*. And when the young men had finished the trench as he had wished, while *we* were kept in ignorance, he took off the clothes he had on ...' (111.5-10)[30] We see that John only takes Byrrhus and two boys with him, who are consistently referred to as 'they', until suddenly the first person plural resumes. This form also occurs in the final chapter (115), but even there the identity of the narrator is not revealed.

This inconsistent use of the first person forms in the AJ must have always been a characteristic of our text. The possibility that scribal errors have introduced changes into the text is not excluded and a few occurrences of the first person may have disappeared or, conversely, been added; there indeed seems to be an error in 86.7. But all the over forty first

[28] Van Kampen, *Apostelverhalen*, 122. The *Virtutes Johannis* have *vidimus*, a first person plural which proves that a first person form is appropriate here at the corresponding place in the AJ.

[29] *Ibid.*

[30] καὶ προετρέπετο τοὺς σὺν αὐτῷ ἀπὸ τῆς οἰκίας ἐξεληλυθότας ... καὶ ἐπευχόμενος ἑκάστῳ ἡμῶν. ὡς δὲ ἐτέλεσαν τὸ σκάμμα οἱ νεανίσκοι τετυπωμένον ὡς ἐβουλήθη, ἡμῶν μηδὲν εἰδότων ἀποδύεται τὰ ἱμάτια αὐτοῦ ...

person forms of the verb cannot be reduced to mistakes; on the other hand within the text as a whole they are clearly less frequent than the third person forms and we cannot say that they once dominated the whole text.

The above discussion was limited to section A. Sections B and C lack the type of first person forms studied here. They are dominated by the 'I' and 'we' of John's direct speech. The difference between the two main parts of the AJ in this respect is so clear that it needs no further discussion. The beginning of section B (87) and the end of section C (105) could reasonably be expected to have a first person form of the type that would link them to section A, but there is none. Evidently the author of the second main part of the text did not feel bound by the narrative perspective of the first part.

Several scholars have briefly commented on the use of the we-form in section A of the AJ. The majority of them assume that it is an imitation of the we-form in the NT book of Acts, although they do not explain the form in Acts.[31] Junod and Kaestli reject this dependence on Acts and see the use of the first person plural, which they label sporadic and hardly important, as an imitation of the style of ancient historiography as well as the result of 'le bon plaisir de notre auteur'.[32] However, an appeal to unspecified ancient historiographical practices or the free choice of the author is not satisfactory.

Van Kampen holds that the use of the first person in the AJ is a consistent, pervasive and meaningful feature. He even states that the AJ is an I-story.[33] In his opinion, this form was not taken over from Acts. The function of the form is not so much to suggest historical authenticity as the possibility of identification of the reader with the narrator. From 61.1, 111 and 115.3 he concludes that a young man close to Byrrhus, the servant of John, must be the implied author.[34]

This conclusion cannot be correct, since the use of 'we' and 'I' is too sporadic and inconsistent for an I-story. Moreover, in several episodes in which the first person occurs (cc.18-25, 56-57, 110-115), the question whether the narrator is one of those present or not cannot be satisfactorily answered. To a lesser extent cc.63-86 leave us with the same problem. The narrator cannot be Byrrhus because the text has spoken *about* him twice (cc.30, 61) without introducing him as a narrator. But Van Kampen's

[31] E.g. Findlay, *Byways*, 210; Plümacher, 'Apostelakten', 54; Bauckham, 'Sequel', 138 n.91.

[32] JK, 533, cf. 527-528, 530-533.

[33] So also Zahn, 'Wanderungen', 211 with n.1, who thinks that the narrator is the author Leukios. Notice that the *Acts of John by Prochorus* is an I-story.

[34] Van Kampen, *Apostelverhalen*, 121-122.

suggestion that it is one of the young men is equally problematic. Will a comparison with Acts of the Apostles, to which we now turn, help us to understand the use of this form in the AJ?

2.2.2.2 The we-form in Acts of the Apostles

In the several passages in the second part of Acts that deal with the travels of Paul, the narrative changes from third person to first person plural. This we-form is not used consistently, but begins and ends rather abruptly. The narrator seems to be a travelling companion of Paul but does not mention his name, and from the text alone the reader is unable to guess who he is. The name traditionally suggested is Luke, a name that appears in the NT only in Col 4:14, Phm 24 and 2 Tim 4:11. The reader is likely to refer to the preface (1:1-2) where the author introduces himself in the first person singular, although it must be noted that the preface is also anonymous.

A complete survey of the historical and literary aspects of the use of the first person plural in Acts would exceed the scope of the present study.[35] In the present context we are not interested in the historical aspects of the matter (the person of the author, the implied narrator and the question of sources), but in the literary question how a second-century reader would think of this feature in Acts.[36] The discussion will therefore be based on the thesis of Jürgen Wehnert, who demonstrates by what he calls an actor analysis that in the 'they' and 'we' passages in Acts the same people are present. This fact means that the author changes the internal perspective of the writing without changing the external perspective[37] and it implies that the author, without introduction, turns an anonymous person

[35] See W.C. van Unnik, 'Luke's Second Book and the Rules of Hellenistic Historiography' in *Les Actes des Apôtres*, 41-42; S.M. Praeder, 'The Problem of First Person Narration in Acts', *NT* 29 (1987) 193-218, points to the existence of sea-voyage narratives in the first person as well as in the third person; J. Wehnert, *Die Wir-Passagen der Apostelgeschichte: ein lukanisches Stilmittel aus jüdischer Tradition*, Göttingen 1989, 48-124; S.E. Porter, 'The "We" Passages', in D.W.J. Gill and C. Gempf (eds.), *The Book of Acts in Its Graeco-Roman Setting*, Grand Rapids/Carlisle 1994, 545-574. Most recently, J.M. Gilchrist, 'The Historicity of Paul's Shipwreck', *JSNT* 61 (1996) 29-51, esp. 30-38, upholds that the we-passages are really the work of an eye-witness.

[36] We have no patristic commentaries on Acts; the Catenae have nothing substantial on Acts 16:10. Irenaeus, *AdvHaer* 3.14.1, has signalled the occasional we-form and interprets it as a sign of Luke's presence with Paul in the pertinent episodes.

[37] Wehnert, *Wir-Passagen*, 140: '... das Skandalon, dass der Verfasser unvermittelt von einer bis dahin bruchlos durchgehaltenen Aussenperspektive in die Binnenperspektive wechselt, d.h., eine Person, die er zuvor zum Objekt seiner distanzierten auktorialen Erzählung gemacht hatte, tritt nun selber als Berichterstatter auf und löst den Autor gleichsam ab, ohne dass dies durch ein zusätzliches Textsignal erklärt wird.'

who formerly was an object of description into the narrating subject.[38] Why he makes this switch is not immediately evident, nor is it very relevant in this context; it may briefly be said that most scholars believe that the change is meant to suggest that the author himself was an eyewitness to some of the events which he describes. The possibility that this suggestion conforms with historical reality cannot be ascertained by a mere study of the literary form.[39] In any case, the fact that this strategy is employed several times demonstrates that it is not a mere accident or anomaly.

Although not all of Wehnert's book is equally convincing,[40] his thesis that the use of the we-form in Acts implies a confusion of narrative perspectives is enlightening.[41] In this respect, the Book of Acts violates the rules of classical literature. No wonder, parallels to this aspect of its form have not been found in classical literature.[42] It must explicitly be added that none of the ancient novels has this characteristic. Some novels are I-narratives, but none change from first to third person in a way that resembles Acts.[43]

#### 2.2.2.3 Acts and the Acts of John

Our analyses of the AJ and of Acts indeed demonstrate that they use the we-form in the same way. Contrary to Junod and Kaestli, I cannot believe that this close resemblance is merely accidental. I therefore fully endorse the observation of Wehnert that the remarkable change of narrative perspective in Acts has influenced the AAA, in particular the AJ:

> Obwohl ActJoh nicht vollständig erhalten sind, geht aus dem Vorhandenen zweifellos hervor, dass sich der Verfasser dem Vorbild der Acta-WPP [= Wir-Passagen] angeschlossen und (in analog sparsamer Verwendung) autoptische Erzählpassagen in sein grundsätzlich

[38] Praeder, 'First Person Narration', 209, shows that the first person preface does not prepare for first person plural participation in the narrated events.

[39] So C.J. Hemer, *The Book of Acts in the Setting of Hellenistic History*, ed. C.H. Gempf, Tübingen 1989, ch.8. Recently R. Riesner, *Die Frühzeit des Apostels Paulus*, Tübingen 1994, esp. 366, concludes after wide-ranging research that the author of the we-passages is the same as the author of the Book of Acts.

[40] E.g., his hypothesis (188-189) that the original I-person in the we-passages was Silas. See also B.S. Rosner, 'Acts and Biblical History', in Winter and Clarke, *Book of Acts*, 65-82, esp. 77-78.

[41] Cf. also Van Kampen, *Apostelverhalen*, 227-228.

[42] Wehnert, *Wir-Passagen*, 139-140; Praeder, 'First Person Narration', 214, also states that the use of the we-form of Acts is unparalleled.

[43] See on *Leucippe and Clitophon*: B.P. Reardon, 'Achilles Tatius and Ego-Narrative', in Morgan and Stoneman, *Greek Fiction*, 80-96.

> aussenperspektivisch konzipiertes Werk eingebaut hat. ... dass die für die Apg charakteristische Doppelfunktion eines Aktanten als Objekt der Darstellung und Subjekt der Wir-Rede auch in ActJoh vorliegt.[44]

There are two minor differences between Acts and the AJ. The we-form of the AJ is not limited to travelogues. Again, as we have seen, the AJ even uses the word 'I' next to 'we'.[45] But these points do not affect my conclusion that the AJ resembles the canonical Acts in the peculiar use of the first person narrative form.[46]

The convergent elements under review are so important that it is worth while to stop for a moment and to see if the we-form of Acts and the AJ is really as unique as Wehnert argues and as commentaries on Acts tend to assume.

**Excursus: the we-form in other texts**

For the sake of clarity let me repeat that the use of the we-form in Acts and in the AJ is a conscious and repeated alternation between the first person form and the third person without a concomitant change of perspective. What we now look for are other prose texts that, in a situation in which there is no change in those present, suddenly change from the third person to the first person form, or the reverse. In other words, texts in which the internal perspective of the writing changes without a change in the external perspective, so that we can say that the author without introduction turns a person who formerly was an object of description into the narrating subject.[47] As we look for a deliberate authorial device, cases in which only one single unexpected we-form appears cannot automatically be included. In Acts and the AJ the repetition demonstrates in particular that the procedure is deliberate. We first look at possible parallels in the Graeo-Roman environment of early Christianity and then at Jewish as well as early Christian texts.[48]

[44] Wehnert, *Wir-Passagen*, 144, who states that the same is true of the APe, ATh, Acts of Philip, and of later Christian texts.

[45] It is possible that the use of 'I' reflects the author's knowledge of Acts 1:1 as well as Lk 1:1-4; see the section on the Synoptics, p. 123ff. below.

[46] In the opinion of Thornton, *Zeuge*, 142-147, the above implies that - just like Acts (!) - the lost beginning of the AJ must have contained a first person singular introduction in which the author also mentioned his name.

[47] Thus my definition is sharper than that of E. Norden, *Agnostos theos. Untersuchungen zur Formengeschichte religiöser Rede*, Leipzig/Berlin 1913, 313-331, esp. 317, who looks for 'Schriftwerke, die so, wie es in der Grundschrift der Acta geschieht, eine Kombination von Berichten in erster und in dritter Person aufweisen'.

[48] R. Scholes and R. Kellogg, *The Nature of Narrative*, New York 1966, 72-73, 243-244, argue that first person narrative was developed by the Romans and mainly used in fiction.

Normally, historians who introduce themselves in the third person, like Caesar, refrain from the use of abrupt we-passages. Eduard Norden argues that the combination of a first person narrative with a third person account exists in the report of Ptolemy III's military campaign against Syria in 247/6 BC.[49] This text, which survives on a papyrus of which the beginning is lost, contains Ptolemy's own report of the events.[50] It has a consistent we-form; the third person section it contains describes the actions of others, in which the king was not present. I therefore conclude that this text has normal changes of narrative perspective and thus differs from Acts.[51]

Norden also refers to three Roman historians who allegedly connect their third person narratives with first person eye-witness reports: Velleius Paterculus, Dio Cassius and Ammianus Marcellinus. Norden furthermore suggests that this habit resembles that of Acts.[52] But an attentive reading of e.g. Dio Cassius' *Roman History* 73 would soon reveal how much his style differs from that of Acts. Time and again Dio (2nd - 3rd century, writing in Greek), inserts brief first person sentences into his narrative, announcing what will come next, giving his opinion, or - what is different - noting his presence at the event being described.[53] These editorial comments are always perspicuous and can be compared with narrative asides.[54] Moreover - a fact not mentioned by Norden - Dio also refers to companies of which he is part, most often the senate, in the first person plural, but even in these cases the change of perspective is clear.[55] The same applies to all of Dio's work as well as that of Velleius Paterculus.

[49] Norden, *Agnostos theos*, 320-321.

[50] Also known as Papyrus Gurob; first published in J.P. Mahaffy, *The Flinders Petrie Papyri* II, Dublin 1893, 145-149, with an addition in III, 1905, 334-338; see now Jacoby, *FGrHist* 160 [2B, 885-887 (text), and 2D, 589-591 (comment)].

[51] Cf. Mahaffy III, 336: 'The consistent use of the first person plural in the document ...'; Jacoby 2D, 589: 'Wir-bericht'.

[52] Norden, *Agnostos theos*, 321-323. [On p.322 l.13 for LXXII read LXXIII.] In fact Norden is concerned with an alleged source for Acts, but admits that in this source the we-episodes were already linked with third person narratives (35, 314). On Velleius see Thornton, *Zeuge*, 177-178.

[53] Ed. E. Cary (Loeb). See 73.18.3-4; also selection in 7.3; 10.3; 11.2; 23 *passim*; opinion in 1.2; 14.3; presence in 4.2; 7.1. Thornton, *Zeuge*, 101-104, argues that this procedure is rather common in historiography.

[54] Sheeley, *Asides*, esp. 156-157, shows that most asides in Acts are not in the first person sections, but he did not study the combination of asides with first person sections in other books.

[55] E.g. 73.16.3; 17.3; 18.2; 19.4; 20.1; 21.1, 77.5.2; 6.1; 8 *passim* (combined with first person singular).

The *Periplus* of Arrianus, also mentioned by Norden, begins as a first person plural narrative and switches to the third person - not quite like Acts with its sudden changes *in medias res*.[56] More complicated but also more explicit is the *Ephemeris belli Troiani* of Dictys of Crete. The narrator places himself squarely in the center of attention and presents his work as an eye-witness account.[57] Nonetheless, the actual story is largely in the third person form, as is explained by the I-person himself (1.13; 5.17).[58] Many readers of Acts have sought in vain for a comparable statement of intent.

Norden's statement that in Ammianus Marcellinus, *Res gestae*, 18.6.5 the we-form appears very abruptly is not correct because the author, who constantly describes several events simultaneously, uses *interea* - a word quoted by Norden himself - to introduce the shift in perspective. Just like Dio and other ancient historians - and unlike the author of Acts - Ammianus refers to himself (and other Romans) in brief asides.[59] Earlier in his work, at the beginning of Book 15, he has extensively informed the reader about his competence.

But there is more to Ammianus. Thornton's statement that in *Res gestae* books 23-25 we have 'die einzige echte Parallele zur Erzählweise des "Lukas" in Acta' is not far from the truth.[60] The subject of these books is a single military campaign; without specific introduction this enterprise is alternatingly told in the third and first person. In addition, there are such first person auctorial side remarks as 'as I told', 'we read' and 'as we Greeks say'. The changes are abrupt and not accompanied by

[56] Norden, *Agnostos theos*, 323-324. Ed. A. Silberman, Paris 1995. Arrian probably only made the first part of the voyage: the use of the first person seems to be connected with his personal experience.

[57] Ed. W. Eisenhut (Teubner); see Thornton, *Zeuge*, 172-174; S. Merkle, *Die Ephemeris belli Troiani des Diktys von Kreta*, Frankfurt 1988, esp. 67-73; *idem*, 'Telling the True Story of the Trojan War: The Eyewitness Account of Dictys of Crete', in J. Tatum (ed.), *The Search for the Ancient Novel*, Baltimore/London 1994, 183-196.

[58] 1.13: *eorum ego secutus comitatum ea quidem, quae antea apud Troiam gesta sunt, ab Ulixe cognita quam diligentissime rettuli et reliqua, quae deinceps insecuta sunt, quoniam ipse interfui, quam verissime potero exponam.*
5.17: *haec ego Gnosius Dictys comes Idomenei conscripsi oratione ea, quam maxime inter tam diversa loquendi genera consequi ac comprehendere potui, litteris Punicis ab Cadmo Danaoque traditis.* (...) *igitur ea, quae in bello evenere Graecis ac barbaris, cuncta sciens perpessusque magna ex parte memoriae tradidi. de Antenore eiusque regno quae audieram retuli. nunc reditum nostrorum narrare iuvat.*

[59] Ed. J.C. Rolfe (Loeb); e.g. 4.1-2; 8.15; 9.1; 14.3.1. For examples of asides from other historians see Thornton, *Zeuge*, 102-104.

[60] Thornton, *Zeuge*, 179, cf. 182. Norden does not discuss these books.

changes in perspective, but, contrary to Acts, there is no doubt about the identity of the narrator, who of course is Ammianus himself, so that the interpretative questions connected with the we-form are limited. Considering this partial parallel, its lateness strikes us: Ammianus wrote in the latter part of the fourth century.[61]

For the sake of completeness it must be repeated that the phenomenon we are studying is not found in the ancient novels.[62] Our conclusion is that we do not find the procedure which is so characteristic of Acts, a change of person without a change of perspective, in any of the texts studied except in part of Ammianus' work.

When we now turn to Jewish texts, we see that Wehnert himself follows Norden in arguing that the Book of Acts was not original in its use of the first person form. In his opinion 'Luke' depends on the style of several Old Testament books and of Hellenistic-Jewish literature.[63] Let us review the relevant texts.

A. From the Hebrew Old Testament the Books of Ezra, Nehemiah, Daniel and Jeremiah are mentioned, from the later books Tobit and Henoch. But the phenomena in these works are not really parallel to those in Acts. First of all, the books in question primarily use the first person singular, not the plural.[64] Secondly, they openly mention the name of their alleged author. In this connection, we must also take into account that the modern separation between the I-person and the actual author was not made in Antiquity. Thirdly, the changes in perspective are easy to follow. Large parts of texts in first person form stand next to third person narratives without any connections.[65] Finally, the I-person in these books is always

[61] Although Ammianus has been subjected to source criticism (esp. by O. Seeck, 'Zur Chronologie und Quellenkritik des Ammianus Marcellinus', *Hermes* 41 [1906] 481-539; see E.A. Thompson, *The historical work of Ammianus Marcellinus*, London 1947, repr. Groningen 1969; G. Sabbah, *La méthode d'Ammien Marcellin*, Paris 1978, 115-155), I find no hypothesis of a we-source. The tacit assumption of Seeck seems to be that 'we' indicates the personal presence of Ammianus.

[62] Norden, *Agnostos theos*, 313, says that Petronius, *Satyricon* 114, offers a sea voyage in we-form. Yet in view of the first person form (which alternates between I and we) of the whole book, that is only to be expected; the *Satyricon* has come to us in a far from complete form. Thornton, *Zeuge*, 150-184, discusses the practices of other Greek and Roman authors.

[63] Norden, *Agnostos theos*, 328-331; Wehnert, *Wir-Passagen*, 145-146, cf. 146-158.

[64] Some passages of Ezra being the exception.

[65] Rosner, 'Acts and Biblical History', 78. The Book of Ezra, e.g., indeed changes from the third person of the narrator to the first person in 7:28b, but the reader can have no doubts about the identity of the I-speaker, since Ezra has been amply introduced. And when the

the main character and, for that reason, easily identifiable. In Acts, on the other hand, the first person form is not that of Paul but of an anonymous person of secondary importance. Had 'Luke' imitated the Old Testament, he would have placed his narrative into the mouth of (Peter and) Paul).[66] Thus while Acts uses a sophisticated strategy, the Old Testament books are extremely simple in this respect.[67]

B. Wolfgang Speyer suggested that the *Testament of Isaac* (2nd or 4th century AD?) is a case in point, and indeed one translation suggests that this text frequently changes from the third to the first person and back again.[68] Although (modern translations of) the ancient versions differ considerably,[69] the distribution of the verb forms that we are studying is less confused: the text tells about Isaac in the third person, while in the middle there is one long unintroduced speech by Isaac.[70] Thus the general pattern of the text resembles that of the Old Testament books just discussed.[71]

C. The Greek *Apocalypse of Ezra* is extremely inconsistent in its use of the

narrator takes over again in c.10 this change is abrupt but not against any convention.

[66] Cf. the verdict of Porter, 'We passages', 547 n.4: no direct influence from these books on Acts has ever been shown; and the we-sections in Acts are much shorter than the I-pieces in these books. Even if Acts was influenced by these Jewish books, Acts would still be the filter through which the we-form reached the AJ. It is extremely unlikely that the author of the AJ was influenced by the Jewish literature in question. As I will show below, the AJ betrays hardly any knowledge of the OT or other Jewish books.

[67] Tobit is made up as follows: 1:1 - 3:6 I-story, 3:7 - 14:15 he-story.

[68] W. Speyer, 'Religiöse Pseudepigraphie und literarische Fälschung im Altertum', *JbAC* 8/9 (1965/66) 88-125, repr. in N. Brox (ed.), *Pseudepigraphie in der heidnischen und jüdisch-christlichen Antike*, Darmstadt 1977, 195-263, esp. 211, who apparently uses the translation in P. Riessler, *Altjüdisches Schrifttum ausserhalb der Bibel*, Augsburg 1928, 1135-1148.

[69] It is disputed if Greek or Coptic was the original language; in any case no Greek text is known.

[70] See K.H. Kuhn, 'The Sahidic version of the Testament of Isaac', *JTS* n.s. 8 (1957) 225-239; *idem*, 'An English translation of the Sahidic version of the Testament of Isaac', *JTS* 18 (1967) 325-336; W.F. Stinespring in J.H. Charlesworth (ed.), *The Old Testament Pseudepigrapha*, Garden City NY 1983, 903-911 (translation from the Arabic); M. Delcor, *Le testament d'Abraham. Suivi de la traduction des Testaments d'Abraham, d'Isaac et de Jacob d'après les versions orientales*, Leiden 1973, 196-205 (from Bohairic), 224-233 (from Ethiopic), 252-261 (from Arabic).

[71] Likewise, the long version of the *Testament of Abraham* (ed. Delcor) contains one chapter (12) in the first person singular, whereas all the rest is in the third person; the shorter version is completely in the third person. The *Hebrew Book of Elijah* (trans. Riessler) is also not completely consistent.

I- and the he-form.[72] Alternatingly, Ezra speaks himself and is spoken about; there is no we-form. This book is an extreme example of the Old Testament type discussed above.[73]

D. We now come to texts of different types.[74] The *Protevangelium Jacobi*, principally a third person narrative, contains an I-section (c.18) from Joseph's perspective, followed in 19.2 by a single we-form.[75] There are two important differences from Acts. The first is that the change in person is clearly introduced, viz. by the phrase 'Now I, Joseph', after which the text indeed changes from external perspective to internal perspective, and back to the former after 19.2. The second difference is that Joseph is not the alleged narrator of the rest of the text, for the colophon (c.25) claims that this is James, from whom the text received its name. Thus the *Protevangelium* displays an inconsistency of another kind than Acts. It must however be noted that the whole section under discussion is absent from the most important and earliest textual witness, the Bodmer Papyrus, so that it may be an insertion by someone other than the author.[76]

E. In the *Testament of Levi* 19.2-3 the sons of Levi, who have so far been addressed by their father, answer his speech so that a sudden we-form is introduced. But these sons did not need any introduction and the change of perspective, though unexpected, is clear and easily explained.[77]

F. The *Gospel of Peter* does not really belong in this discussion,[78] since everything suggests that it is consistently written in the first person, allegedly by Peter, and also since the change in person (vss. 26, 59, 60) is accompanied by a satisfactory identification of the persons concerned.

[72] Noted by Speyer, 'Pseudepigraphie', 211. Trans. M.E. Stone, in Charlesworth, *Pseudepigrapha* I, 561-579.

[73] More examples of this type in Thornton, *Zeuge*, 127-128, who however denies that we are dealing with a biblical narrative model.

[74] In his review of H.W. Hollander and M. de Jonge, *The Testaments of the Twelve Patriarchs*, Leiden 1985, A. Hilhorst discusses several possible parallels to unexpected we-forms in a number of Jewish and Christian writings, see *Journal for the Study of Judaism* 17 (1986) 252-255, esp. 255; Hilhorst orally provided most of the other references given here and kindly discussed them with me.

[75] Ed. G. Schneider, *Evangelia infantiae apocrypha. Apokryphe Kindheitsevangelien*, Freiburg 1995; E. de Strycker, *La forme la plus ancienne du Protévangile de Jacques*, Bruxelles 1961; Elliott, *Apocryphal NT*, 50, states: 'Joseph's first person narrative in 18.2-7 probably came from an earlier written source, and invites comparison with the "We" sections of the Acts of the Apostles.' See also Thornton, *Zeuge*, 128.

[76] Cf. Schneider, *Evangelia, ad loc.*; De Strycker, *Protévangile*, 404-406.

[77] Ed. M. de Jonge, Leiden 1978.

[78] *Pace* Speyer, 'Pseudepigraphie', 213.

G. The we-form in *Martyrium Pionii* 1.2, 10.5, 18.13, 22.2 is closer to that in Acts than any of the other texts mentioned, although the two are not completely similar.[79] The identity of the 'we' is readily apparent: the pronoun designates those present at the trial and death, who indeed identify themselves at the beginning of the text (1.2) and again when the we-form occurs for the last time (εἴδομεν οἱ παραγενόμενοι).[80] Yet the way in which the text alternates between the first and third person forms reminds us of Acts. Indeed, it is likely that it was directly influenced by Luke's book.[81] In my opinion *Mart. Pionii* underlines our thesis, since its use of the we-form, like that of the AJ, is modelled on Acts.[82]

H. In its present form the Antiochene version of the *Acts of Ignatius*[83] (cc.5 and 7) has the same use of we-passages as Acts: the we-form begins and disappears suddenly, the first time during travel at sea, without change of perspective and without identifying the persons being indicated. Although the *Acts of Ignatius* contains second-century materials, its final version was composed considerably later, certainly after Eusebius.[84] I would argue that the formal similarities with Acts are due to influences from this book.[85]

I. The single 'we' in *Passio Fructuosi* 3.5 stands isolated and it is doubtful if it is attributable to the author. If not, we cannot and need not explain it here. But if so, it may be seen as a remnant of the we-form like that which occurs in *Mart. Pionii* (see above).

We find that in *Mart. Pionii*, *Acts of Ignatius* and *Passio Fructuosi* the we-form denotes 'the followers of the story's main character'.[86] This use seems to have developed under the direct influence of Acts.[87] A similar

[79] Ed. L. Robert, Washington D.C. 1994; also H. Musurillo (ed.), *The Acts of the Christian martyrs*, Oxford 1972; A. Hilhorst in A.A.R. Bastiaensen *et al.*, *Atti e passioni dei martiri*, no place [Milano] 1987, 149-191 (text), 453-477 (commentary).

[80] The introductory c.1 has τῶν καθ' ἡμᾶς, which could be read as 'being one of us' or 'in our days'. In the former case it is an implicit identification of the 'we'.

[81] Robert, *Pionios*, in his commentary points to passages that echo the NT; influence from Acts is mentioned 56, 63, 68, 116, 118.

[82] Robert, *Pionios*, 73, argues that the first person form in 10.5 goes back to Pionios himself.

[83] Ed. G.A. Bisbee, *Pre-Decian Acts of Martyrs and Commentarii*, Philadelphia 1988, 136-142; discussion *idem*, 133-162; cf. J.B. Lightfoot, *The Apostolic Fathers* II.2, London/New York [2]1889, repr. Hildesheim/New York 1973, 363-391, 473-495; Thornton, *Zeuge*, 144.

[84] Th. Zahn, *Ignatius von Antiochien*, Gotha 1873, 41-54; Lightfoot, *Apostolic Fathers* II.2, 386, 450, 480.

[85] Zahn, *Ignatius*, 51 ('die Nachäffungen der Apostelgeschichte').

[86] An expression suggested to me by Dr. A. Hilhorst in a private conversation.

[87] Hilhorst is not convinced of this thesis.

'we' occurs in the *Martyrium of Matthew* 24 and 30[88] and in the other Apocryphal Acts (see below).
J. In the *Acts of Peter and the Twelve Apostles* the changes of person coincide with clear changes in perspective, so that this text contains no parallels to Acts.[89]

2.2.2.4 The reason for the use of the we-form
This curious use of the we-form first occurs in Acts of the Apostles and then in the AJ and in other texts that depend on Acts, such as other AAA, *Mart. Pionii* and *Acts of Ignatius*. Its occurrence in Ammianus Marcellinus requires a separate explanation.

When we ask *why* the AJ and others copied Acts in this respect, it seems most likely that this we-form was regarded as the testimony of an eye-witness. 'Luke' was allegedly communicating his personal experiences to the readers, thus both increasing his reliability and bridging the gap between them and the story's hero. The first author of the AJ probably intends to convey a similar impression to his readers.

*2.2.3 Other structural parallels*
It so happens that among the passages in the AJ that deserve attention because they are structurally related to Acts, the first two also contain the we-form. But now our attention must shift to other aspects of the texts.

2.2.3.1 Acts of John 18-19
The occurrence of visions in cc.18-19 reminds the reader of the AJ of the story of Paul's dream and subsequent crossing over to Europe with which the first we-passage in Acts begins (16:9-12). The visions also echo other episodes in Acts: the stories about Peter and Cornelius (Acts 10) and about Paul's conversion (Acts 9:3-19; 22:6-16; 26:12-18).[90] In AJ 18 John is compelled by a vision (ὅραμα, 18.1) and by a voice that speaks from heaven (18.7-10) to go to Ephesos. The trip is narrated in the we-form. The fact that John is hurried is suggested by the verb 'to hasten' (ἐπείγομαι, 18.1). In Acts 16 it likewise is a vision (vs.9-10) that informs Paul where to go; with that fact and with a word that expresses haste ('-immediately', εὐθέως, 16:10) a we-passage begins (16:10-16). These

[88] Bonnet, *AAA* II.1, 250.9 Greek, 19 Latin; 261.26 Latin only.
[89] S.J. Patterson, 'Sources, Redaction and *Tendenz* in the *Acts of Peter and the Twelve Apostles* NH VI,1)', *VigChr* 45 (1991) 1-17, 6-7, identifies each perspective as a separate source and assumes a redactor, 10-15.
[90] Zahn, 'Wanderungen', 195, for Acts 10; Hennecke, *Handbuch*, 494; JK, 443; Wehnert, *Wir-Passagen*, 145, 244-245; Sirker-Wicklaus, *Untersuchungen*, 41.

combined elements strongly suggest that the episode in the AJ was influenced by the story from Acts.

But in AJ 18-19 John is not the only character who hears a heavenly voice. The person whom John is to meet and convert, Lycomedes, likewise hears a voice which asks him not to commit suicide and which announces the arrival of John from Miletus (19.7-13). Twice in the Book of Acts, in the more or less parallel episodes Acts 9 and 10, two characters independently from one another receive a message which prepares their meeting. In both stories an apostle (Paul, Peter) and another person (Ananias, Cornelius) hear the voice of the Lord before they meet each other.

A.Wikenhauser has shown that the motif of double dreams was popular in ancient literature: he lists 19 parallels to Acts 9 and 10, of which AJ 18-19 is one.[91] In view of the frequency of the motif it might appear difficult to argue confidently that its occurrence in the AJ has been influenced by Acts. But it is remarkable that all parallels collected by Wikenhauser, except the AJ, explicitly concern dreams (dream visions).[92] Only the visions in Acts 9 (implicitly, since Paul is on the road) and in Acts 10 (explicitly in vss.3, 30!) are said to have occurred while the recipients were awake.[93] When we return to the AJ, we see that neither John (18.1, 7-8) nor Lycomedes (19.7-8, cf. 13) were asleep. It can be concluded that among the passages collected by Wikenhauser those from Acts and the AJ occupy a special position and that the other passages are not fully parallel with them.[94]

The relationship between the stories from Acts and from the AJ is close.[95] I surmise that AJ 18-19 borrowed several of its characteristic features from Acts 9, 10 and 16. Acts is likely to be the literary model for this part of the AJ, but the influence of Acts does not surpass the thematic

[91] A. Wikenhauser, 'Doppelträume', *Biblica* 29 (1948) 100-111. Some parallels are roughly contemporary with the AJ (Pausanias, Apuleius, Aelius Aristides) or later (ATh 29-34, etc.), others are earlier: an inscription from Epidaurus (4th century BC), Livy, Dionysius of Halicarnassus, Tacitus and Josephus, *Ant Jud* 11.8.4-5.

[92] Using phrases like ἐνύπνιον, κατὰ τὸν ὕπνον, ὄναρ, κατὰ τοὺς ὕπνους and *per quietem*.

[93] Cf. Wehnert, *Wir-Passagen*, 156. The presence of the word ὅραμα does not imply a state of sleep because Acts 7:31; 11:5; 12:9 also use the word to suggest a vision received while awake, whereas in 16:9 and 18:9 'at night' is explicitly added.

[94] Wikenhauser's thesis, 'Doppelträume', 100, that Acts 9 contains double dreams and Acts 10 double visions is not correct, since both texts speak of visions.

[95] In Acts 10:25 Cornelius performs a προσκύνησις for Peter, and Lycomedes does the same thing for John (AJ 19.3), although the words used differ. Both the stories in Acts 9 and in AJ 19 find a provisional end with the word εὐθέως (Acts 9:18; AJ 19.15).

level. The episodes in the AJ are not unintelligible to a reader who misses the intertextual connections.

2.2.3.2 Acts of John 58-62

In AJ 58-62 many things happen in a short piece of text. Cc.58-59 describe a farewell speech which John gives before leaving Laodicea[96] for Ephesos. The speech is followed by a list of travelling companions (59.3-10) which, in turn, is followed by a short we-narrative (cc.60-61). A second episode in we-form tells that on John's return to Ephesos many of the brothers there are healed by his mere touch (c.62).

This whole cycle corresponds with the contents of Acts 19-21. Acts 19:11-12 contains a brief note on healing which states that people in Ephesos are healed when they touch the apostle Paul. Soon after this note, Acts includes a list of Paul's travelling companions, followed by a narrative in the we-form (20:5-21:18) that contains a farewell scene.[97] In this scene (20:17-38), Paul says farewell to the elders of Ephesos who have come to Miletus to see him. Thus within the same context we have not only the list of companions immediately followed by a we-narrative,[98] but in addition a healing story and a farewell scene. These resemblances between Acts 19-21 and AJ 58-62 are remarkable and lead to the conclusion that the AJ has been influenced by Acts.[99]

One element of the two cycles deserves further treatment, viz. the idea expressed in both stories that the apostle's touch or belongings have healing power. This idea also occurs in the Synoptics, but the verbal similarities between AJ 62 and Mk 6:56 (cf. Mt 14:36) as well as Mk 5:27 (cf. Mt 9:20-21, Lk 8:44) are limited to the key words 'to touch' (ἅπτομαι) and 'clothes' (ἱματία). Despite what one might be inclined to think, this idea of a healing touch, whether it is the healer or the sick who initiates it, is nearly absent from Hellenistic pagan sources;[100] ἅπτομαι in the sense

[96] The name of Laodicea occurs only in the heading of the passage. JK, 101-104, cf. 93, show that this heading is very old and, therefore, not a later addition.

[97] For the topos of the farewell scene see JK, 430-431 (n.1), 533 n.1, and n.103 below.

[98] Wehnert, *Wir-Passagen*, 145, likewise notes the correspondence: the list of the apostle's companions is followed by a we-narrative.

[99] Two of the elements of this cycle also occur in APl 5 (PHeid 35), viz. a farewell scene followed by a list of travelling companions, cf. F.S. Jones, 'Principal Orientations on the Relations between the Apocryphal Acts' in Lovering, *SBL 1993 Seminar Papers*, 485-505, 501.

[100] The title of the paper by S.C. Muir, 'Touched by a God: Aelius Aristides, Religious Healing, and Asclepius Cult', in E.H.Lovering (ed.), *Society of Biblical Literature 1995 Seminar Papers*, Atlanta 1995, 362-379, creates an impression which is not justified by its contents. Asclepius most often healed by means of dreams that, granted to those who slept

of to touch-for-healing is really a word belonging to the Christian vocabulary.[101] As far as the relation between Acts and the AJ is concerned, the Ephesians in Acts touch the apostle Paul, 'so that handkerchiefs or aprons were carried away from his body to the sick' (19:12). A similar rush to touch John occurs in the AJ. In both stories a touch of the apostle or some of his belongings has healing power. It is therefore rather surprising that, despite the fact that both stories are situated in Ephesos, there are no lexical similarities between Acts 19 and AJ 62 except for the very general word 'hands'. Nevertheless, one can not help thinking that the AJ consciously has John perform the same miracles as Paul did. The author of the AJ knows the specific use of the word ἅπτομαι from the Christian tradition, but composes his story without open references to the gospels and Acts. This procedure is illustrative of his attitude towards the books of the NT.

2.2.3.3 The end of the apostle's life

From c.58 onwards the AJ indicates that John's death is near. The farewell address c.58 resembles a last farewell. Twice John has to explain that his departure does not mean the departure of God's presence, but still the brothers cry at the moment of leave taking (59.2-3).

The final episode (106-115) contains several announcements of John's death, first of all in the speeches of cc.106-107 which are true farewell speeches.[102] And what are the prayers in cc.108 and 113 if not preparations for a final departure?[103] John even states: 'These things, brethren, I communicate to you, pressing on to the work prepared for me ...' (107.10-11).[104] After these words, the narrator declares that he and his com-

in his temple, either cured them directly or revealed an adeaquate therapy. I verified this verdict by examining E.J. Edelstein and L. Edelstein, *Asclepius. A collection and interpretation of the testimonies*, 2 vols., Baltimore 1945, repr. 2 vols in 1, New York 1975, and C.A. Behr, *P. Aelius Aristides. The Complete Works*, Leiden 1986, as well as by searching the Pandora Greek database for ἰάομαι as well as the roots ἀπ- (ἡπ-, ἀψ-) and θιγγ-.

[101] See P.J. Lalleman, 'Healing by a mere touch as a Christian concept', *TynB* 48 (1997) 355-361.

[102] *Contra* JK, 564-565, who think that the final outcome of the AJ, the death of John in Ephesus, is not anticipated in the narrative.

[103] J. Lambrecht, 'Paul's Farewell-Address at Miletus (Acts 20, 17-38)', in Kremer, *Actes des Apôtres*, 332-333, provides a list of elements typical of the genre of the farewell-address. These elements are also found in the AJ: a specific group of addressees (106.1-3), reference to speaker's good life (106.3-10, 113), emphasis on his innocence (*ibid.*), announcement of the future (107.10-11), warnings (106.10-17, 107.1-10, 14-18), the question of succession (absent), benediction (110.1-3), and (intercessory) prayer (108).

[104] ταῦτα ὑμῖν, ἀδελφοί, ὁμιλῶ νῦν ἐπειγόμενος εἰς τὸ προκείμενόν μοι ἔργον ...

panions had not known what would happen[105] in order to confess his disbelief in the foreshadowings and parallel to the canonical Gospels, in which the disciples fail to see the signs and to understand the predictions of Jesus' death (e.g. Mk 9:32, Lk 18:34, Jn 12:16).

Both the gospels and Acts have a similar sense of the main character's approaching demise. From 19:21 on, Acts focusses on the 'last voyage' of Paul, who must first go to Jerusalem and thereafter to Rome. Wherever he goes, he says goodbye until, in the end, he indeed arrives in Rome. Paul is consciously moving towards his end. Van Kampen argues that the last part of Acts was written with an eye on the final parts of the gospels, so that the description of Paul's fate is modelled on Jesus's.[106] It is equally probable that the author of the AJ knew both the gospels and Acts and was influenced by both in writing about the imminent death of John; due to the AJ's independent style we cannot say which influence was greatest.

2.2.3.4 Passages which distinguish the AJ from Acts

Now we come to several elements in the AJ for which parallels in Acts might be expected but do not exist. First we consider how the AJ relates to the Ephesian episodes in Acts.[107] AJ 19-55 and 62-115 are situated in and around Ephesos. Within these chapters, only two stories are specifically related to the city: cc. 30-36 about John's inviting the city's old women to the theatre in order to heal them and the story of the destruction of Artemis' temple (cc.37-45). The AJ never informs us about the church in Ephesos as such and displays a general lack of interest in ecclesiastical affairs.

According to Acts, Paul played a leading role in the origin of the church in Ephesos and visited the city several times.[108] There is only one scene clearly situated in the city, Acts 19:23-40, which tells how Paul and his missionary work are threatened by a mob gathering in the theatre. No word from Paul or any other Christian is recorded in this passage in Acts. With the exception of the reference to the theatre, the Ephesian scenes in Acts and the AJ are not analogous.

The same disparity is revealed by comparing the travelogues in the AJ

[105] ἡμῶν μηδὲν εἰδότων, 111.10.

[106] According to Van Kampen, *Apostelverhalen*, 230-232, Paul's shipwreck and survival mirrors death and resurrection.

[107] JK, 506, see no relation. On the knowledge of Ephesos displayed in the AJ, see chapter 6.

[108] Acts 18:19-21 and Acts 19, esp. :10 which says that he was in the city for two years; cf. 20:16-21 and the situation envisaged in 1 and 2 Tim, which is important regardless of the authorship of the letters.

and Acts.[109] In chapter 1 we saw that the AJ originally was as much a story about John in Ephesos as a story about his travels. The travelogues in Acts differ from those in the AJ in that they are full of local and historical details. Luke mentions the names of officials and local converts, gives details about synagogues and other buildings, and explains alien customs. The narrative of the sea-voyage is full of geographical and technical details. The AJ, on the other hand, contains hardly any local colour. Of the cities John visits, Miletus and Laodicea are named without any details about them being given. For Ephesos we learn the names and sometimes the official positions of several people. But the temple and the theatre, though important buildings, are not described in any detail. I conclude that travel is more important in Acts than in the AJ and that it is described in a different manner.

*2.2.4 Lexical similarities*

On the lexical level, the intertextual relation between Acts and the AJ is less conspicuous. In fact there are only three cases worth mentioning:

2.2.4.1 Acts of John 22

AJ 22 narrates the revivification of Cleopatra. Four sentences in this chapter have corresponding elements in Acts 3, the story about the healing of the paralytic and the consequent sermon of Peter in the presence of John.

1. In 22.4 John in his prayer uses the phrase 'Now the time of refreshing ...' (Νῦν καιρὸς ἀναψύξεως ...), which recalls the rare expression 'times of refreshing' (καιροὶ ἀναψύξεως) from Acts 3:20. In Acts the meaning of the phrase is eschatological while in the AJ it refers to the present salvation. The phrase is rare enough to suggest that the AJ consciously or unconsciously adopts the wording of Acts, although its meaning is distorted.

2. Then in lines 12-13 John prays: 'We therefore beseech you, O King, not for gold, nor for silver, nor for riches, ...'[110] This recalls Peter's claim, 'I have no silver and gold' (ἀργύριον καὶ χρυσίον οὐχ ὑπάρχει μοι), in Acts 3:6. Though the words differ slightly, the mentioning of gold and silver connected with a form of ὑπαρχ- in the context of a healing story indicates an intertextual connection. The AJ alludes to the fact that, according to Acts, an apostle denigrates the value of silver and gold.

[109] Van Kampen, *Apostelverhalen*, 272-273, holds that travel is not important in the AJ. He states that the same is *mutatis mutandis* true of the other AAA as well: travel is unimportant as a means of structuring the narrative. See my chapter 1.

[110] Αἰτούμεθα οὖν σε, βασιλεῦ, οὐ χρυσόν, οὐκ ἄργυρον, οὐχ ὕπαρξιν κτλ.

3. Peter continues by saying: 'In the name of Jesus Christ of Nazareth, arise and walk' (Acts 3:6b).[111] At the corresponding place in the narrative in the AJ, one finds the command 'Arise, in the name of Jesus Christ' (22.20). The occurrence of these phrases in itself does not prove much as they are not rare, but in the context of the other allusions it is one more indication of an intertextual relationship.
4. Finally, both writings use the verb συντρέχω (to run together) in the same tense συνέδραμεν (Acts 3:11; AJ 22.1-2) in order to refer to a big crowd that gathers to watch an event. Again, this resemblance is not by itself very significant, but in the present context it strengthens our conclusion that the texts are related.

In this case, the combined occurrence of these four points of comparison strongly suggests that the episode in the AJ depends on the wording of the story in Acts 3. But the function of the architext within the phenotext is not easy to indicate. The phenotext itself does not explicate the allusions and, in fact, the reader who misses them cannot be said to have any disadvantage over the reader who identifies them. The structure of the phenotext has not notably been influenced by the architext. It is not even certain that the allusions were introduced consciously by the author. He does not exploit the fact that Acts 3 is one of the few parts of Acts in which the apostle John is (silently) present at Peter's side, whereas he might have contrasted Peter and John. On the other hand, the role of John in Acts 3 may well be responsible for the fact that this precise episode exercised a strong influence on the author's vocabulary; he had read the story in Acts and it was in his mind when he composed his own narrative. Nonetheless, he still managed to display his own realm of thought that differs so radically from that of Acts.

2.2.4.2 Christianity as 'the way'

Acts of the Apostles tends to refer to the Christian faith as 'the way'.[112] In the same very pregnant sense the word 'way' appears in AJ 59.7, where it says that Aristobula heard about the death of her husband Tertullus on

[111] ἐν τῷ ὀνόματι 'Ιησοῦ Χριστοῦ τοῦ Ναζωραίου ἔγειρε καὶ περιπάτει.

[112] Acts 9:2; 19:9, 23; 22:4; 24:14, 22. ὁδός has the definite article but no adjective in these verses. The combination with qualifiers (ὁδός τῆς πλάνης Justin, *Dial* 39.2; τῆς ἀληθείας 2 Pe 2:2, κτλ) is not parallel with this specifically Christian use. Cf. J. Pathrapankal, 'Christianity as a 'Way' according to the Acts of the Apostles', in Kremer, *Actes des Apôtres*, 533-539.

the way.[113] The use of 'way' in 22.15 ('convert those present to your way') is equally pregnant, despite the fact that the word has a possessive pronoun with it.[114] The word 'way' here stands for the Christian conviction of the text. It would seem that its use in the AJ derives from Acts - but does it?

Christians in the second century nearly never denote the community and/or its faith with the word 'way'.[115] In the Qumran texts, 'way' is used to describe religious convictions,[116] but apart from the fact that this use is less exclusive, it is highly unlikely that the AJ has any direct relation with the Qumran texts. I conclude that the specific use of the word 'way' in the AJ must echo the terminology of Acts.[117] The AJ does not allude to Acts as a text but shares some of its specific vocabulary.

2.2.4.3 The 'wonderful works of God'

The news about John spreads, his companions from Miletus say, since 'the wonderful works of God' (τὰ μεγαλεῖα τοῦ θεοῦ, 37.3) have become known in Smyrna. The expression τὰ μεγαλεῖα τοῦ θεοῦ is typical 'Bible language', an echo from Scripture. Specifically, it echoes Acts 2:11 rather than Dt 11:2, Ps 70:19 LXX, or Lk 1:49 v.l. In Acts 2:11 the expression is accompanied by the verb 'to hear' (ἀκούομεν) and the context contains the list of all the people who hear the disciples. The naming of the people from Miletus and the cities Smyrna and Ephesos (AJ 37.1-2) may have been inspired by the author's recollection of Acts 2.

We see that the lexical relations between Acts and the AJ are

[113] Junod and Kaestli, *Histoire*, 53 n.17: This 'signifie non pas qu'Aristoboula a appris que son mari Tertullus était mort "en chemin", alors qu'il faisait route (pour la rejoindre?), mais qu'elle sait qu'il est mort "dans la Voie", c'est-à-dire converti à la foi qu'il avait d'abord combattue en personne de sa femme.'

[114] JK, 95 n.2.

[115] W. Michaelis in *Theologisches Wörterbuch, s.v.* The only occurrence is Eusebius *HE* V.1.48 (Letter of the churches in Vienna and Lugdunum): ἀλλὰ καὶ διὰ τῆς ἀναστροφῆς αὐτῶν βλασφημοῦντες τὴν ὁδόν.

[116] E.g., 1QS 9.18; CD I.13; II.6. It is questionable if Acts of the Apostles depends on the terminology of the Qumran sect (so J.A. Fitzmeyer, *Luke I,* Anchor Bible 28, 242-243; S. Lyonnet, '"La voie" dans les Actes des Apôtres', *RSR* 69 [1981] 149-164), or if it is a Lucan creation (so Michaelis in *Theologisches Wörterbuch, s.v.*, followed by JK, 95).

[117] Junod and Kaestli assign less weight to the similarity than I do. 'Way' occurs in Lucian's *Hermotimos* (MacLeod) 1-30, cf. 46-47, as a key term in describing the search for wisdom, which itself is designated e.g. as τὸ ἄκρον (2-7), ἡ ἀρετή (10) and ἡ φιλοσοφία (14). Lucian may represent a popular second-century usage of 'way' that is to be distinguished from the absolute use made of it in Acts. (*Contra* the reference to *Hermot* 46 in Bauer/Aland s.v. 2c.)

unmistakable but few in number.[118] Despite his familiarity with Acts, the author of the AJ evidently wished to write his own text. Structural dependence on Acts goes hand in hand with independence *qua* vocabulary and theology.

*2.3 Sections B and C*

We saw that section A belongs to the genre of acts. A similar relation between section C and this genre is not likely because section C is a gospel-like text. Section B on the other hand originated in the same circle as section A, so that here the influence that Acts had on section A may still be felt, although the genre differs.

My investigations demonstrate that there are no structural connections between the gospel flashback in the AJ and the Book of Acts. On the lexical level, in 88.1 John addresses his audience as ἄνδρες ἀδελφοί. This phrase is characteristic of the Book of Acts, in which it occurs thirteen times, though it was probably derived from the language of the synagogue.[119] The phrase is never found in classical Greek texts or in the LXX[120] with the exception of 4 Macc 8.19. It occurs in 1 Clem and the APl and then in ecclesiastical authors. I conclude that section B of the AJ here echoes the language of Acts, just as does the APl.[121]

There are a few more resemblances between sections A and B which are indicative of their associations with the genre of AAA. The motif of polymorphy, which also occurs in the other AAA but not in the canonical Acts, is more important in section B than in section A. Again, the novelistic motif of curiosity (περιεργία) occurs several times in cc.89-93.[122] The Johannine saying 'Do not be unbelieving but believing' (20:27) is extended by 'and (be) not curious' (90.16-17). At times, John's curiosity may even be called voyeurism, which is also a motif from the novel.[123]

[118] AJ 84.17 combines the virtues of continence (ἐγκράτεια) and righteousness (δικαιοσύνη) which occur in reversed order in Acts 24:25.

[119] So Th. Zahn and F.F. Bruce in their commentaries on Acts.

[120] This verdict is based on a search in Pandora.

[121] On the relations between the AJ and the APl see the next paragraph.

[122] On this motif in *The Ass* and Apuleius' *Metamorphoses* see H.J. Mette, '*Curiositas*', in *Festschrift Bruno Snell*, München 1956, 227-235; B. Wesseling, *Leven, liefde en dood: Zelfmoord, vermeende dood, huwelijk en dood: motieven in antieke romans*, Dissertation Groningen 1993, 56-60; Swain, 'Dio and Lucian', 178; Harrison, 'Apuleius' *Metamorphoses*', 512; V. Schmidt, '*Revelare* und *Curiositas* bei Apuleius und Tertullian', in H. Hofmann (ed.), *Groningen Colloquia on the Novel Volume VI*, Groningen 1995, 127-135.

[123] B. Egger, 'Looking at Chariton's *Callirhoe*', in Morgan and Stoneman, *Greek Fiction*, 31-48, esp. 38.

As for section C, the idea that the death of Jesus could be blamed on 'lawless people' occurs in Acts 2:23 (διὰ χειρὸς ἀνόμων) and in AJ 94.1-2.[124] It has been suggested that the wording of the AJ has been influenced by Acts,[125] but the AJ lacks the accompanying word 'hands' or a synonym for it, whereas the word lawless occurs elsewhere to refer to the murderers of the Christians (APlCor 1.8; *MartPol* 9.2, 16.1). I conclude that an intertextual relationship cannot be demonstrated.[126] This conclusion confirms our hypothesis that Acts had no influence on the composition of section C.

*2.4 Ideological connections?*

There are no specific ideological resemblances between Acts and any section of the AJ. In Acts, dominant motifs are the work of the Holy Spirit, especially his guiding role in the lives of individuals and communities, the relationship between the Jewish and the gentile believers, the different attitudes of people towards the Gospel, the opposition to the Gospel and the resulting defence of Christianity as a religion that does not threaten the Empire, and the trajectory of the Gospel from Jerusalem to Rome. None of these motifs resounds in the AJ, of which the first main part focuses on the grace of God, the spiritual resurrection of believers and an ascetic lifestyle, while the second main part is centered on the identity and the suffering of Christ.

*2.5 Preliminary conclusion*

The author of the AJ has used Acts of the Apostles, which itself belongs to the genre of the historical monograph,[127] as a model for writing a text in

[124] Πρὶν δὲ συλληφθῆναι αὐτὸν ὑπὸ τῶν ἀνόμων καὶ ὑπὸ ἀνόμου ὄφεως νομοθετουμένων 'Ιουδαίων συναγαγὼν πάντας ἡμᾶς ἔφη κτλ. Thus the reading of the Acts of the Council of Nicea, which is to be preferred; manuscript **C** reads ὑπὸ τῶν ἀνόμων 'Ιουδαίων. I think that the text is improved on the assumption of a case of haplography in the pre-Nicene transmission: καὶ ὑπὸ τῶν ὑπὸ became καὶ ὑπὸ. In this way the first part of the phrase refers to the Roman authorities and the second to the Jews; the Jews come off slightly better, because the words 'lawless ones' refer to the Romans.

[125] Koschorke, 'Pfingstpredigt', 332 n.22, who also refers to the *Letter of Peter to Philip* (NHC VIII.2) 139.28-30: 'My brothers, let us therefore not obey these lawless ones (ἄνομος) and walk in ...'

[126] A separate discussion of ideological affinities can be left out because on the theological level the second main part of the AJ and Acts are worlds apart.

[127] See pp. 39-42 above.

which he could transmit his own message.[128] The AJ is related to the very text of Acts; the author knows Acts not *via* another text (e.g. one of the other AAA) but directly. The similarities in details are best explained by the supposition that he somehow had a copy of the book available.[129]

To some, the conclusion that the AJ depends on Acts may seem improbable, but external arguments support the above internal arguments. The fact that the book of Acts became a part of the canon at a later moment than the Gospels and the Epistles of Paul does not mean that it did not yet exist in the second century. Justin, the *Epistula Apostolorum*, the believers in Lyon and Vienne (± 177 AD), and the authors of the APe and APl all demonstrate that they had a working knowledge of Acts.[130] As Haenchen says in his commentary on Acts (7), the book was well known but it had no 'Sitz im Leben', no role of its own in the life of the church. Its recognition as authoritative by Irenaeus, Clement and Tertullian at the end of the second century was no doubt stimulated by a wide circulation.[131]

I would add proleptically that my research into the relationship between the AJ and the Synoptic Gospels (see below) leads to the conclusion that section A was influenced by the Gospel according to Luke. It is possible that in those early days the Gospel and the Acts circulated together. These observations indicate that there is nothing inherently unlikely in our conclusion that Acts was known to the author of section A (and B) of the AJ and served as a model for his own work.

[128] The following statements of Stoops, 'Departing', 404, are also valid if one replaces *AcPet* with AJ: 'The author of *AcPet* apparently knew Acts, but (s)he did not, and probably could not, assume familiarity on the part of the intended audience.' '... the canonical Acts, therefore, is neither the controlling authority nor the sole literary model for *AcPet*' and 'the author of *AcPet* felt free to modify, develop, or contradict whatever elements were borrowed from Acts.'

[129] Of the alternative explanations, indirect knowledge is unsatisfactory. Knowledge *via* the liturgy is unlikely because of the unrecognised status of Acts, a point that will be discussed below. Memorization of the text is less likely than the presence of a copy in the community.

[130] The mere fact that the authors of APl and APe were familiar with Acts (see also note 24 above) should be sufficient to suggest the possibility of the same for the author of the AJ.

[131] When Pervo, 'Ancient novel', 700, states that 'during the last half of the second century *APl* was more popular among Christian readers than the Acts that eventually entered the Christian canon', his personal preferences trouble his vision.

## 3 The Acts of John and the other Apocryphal Acts

### *3.1 The AAA as a group*

There are four other major Acts (APe, APl, ATh, AAn) that originated in the second or third century.[132] The links between the five AAA have so far been insufficiently studied, so that hypotheses about their interconnectedness lack firm backing. The present work cannot make more than a limited contribution to the debates.[133] Unfortunately, the fact that Photius had the five main AAA in one volume has too often led to the conclusion that they can be dealt with *a priori* as one corpus.[134] On the other hand, in some contemporary studies there is no discussion of the question of the possible interdependence among the AAA at all.[135]

In chapter 2, I approvingly quoted Bauckham's thesis that the AAA are novelistic biographies. A shared influence by Acts characterises all these writings, but they are at the same time more biographical and more

[132] Other Apocryphal Acts, e.g. the *Acts of Philip*, are later than these five; see Elliott, *Apocryphal NT*, 512-537; A. de Santos Otero in *NA*[5], 381-438. F.W. Weidmann holds that the text about Polycarp of which we have only the Coptic translation's fragmentary remains, dates from the late second century and also belongs to the acts genre; see his *The Martyrdom of Polycarp, Bishop of Smyrna in early Christian literature: A Re-evaluation in light of previously unpublished Coptic fragments*, Dissertation Yale University 1993, esp. 83-85, and his 'Intertextuality and Intent: John and the Apostolic Mission in the Harris Fragment on Polycarp', in Lovering, *SBL 1995 Seminar Papers*, 394-398.

[133] An excellent account of the situation is provided by Jones, 'Orientations', though his comparison of the mutual relations of the AAA with the Synoptic problem seems a bit exaggerated.

[134] E.g. Söder, *Apostelgeschichten*, and Elliott, 'Apocryphal Acts'. Especially scholars with interest in the women of the AAA assume *a priori* that all five works constitute a corpus. Hamman, 'Sitz im Leben', is an example as he locates this corpus in Syrian Jewish-Christian encratitic circles that were influenced by the Diatessaron and in which women were very important. He seems heavily indebted to Peterson, 'Hamburger Papyrusfragment'; Davies, *Social World*, esp. 10, 93-94, 116, who holds that the corpus of AAA was written between 160 and 225 AD by women for women(!); see also Burrus, *Chastity as Autonomy*; Niederwimmer, *Askese und Mysterium*; M. Van Uytfanghe, 'Encratisme en verdrongen erotiek in de apocriefe 'apostelromans'. Omtrent de christelijke problematisering van de sexualiteit', *Handelingen der Koninklijke Zuidnederlandse Maatschappij voor Taal- en Letterkunde en Geschiedenis* 45 (1991) 175-194. A healthy corrective to the tendency to efface the differences is provided by Pervo, 'Ancient novel'.

[135] Schäferdiek, *NA*[5], and Sirker-Wicklaus, *Untersuchungen*, propose late dates for the AJ without taking any of the other AAA into account. Junod and Kaestli, *Histoire*, 36-39, are convinced that the AJ is the oldest of the AAA and that at least the ATh is influenced by it; cf. JK, 697.

fictional than Luke's second volume. Like Acts, they describe the activity of one or more apostles after the end of the ministry of Jesus. In order to support this thesis of a common genre, we will first survey the most important characteristics of the five AAA as a group and then compare the AJ with each of them separately.

*3.1.1 Structural resemblances*

There are numerous structural elements that two or more of the AAA share:

* The AAA combine travelogues with narratives about the apostles' activities in certain cities (πράξεις). The possibility that the latter may originally have existed independently in oral form is both disputed and irrelevant.[136] Important is the fact that, contrary to what we find in the ancient novels, travel in our texts is not exploited for literary aims such as separation and recovery. It rather symbolises the advance of the Gospel and marks the AAA as missionary writings.

* Closely connected with the former element is the fact that, in the AAA, the stress falls on the individual episodes (πράξεις). Especially in AJ, APl and AAn, an episode can easily be left out and/or circulate separately.

* The apostle speaks about Jesus as Lord and calls people to conversion. The message of the text - which is not meant for entertainment but for proclamation[137] - is put into the mouth of the apostle.

* The hero-apostles are also teachers, healers and miracle-workers. In fact, they are imitators of Christ himself.[138] But like the actors in the ancient novels they are flat characters who are little more than their roles, in this case preachers of the divine message.

* Actors often express themselves in monologues that are typical of novels but atypical of other early Christian writings.[139]

* A kind of retrospective prayer is said near the end of the story (AJ 113,

[136] See e.g. Vielhauer, *Literatur*, 716-717; Schneemelcher, *NA*[5], 76; Van Kampen, *Apostelverhalen*, 276-277; E. Junod, 'Créations romanesques et traditions ecclésiastiques dans les Actes apocryphes des Apôtres. L'alternative fiction romanesque - vérité historique: une impasse', *Augustinianum* 23 (1983) 271-285, esp. 276-277. The best known statement of the orality hypothesis is D.R. MacDonald, *The Legend and the Apostle. The Battle for Paul in Story and Canon*, Philadelphia 1983.

[137] *Contra* Schmeemelcher, *NA*[5], 78, 81. Cf. Van Kampen, *Apostelverhalen*, 276-278.

[138] Cf. Elliott, 'Apocryphal Acts', 74-75. Theologically, their death is not a defeat but a triumph, the peaceful death of John no less than the martyrdoms of the others.

[139] Vielhauer, *Literatur*, 714-715.

ATh 144-148, less certain the Bodleian Coptic Fragment of the AAn).[140]
* The use of the first person plural form characterises parts of the AJ, as we have seen above. Remains of this form also occur in three of the four other Acts: APe 4, 21,[141] AAnGr 64.1, 65,[142] ATh 1,[143] as well as in the late *Acts of Philip* 3.12.[144] Furthermore, the *Acts of John by Prochorus* makes extensive use of it throughout.[145] This fact suggests that the five main Apocryphal Acts, none of which have been preserved in their entirity in the original Greek, were once characterised by the un-classical use of this form which is so typical of Acts. Of course, later redactors omitted it, presumably because they did not understand it.
* An initial scene describes the division of the world as a field of mission among the apostles, after which each travels to his allotted area (AAnLat 1, AAnMat 1, ATh 1). The presence of similar scenes in the lost originals of the other AAA is disputed.[146]
* With the notable exception of the AJ, the AAA end with the martyrdom of the apostle. In the AJ John dies peacefully.[147]

Comparison of this list with the corresponding qualities of the canonical Acts shows that half of the items are common to Acts and the AAA. The most important feature involves their unique use of the first person plural form. Secondly, there is the importance of travel, although it is in neither case undertaken for its own sake; in Acts travel records rather

[140] The first editor, J. Barns, 'A Coptic Apocryphal Fragment in the Bodleian Library', *JTS* NS 11 (1960) 70-76, rather arbitrarily thinks that the fragment stems from the beginning of the AAn; see Prieur, *NA*[5], 99; *idem*, *Acta Andreae*, 24-25.

[141] See pp. 106-107 below.

[142] AAnGr = the Greek remains of the AAn, ed. J.-M. Prieur, *Acta Andreae*, Turnhout 1989, 441-549; AAnLat = the Latin epitome of the AAn by Gregory of Tours (*ibid.*, 564-651; not in *NA*[5]).

[143] See Prieur, *Acta Andreae*, 37-38, 56-57, and *NA*[5], 102; the first person frame chosen by Gregory of Tours (AAnLat prol., 37, 38) may still reflect the style of the underlying original. In fact the case of ATh 1 (Greek text, which preserves the oldest form, only) is different because it involves only one word and because it means no sudden change in the middle of the narrative.

[144] F. Amsler, F. Bovon, B. Bouvier, *Actes de l'apôtre Philippe*, no place [Turnhout] 1996.

[145] Söder, *Apokryphe Apostelakten*, 213; cf. n.33 above.

[146] See Kaestli, 'Scènes d'attribution'. Despite Kaestli's *caveat*, Weidmann, 'Intertextuality and Intent', 397, supposes that departure narratives function as an indication of genre in the AAA.

[147] The most likely explanation why the AJ deviates from the pattern is that it (like the comparable text Jn 21) reflects the actual death of the leading person in the Johannine movement. I think that, in this respect, the AJ preserves an ancient tradition and is not based on free invention.

than symbolises (AAA) the spread of the Gospel.[148] Compared with Acts, the AAA proclaim the Gospel in even longer homilies, speeches and prayers. The speeches in Acts contain more 'salvation history' than those found in the AAA.[149] The message of both Acts and the AAA is largely articulated by the main characters of the book.

*3.1.2 Literary motifs*

We now come to some of the literary motifs that typify the AAA. Again the treatment must be brief.

* Appearances of Christ in metamorphosis occur in all five AAA. Sometimes he takes on the form of the hero-apostle of the text (AJ 87, APlTh 21, AAnGr 46, ATh 11, 27, 151-153); at other times he assumes the looks of a beautiful young man (AJ 73, 76, 87, APe 5, APl 7 [PH 3], AAnGr 32, ATh 27, 154-155).

* A related yet very specific form of metamorphosis is the polymorphy of Christ (AJ 82, 88-93, 97-98, APe 20-21, suggested ATh 48, 153) and of satan (AJ 70, ATh 43-44), which is also implicitly predicated upon Thomas Didymus (ATh 34).[150]

This complex of motifs is a very characteristic feature of the AAA which marks them out among early Christian writings. Polymorphy explicitly occurs in both sections A and B of the AJ; in the next chapter we will see that it is also present in section C, and discuss its theological implications. From the AAA it seems to have spilled over into a few other writings, like the *Gospel of Philip* and Origen, *Contra Celsum* 2.62-66, 4.14-19, 6.68-77.

* There is a tendency to elevate the apostle above the human level and to give him divine traits, especially in the AAn and ATh. It is not only evident from his polymorphy that Thomas is more than human, but also from his transfiguration (ATh 8). In this respect the *post mortem* appearances of apostles (APe 40, APl 11 [MP].5-6, ATh 169-170), which distance them from ordinary people, can also be mentioned.[151]

* Equally characteristic of the AAA are the miracle stories, which occupy

[148] Though note the symbolic function of Rome.

[149] Vielhauer, *Literatur*, 714.

[150] See my 'Polymorphy'. Dr. Hilhorst has suggested in conversation that this passage is an echo of 2 Cor 11:14, ὁ σατανᾶς μετασχηματίζεται εἰς ἄγγελον φῶτος.

[151] See for 'the apostle as saviour' in the AJ, AAn, APe and ATh, Sturhahn, *Christologie*, 90-161.

a very prominent position.[152] A specific feature of these stories is that persons who have just been resurrected or converted, personally perform miracles for others (AJ 24, 47, 81-83, AAnLat 12, 15, 19, ATh 54, 73-74).
* One of the miraculous events involves wild animals who, when let loose against condemned Christians, leave them unharmed (APlTh 28, 33-35, AAnLat 18).
* In all the AAA there is a tendency towards asceticism. This tendency is evident in their treatment of the Eucharist, marriage and sexuality. The Lord's Supper is never celebrated with wine. Sometimes there is only bread; if there is a cup, it contains water.[153] The apostles prevent marriages (the three fragments of the first part of the APe, APlTh 5-11, AAnLat 11,[154] ATh 11-16), while existing conjugal relationships come under pressure as wives are converted and persuaded to remain aloof from their husbands (AJ 82, APe 34, AAnGr 14-17, ATh 51-52); a special but very characteristic development in the second sphere is the continence of the baptised lion (APlPG).[155]
* The apostles witness before large crowds and, even more characteristically, before leading people such as government officials. Crowd scenes and court scenes also occur frequently in the novels.
* The former point notwithstanding, official opposition to the apostle occurs in all texts except the AJ. Arrests and reports of trials are frequent.[156] On closer inspection it appears that in the APl the Roman government is opposed to the Gospel as such, so that many Christians are killed. In the APlTh, APe, AAn and ATh on the other hand, it is the apostle's message of sexual renunciation which annoys individual officials, who therefore punish the apostle alone. The latter motif is rather stereotypical.
* The words σφραγίς and σφραγίζω denote a kind of sacrament (AJ 115.1, APe 5, APlTh 25, APl 4 [PHeid 29], 11.5,7, AAnGr 10-11, ATh 26-27, 49, 54, 87, 120, 131). This rite(s) must have been well known to the intended readers. Due to our lack of knowledge its nature is disputed by present day scholars, although many suggest that it is simply the Christian

[152] J.V. Hills, 'Tradition, Redaction, and Intertextuality: Miracle Lists in the Apocryphal Acts as a Test Case', in D.J. Lull (ed.), *Society of Biblical Literature 1990 Seminar Papers*, Atlanta 1990, 375-390, reaches the largely negative conclusion that the lists in the AAA have no common features when compared with the many lists in other literature. See Gallagher, 'Conversion and Salvation'; F. Bovon, 'Miracles, magie et guérison dans les Actes apocryphes des apôtres', *JECS* 3 (1995) 245-259.

[153] Roldanus, 'Eucharistie', puts the practices in the AJ in a wider historical perspective. I found, however, no intertextual relations in this respect.

[154] Not in the preserved version but in its *Vorlage*, see Prieur, *NA*$^5$, 100.

[155] More on this subject in chapter 5.

[156] With respect to Acts, see Pervo, *Profit*, 18-24.

baptism.[157] It is even suggested that different practices are meant in the different AAA.[158]

* Last but not least, the AAA avail themselves of literary topoi from the Hellenistic novels such as the shipwreck, the beauty and youth of the women, speaking animals and suicides.[159] On the subject of women the AJ is rather reticent: there are no descriptions of their beauty and although Drusiana remains attractive even after her death (cc.70-71), Cleopatra's illness affects her outer appearance (20:3-5).[160]

Most of these motifs are not found in Luke's Acts. Only miracles, crowd scenes and persecution might be traced back to that writing. This relative scarcity of parallels points to the difference between Acts as an historical monograph and the AAA as largely fictional novelistic biographies. The function of Acts as a model for the authors of the AAA is limited.

### *3.1.3 Preliminary conclusion*

For all their individuality, the five AAA form a specific group of writings which have both important elements in common with the canonical Acts and specific narrative motifs as well as conceptual elements of their own.[161] Bauckham's thesis holds true: although they have been influenced by Acts, they are more fictional and biographical. Special emphasis must fall on the fact that the above discussion was almost completely limited to section A and the generic similarity with the other acts may only pertain to this section.

[157] E.g. Peterson, 'Hamburger Papyrusfragment', 190, with reference to Hermas, *Sim* 9.16; J. Ysebaert, *Greek baptismal terminology. Its origins and early development*, Nijmegen 1962, esp. 390-395.

[158] Prieur, *Acta Andreae*, 190-191; Klijn, *Thomas*, 55-57. The fact that in AJ 115.1 John seals himself at the end of his life at least shows that the terminology does not always denote baptism (cf. JK, 579-580, and R. van den Broek, *Studies in Gnosticism and Alexandrian Christianity*, Leiden 1996, 110-113). Van Kampen, *Apostelverhalen*, 142, points out the essentially spiritual character of the seal in the AAn.

[159] JK, 547-550, offer a list of novelistic motifs which have parallels in AJ 63-64, 70-71.

[160] *Contra* Pervo, 'Becomes Christian', 699.

[161] This conclusion is supported by studies in the relationship between other AAA such as the APe and the APl; see e.g. C. Schmidt, Πράξεις Παύλου, Hamburg/Glückstadt 1936, 127-128; Peterson, 'Hamburger Papyrusfragment'; Klijn, *Thomas*, 22-25; Prieur, *Acta Andreae*, 388-403; D.R. MacDonald, '*The Acts of Paul* and *The Acts of Peter*: Which Came First?', in E.H. Lovering (ed.), *Society of Biblical Literature 1992 Seminar Papers*, Atlanta 1992, 214-224; R.F. Stoops, Jr., 'Peter, Paul, and Priority in the Apocryphal Acts', *ibid.*, 225-233.

### *3.2 Comparison with individual Acts*

The following brief comparisons of the AJ with each of the other AAA separately make no strict distinction between structural and lexical parallels.

#### *3.2.1 The Acts of Paul*

Although the APl is badly preserved, it evidently is much more a travelogue than the AJ. Whereas the APl is traditionally regarded as a text influenced by the AJ, it has recently been suggested that the influence may have been the other way round.[162] This state of affairs in any case suggests a connection between the two texts!

An obvious parallel is that in both texts half a temple is destroyed. According to the AJ one half of the Artemision collapses (42.4-5), whereas in APl 5 [PHeid 38] half the temple of Apollo in Sidon is brought down. Who imitates who?[163] The continuation of the story in the AJ tells us that the other half of the building was taken down by the newly converted believers (44.1-2). This detail is fully in line with the text's stress on the cooperation of the believers in their own salvation and in resurrecting others (to be discussed in the next chapter), so that we may conclude that the story is a well-integrated part of the AJ.[164]

The designation of important people as 'first of' (πρῶτος) a city occurs in APl and AJ as well as in the canonical Acts.[165] Jan N. Bremmer thinks that this terminology is particularly Asiatic and suggests

[162] For (criticism of) the traditional view see Jones, 'Orientations', 486-491. The recent effort is D.R. MacDonald, '*The Acts of Paul* and *The Acts of John*: Which came First?', in Lovering, *SBL 1993 Seminar Papers*, 506-510, who in his first page reduces intertextuality to literary dependence and then looks for literary parallels without considering (differences in) theology, attitude towards the developing NT, and social background. He points to four pairs of passages which he deems parallel, but only the first pair forms a real parallel. MacDonald overlooks that John is not imprisoned in AJ 63-87. If one nevertheless wants to see APl 7 (PH 3) and AJ 63-87 as parallels, the more logical explanation is that the tomb (AJ) was changed into a prison (APl).

[163] MacDonald, 'Paul and John', 507-508, suggests that the AJ imitates the APl.

[164] In AAn Mart.pr. 6 the believers themselves destroy temples.

[165] In AJ 31.7 ('Ανδρόνικος δέ τις στρατηγός πρῶτος ὢν τῶν 'Εφεσίων κατ' ἐκεῖνο καιροῦ), 56.3 (τις ἀνὴρ 'Αντίπατρος ὀνόματι Σμυρναίων πρῶτος) and 73.10 (νεανίσκον πρῶτον τῶν 'Εφεσίων Καλλίμαχον); APlTh 11, 26; AAnLat 3; Acts 13:50, 28:7 (regarding Malta, cf. *IGRR* I 512). The designation πρῶτος τῆς πόλεως/ἐν τῇ πόλει - though admittedly in a less technical sense - also occurs in inscriptions not only from Phrygia but also from Thracia and Arabia, see *IGRR* I 652 Acmonia, 666 Dioclea (Phrygia), III Gerasa (Arabia), IV 798 Heraclea, 816 Callipolus.

that both AJ and APl were written in Asia Minor.[166] In that case, Luke was well informed about conventions in this area.

More parallels between AJ and APl have been suggested, some of which are real - such as the laying down of a dead or ill person at the apostle's door, AJ 46 and APl 4 [PHeid 33]. Others are merely apparent.[167] Together they justify the conclusion that the authors of the AJ and the APl are not only familiar with the canonical Acts but that these works are also closely related to each other, although the direction of the influence could be in either way.[168]

### *3.2.2 The Acts of Peter*

I have dealt with the relationship between the AJ and the APe in a separate essay, the conclusions of which I will now only summarise.[169] Both texts are closely related; there are some partly parallel episodes and quite a few verbal parallels. The conclusion of Dennis MacDonald that the APe is the architext is ill-founded,[170] since two observations suggest that the AJ is the text which influenced the APe. First of all, the theology of the APe is inconsistent; sometimes it is proto-Orthodox, but when the text has a parallel with the AJ it adopts the views of the latter.[171] Secondly, parallels to both major parts of the AJ occur in the APe. Because it is unlikely that both authors of the AJ used the APe, the best explanation of the data is that the author of the APe knew the AJ in its final form.

The overal structure of the APe resembles that of the AJ and the AAn: in the lost first part Peter gradually travels to Rome. Once there, he has a lengthy confrontation with Simon, after which he tries to escape the city to be sent back by the Lord for a second stay resulting in his death. As for the literary form, a sudden first person plural occurs once in c.4 and several times in c.21.[172] Although this number is considerably lower than that in Acts and the AJ, the we-form is due to the influence of Acts and/or the AJ, since it is reasonable to suppose that the lost Greek text contained more we-forms.

[166] Bremmer, 'Magic', esp. 56.

[167] See the list in Jones, 'Orientations', 501-502.

[168] I noted on p. 96 above that both texts use the phrase ἄνδρες ἀδελφοί from Acts.

[169] Lalleman, 'Acts of John and Acts of Peter'.

[170] '*The Acts of Peter* and *The Acts of John*: Which Came First?', in Lovering, *SBL 1993 Seminar Papers*, 623-626.

[171] So already Schmidt, *Petrusakten*, 90-96.

[172] Vielhauer, *Literatur*, 698.

### 3.2.3 *The Acts of Andrew*[173]

A comparison of the overall structure of the AAnLat - in which the story line of the original AAn largely remains intact[174] - with the AJ reveals the clear resemblances between the two texts. In the AJ John first travels to Ephesos and then stays there for a while. His stay is interrupted by a trip around the city's area. Likewise Andrew needs some time to come to Patras, the city in which he will stay twice.

Moreover, we can list several episodes in the AAnLat which recall scenes from the AJ:

| AJ | AAnLat | Subject |
|---|---|---|
| 19 | 11, 22 | supernatural announcement of the arrival of the apostle (double vision) |
| 19-20 | 30 | a husband threatens to commit suicide because of the fate of his wife |
| 56 | 7, 14, 16, 26, 30 | performance of a healing miracle in exchange for conversion |
| 58 | 20 | departure, sadness, farewell speech |
| 59 | 21 | reference to travelling companions |
| 90 | 20 | appearance of the cross on a mountain |

Some (AJ 19, 58 and 59), but not all, of these episodes were probably inspired by Acts of the Apostles, as we have seen above. Those that were not written in this way still indicate the clear parallels between the AJ and the AAn.

In the third place, the literary style of prayers and speeches in the AJ and the AAnGr is often similar, with ample use of enumerations and a repeated exclamatory ὦ. There are also other striking verbal similarities between the AJ and the AAnGr.[175] Also common to both acts is the idea of a relation between the apostle's success and his attainment of rest.[176] Adding these observations to the list of generic characteristics above, I can safely conclude that on the literary level both writings are closely related.[177]

[173] Cf. Prieur, *Acta Andreae*, 394-400; A. Hilhorst, 'The Apocryphal Acts as martyrdom texts: the case of the Acts of Andrew', in Bremmer, *Acts of John*, 1-14, esp. 4-5.

[174] So Prieur, *Acta Andreae*, 8-12; *idem*, *NA*[5], 96-103; but L. van Kampen, '*Acta Andreae* and Gregory's *De miraculis Andreae*', *VigChr* 45 (1991) 18-26, 22, disagrees with this conclusion.

[175] See Prieur, *Acta Andreae*, 396-397; similarities with AJ section C: 399 n.5.

[176] Use of a form of ἀναπαύομαι in AAnGr 40, 43, and AJ 45.

[177] Cf. Prieur, *Acta Andreae*, 394-400, and *NA*[5], 107 n.47.

### *3.2.4 Acts of Thomas*

Opinions on the existence of a relationship between the AJ and the ATh are divided.[178] In my opinion such parallels as the similar structure of some of the prayers, the presence of a final prayer (AJ 112-114, ATh 144-148), the theme of polymorphy and the performance of miracles by recently saved persons are common generic features. But the specific parallels between the AJ and the ATh signalled by Junod and Kaestli are such as to suggest stronger ties.[179]

### *3.3 Ideological relations among the AAA*

Theologically the AJ is distinct from the other AAA, though it is perhaps best to say that theologically these writings are all different from one another. The APl and the APe both openly combat heresies and can be seen as expressions of a popular, proto-orthodox faith. Closer inspection reveals, all the same, marked differences between them. In their own ways, the AAn and the ATh are representatives of a rather dualistic attitude which can easily be seen as Gnostic. To a greater extent than the other acts, both identify their hero-apostles with Christ and both show clear philosophical influences, the AAn from Greek and the ATh from Syriac traditions.[180]

A brief remark about Christology illustrates the differences among the AAA. The APl never calls Jesus Christ 'God' and the APe is ambivalent in this respect. The position of canonical Acts would seem to resemble that of the APl. The AAn agrees with (at least a part of - see next chapter) the AJ in that it makes no distinction between God and Christ, although the latter is only once called 'God'. For the ATh, Jesus Christ is, on the other hand, fully God.

One may go further and assert that even within the individual AAA conceptual consistency is not always to be found. The internal inconsistencies within these writings have several different causes: the oldest forms of the texts were already a composite whole;[181] incompetent authors;[182]

[178] Schäferdiek, 'Herkunft', 249-251, and 'Johannes-Akten' (*RAC*) 578-579, thinks of a common environment; Junod and Kaestli, *Histoire*, 36-40, argue that the AJ influenced ATh; Klijn, *Thomas*, 25, denies any connections whatsoever.

[179] See JK, 517 n.2; Junod and Kaestli, *Histoire*, 38-39 with n.21. To mention just two cases, compare AJ 48-54 with the third act ATh 30-38, and AJ 113 with ATh 144-145.

[180] For the AAn see Prieur, *Acta Andreae*, 372-379. For the ATh and the Syriac milieu see H.J.W. Drijvers, 'Thomasakten', in *NA*[5], 300-302.

[181] For the APl, where the APlTh differ from the rest, see my 'Resurrection'. And of course there is the difference between the Gnostic and non-Gnostic parts of the AJ.

[182] Generally assumed to be the case for the APe.

later redactions with a catholicising tendency were incomplete.[183] In any case, the discussion about the alleged Gnosticism of the AAA is not only the invention of the present-day readers!

We conclude that the common genre to which the AAA belong did not prescribe the ideological directions that the individual writings had to take; or, to state it differently, authors with diverse convictions availed themselves of the same genre in order to express and to propagate the Christian faith.[184]

*3.4 Conclusions: the AJ, the other AAA and the canonical Acts*

The five AAA display great generic similarities with each other and with the canonical Acts. *Qua* genre, section A of the AJ can indeed be counted among the acts, but sections B and C are not related to the group of acts. Section A is a text in the model and style of the canonical Acts. Indeed, the connection between section A and Acts is much closer than previous research has assumed. But despite this influence from Acts, the author of section A never followed it slavishly. The older text is not normative nor treated as 'scripture', but it just serves as a model for the composition. The AJ is fully independent in the sense that it can very well be understood without any knowledge of Acts.

It is not necessary to be dogmatic about the difficult question of the interrelations among the AAA. It is possible that the author of the AJ not only knew Acts but also one of the other AAA, most probably the APl. It may even be the case that the idea of taking Acts as a model occurred to the author of the AJ when he noticed how the APl had made use of this book. Conceptually the APl and Acts have much more in common than the AJ and Acts. But although the hypothesis that APl served as a bridge between Acts and AJ is somewhat attractive, there is no way to prove that it actually served this function, nor is it a necessary hypothesis. Our author not only demonstrates his great independence of mind, but also his direct knowledge of Acts. Having Lk and Acts at hand would be enough for him to develop his own writing.

The place of the AJ among the AAA is marked by its adoption (or preservation) of more of the we-form found in Acts than the others. It also contains a sermon about Christ (section B), which was later developed into an even larger-scale gospel, and it makes the most effective use of the

[183] In this respect, Gregory's Latin epitome of the AAn greatly differs from the parts preserved in Greek.

[184] This suggests that ideological differences cannot be used to argue against a literary relation between one of the AAA and Acts.

motif of polymorphy.[185] Persecution hardly has a place in it and its hero-apostle is not martyred. Conceptually it goes its own way and in this respect it is a real Johannine text.

## 4 The Acts of John and the Gospel of John

### *4.1 History of research*

In previous research on the relationship between the Fourth Gospel and the AJ, three phases can clearly be distinguished. The first phase began when, about a century ago, the ancient AJ had just been reconstructed and the relationship between this writing and John's Gospel was hotly debated. In that period, when many advocated a date for the Gospel in the middle to late second century,[186] Peter Corssen and Adolf Hilgenfeld held the opinion that the AJ is older than the Gospel and that the latter was influenced by the former. To prove their point, they tried to demonstrate that all elements pertaining to the life of Christ in the AJ merely repeat what we are told in the Synoptic Gospels, but not what is mentioned in John.[187] Strong opposition to this view came from James, who went so far as to state: 'Leucius is writing a commentary upon St. John's narrative, with the view of explaining it all away.'[188]

Corssen and Hilgenfeld found no supporters.[189] Worse, Johannine scholarship in the subsequent period paid no attention to the possibility of a connection between the Johannine literature inside and outside the NT. This attitude still prevails in the work of Junod and Kaestli up to and including their 1983 edition of the AJ. In the latter work they merely state, when opting for a second-century date for c.94-102 + 109, that this date is verified by the connection this text has with the Johannine tradition.[190]

[185] Indeed, in my 'Polymorphy' I argue that this motif originated with the AJ.

[186] The publication of Papyrus Rylands 457 (Aland P 52) disallows this possibility, as the papyrus dates from the first half of the second century: C.H. Roberts, *An unpublished fragment of the Fourth Gospel in the John Rylands Library*, Manchester 1935.

[187] P. Corssen, *Monarchianische Prologe zu den vier Evangelien. Ein Beitrag zur Geschichte des Kanons*, Leipzig 1896, 118-134; Hilgenfeld, 'Johannes', 22-43.

[188] James, *Apocrypha anecdota*, 144-154; citation from 149. Leucius is the alleged author of the AJ. Cf. Zahn, 'Wanderungen', 199-200. Instructive reviews of Corssen's book by A. Jülicher in *GGA* 158 (1896) 841-852 and by H. Holtzmann in *ThLZ* 22 (1897) 331-335.

[189] See Loewenich, *Johannes-Verständnis*, 102-109; F.-M. Braun, *Jean le Théologien et son Évangile dans l'église ancienne*, Paris 1959, 203.

[190] JK, 632: 'Nous pensons en effet qu'il contient encore des traces des querelles christologiques qui ont marqué le développement du christianisme de type johannique, notamment à l'époque de la rédaction des trois épîtres canoniques.'

A few years earlier Helmut Köster had already initiated the third phase, in which the AJ is studied in closer connection with the Johannine literature as a phase of the Johannine trajectory. His New Testament *Introduction* discusses the AJ as part of the treatment of the Johannine literature and labels the apocryphal work as a gnostic continuation of the Johannine tradition. Köster suggests that the hymn cc.94-96 was probably sung in the Johannine churches before it was included in the AJ.[191] Subsequently, Schäferdiek suggested that the *Sitz im Leben* of the AJ is in the Johannine circle, but he did so without stating his grounds.[192] Kaestli came round to a position which resembles that of Köster insofar as cc.94-102 are concerned.[193] He now explicitly says that he thinks not only of a theological but also of a socio-historical continuity between the Gospel of John and AJ.[194] The term 'trajectory', introduced into New Testament studies by Köster and Robinson,[195] is used for a theological tradition which has socio-historical as well as literary features. The word 'trajectory' was first used in a discussion about the AJ by Kaestli and it has also been used by Sirker-Wicklaus, Pervo, and Garcia.[196]

It is important to see that opinions are divided over the question whether the AJ in its entirety forms a part of the trajectory. Kaestli and Jean Zumstein limit the extent of the trajectory to cc.94-102.[197] In

[191] Köster, *Einführung*, 635-637.

[192] Schäferdiek, 'Herkunft', 267. In *NA*[5] he is nearly silent on the relationship.

[193] Kaestli, 'Response', 86-88; *idem*, 'Le mystère de la Croix de lumière et le johannisme. Actes de Jean ch. 94-102', *Foi et Vie 86 (Cahier biblique 26)* 1987, 35-46. H. Köster, 'Les discours d'adieu de l'évangile de Jean: leur trajectoire au premier et deuxième siècle', in Kaestli, *Communauté*, 277, calls this essay convincing.

[194] Kaestli, 'Mystère', 46, who specifies this as 'une communauté héritière des 'dissidents' combattus par la première épître de Jean.' Cf. J.-D. Kaestli, 'Remarques sur le rapport du quatrième évangile avec la gnose et sa réception au IIe siècle', in *idem*, *Communauté*, 354-355.

[195] H. Köster and J.M. Robinson, *Trajectories through Early Christianity*, Philadelphia 1971 = *Entwicklungslinien durch die Welt des frühen Christentums*, Tübingen 1971. The chapter on Johannine research in this volume (216-250, by Robinson) ignores the AJ.

[196] Kaestli, 'Response', 87; Sirker-Wicklaus, *Untersuchungen*, 221-224, 229-231; Pervo, 'Trajectories', *passim*; H. Garcia-Iberg, *Polymorphie du Christ dans la tradition johannique gnostique*. Mémoire de D.E.A., École pratique des hautes études Paris, V[e] section, 1993-'94, *passim*, esp. 21. Schneider, *Mystery*, pays no attention to the trajectory approach.

[197] J.-D. Kaestli, 'Le rôle des textes bibliques dans la genèse et le développement des légendes apocryphes. Le cas du sort final de l'apôtre Jean', *Augustinianum* 23 (1983) 323-324, emphatically denies that AJ 115 depends on Jn 21. J. Zumstein, 'L'interprétation johannique de la mort du Christ', in F. Van Segbroeck *et al.* (eds.), *The Four Gospels 1992. FS Neirynck* III, Leuven 1992, 2137.

contrast, Sirker-Wicklaus, Pervo and Garcia consider the whole of the AJ as Johannine literature. Pervo's essay 'Johannine Trajectories in the Acts of John' is original in that it aims to show that the AJ as a whole (not just cc.87-105) is a commentary on the Gospel of John if not a parody of it.[198]

*4.2 Sections B and C*

Because of the generic similarities discovered in chapter 2, we begin with the gospel flashback in the AJ (sections B and C, i.e. cc.87-105), the part of the text which structurally resembles the Fourth Gospel. Section A, which resembles Acts, will be reviewed later. The gospel flashback consists of section B, which probably originated together with section A, and the Gnostic section C. Junod and Kaestli divide section B into twelve so-called testimonies and I also use this designation.[199] These testimonies occur in roughly chronological order because the first two deal with the calling of disciples and two in the middle with the transfiguration of the Lord.[200]

*4.2.1 Structural affinities*

In chapter 2 we saw that the structure of the gospel flashback resembles the structure of the Gospel of John. Both writings contain a description of the public activity of Christ, followed by private teaching and a section concerning the cross.[201]

Apparently, one of the characteristic parts of cc.87-105, the first testimony in section B (c.88), has been modelled on c.21 of the Fourth Gospel.[202] In section 5 below I will demonstrate that this testimony also borrows some of its contents from the story in Mt 4:18-22 par. Mk 1:16-20. But the explicit statement that Jesus stands at the shore and the suggestion that John and James are sailing both strongly remind us of Jn 21. Moreover, the whole atmosphere of the story in the AJ resembles that of Jn 21. The Fourth Evangelist uses the expression 'he showed himself' (ἐφανέρωσεν ἑαυτὸν), which exactly expresses what occurs in the AJ: Jesus is not present with his disciples, he just appears momentarily. It

[198] Pervo, 'Trajectories', 68.

[199] The label 'testimonies' was introduced by JK, 468, 474-475. Neither the text nor JK attach significance to the number twelve.

[200] Sirker-Wicklaus, *Untersuchungen*, 101-104, rather sees a logical order in the testimonies, but I fail to understand her reasoning; JK, 475, simply state: 'La structure de l'ensemble du témoinage défie toute logique.'

[201] Cf. pp. 43-46, esp. the table on p. 45.

[202] By using the final, post-resurrection chapter of the Fourth Gospel for the beginning of his 'gospel', the author suggests that the body of Jesus was always such as the canonical gospels suggest that it was only after Easter.

therefore strikes me as more than accidental that this testimony and its immediate sequel (88.9-89.7) consist of 153 words, which is exactly the number of fish caught according to Jn 21:11![203] These observations taken together suggest that AJ 88-89 is an ingenuous and remarkable combination of Synoptic and Johannine elements, which can nevertheless be understood without knowledge of these Gospels. The combination of an episode from Jesus' public ministry and a post-resurrection appearance strongly suggests that Jesus' life was nothing else than one great supernatural appearance.

We saw in the last chapter that the AJ originally existed without cc.94-102. In that form, the story about the Lord just consisted of cc.87-93 and 103-105. We now focus on 93.14-17, which forms the epilogue to the narrative part of this Christological section and the original transition to the hortatory cc.103-105. These lines strongly remind us of the first epilogue to the Gospel, Jn 20:30-31. Both pericopes state the limitations and selectiveness of what preceded in the respective texts, as well as the aims with which they were written; both moreover refer to the deeds of Christ in neuter plural form. For these reasons it is very likely that 93.14-17 was inspired by Jn 20:30-31.

The first part of section C (cc.94-96) parallels Jesus' farewell to his disciples in Jn 13-17. In both Jn and the AJ the Lord performs an act which appears to replace the Synoptic institution of the Lord's Supper (AJ 94-95, Jn 13:1-30) and which is followed by an explanation (AJ 96, Jn 13:31-17:36).[204] The absence of any further structural parallels between cc.97-102 and Jn 18-20 is caused by the fact that the texts deal with totally different things; the cross is the only common denominator.

It appears that the similarity in overall structure between the gospel flashback of the AJ and the Gospel of John is accentuated by the presence of several corresponding passages.

[203] The number 153 has always fascinated readers. Admittedly, the text in manuscript **C** is not completely certain. Leaving out all that qualifies for deletion, I count 149 words; if I include as many words as possible, there are 154.

[204] Hilgenfeld, 'Johannes', 28-34, wishing to prove that the AJ is completely independent from John's Gospel, in fact shows that AJ 94-95 resemble Jn 13:1-30, and c.96 Jn 13:31-17:36. Cf. JK, 624: 'Le mystère décrit en *AJ* 94-96 prend la place du récit de la dernière Cène dans les évangiles synoptiques. La dernière réunion du Christ avec ses disciples (*AJ* 94,2) a été consacrée à l'institution d'un rite, mais, comme dans le IVe évangile, ce rite n'est pas l'eucharistie.' See also Kaestli, 'Response', 87; *idem*, 'Mystère', 37, and Roldanus, 'Eucharistie', 90. The rite of the dance is called 'the Last *dîner dansant*' by Pervo, 'Trajectories', 63 n.95.

*4.2.2 Lexical intertextuality*

The lexical similarities between the Fourth Gospel and section B of the AJ are clear. We begin with some generally acknowledged quotations. In the fifth testimony John tells that Jesus 'would take me upon his breast' (ἐπὶ τὰ ἴδια στήθη, 89.11). These words evoke Jn 13:23, in which the beloved disciple is said to be 'close to the breast' (ἐν τῷ κόλπῳ) of Jesus, and even more vs.25, according to which the disciple fell ἐπὶ τὸ στῆθος of Jesus. The use of the word στῆθος in combination with the preposition ἐπὶ demonstrates that the author of this section knows the Gospel of John.[205] The fact that John designates himself as the one whom Jesus loved (90.7 = Jn 20:2, cf. 13:23; 19:26), a remarkable statement which moreover seems somewhat inappropriate in view of his misbehaviour (90.15-22), leads to the same conclusion. Third, AJ 90.16 (testimony 7) is also a clear quotation from the Gospel of John. 'Do not be faithless, but believing' (μὴ γίνου ἄπιστος ἀλλὰ πιστός), Jesus commands Thomas in Jn 20:27; literally the same words are spoken to John in the AJ: Ἰωάννη, μὴ γίνου ἄπιστος ἀλλὰ πιστός. The function of the quotation is less obvious, for Thomas does not play any role in the AJ. The point seems to be that, just as Thomas was wrong in asking for proof of the resurrection, John should not seek proofs of the incorporeality of the Lord but must believe in his identity.[206]

In addition to these quotations I wish to discuss an allusion to the Fourth Gospel as such that occurs right at the beginning of section B. The John of the AJ says that he has, up to that point, been unable to (speak or) write about his personal encounters with Christ.[207] In my opinion, the reference to writing must be taken seriously. John's phrase can imply two basic meanings. Either the author suggests that John refrained from writing until now, or he hints that his previous writing was insufficient. To answer the question, it is important to note that the verb χωρεῖν ('to hold, contain, be able') occurs also in Jn 21:25, the verse which deals with the writing of gospels.[208] I would therefore translate AJ 88.4 as 'I was unable to write

[205] Cf. Beyschlag, *Überlieferung*, 101-102.

[206] Cf. Garcia, *Polymorphie*, 63-64.

[207] ἐγὼ μὲν ὑμῖν <οὔτε> προσομιλεῖν οὔτε γράψαι χωρῶ ἅ τε εἶδον ἅ τε ἤκουσα, 88.3-5, cf. 88.6: καθ' ἃ χωρεῖ ἕκαστος ἐκείνων ὑμῖν κοινωνήσω ὧν ἀκροαταὶ δύνασθε γενέσθαι. The precedence of speaking over writing may reflect the priority of oral transmission over written sources in Early Christianity.

[208] The verb is used in another way than in the AJ: ἔστιν δὲ καὶ ἄλλα πολλὰ ἃ ἐποίησεν ὁ Ἰησοῦς, ἅτινα ἐὰν γράφηται καθ' ἕν οὐδ' αὐτὸν οἶμαι τὸν κόσμον χωρῆσαι τὰ γραφόμενα βιβλία. About these words Zahn writes in his Commentary, *ad* 21:25: 'Die Verwunderung über die naive Hyperbolie des Ausdrucks ... trug nicht wenig dazu bei, die uneigentliche Fassung von χωρεῖν im Sinn von 'mit dem Verstand begreifen' beliebt zu

...'[209] This denigrating remark is aimed at John's writing about Christ, which must be the Gospel that bears his name. Therefore, M.R. James correctly notes:

> ... the use of the first person singular seems to me to indicate that the speaker has actually written something. And the phrase contains a further implication: namely, that the written work was in a certain way incomplete. 'In my published writings', says St John, 'you will not find the mysteries which I am now going to lay before you: they were too deep for me to record in writing.'[210]

Consequently, the statement in c.88 confirms our impression that the quotations and echoes in the later parts of section B are meant as *pars pro toto* to indicate the author's familiarity with the Fourth Gospel.

Section B as a whole is an effort to replace other gospels, an act that has authority because it is allegedly carried out by one of the previous evangelists, John. Instead of a straightforward contradiction of these gospels, the author opts to reveal new knowledge that had not yet been expressed in writing before. But again we encounter a characteristic of the chapter's intertextual references: readers who do not know any other gospel will hardly notice the polemical attitude towards the Fourth Gospel; for them the AJ can well serve as *the* gospel.

The lexical relations between section C and John's Gospel have been studied in one of Kaestli's essays, in which he demonstrates that this section is replete with Johannine vocabulary.[211] As for the hymn (cc.94-95), the Christological titles used in its beginning (Logos, Father,[212] grace, spirit, glory) are all characteristic of the Fourth Gospel. Several lines in it have the characteristic form of the Johannine 'I am' sayings, a parallel that can hardly be accidental.[213] In its final lines (95.47-50) Christ calls himself 'door' and 'way', which are allusions to Jn 10:9, 14:6. The whole of c.96 has an even more Johannine style. AJ 96.5-6 recalls the stress that the Gospel places on the fact that Christ was sent by the Father. The

machen'; in *Apostel und Apostelschüler*, 195 n.3, he refers to the first part of APe 20, *quod cepimus scripsimus* (ἃ ἐχωρήσαμεν ἐγράψαμεν), and three other occurrences of *capere* in that chapter.

209 The καὶ νῦν μὴν in 88.5 implies that the preceding present tense χωρῶ refers to a past event.

210 James, *Apocrypha anecdota*, 151; this view is rejected by Loewenich, *Johannes-Verständnis*, 103-104.

211 Kaestli, 'Mystère'.

212 In chapter 4, pp. 179-181, I discuss Father as a Christological title.

213 Pervo, 'Trajectories', 63.

vocabulary of 96.11-13 echoes Jn 8:28; 16:7; 13:7. More examples of quotations and allusions are given by Kaestli.

Let us now turn to examples from the revelation about the cross, in which Christological predicates from the 'I am' sayings are echoed several times.[214] 'The sixth hour' (97.6) is directly derived from Jn 19:14-16 (the AJ is otherwise not too exact about chronology). The luminal character of the cross may have developed from Christ's claim to be the light of the world (Jn 8:12; 9:5; 12:35; cf. 1:4-5). The list of predicates in AJ 98.8-12 contains many Johannine words; it is especially notable that λόγος occupies the first place. The self-designation of Christ as the one who descended (100.3) is possibly based on Jn 3:13, 31; 6:62, and the designation of the believers as those who obey his voice on hearing it on Jn 10:16, 27. The phrase 'Know that I am wholly with (παρὰ) the Father, and the Father with me' (100.11-12) cannot be understood apart from the Johannine phrases 10:38; 14:10-11; 17:21.[215]

Jn 19:34 is alluded to twice; the first time (c.97) will be discussed in connection with the *Gospel of Peter* and leads to the conclusion that the AJ is related to John's Gospel. The second allusion consists in the denial that blood flowed from Christ (101.8-9). This is unmistakably a form of substitution which implies a direct refutation of the verse from John. A third allusion is the occurrence of the verb νύσσομαι (also Jn 19:34) in 'pierced, yet not wounded' (νυγέντα καὶ οὐκ ἐπλήγην, 101.7-8).[216] The pattern of the literary relationship is clearly polemical.

When taken by themselves, several of the above cases would support the conclusion that the similarities between the two writings indicate that the Johannine words and ideas were still being orally transmitted in the second century. Other references manifest a detailed knowledge that most likely resulted from a reading of the Gospel. On the whole, section C of the AJ is both familiar with the Gospel of John and opposed to it. It is a critical revision of the gospel.

[214] JK, 599 n.4.

[215] The next chapter, p. 181, will discuss the choice of παρά as a preposition instead of the Johannine ἐν, although I can here refer to Jn 17:5; cf. Kaestli, 'Mystère', 45.

[216] Schäferdiek, 'Herkunft', 252-253, thinks that this phrase is the result of a later redaction because it does not match with the surrounding antithetical phrases, which have the same verb in both parts and because, in view of the order of events, the phrase cannot refer to the piercing of Christ's side (John 19:34) but has to refer to the flogging (Mk 15:15 par John 19:1). Neither of these arguments is compelling, especially because Schäferdiek does not take the *Gospel of Peter* into account.

### *4.2.3 Theological relations*[217]

The Fourth Gospel has a specific theological view of the cross, which focuses less on the shame and the suffering of death by crucifixion than on Christ's victory. Jesus' departure does not take away his glory but only serves to demonstrate it. The affirmations of his elevation are inherently open to a spiritual interpretation (Jn 3:14; 8:28; 12:32-34). It is this line of thought that has been developed in section C of the AJ at the cost of the other part of the story, the reality of Christ's physical suffering. The AJ devalues the wooden cross and replaces it by the cross of light in cc.98-100.[218] In the Gospel as well as in section C of the AJ it is the cross which separates believers and non-believers, although in this respect the AJ has a more literal conception of separation than the Gospel has. According to section C, when Gnostic Christians are united into the cross of light, they regain their original status. This idea may owe something to Jn chapters 11 and 14-17, which stress both the importance of being 'in Christ' and the unity among the believers. Christ's request that believers will be 'in us' (i.e. in God and Christ, Jn 17:21) especially seems to have influenced the conception of the cosmic cross. But in addition, the AJ has no room for the reality of the wooden cross and the resurrection of Jesus.

In section C, a polemical attitude denies the very fact of Christ's physical crucifixion and even ridicules those who believe in it (c.102).[219]

In section B the polemical remark about the Gospel (88.3-5) just discussed is not followed by an open polemics, but the subsequent text is nonetheless an interpretation of the Gospel that would not be acceptable to many of its readers. The human aspects of the Johannine Jesus and the physical reality of his life on earth have been removed so that attention falls only on his divinity. Another conspicuous difference is the role attributed to the apostle John. As if to compensate for the Fourth Gospel's silence about him, the AJ places him in the spotlight, albeit not without some critical commentary from the Lord (90.16-17, 21-22; 92.4, 6-8).

I conclude that Sections B and C both contain many clear echoes of and references to the Fourth Gospel; section C shares much of its structure with it and c.101 is clearly a critical dialogue with it. In view of the structural and lexical resemblances, the differences in theological content between the two texts are all the more remarkable. They point to the existence of great theological differences among members of one 'family',

[217] More on Christology in chapter 4.

[218] Kaestli, 'Response', 87.

[219] Cf. Kaestli, 'Mystère', 40. JK, 596, 600, state that of all the Gnostic texts they know, the AJ is the one that most fiercely combats the canonical view of Christ's passion.

i.e. among recipients of the Fourth Gospel. Section C is a critical revision of that Gospel.

In order to solve the tension, it was suggested that section C may be sourced in an early phase of the Johannine movement, when the text of the Gospel was not yet 'orthodox'.[220] I think that this is not a helpful suggestion and I would rather keep the source criticism and redaction criticism of the Fourth Gospel distinct from the present research, since I am very sceptical about the results of these forms of criticism.[221]

### *4.3 Section A*

At first sight there are hardly any indications of literary connections between the Fourth Gospel and section A. But Junod and Kaestli's hypothesis that section A derives from the same author as section B is valid and, therefore, section A is likely connected with John's Gospel in the same way as section B is.

In section A the first certain echo only occurs in John's autobiographical note (113.7-10): 'who for two years blinded me ...; who in the third year opened up the spritual eyes, and gave me back my visible eyes.'[222]

[220] Kaestli, 'Mystère', 40-41, who argues that the divergences between Jn and the AJ need not mean that the latter text simply contradicts the former: '... les divergences constatées pourraient remonter à un stade ancien de la tradition ...' 'La communauté d'origine de notre texte serait l'héritière de cercles johanniques se réclamant d'une forme "primitive" de l'évangile, encore exempte des correctifs "orthodoxes" apportés par le dernier rédacteur. L'épisode du coup de lance et la présence du disciple bien-aimé au pied de la croix peuvent avoir fait partie de cette rédaction "anti-docète" ...' Nowadays many scholars think that several redactional layers can be distinguished within Jn and that these layers can be related to distinct moments in the history of the Johannine community. See J.L. Martyn, *History and Theology in the Fourth Gospel*, Nashville 1968, followed by Brown, *Community*, and M.C. de Boer, *Johannine Perspectives on the Death of Jesus*, Kampen 1996.

[221] The reconstructions of the textual layers and the communal history are mutually dependent; there are no external data to support or to falsify them; cf. Hengel, *Johanneische Frage*, 157, 163-164. Independent historical evidence for intra-Johannine developments allegedly exists in the form of the expulsion of Jewish Christians from the synagogues (allegedly reflected in Jn 9:22, 12:42, 16:2); but the *birkat h^aminim* which allegedly documents this event was - at least in its present form - almost certainly written later; see P.W. van der Horst, 'The Birkat ha-minim in Recent Research', *ExpT* 105 (1993-'94) 363-368; P.S. Alexander, '"The Parting of the Ways" from the Perspective of Rabbinic Judaism', in J.D.G. Dunn (ed.), *Jews and Christians. The Parting of the Ways A.D. 70 to 135*, Tübingen 1992, 1-25, esp. 7, 10. The whole reconstruction of Martyn, Brown and De Boer requires a Palestinian or Syriac environment for Jn.

[222] The multitude (τὸν ὄχλον τὸν περιεστῶτα) and the loud voice in AJ 24.15-17 may allude to Jn 11:42-43.

These words imply that the length of the period which John spent with Christ was three years. As the same period is suggested in the biography of Jesus provided in John's Gospel, it becomes evident that the author of the AJ knew the Johannine tradition, in which the period of Christ's public activity is said to be about three years.[223]

According to AJ 106-115, John died peacefully at old age in Ephesos. The end of his life contrasts with what the other AAA tell us about their hero-apostles. John's fate is probably derived from Jn 21:18-23, where Christ speaks about the death of Peter and of the beloved disciple, who was soon - when exactly is highly disputed - identified as John the Son of Zebedee and as the author of the Fourth Gospel. Christ *says* that the beloved disciple will grow old[224] and *implies* that, unlike Peter, he will not die a violent death. It would seem that the author of the AJ knew Jn 21 at least indirectly. In what the AJ tells us about the beloved disciple John, the traditions about him preserved in Jn 21 play a decisive role.[225] This fact is no real surprise in view of the familiarity of the author of sections A and B with John's Gospel.

The only real lexical similarity[226] - but a striking one - concerns the

[223] Pervo, 'Trajectories', 51-57, focuses on the 'resurrection stories' of Lycomedes and Cleopatra (cc.20-25) and of Drusiana and Callimachus (63-86) as developments of Jn 11 and 20. On the structural and - as we will see below - lexical levels, he fails to demonstrate a direct intertextual relationship. Nobody in the AJ is dead for four days like Lazarus was. Again, the tomb of Drusiana has no stone, but a door operated by a key (70.13; 72.8; 73.2). Unlike what Pervo states, in these stories in the AJ δόξα (18.8, 43.2, 52.4, 68.5, 77.7, 78.2) has a general sense, quite in contrast with the pregnant Christological meaning that the word has in Jn ('Trajectories', 51 with n.24; S.S. Smalley, *John: Evangelist and Interpreter*, Exeter 1983, 220-223).

[224] Cf. the self-designation ὁ πρεσβύτερος in the Johannine letters.

[225] Kaestli, 'Le rôle des textes bibliques', 323-324, denies this for two reasons: he reads Jn 21 as stressing not the old age that 'John' would reach but the 'idée d'un destin privilégié de Jean dans l'au-delà', and he presupposes that the AJ depends on an ecclesiastical tradition concerning John in Ephesos. Both grounds cannot be held. The Fourth Gospel does say that John, contrary to Peter, will not die violently and will become so old that people will wonder if he will ever die (21:21-23). Another element from this pronouncement also entered into the AJ in which John is old (27.9). The conviction of Junod and Kaestli that the AJ *presupposes* a late second century tradition concerning the activity of John in and around Ephesos has not been proven; cf. chapter 6.

[226] In places were we would expect the AJ to show knowledge of the Gospel, it does not. A few examples: - The wordplay on παρακαλέω in c.57 contains no allusion to the Paraclete. - The story about the temple in Ephesos does not refer to Jesus' words and deeds regarding the temple of Jerusalem and his own body. The story of Lazarus is never alluded to verbally, although resurrection is one of the central concepts in the text.

final sentence of the text: 'He then said to us, "Peace be with you, brothers", and joyfully gave up his spirit' (115.4).[227] First of all, the risen Christ uses the phrase 'peace be with you' in Lk 24:36 and Jn 20:19, 21, 26. As this expression is absent from the Apostolic Fathers and the Apologists, its occurrence in the AJ must allude to the gospels. Secondly and more specifically, the words used to describe John's death - 'giving up his spirit' - are those used of Christ in Jn 19:30, which differ from the formulations of the Synoptics and are very rare in Greek texts (cf. APe 40, AAn 63). Thus the final sentence in section A clearly owes its wording to the Gospel of John. In combination with the structural affinities with the Gospel, it functions as a signal of the author's acquaintance with it.

Ideologically, this section of the AJ presents us with a spiritualising interpretation of the Fourth Gospel that is closely akin to the one given by Ernst Käsemann in our time.[228] This interpretation is not without its sources in the Gospel: characteristic of both the Gospel and the AJ is their lack of references to the constitution and organisation of the Christian community; instead of a church fellowship we meet individual believers.[229] In the AJ John neither has a successor nor installs leaders for the churches. This silence with regard to community life points to a low degree of organisation, possibly associated with a notion of authority that is sourced in a sole leading person.

Sacraments are not explicitly mentioned in the Fourth Gospel: baptism is not prescribed nor the Lord's supper instituted. We may say that Jn is neither anti- nor hyper-sacramental.[230] In the AJ the position of baptism is very marginal. It is referred to once (84.15, λουτροῦ ἁγίου), but newly converted people are not baptised. Bread is broken in the community and

[227] καὶ εἰπὼν ἡμῖν Εἰρήνη ὑμῖν, ἀδελφοί, παρέδωκε τὸ πνεῦμα χαίρων (115.4) - my translation.

[228] E. Käsemann, *Jesu letzter Wille nach Johannes 17*, Tübingen ²1967 (ET *The Testament of Jesus*, London 1968), never refers to the AJ. He holds that the Gospel is a Gnostic or at least Gnosticising document. In this study it is assumed, in contrast, that the Fourth Gospel, read against the background of the Old Testament and of Judaism (cf. J. Painter, *The Quest for the Messiah. The History, Literature and Theology of the Johannine Community*, Edinburgh 1991), as well as through the lenses of 1 Jn, is far from Gnostic; cf. G.P. Luttikhuizen, 'Johannine Vocabulary and the Thought Structure of Gnostic Mythological Texts', in H. Preissler and H. Seiwert (eds.), *Gnosisforschung und Religionsgeschichte. FS K. Rudolph*, Marburg 1994, 175-181, esp. 175.

[229] For Jn see Käsemann, *Jesu letzter Wille*, 53-61.

[230] R.W. Paschal, Jr., 'Sacramental symbolism and physical imagery in the Gospel of John', *TynB* 32 (1981) 151-176, 175, concludes that 'the sacraments stand as symbols of our participation in and acceptance of Christ's sacrifice and humiliation.'

even at the grave of Drusiana, but this ritual would not seem to have a sacramental meaning. Although it is not connected with the suffering and death of Christ, during the celebration the Lord receives praise for the salvation he brought.[231]

The absence of salvation history in the AJ marks a definite contrast with Jn, but one that can again be understood from the Gospel itself. In the Gospel the polemics against the Jews occupy a very important position. In the AJ they are replaced by silence on the subjects of Israel, prophecy and covenant.[232] This omission shows that the polemics have in a certain way been effective and that (at least this branch of) the Johannine community has gained a considerable distance from the Jewish context in which its Gospel originated. In the environment in which the AJ originates, the Jews are at most marginal and the believers no longer remember their roots. The only traces of the old covenant that we find in section A are reminiscences of stories about Moses and Elijah (cf. section 7.1 below).[233] The spiritualising interpretation of the Johannine theology in the AJ probably results, at least in part, from the fact that the Gospel is being read outside its original Jewish context.[234]

Finally, there is the occurrence of dualistic language in both texts, which both make ample use of pairs of contrasts.[235] In Jn Jesus descends from heaven in order to reveal the eternal light. The use of pairs of ideas creates sharp antitheses: light - darkness, seeing - blindness, heaven - earth, above - below, life - death, truth - falsehood, love - hate, etc. Some take these antitheses as evidence of Gnosticism;[236] the element of truth in this view is that dualism was much appreciated by the Gnostics. The same type of language returns in the AJ. Characteristic pairs of contrasts are: the human and the divine spheres;[237] life - death (cc.18-25), soul/the invisible

[231] Roldanus, 'Eucharistie', 96, thinks that the author of the AJ places a one-sided stress on Jn 6:63 at the expense of vs.57.

[232] Cf. Käsemann, *Jesu letzter Wille*, 31-37; Pétrement, *Dieu séparé*, 232-233; for the AJ, Schäferdiek, 'Herkunft', 265.

[233] In section C there is an oblique hint at the 'lawless Jews' (c.94).

[234] Painter, 'Opponents', 49, points out that the opponents combatted in 1 Jn lacked the Jewish background of the Gospel and its first readers.

[235] Following B.B. Wolters, *Alzo lief heeft God de wereld gehad ... Dualisme in het evangelie van Johannes?*, Doctoral Essay Groningen University 1993, I distinguish between a dualistic worldview (not in Jn) and dualistic language.

[236] Käsemann, *Jesu letzter Wille*, 118, 124, 129, 130, uses the label Gnostic several times but his arguments consist largely of elements of docetism and realised eschatology, ideas that are hardly characteristic of Gnosticism; M.F. Wiles, *The Spiritual Gospel. The Interpretation of the Fourth Gospel in the Early Church*, Cambridge 1960, 101-105.

[237] Sirker-Wicklaus, *Untersuchungen*, 211-212.

inner - body/outer appearance (cc.26-29, 54)[238], chastity - sexuality, rest - unrest (cc.48-54), God/Christ - satan, and (on the narrative level) stay - go away.[239] Moreover, several pairs of characters form deliberate contrasts: Cleopatra - Lycomedes, the lice - mankind, Andronicus - Fortunatus. In its use of dualistic language, the AJ displays a clear influence from Jn.

From the viewpoint of the later canon and of Orthodoxy, the type of intertextual relationship between John's Gospel and the AJ is that of distortion. Our author's specific outlook opposes 'orthodox' readings of the Gospel and has rightly been called ultra-Johannine.[240] Conversely, the author of the AJ would probably argue that his spiritualisation is the legitimate continuation of the trajectory.

### *4.4 Conclusions*

The hypothesis that the AJ is a part of the Johannine trajectory is confirmed in so far as sections B and C of the AJ display that their authors were familiar with the Gospel of John. Section C adopts the general outline of the Gospel but it is involved in a very intense intertextual relationship with the Fourth Gospel since it rejects main ideas of the canonical text.[241] In the AJ, John has become an opponent to the Gospel that bears his own name. Section C probably reflects a situation in which the Gospel is largely interpreted along Proto-orthodox lines. The ultra-Johannine group which presents itself in section C is forced to combat the very Gospel that was formative of their thought. The polemics imply that the AJ also testifies to the fact that the Fourth Gospel was accepted and used in the non-Gnostic part of the church.

The intertextual relationship between section B and John's Gospel is less intense. This section avoids direct contradiction and presents itself in an unpolemical manner as a new gospel which hopes to replace the existing ones. This state of affairs points to a difference in the background of the two sections.

As expected, the intertextual links between John's Gospel and section A are not particularly strong, but there is a clear conceptual influence. The differences between sections A and B, which according to our hypothesis

[238] On cc.26-29 see Van Kampen, *Apostelverhalen*, 111.

[239] JK, 428-438.

[240] Vielhauer, *Literatur*, 472, where the term denotes those combatted in 1 Jn, whom Vielhauer sees as Gnostics.

[241] M. Pfister, 'Konzepte der Intertextualität', in U. Broich and M. Pfister (eds.), *Intertextualität. Formen, Funktionen, anglistische Fallstudien*, Tübingen 1985, 1-30, 29, argues that the dialectic situation in which a text at the same time interacts with and distances itself from another text creates an 'Optimum an Dialogizität'.

have the same author, are not so great that they could not be explained by attributing them to their respective subject matters and genre.

## 5 The Acts of John and the other Gospels

It is worth asking to which extent there is a relationship between the non-Johannine gospels and the AJ. Previous research already collected evidence for such a relationship, but has largely limited itself to listing textual references. We will go over the evidence once more and evaluate the relationship, answering questions such as whether the AJ recognises the Gospels as authoritative or as writings with a special status.

Besides the Synoptics I will also deal with the non-canonical *Gospel of Peter*, which may briefly be introduced here. The original length of the writing is unknown. What we have are 60 verses, which deal with the passion and resurrection of Jesus, and the beginning of one more scene, probably a post-resurrection appearance.[242] The Old Testament plays a rather large role in the *Gospel of Peter*, but the view that this Gospel is only related to the Old Testament and not to the canonical gospels[243] is unconvincing.[244] Most scholars hold that *Peter* was written under the

[242] This implies that any structural comparison with the AJ can only involve its section C. I do not use the now unnecessary division of the text into fourteen chapters, only the division into verses.

[243] A view held by J. Denker, *Die theologiegeschichtliche Stellung des Petrusevangeliums. Ein Beitrag zur Frühgeschichte des Petrusevangeliums*, Bern/Frankfurt 1975; H. Köster, 'Apocryphal and Canonical Gospels', *HTR* 73 (1980) 105-130; *idem*, *Ancient Christian Gospels. Their History and Development*, London 1990; J.D. Crossan, *Four Other Gospels*, Minneapolis 1985, 125-181. *Idem*, *The Cross That Spoke. The Origins of the Passion Narrative*, San Francisco 1988, esp. 16-30, 409-413, paints a more complicated picture of the origin of the *Gospel of Peter*: an original 'Cross Gospel' was enlarged with material from the four canonical gospels and redactional transitory phrases. The idea that the *Gospel of Peter* contains 'a primitive and less crystallized form of the Christian tradition' was already expressed upon its rediscovery in 1892, see Findlay, *Byways*, 96, 314-315.

[244] J.B. Green, 'The Gospel of Peter: Source for a Pre-Canonical Passion Narrative?', *ZNW* 87 (1987) 293-301; Schneemelcher in *NA*[5]; Brown, '*Gospel of Peter*', rebuts Crossan's first book. Crossan, *Cross That Spoke*, is unconvincing. For this statement I can here give only two reasons in draft form. First, as the author himself says (e.g. 198-207, 335, 387), nearly every verse ascribed to the 'Cross Gospel' derives from or recalls the OT so that Crossan has reconstructed a modern version of Rendell Harris's 'Testimony Book' rather than a *Christian* gospel. Secondly, his hypothesis that *Peter* originated in two stages, first influencing and later being influenced by all four canonical gospels, is unduly complicated. For a more vigorous criticism see Hengel, *Johanneische Frage*, 56 n.159, who states:

influence of the canonical gospels[245] and that the unknown author also made use of independent oral traditions[246] - a possibility that we will discuss below. Some believe that there is a special relationship between *Peter* and the Fourth Gospel.[247] The date of the *Gospel of Peter* is uncertain. Evidence from the Early Church only demonstrates that it originated before the end of the second century.[248] A second-century date fits with the internal evidence, such as a notable lack of knowledge about the first-century situation.[249] On the other hand the four gospel canon was not yet inviolable when this gospel originated, so that we cannot move beyond the second century.[250] As place of origin, Syria (Antioch) and Asia Minor have both been proposed.[251]

### *5.1 Sections B and C*

Because there is a generic similarity between section B and C of the AJ and the gospels, it is a priori likely that this so-called gospel flashback is much closer to other gospels than section A. We will therefore start with this flashback.

#### *5.1.1 Structural relations*

From section B (cc.87-93) we discuss the testimonies that seem to be related to the Synoptics. Testimony 1 (88.9-20), in which four disciples are

'Barnabasbrief und Petrusevangelium zeigen die typische, den Antijudaismus steigernde Weiterentwicklung der Erzähltradition wie des Schriftbeweises im frühen 2.Jh.'

245 The author knew of them either by oral transmission (so Brown, 'Gospel of Peter', 334-337) or he had the texts (so Th. Zahn, *Das Evangelium des Petrus*, Erlangen/Leipzig 1893; Findlay, *Byways*, 79-116, esp. 96-98; Hengel, *Johanneische Frage*, 56-57 n.159; A. Kirk, 'Examining Priorities: Another Look at the *Gospel of Peter*'s Relationship to the New Testament Gospels', *NTS* 40 [1994] 572-595).

246 Kirk, 'Priorities', 594 n.66; P.M. Head, 'On the Christology of the Gospel of Peter', *VigChr* 46 (1992) 209-224, 218. M.K. Stillman, 'The Gospel of Peter. A case for oral-only dependence?', *EphTheolLov* 73 (1997) 114-120, argues that *Peter* was influenced only by hearing, not reading, the canonical Gospels.

247 M.G. Mara, *Évangile de Pierre* (SC 201), Paris 1973, 214-218, followed by Hengel, *Johanneische Frage*, 56-57 n.159.

248 A full survey of the evidence in Denker, *Petrusevangelium.*

249 Esp. Brown, 'Gospel of Peter', 338.

250 Denker, *Petrusevangelium*, 57, 89; Kirk, 'Priorities', 595.

251 In favour of Syria see T.V. Smith, *Petrine Controversies in the Early Church*, Tübingen 1985, 136; Denker, *Petrusevangelium*, 126-130, who thinks of the circles of docetic adversaries of Ignatius and who rejects (255-256) Mara's idea of much Johannine influence on the *Gospel of Peter*. Relations with Melito of Sardes would favour the latter possibility, see O. Perler, 'L'Évangile de Pierre et Méliton de Sardes', *RB* 71 (1964) 584-590.

called by Jesus, resembles the story in Mk 1:16-20 par. Mt 4:18-22.[252] There are a good many parallel elements. Jesus first calls Peter and Andrew, followed by John and James; our author thus maintains the Synoptic order. Peter/Simon and Andrew are seen as brothers, just as John and James are. The names themselves can be considered allusions to Mt/Mk in the AJ, a fact that reveals an exact knowledge of how the disciples are related to each other.[253] The command to 'come behind' Jesus (Mt/Mk) becomes 'come to me' (AJ). Both versions of the story are situated on the shore and both tell that the disciples are fishermen. The real difference between Mt and Mk on the one hand and the AJ on the other involves the elements that the latter adds to the story, viz. a polymorphous appearance of Christ which is told much more elaborately than the call-story itself is (88.11-20). The simple calling scene (Mt/Mk) is thus the basis from which the narrator develops his own interest.[254] We may safely conclude that the AJ was familiar with this story from Mt or Mk. It functions as a platform on which the author of the AJ, with his own vocabulary, builds his own narrative. I would classify this use of the architext as a paraphrase.

Testimony 6 (90.1-4) is the first of two transfiguration scenes in the AJ.[255] Like 1, the beginning of this testimony closely parallels the opening sentences of the three Synoptic stories about the transfiguration:[256] An indication of time is followed by the introduction of the characters of the story, reference to the mountain and a description of a visionary experience. The resemblance is heightened by several verbal parallels: all stories open with the same verb, παραλαμβάνω, and mention the same three disciples who accompanied Jesus - AJ placing John first. There is a parallel with Mt which mentions the light (Mt 17:2 = AJ 90.3). More notable is the fact that Lk and the AJ say that Jesus climbed the mountain in order to pray (προσεύξασθαι, Lk 9:28; compare 90.2 where it says that he used to pray [εὔχεσθαι] there). Prayer recurs again in the

[252] I showed on pp. 112-113 above that this testimony depends on Jn 21. The call narrative has a rather different form in Lk 5:1-11.

[253] Besides John, only James, Peter and Andrew are presented, a fact that is inexplicable without knowledge of what the NT gospels (Mk 1:29; Lk 6:14a; Jn 1:40-42) say about their relations. Influence by oral traditions is unlikely.

[254] We saw above that the same testimony is also closely connected with Jn and that it owes a lexical detail to Lk.

[255] The other is testimony 7 (90.4-22).

[256] Mt 17:1-9; Mk 9:2-13; Lk 9:28-36.

second transfiguration story. The similarity in structure is evident.[257] After the common beginning, the AJ abbreviates the original story and continues with a new, second transfiguration scene.

I conclude that in two cases this section of the AJ gives evidence that its author had a good knowledge of the Synoptics.[258] Yet on the whole the author avoids the impression that he saw these writings as important. He neither openly combats the NT gospels nor recognises them as authoritative. Our author is consciously independent, but the two testimonies that are partly modelled on the Synoptics do suggest that the present text is intended to function as an alternative gospel.

The structure of section C contains no specific agreements with any other Gospel than that of John (see above).

*5.1.2 Lexical relations with section B*

One detail at the end of the first testimony (88.9-20) parallels the end of Luke's version of the call narrative:[259] The phrase καταγαγόντες τὰ πλοῖα ἐπὶ τὴν γῆν in Lk 5:11 reappears as εἰς γῆν τὸ πλοῖον ἀγαγόντες in 88.19.

Testimony 7 (90.4-22) is a second, much longer transfiguration story.[260] The fact that the Lord's feet are whiter than snow seems to reflect Lk's account of the transfiguration (9:29).

Two passages in the AJ describe the enormous length of Christ. The same idea occurs in the *Gospel of Peter*:

AJ 89.10 τὸ πᾶν εἰς οὐρανὸν ἀποβλέπων.

AJ 90.13 τὴν δὲ κεφαλὴν εἰς τὸν οὐρανὸν ἐρειδομένην.

GPe 40 καὶ τῶν μὲν δύο τὴν κεφαλὴν χωροῦσαν μέχρι τοῦ οὐρανοῦ, τοῦ δὲ χειραγωγουμένου ὑπ' αὐτῶν [sc. Χριστοῦ] ὑπερβαίνουσαν τοὺς οὐρανούς.

The stories use different verbs, but the fact that both specifically have the nouns 'head' and 'heaven' in their statements about Christ's length is more than accidental. A common tradition is likely. Notice that the AJ has developed several ideas about the Lord's appearances into a unique pattern of polymorphy.

The only toponym in section B is Gennesaret (92.1-2), which is ap-

[257] *Contra* the conclusion of Cartlidge, 'Transfigurations', 54: 'Attempts to show a literary relationship between the synoptics' transfiguration stories and those in the apocryphal Acts have not been convincing.'

[258] See also the discussion of 90.22 in connection with James on p. 146 below.

[259] We just saw that the structure is based on Mt/Mk.

[260] JK, 482, call it the pearl of the AJ. Hennecke, *Handbuch*, 523, observes that the author's preference for nudity indicates his pagan rather than Jewish background.

parently used to designate a village, whereas the name was more commonly used for an area.[261] Rather than demonstrating a personal acquaintance with Palestine, this use of the name seems to be based on its occurrence in the Synoptics.

In the tenth testimony John narrates the following about his life with Christ: 'Sometimes when I wanted to touch (κρατῆσαι) him, I met a material and solid body; and at other times again when I felt him (ψηλαφῶντός μου), the substance was immaterial and bodiless and as if it were not existing at all' (93.1-4). These words contrast sharply with two cases in which the verb ψηλαφάω occurs in the NT: 1 Jn 1:1 '... which we have seen with our eyes, which we have looked upon and which our hands touched (ἐψηλάφησαν) ...'; and Lk 24:39 'handle (ψηλαφήσατέ) me and see; for a spirit has not flesh and bones as you see that I have.' The use of ψηλαφάω seems to be a conscious allusion,[262] but the fact that Ignatius uses the same word in a comparable context in *Smyr* 3.2 makes this suggestion uncertain. The word may have been used by early Christians apart from its occurrence in (later) canonical writings. If it is an allusion, it is impossible to say whether it alludes to Lk or 1 Jn, or both. As this chapter makes the second author's acquaintance with both books relatively certain, he may even have had both in mind. In that case the AJ typically presents a critical revision of the relevant texts.

Testimony 11 (93.4-10) is a remarkable mixture of elements about Jesus' table fellowship with the Pharisees (Lk 7:36; 11:37; 14:1) and the miraculous feeding of several thousand people (Mk 6:35-44; 8:1-10 par.). The point of the testimony is that Christ needs no food, which is in obvious contradiction with the implicit view of the gospels. The stories about the Pharisees are clearly echoed but not really used in a positive way.[263] The words about the miraculous feeding echo the Synoptic account of the first feeding. Indeed, the sequence of verbs in AJ 93.7-9 exactly corresponds with Mk 6:41-42: λαβὼν ... εὐλόγησεν ... ἐμέρισεν ... ἐχορτάσθησαν,[264] a parallel that suggests an acquaintance with Mk, though the evidence is not enough for a firm conclusion.

In view of the fact that section B is a gospel-like text and that its author was familiar with synoptic traditions, the lexical parallels are surprisingly unimportant and few in number.

[261] See, besides the commentaries, D.J. Edwards, 'Gennesaret', *ABD* 2 (1992) 963.

[262] It also occurs in Acts 17:27.

[263] Compare Lk 7:39 ὁ καλέσας αὐτὸν - 14:7 τοὺς κεκλημένους - 14:12 τῷ κεκληκότι αὐτόν with AJ 93.5 κληθεὶς εἰς κλῆσιν ἐπορεύετο - 93.6-7 ὑπὸ τῶν κεκληκότων - 93.10 τοὺς καλοῦντας αὐτόν.

[264] Mt and Lk do not have ἐμέρισεν, the AJ has διεμέριζεν.

*5.1.3 Lexical relations with section C*

The phrase 'let us sing a hymn to the Father' (94.3) is a clear quotation of the singing in Mk 14:26 par. Mt 26:30.[265] The author underlines his interest in the word hymn by repeating it somewhat redundantly in 94.7 (Ἤρξατο οὖν ὑμνεῖν καὶ λέγειν). The intertextual relation in this description of comparable situations is one of paraphrase.

The fact that the four verbs in Mt 11:17 return in the same order in AJ 95.19-22 leaves no doubt about the parallels between these verses,[266] which are stronger than the ones we encountered in section B. But given the spiritualising tendencies of the AJ, it is remarkable that what is metaphorical in Matthew is here taken quite literally. The words now function as a justification of the institution of the dance.[267] On the level of meaning the architext is distorted.

After Jesus' arrest, the disciples flee. In telling us this detail, AJ 97.2-3 depends on Mt 26:56 par. Mk 14:50. The use of the word 'flee' is an unmistakable allusion in a context of denial. The same is true of the reference to darkness (Mk 15:33/Mt 27:45 = AJ 97.6-7).[268]

The only geographical names from the canonical gospels to be used in section C are Jerusalem and the Mount of Olives in c.97. The reference to the Mount is remarkable because it suggests that the text here depends on traditions other than the gospels. John is said to receive Christ's revelation in a cave on the Mount, but the NT never mentions the existence of this cave. The earliest written mention of its existence outside the AJ dates from the fourth century, when the cave is connected with the ascension.[269]

At the end of section C it is said that the Lord was taken up (ἀνελήφθη, 102.2). The ambiguous word ἀνελήφθη is used with reference to the Lord in the *Gospel of Peter* 19 in the sense of 'to die'; but in Mk 16:19 (long end) and Acts 1:2, 22 - again with reference to Christ - the predominant aspect of meaning is 'to be taken up'. There can be no doubt that the latter nuance is the one intended in the AJ. By the use of this one word, the AJ skips the death, burial and resurrection stories and

[265] Zahn, 'Wanderungen', 202; Kaestli, 'Mystère', 36-37.

[266] ηὐλήσαμεν ὑμῖν καὶ οὐκ ὠρχήσασθε, ἐθρηνήσαμεν καὶ οὐκ ἐκόψασθε. In Lk 7:32 the last verb is ἐκλαύσατε.

[267] JK, 598, 623.

[268] JK, 597.

[269] Viz. in Eusebius, *Vita Constant*, 3.41. See K. Schmaltz, 'Die drei "mystischen" Christushöhlen der Geburt, der Jüngerweihe und des Grabes', *Zeitschrift des Deutschen Palästina-Vereins* 42 (1919) 132-165, esp. 150-154; G. Kretschmar, 'Festkalender und Memorialstätten Jerusalems in altkirchlicher Zeit', *ZDPV* 87 (1971) 183-187.

come right to the end of the Lord's appearances. The AJ differs, at this point, markedly from the *Gospel of Peter*, which deals extensively with the burial and the resurrection.

We come, last but not least, to the phrase in which the Lord tells John that the people think that he is pierced with lances and reeds (λόγχαις νύσσομαι[270] καὶ καλάμοις) and that he receives vinegar and gall to drink (ὄξος τε καὶ χολὴν ποτίζομαι, AJ 97.8-10). The piercing of the Lord and the drinking that he is given are described as elements that the multitude down in Jerusalem believe but that do not belong to the true faith. John should not believe that they were real. There is no doubt about the author's interest and intentions: The phrase is an intense polemics against earlier traditions, which are both quoted and rejected.[271]

This conclusion leaves us with the intriguing question, which earlier tradition(s) is/are in the author's mind? The question is the more interesting because the *Gospel of Peter* is involved in the intertextual comparison. It should be noted that the *Gospel of Peter*'s treatment of the piercing of the Lord and the drinking given him complies with the canonical gospels, while the AJ contradicts them.

The first part of the phrase has the following parallels:

Jn 19:34: λόγχῃ αὐτοῦ τὴν πλευρὰν ἔνυξεν
Mk 15:19: ἔτυπτον αὐτοῦ τὴν κεφαλὴν καλάμῳ (cf. Mt 27:31).
GPe 9 : καλάμῳ ἔνυσσον αὐτὸν

Both GPe 9 and AJ 97 make use of the words from the canonical texts, combining an element from Mt/Mk, the reed (κάλαμος), with an element from Jn, the piercing. The combination is remarkable because Mt/Mk and Jn employ the key word in different contexts: In Mt/Mk it occurs in a report of the beating before the crucifixion, while what Jn's account tells us, happened at the end of the crucifixion.[272]

The second part of the phrase forms a difficult case because Mt/Mk mention two drinks, one offered before the crucifixion and one just before the Lord's death. The following table visualises what the gospels narrate:

[270] The second occurrence of the verb to pierce (νύσσω) in the AJ (101) was discussed in the section on John's Gospel (p. 116).
[271] Cf. above n.241.
[272] This shows the secondary character of the *Gospel of Peter* in comparison with the canonical gospels.

| | drink before | drink at the end |
|---|---|---|
| Mt 27 | wine with gall (οἶνος[273] μετὰ χολῆς, vs.34) | vinegar (ὄξος, vs.48) |
| Mk 15 | wine (vs.23) | vinegar (vs.36) |
| Lk 23 | vinegar (vs.36) | none |
| Jn 19 | none | vinegar (vs.29-30) |
| GPe | none | gall with vinegar (χολὴν μετὰ ὄξους, vs.16) |

Ps 68:22 LXX probably stands behind the words used:
καὶ ἔδωκαν εἰς τὸ βρῶμα μου χολὴν
καὶ εἰς τὴν δίψαν μου ἐπότισάν με ὄξος.[274]
The episode also has parallels in other writings.[275]

Returning now to the first element of the phrase, the beating, the AJ conflates Mt/Mk with Jn and the same conflation occurs in the *Gospel of Peter*.[276] It is unlikely that the authors of the *Gospel of Peter* and the AJ independently produced the same phenomenon.[277] Was the AJ, then, influenced by the *Gospel of Peter* or vice versa, or is there a common source? The key to the answer is that we may assume that the word λόγχαις in the AJ derives directly from Jn because it occurs neither in Mt/Mk nor in the *Gospel of Peter*.[278] Does the *Gospel of Peter* therefore borrow from the AJ? Indeed, the text in the *Gospel of Peter* could be explained on that basis. But we know that the *Gospel of Peter* had in-

[273] An important variant reads ὄξος, see Nestle-Aland apparatus, to which add Orig. *In Matth ser* 127, and Diatessaron.

[274] Green, 'Gospel of Peter', 296 would relate the words in the gospels to Prov 31:6,7 rather than to Ps 68.

[275] See W. Bauer, *Das Leben Jesu im Zeitalter der neutestamentlichen Apokryphen*, Tübingen 1909, 217-220. Melito, *Peri Pascha* 79, the anonymous second-century *In Pascha*, and *Visio Pauli* 44 (*dederunt mihi acetum cum felle mixtum*) have the order vinegar and gall. *Barnabas* 7.3 has the same order as the AJ (ὄξει καὶ χολῇ) but 7.5 shows the reverse order found in the *Gospel of Peter* (χολὴν μετὰ ὄξους). Notice, *contra* Crossan, that the *Gospel of Peter* sides with the secondary witnesses over against the canonical gospels. *Peri Pascha* and *In Pascha* (on which see p. 189 below) were written in second-century Asia Minor, which is also the most likely place of origin for the *Gospel of Peter*, *pace* Crossan. In chapter 6 I will reconsider second-century Asia as the date and location of the AJ's composition.

[276] And in *Oracula Sibyllina* (ed. Geffcken, GCS, Leipzig 1902) 2.373-374 (πλευρὰν νύξωσιν καλάμοισιν) and 8.296 (πλευρὰς νύξουσιν καλάμῳ διὰ τὸν νόμον αὐτῶν).

[277] Though Schneider, *Mystery*, 85-86, seems to make this suggestion.

[278] Kaestli, 'Mystère', 40, affirms that this is a case of polemics against Jn 19:34-35; cf. JK, 599. Moreover, we saw above that other elements from Jn 19 have influenced the AJ.

dependent access to the canonical gospels, so that we cannot prove that the *Gospel of Peter* was influenced by the AJ in this specific case.[279]

The second part of the phrase is also a case of conflation. Here two elements that are separate in Mt/Mk have been combined both in the *Gospel of Peter* and in the AJ. Again it is not likely that this combination was wrought independently by the two authors. Dealing with the *Gospel of Peter* in relation to the Synoptics, Brown convincingly argues that the wording in Mk and Mt is more original and that the *Gospel of Peter* reflects a secondary harmonization with Ps 68.[280] But that explanation will not do for the AJ, which is too far away from the Jewish Scriptures to reflect a Psalm. The question remains: does the AJ depend on the *Gospel of Peter* or was there a oral tradition underlying both texts?[281]

From the treatment of the lexical affinities I conclude that, contrary to section B, section C openly polemises against the earlier gospels by quoting and subsequently rejecting several phrases from them. The intertextual relationship between C and the gospels is therefore more intense than that between B and the gospels. A second conclusion is that the resemblances between the AJ and the *Gospel of Peter* are unmistakable but difficult to explain.[282]

### *5.1.4 Conceptual intertextuality*

The gospel section in the AJ denies the death of Christ and the reality of his suffering, while the resurrection is passed over in silence. Therefore the AJ must be regarded as a polemical text. In section B the polemical attitude is hidden because its author largely ignores rather than quotes the earlier gospels. In section C the views of others about the 'events' are contradicted: in 97.8-10 the multitude in Jerusalem stands in opposition to John; in 99.3-6 the wooden cross contrasts with the cross of light, while the real Christ differs from the lowly things people say about him; in 101.1 the Lord denies that he suffered the things 'they' mention; and in 101.6-11 there is an elaborate contrast between what 'they' say and the reality according to the AJ. In the second and third of these instances, the wording is independent from the canonical gospels except for the common words 'cross' and 'suffer'. But 'the things they say about me' refers to gospel traditions about which, as we have seen, the author was well informed.

[279] Braun, *Jean le Théologien*, 208, argues for this dependence.

[280] Brown, 'Gospel of Peter', 327. That the *Gospel of Peter* used the Psalm is also held by L. Vaganay, *L'Évangile de Pierre*, Paris 1930, 99-101, 251.

[281] In this case *Oracula Sibyllina* (1.367-368, 8.303) does not constitute a parallel, because it distinguishes between the χολή as food and the ὄξος as drink.

[282] Schneider, *Mystery*, 105, assumes a common Syrian source.

Even if some of the elements against which the AJ polemises derive from oral traditions, my research shows that the author was familiar with the written gospels.

The treatment of the cross in the AJ resembles its 'docetic' description in the *Gospel of Peter*. In both writings the cross shares in the glorification of Christ. Both texts tell how a voice came from the cross (GPe 42; AJ 98.4-6, cf. 99.5; both avoid saying that it is the cross itself that speaks!). Though other early Christian texts also contain a theology of the glorious cross,[283] the writings compared here form a unique twosome because of the textual relations discussed above.

*5.1.5 Conclusion regarding sections B and C*

My designation 'gospel' for this part of the AJ led me to expect more open interaction with earlier gospels than can be found in section B. This section shares some structural characteristics with the Synoptics. Section C more openly uses words from the Synoptics and from another tradition which it shares with the *Gospel of Peter*; however, the structure of C is not determined by these Gospels but by John's alone, as we have seen above. The attitude of the author(s) of the AJ towards the gospels is clearly negative, in section C even more than in B. This attitude explains why no quotations are made and why the wording of the earlier gospels is avoided.

As for the relationship with the *Gospel of Peter*, a firm conclusion cannot be reached. Section C recalls *Peter's Gospel* in three places, section B only once. For the words describing the beating of the Lord, priority should be granted to the AJ; as far as the passage about the drink is concerned, the *Gospel of Peter* seems the more original text. The comparison of GPe 19 with AJ 102 yields more differences than similarities. Perhaps the existence of a common source explains the situation best, if we assume that the AJ moved away from the description of Christ's passion which this source must have presented.

*5.2 Section A*

The Synoptics play only a minor role in section A, although the author at least knew the Gospel of Luke. In a few scattered places, an echo of gospel words may be detected, but these are remarkably seldom in this relatively long text. None of the episodes in the AJ have formal or structural parallels with any passages in the Synoptics.

As far as Lk is concerned, in *Virtutes Johannis* VI John pronounces a long sermon against the rich,[284] which quotes the parable of the rich man

[283] See Vaganay, *Évangile de Pierre*, 299.

[284] On the *Virtutes*, see chapter 1.

and the poor Lazarus (Lk 16:19-31) in full.[285] As the sermon in AJ 34-36 contains a similar motif, one might wonder if AJ 34-36 also makes use of the parable.[286] Several phrases indeed echo Luke's Gospel, and these echoes suggest that the author of the AJ knew the parable, which belongs to Luke's *Sondergut*.[287] We cannot in any way prove that these echoes are the result of deliberate allusions; they may just as well have flown spontaneously from the memory of the author.

The wording and contents of the second half of AJ 77 resemble the parable of the prodigal son (Lk 15:11-32).[288] I quote AJ 77.13-16: 'Who did not send away the one who had spoiled (σκορπίσαντα, cf. διεσκόρπισεν Lk 15:13) his riches, nor turned his face from the repentant one; father who had mercy and compassion (σπλαγχνισθεὶς, cf. ἐσπλαγχνίσθη Lk 15:20) for the man who had not taken care of himself.'[289] It is clear that the parable, another example of Luke's *Sondergut*, made a lasting impression on the person(s) who wrote the AJ.

The most overt reference to authority in the AJ occurs in 22.11-12, where John prays: 'For you said yourself, O Christ, "Ask and it shall be given you".'[290] The wording of this short saying of Christ conforms literally with Mt 7:7 par. Lk 11:9. But such a short saying can have been

[285] There are no *structural* parallels between these texts. Lk 16:19-31 combines several themes: warning against the dangerous side of richness; consolation of those who are poor on earth; warning against the impossibility of conversion after death; refusal of special miracles for the living. The AJ (35.3-5, 8-11; 36.4-10) contains only several warnings for the rich. The situation of the dead is not depicted in 'Lukan' but rather in pagan terms: they will be spirits without a body!

[286] A. Westra, *De gelijkenis van de Rijke Man en de Arme Lazarus (Lk.16, 19-31) bij de vroeg-christelijke Griekse schrijvers tot en met Johannes Chrysostomus*, Dissertation Leiden 1987, does not deal with the AJ and the *Virtutes Johannis*. H. Gressmann pointed to a possible source of this parable, viz. an Egyptian (Demotic) story in 'Vom reichen Mann und armen Lazarus', *Abhandlungen der preussischen Akademie der Wissenschaften Jahrgang 1918, Philosophisch-historische Klasse*, Nr.7, Berlin 1918. In view of Junod and Kaestli's thesis that the AJ originated in Egypt, I made a brief comparison, but I found no relationship between this story and the AJ.

[287] 1. The word 'comfort' in AJ 35.8 (οὐχ ἕξεις τὸν ἐλεοῦντα) and in Lk 16:24 (ἐλέησόν με καὶ πέμψον Λάζαρον). 2. The phrase ἐν πυρὶ φλεγόμενος (35.7-8) resembles ἐν τῇ φλογὶ ταύτῃ (Lk 16:24) as well as τόπον τῆς βασάνου, Lk 16:28. 3. The ὀδυνῶνται (36.13) echoes ὀδυνῶμαι (Lk 16:24) and σύ δὲ ὀδυνᾶσαι (Lk 16:25).

[288] JK, 280 n.4. The text in JK is based on manuscript **O**, which offers a much longer text than **R**, **Z** and **M**. Elliott's *Apocryphal NT* reflects Bonnet's text, which is based on **R** and **M**.

[289] Cf. ἐν εὐφρασίᾳ (77.1) with εὐφραίνεσθαι (Lk 15:23, 24, cf. 29, 32).

[290] αὐτὸς γὰρ εἶπας, Χριστέ· Αἰτεῖτε καὶ δοθήσεται ὑμῖν.

transmitted orally into the second century, so that it does not necessarily provide any evidence of a written gospel's influence on the AJ. The word of Jesus as such is authoritative for the author and is presented to his readers in the conviction that they would share his opinion. The idea of a written authority is completely absent.

One cannot fail to notice the similarity between John's exhortation of the rich (AJ 34.4-5)[291] and Mt 6:19,[292] but the AJ does not quote the Gospel: it leaves out the object 'treasures' and has ἔνθα instead of ὅπου. There is nothing in the AJ that would make a reader who does not know Mt think that the AJ echoes an earlier text. Yet the similarities are not only in the wording, but also in the context and the function of the corresponding phrases. I think that the author uses authoritative words that have came down to him, either in written or in oral form.[293]

*5.3 Conclusion about the other gospels*

The authors of both parts of the AJ are familiar with the Synoptic Gospels, that is, with Lk and one of the other two, but the Gospels are in no way recognised as authoritative. Just as we saw with the Gospel of John, section A hardly pays any attention to these writings, a characteristic that is typical of its genre. Surprisingly, section A nevertheless contains clear reminiscences of specific material from Lk; it is likely that the author used Lk together with Acts, his model.[294] Due to its subject matter, section B, which was composed by the same author as A, could not avoid some echoes of the existing gospels, but the author keeps the interaction to a minimum. Indeed, the intertextual links are such that they do not always allow us to say which of the Synoptics is echoed. Our author seldom shows if he used the exact text of Mt and/or Mk, or drew on oral traditions. The AJ has no value for the textual criticism of the Synoptics.

Section C is more open about both the existence and the supposed deficiencies of the Synoptics than B is. The polemical attacks on them are important to the author of C, who thus displays an attitude which differs from that of the first author. The present conclusion is in harmony with

[291] μηδὲ θησαυρίζειν ἐπὶ τῆς γῆς ἔνθα ἅπαντα μαραίνεται [...] μηδὲ ἡγεῖσθαι παίδων ὑμῖν συγγινομένων αὐτοῖς ἀναπεπαῦσθαι. Manuscript **H** has about 35 illegible letters between the two phrases, while **R** and **Z** do not indicate any lacuna.

[292] Lk 12:33 has different wording.

[293] H. Riesenfeld, 'Vom Schätzesammeln und Sorgen - ein Thema urchristlicher Paränese. Zu Mt VI 19-34', *Neotestamentica et Patristica. FS Cullmann*, Leiden 1962, 47-58, argues that Mt 6:19-34 recurs in many and diverse ways in texts from the first and second centuries.

[294] On the close connection between Lk and Acts see I.H. Marshall, 'Acts and the "former treatise"', in Winter and Clarke, *Book of Acts*, 163-182.

that of chapter 2.

## 6 The Acts of John and other Gnostic literature

The Gnostic part of the AJ, i.e. section C, has many ideas in common with Gnostic writings, but the present chapter is limited to the quest for intertextual connections. Any effort to trace these is beset with the problems of language (Greek - Coptic), chronology and definition.[295] The dates of origin of other Gnostic texts are even more uncertain than the date of the AJ, though nowadays most of them are dated between 150 and 250 AD, which makes them contemporary with and somewhat later than the AJ. The question of the position of the AJ vis-à-vis the Gnostic writings would of course be settled if there was an Archimedean point from which to judge. But despite the numerous correspondences between ideas expressed in the Gnostic part of the AJ and in other Gnostic texts, so far no real lexical or structural parallel that would settle the question has yet been found.[296]

The search for parallels in this paragraph is necessarily limited. It is e.g. noteworthy that the final part of the late *First Book of Jeu* contains a song and dance that closely parallel elements in cc.94-96, but chronological considerations make this text uninteresting.[297] I limit myself to the *Secret Book* or *Apocryphon of John*, the Excerpts from Theodotus, the fragments of Valentinus (which strictly speaking do not fit under the heading 'Gnostic' - see below), the *Letter of Peter to Philip*, and the *Apocalypse of Peter* because these texts are closest to the AJ. On the side of the AJ, the non-Gnostic sections A and B are only involved in the comparison with the

[295] For a definition of 'Gnostic' see pp. 32-34 above.

[296] JK, 594 n.1, cf. 644, 653, 655, show that the order of events in the *First Apocalypse of James* (NHC V.3) resembles that in AJ 87 (or 94)-102. The text consists of two parts in which the Saviour speaks with James; the bridge between both parts reminds us particularly of the AJ: 'The Lord said farewell to him and fulfilled what was fitting. When James heard of his sufferings and was much distressed, they awaited the sign of his coming. And he came after several days. And James was walking upon the mountain, which is called "Gaugelan" ...' (p.30.12-20, trans. W.R. Schoedel, in J.M. Robinson, *The Nag Hammadi Library in English*, Leiden/San Francisco [3]1988, 245). But W.-P. Funk, *NA*[5] I, holds that the text has a tripartite structure.

[297] C. Schmidt and V. MacDermot (eds.), *The Books of Jeu and the Untitled Text in the Bruce Codex*, Leiden 1978, 92-98; also considered late by Rudolph, *Gnosis*, 32. Other examples include influence of the AJ on later Gnostic writings such as the *Gospel of Eve* and *Pistis Sophia*, see Beyschlag, *Überlieferung*, 118-131.

*Apocryphon.*[298]

### *6.1 The Secret Book of John*[299]

The *Apocryphon of John* went through a complicated process of transmission; it was known to Irenaeus in some form.[300] The form of the text which interests us here is that which is enclosed by a narrative frame. This frame, best preserved in the Berlin codex (BG 20.5- 22.16, 76.16-77.5), shows remarkable similarities with parts of the AJ.[301] The following correspondences can be listed:

* flight of John from Jerusalem
* meeting of John and the Revealer on a lonely mountain
* polymorphous appearance of the Lord in which light also plays an important role
* John receives a revelation, followed by a command to hide its contents
* disappearance of the Saviour ends the conversation[302]

It is remarkable that the frame of the *Apocryphon* combines elements found in AJ 90 (polymorphy), 97 and 103 and is thus intertextually related to the

[298] As the AJ contains a kind of gospel, it seemed right to compare it with the *Gospel of Thomas*, but in fact there is no relationship at all between the texts. Indeed, there could hardly be a greater contrast than that between the esoteric-philosophical view of Christ in *Thomas*, in which all stress is on his sayings, and the one-sided attention for his outer appearance in section B of the AJ, which does not contain any sayings.

[299] M. Waldstein and F. Wisse (eds.), *The Apocryphon of John. Synopsis of Nag Hammadi Codices II,1; III,1; and IV,1 with BG 8502,2*, Leiden 1995. On the importance of this text see Luttikhuizen, *Gnostische geschriften* I; *idem*, 'The Jewish Factor in the Development of the Gnostic Myth of Origins: Some Observations', in *Text and Testimony. FS A.F.J. Klijn*, Kampen 1988, 152-161; and *idem*, 'Gnostic Reading', 124-126. For opinions regarding connections with the AJ, see P. Weigandt, *Der Doketismus im Urchristentum und in der theologischen Entwicklung des zweiten Jahrhunderts*, typescript Dissertation Heidelberg 1961, 51-52; Schneider, *Mystery*, 87-88; Schäferdiek, 'Herkunft', 255-256; *idem*, *NA*[5], 138.

[300] The general accuracy of Irenaeus' descriptions of Gnostics was recently confirmed by D. Voorgang, *Die Passion Jesu und Christi in der Gnosis* (Europäische Hochschulschriften XXIII /432), Frankfurt 1991, 251: '... dass das Referat des Irenäus über gnostische Systeme mit den gnostischen Selbstzeugnissen aus Nag Hammadi weitgehend konform geht, also zuverlässig ist.' Logan, *Gnostic Truth*, is largely based on the trustworthiness of Irenaeus.

[301] As I noted on p. 46, Layton, *Gnostic Scriptures*, 24, compares the narrative frame of the *Apocryphon* to the novelistic form of the AAA. This observation makes the *Apocryphon* similar in form to the AJ, which also has other genres ('gospel', song and dance) within a novelistic frame.

[302] Most of these correspondences are signalled in Beyschlag, *Überlieferung*, 134-136. I fail to find an 'Aussendung des Jüngers' as a final element in the AJ. See also Schneider, *Mystery*, 57-60, 87-89.

final version of our text. A notable difference between the two works concerns the appearances of the Lord, which in the AJ take place in contrasting pairs, whereas in the *Apocryphon* he is seen in three forms at a time.

In case there is an intertextual relation here - and this is quite probable - there are several reasons why the AJ must be the architext.[303] First it is less likely that the authors of both parts of the AJ would have known and used the *Apocryphon* than that the compiler of the *Apocryphon* knew the final text of the AJ.[304] Secondly, the threefoldness of the appearances in the *Apocryphon of John* suggests that at least in this form it represents a later development of ideas than the dual appearances of the AJ. From the fact that the body of the *Apocryphon* does not contain the name of John, it is generally gathered that the narrative frame was added by a redactor. It can now be said that this novelistic frame was created under the direct influence of the AJ, whereas there are no indications that the body of the *Apocryphon* was subject to a similar influence.[305]

### *6.2 Valentinus*

It is noteworthy that three of the topics addressed in the fragments that we have of Valentinus also occur in the AJ, and that they occur in the non-Gnostic sections A and B. They are the specifically Christian questions of the eating of the Lord (fr. 3), the physical appearance of Christ (fr. 7), and the Platonic topic of the value of a painting in comparison with the painted reality (fr. 5).[306] The latter topic, however, is too common and its use by the AJ differs too much from Valentinus' to be significant for the present intertextual analysis.[307]

Valentinus says that Jesus ate and drank but had no digestion. Markschies thinks that this viewpoint mediates between the naive docetism of some and a denial of Jesus' divinity: Because he was human he ate and

303 Schäferdiek, 'Herkunft', 255-256, thinks that there was a common tradition motif although he admits that in the AJ the scene is better integrated into its context.

304 Cf. the discussion of the APe, which also relates to the final version of the AJ, in par. 3.2.2 above.

305 I reached a similar conclusion in my 'Polymorphy', 117-118. Schneider, *Mystery*, 124-127, 131-143, does see parallels because he views all of the AJ as Gnostic and discovers the 'Sethian' Gnostic motif of the immovable race in them. For this reason he contradicts Junod and Kaestli's classification of the AJ as 'Valentinian'.

306 Fragments edited, translated and commented upon by Markschies, *Valentinus*, 11-290, esp. 83, 205, resp. 153. English translation in Layton, *Gnostic Scriptures*, 238-239 (Markschies 3 = Layton E), 230-231 (M 7 = L A), resp. 226-227 (M 5 = L D).

307 Markschies, *Valentinus*, 155-156, 168-171, stresses the Platonic background; JK, 448-452, point to parallels with Plotinus.

drank, but because he was also God there was no motion.[308] This view implies that the position of Valentinus differs from that of the AJ. There are no verbal parallels.

On the topic of Christ's physical appearance, Valentinus says that a new-born child appeared to him and, upon his questioning, stated that it was the Logos.[309] This anecdote reminds us of the twelve testimonies in AJ section B, but it has no exact parallel there. Furthermore, a child is a common image for Christ.[310]

I conclude that despite the remarkable thematic similarities, the ideas expressed are less similar. A textual link between Valentinus and the AJ cannot be demonstrated. Yet it is interesting that the author of the first main part of the AJ and the Valentinus of the fragments, who both stand on the brink of the earliest Gnosticism and who probably were instrumental in the origins of this Gnosticism, deal with the same topics.[311]

### *6.3 Theodotus*

Theodotus allegedly was a pupil of Valentinus. What we have of his writings are excerpts preserved by Clement of Alexandria. These excerpts are in small segments which are difficult to use for several reasons. First, they are intertwined with Clement's own words. Second, it is common to follow Hippolytus in distinguishing a Western and an Eastern Valentinian School.[312] It has been found that the major part of the *Excerpta ex Theodoto* (§ 1-42) consists of ideas from the Eastern School. An intermediate section (§ 43-65) has more affinities with the Western School, but

[308] Markschies, *Valentinus*, 105-107, thinks that this opinion was common in the second century.

[309] Fr. 7 ed. Markschies, *Valentinus*, 205: καὶ γὰρ Οὐαλεντῖνος φάσκει ἑαυτὸν ἑωρακέναι παῖδα νήπιον ἀρτιγέννητον· οὗ πυθόμενος ἐπεζήτει τίς ἂν εἴη, ὁ δὲ ἀπεκρίνατο λέγων ἑαυτὸν εἶναι τὸν Λόγον.

[310] Markschies, *Valentinus*, 208-210.

[311] This observation is partly based on Markschies, *Valentinus*, who has shown that the fragments of Valentinus are not Gnostic. This conclusion strongly contradicts the testimonies of the ecclesiastical authors (Irenaeus, Hippolytus) that he was a Gnostic teacher. Rather than doubting the general accuracy of these testimonies, the contradiction can be solved by assuming that Valentinus' thought developed (see also n.300 above and the conclusion to my next chapter). Thus he can really be seen as the *founder* of (Valentinian) Gnosticism. In this hypothesis, the more philosophical form of Gnosticism predates the mythological form.

[312] Hippolytus, *Refutatio* 6.35. The difference turns on the issue of Christ's pneumatic (as the Eastern School claims) or psychic (as the Western School holds) body.

the allegiance of the final part (§ 66-86) is disputed.[313] Thus the proper use of the *Excerpta* for the study of Valentinianism presupposes source-criticism.[314] Thirdly, nothing is known about the life of Theodotus, and there are no other sources for the reconstruction of his thought.

Section C of the AJ shows some clear conceptual resemblances with the *Excerpta*.[315] They include the conception that the Saviour suffers because he temporarily becomes part of the material world (*Excerpta* 30.2-31.1), as well as the equivocation of Christ, Horos and the cross (26.2, 35.1, 42.1). But there are also differences. The most important in my opinion is that Theodotus distinguishes between Jesus and Christ whereas this distinction is not made in the AJ, as the next chapter will make evident. Again, the AJ lacks the concept of pleroma which is typical of Theodotus.

A close relation in wording exists between *Excerpta* 26.3 (ὅταν δὲ καὶ αὐτὸς ['Ιησοῦς] εἰσέρχεται, καὶ τὸ σπέρμα συνεισέρχεται κτλ) and AJ 100.4 (ὅταν δὲ ἀναληφθῇ ἀνθρώπου φύσις καὶ γένος προσχωροῦν ἐπ' ἐμὲ κτλ).[316] The conception reflected in both phrases is the future corporate salvation of the souls by assumption into the world of light. The similarity between the phrases is notable, but not clear enough to enable us to assume an intertextual connection. The same holds for the texts as a whole.

### *6.4 The Letter of Peter to Philip (NHC VIII.2)*[317]

The revelation of the Lord in the *Letter of Peter to Philip* resembles that which occurs in the AJ in several respects:

[313] At least § 60 breaks this neat division, see also Sagnard's note on it. J.-D. Kaestli, 'Valentinisme italien et valentinisme oriental: leurs divergences à propos de la nature du corps de Jésus', in B. Layton (ed.), *The Rediscovery of Gnosticism* I, Leiden 1980, 391-403, reckons *Excerpta* 1-42 and AJ 94-102 among the witnesses to the Eastern School, together with Irenaeus' description of Mark the Magician (*AdvHaer* 1.13-16, 21), parts of the *Gospel of Philip*, and the *Apocalypse of Peter*.

[314] This has been done in the SC edition by Sagnard. See also F.-M.-M. Sagnard, *La gnose valentinienne et le témoignage de Saint Irénée*, Paris 1947, 521-559, and Kaestli, 'Valentinisme'.

[315] Cf. JK, 581-677; Schneider, *Mystery*, 97-98, 103-104. Sections A and B play no role in the comparisons of JK and myself. Reference to Christ as light (*Excerpta* 35.1, 41.2, 44.1) derive from the Fourth Gospel.

[316] JK, 610.

[317] Ed. F. Wisse and M.W. Meyer, in J.H. Sieber (ed.), *Nag Hammadi Codex VIII*, Leiden 1991, 227-251; cf. J.-É. Ménard, *La lettre de Pierre à Philippe*, Laval 1977, and M.W. Meyer, *The Letter of Peter to Philip*, Chico 1981.

1. It takes place on the Mount of Olives (*Letter* 133.15)[318]
2. The Lord is not himself seen
3. Instead a great light appears (134.10-13, 135.4,138.12; cf. φωστήρ 133.27, 139,15, and cf. 134.6), which, in the AJ, is a cross of light
4. Next to the light, the Lord is represented by a voice (134.13, 135.3, 137.18, and again 138.21)
5. It ends with the remark that the Lord is taken up to heaven (138.6-7)

In view of these similarities, which admittedly are not equally weighted, it would seem that these texts are related to each other. This impression finds support in the observation that, the epistolary introduction apart, the genre of the *Letter of Peter to Philip* is almost the same as that of the AAA.[319] Yet the apparent dependence of both texts on themes from the NT (Mt 17:1-9, 2 Pe 1:16-19, Acts 9:1-9, Rev 1:12-16)[320] precludes a definite conclusion. Moreover, the remarkable differences in theology between the texts make an intertextual relationship less likely.[321]

*6.5 The Apocalypse of Peter (NHC VII.3)*[322]

The way in which the *Apocalypse of Peter* denies that Christ died on the cross recalls section C of the AJ. Here the main actor is Peter, who initially sees that the Lord is taken prisoner. The subsequent passage in which Peter receives a revelation must be quoted extensively:

> I said: 'What is it that I see, o Lord? Is it you yourself whom they take and are you grasping me? Or, who is the one who is glad and who is laughing above (?) the wood and do they hit another one on his feet and on his hands?' The Saviour said to me: 'The one you see glad and laughing above the wood, that is the living one, Jesus. But the one into whose hands and feet they are driving the nails is his fleshly part, which is the substitute. They put to shame that which has come into

[318] Other parallels in Meyer, *Letter*, 98-99.

[319] Ménard, *La lettre*, 5-6. Meyer in Sieber, *Codex VIII*, 229, merely notes resemblances to the NT Acts.

[320] Cf. Meyer, *Letter*, 105-108.

[321] 1. Once Jesus is directly called 'God' in the *Letter* (133.8) as is common in the AJ (see next chapter), but a little later there is a clear distinction between God the Father and Christ the Son (133.21-26); the *Letter* also refers to the Holy Spirit as a separate entity; in chapter 4 we will see that the AJ does not do this. 2. The *Letter* deals with many aspects of the Gnostic pleroma, which is nearly wholly absent from the AJ. 3. The *Letter* stresses its continuity with the original Christian message (cf. Meyer in Sieber, *Codex VIII*, 230) whereas the AJ displays an antithetical position.

[322] Ed. and transl. Havelaar, *Apocalypse*; cf. Schneider, *Mystery*, 100-101.

existence after his likeness. But look at him and at me.'[323]
According to Havelaar's analysis, the text distinguishes between the transcendental Christ (intellectual pleroma), the Christ in history who revealed himself through the prophets, the non-corporeal Christ who was temporarily connected with the body, and finally this material body which was created by the archons.[324]

Several elements here recall the AJ; first of all, there is the multiform aspect of the appearance of the Lord, which even includes one form *above* the cross. Christ apparently has these three identities at the same time. His material body is only his temporal abode.[325] This description of the Lord looks like a more sophisticated retelling of the revelation of the Lord in the AJ. More attention is devoted to the being of the Lord than to his outer forms. This type of Christology can be considered as a highly spiritualised polymorphy. The *Apocalypse of Peter* differs significantly from the AJ in that the former suggests that the Lord (temporarily) had a material body.[326]

Other elements that remind us of the AJ are the references to light and to the laughter of the Lord, besides of course the fact that only one apostle receives the revelation. The phenomenon of laughing is meaningful in the AJ but not in the *Apocalypse of Peter*.[327] According to Luttikhuizen, Jesus laughs at the soldiers because they think that they can humiliate the divine redeemer, whereas actually they only crucify the artefact of the archons. The function of the revelation would seem to be the same in both texts: a spiritualising transformation of the traditions about the suffering of the Lord.

It would seem that the crucifixion scene in the *Apocalypse of Peter* is more fragmentary and the Christology of the text more complicated than their counterparts in the AJ. If there is an intertextual relationship between the AJ and the *Apocalypse* - and we cannot prove that there is one! -, then the AJ is the architext, that is paraphrased, largely confirmed, and modified by the *Apocalypse*.

*6.6 Conclusion*

The influence of section C on any other Gnostic writing cannot be demonstrated. The closest parallels are the (heterogeneous) *Excerpta ex*

[323] *ApocPe* 81.7-24, transl. Havelaar, who places a question mark after 'above' (Coptic chijim).
[324] Havelaar, *Apocalypse*, 163; cf. Luttikhuizen, 'Gnostic reading', 141.
[325] Havelaar, *Apocalypse*, 169.
[326] See Havelaar, *Apocalypse*, 160-163, 169.
[327] Havelaar refers to Ps 2:4, but this does not explain its occurrence here.

*Theodoto*. There is evidence that the AJ exercised influence on some texts, notably the frame story of the *Apocryphon of John* and the Christological revelation in the *Apocalypse of Peter*. It is remarkable that the *Apocryphon* reflects the complete form of the AJ, i.e. the form after section C was added to A and B. The tentative conclusion of this survey is that the AJ occupies a position early in the Gnostic movement.[328]

## 7 Other writings

### *7.1 The Old Testament and early Jewish literature*

Our text contains no citations from the Jewish Scriptures. Furthermore, the term 'scripture' or an equivalent does not appear. As Junod and Kaestli stated, for the AJ there is no old dispensation: 'La révélation de Dieu paraît commencer *hic et nunc* avec la venue et la prédication de Jean.'[329] The reference to the Jews in c.94, which I discussed on p. 97 above, is not a reference to the Old Testament, although it is an indirect statement about its origin.

Nevertheless, the initial impression that the AJ is very far from the Old Testament and the Jewish roots of Christianity has to be slightly modified. As for the Old Testament itself, the story about the challenge of Artemis by John (AJ 37-45) has the same theme as the Elijah story about the contest between God and Baal on Mount Carmel in 1 Kings 18.[330] In both cases the main character delivers a speech which challenges the worshippers of a pagan deity.

Elijah is not the only Old Testament character with whom John is equated. The reference to John's view of the back of the Lord (90.8-9) is an allusion to Ex 33:23.[331] This allusion makes John comparable to Moses, who saw the back of God. The fact that both Moses and Elijah appear - albeit anonymous - in the AJ indicates not so much respect for the Old Testament as the author's love of the story of the transfiguration, which he uses in two of the testimonies. On the other hand it implies that the Old Testament stories in question were known to the first author of the AJ, although these stories are not repeated or even alluded to in the

[328] In the next chapter I will come back on the position of the AJ among the Gnostic texts and adduce evidence in support of the present hypothesis.

[329] Junod and Kaestli, 'Théologie', 132, cf. 127.

[330] Cf. Hennecke, *Handbuch*, 506; Findlay, *Byways*, 213; P. Herczeg, 'Sermons in the Book of Acts and the Apocryphal Acts', in Bremmer, *Acts of John*, 153-170, esp. 162.

[331] Cf. I. Karasszon, 'Old Testament quotations in the Acts of Andrew and John', in Bremmer, *Acts of John*, 57-71, esp. 70.

gospels. Evidently, the author did not live outside the sphere of influence of the Old Testament.[332]

In the second place, section C contains several phrases which remind us of Sapientia Solomonis (Sap), a book which does not belong to the Hebrew canon of the Old Testament but is included in the LXX and was well known in the second century. It probably originated in Alexandria in the years just before or after the beginning of the Common Era.[333] The word mirror (ἔσοπτρον) and a light imagery occur together in Sap 7.26 and in AJ 95.43-46, but metaphorical language about seeing and light is very common in Jewish, Christian and other religious texts. Sap 7.24a runs: 'Wisdom is more mobile than all movement',[334] which resembles AJ 96.8-9: 'you have not stood firm but were wholly moved. Moved to become wise, you have me for a support'; however, in the AJ the words are addressed to those watching the dance of the Lord so that a play with words seems unlikely. Both Sap 15.3 and AJ 109.12-13 use the rare combination 'root of immortality' (ῥίζα ἀθανασίας);[335] the fact that both texts often use the word ῥίζα[336] increases the probability that the AJ had some knowledge of the vocabulary of Sap.[337] Because not one

[332] *Pace* Karasszon, 'Quotations', 70, this does not imply continuity of thought. *Pace* J.E. Fossum, *The Image of the Invisible God. Essays on the influence of Jewish Mysticism on Early Christology*, Freiburg CH/Göttingen 1995, 95-108, this does not suggest familiarity with Jewish mysticism. Siegert, 'Analyses rhétoriques', argues that the AJ's style reveals many Semitisms. The reference to the law and the prophets in several manuscripts of c.112 is a later addition. Such additions are more frequent in cc.106-115 than in the rest of the text because these chapters were part of the hagiographical literature of the Middle Ages (JK, 30-31).

[333] *Le Livre de la Sagesse ou la Sagesse de Salomon I*, ed. C. Larcher, Paris 1983, 161; W. Horbury, 'The Christian use and the Jewish origins of the Wisdom of Solomon', in J. Day, R.P. Gordon and H.G.M. Williamson (eds.), *Wisdom in ancient Israel*, Cambridge 1995, 182-196, esp. 185.

[334] Part of Sap 7 is labelled 'nearly Gnostic' by C. Larcher, *Études sur le Livre de la Sagesse*, Paris 1969, 93.

[335] A computer search yielded just two more, but later, occurrences of ῥίζα ἀθανασίας: Gregory of Nyssa, *Homiliae in Canticum canticorum*, 15, and John of Damascus, *Sacra parallela*, quoting Sap.

[336] ῥίζα occurs Sap 3.15; 4.3; 7.20; AJ 84.10, 98.18; 114.9.

[337] Cc.26-29 resemble Sap 14.15, which describes a house cult: 'A father, tormented by too early mourning, having made an image of the child that was taken away so soon, venerated as a god what once was a dead person and instituted rites and ceremonies for his servants.' In the context the practice is vehemently condemned ('Considering idols is the beginning of fornication', 14.12; 'that ungodly custom', 14.16). John's rebuttal of Lycomedes is less sharp (29.18-19). This is a case of parallel motifs; the AJ may depend on early Christian

intertextual relationship is beyond doubt, knowledge of Sap cannot, however, be demonstrated.

Thirdly, the vocabulary of section A displays Old Testament influences, but it it is impossible to say if they were mediated by NT writings. Thus God is addressed with the typically Jewish words 'whom flesh and blood do not know' (79.13-14)[338] and again as 'you who alone can do what is wholly impossible with man' (79.16-17).[339] The metaphor of standing on a rock (στερεὰν πέτραν) in 45.9 also occurs in Ps 40 (LXX 39):3 and Is 50:7[340] where the words are similar but the context different. It is likely that in these cases the text depends on the vocabulary of the early Christian communities.

*7.2 Other books of the New Testament*

Neither the letters of Paul, James, Peter and Jude, nor Hebrews, seems to have had any discernible structural influence on the AJ. It is not easy to say whether the authors of the AJ were ignorant of these writings, disinterested in them, or merely omitted them. What remains are a few lexical reminiscenses of 1 Jn, Rev, Paul and James.

In the AJ John recounts that he sometimes wanted to touch (ψηλαφάω) Christ (93.3) but discovered that the Lord was immaterial. This use of the verb stands in sharp contrast to its use in 1 Jn and in Lk.[341] As noted in the above discussion of Lk, this use of the word can be considered a polemic one, but it is impossible to be certain whether it is an allusion to Lk, 1 Jn or both. 'Light, in whom darkness does not abide' (94.16-17) has generally been recognized as parallel to 1 Jn 1:5, probably reflecting a common background in Johannine Christianity.[342]

and Jewish polemics against dead statues and images, but a relationship with Sap cannot be shown.

[338] Words left out by Elliott. Cf. Mt 16:17 (expressing a different idea), 1 Cor 15:50, Gal 1:16; the phrase is not used by the Apostolic Fathers.

[339] σοὶ δὲ μόνῳ δυνατόν; cf. Gen 18:14, Zach 8:6; Mt 19:26, Mk 10:27, Lk 1:37, 18:27. Literary dependence on a specific text cannot be shown.

[340] Quoted in *Barnabas* 5.14, 6.3.

[341] 1 Jn 1:1: ὃ ἐθεασάμεθα καὶ αἱ χεῖρες ἡμῶν ἐψηλάφησαν περὶ τοῦ λόγου τῆς ζωῆς κτλ. Lk 24:39: ψηλαφήσατέ με καὶ ἴδετε, ὅτι πνεῦμα σάρκα καὶ ὀστέα οὐκ ἔχει καθὼς ἐμὲ θεωρεῖτε ἔχοντα.

[342] AJ 107.15-18 contrasts remarkably with 1 Jn 1:5-2:4 and could have been written with the latter text in mind. The construction (If ... then ...; you have ...) is parallel, though more so in translation than in Greek. There is a similar antithetical parallelism between 103.3-4 and 1 Jn 3:18: the epistle asks for love not with a word or the tongue but in works and truth; the apocryphal Christ ask for worship 'not with our fingers, nor with our mouths, not with the tongue, nor with any part of our body, but with the disposition of our soul.' Both

Rather surprising in a book influenced by the Gospel of John, situated in Asia Minor and with a John as its major character is the absence of relations with Rev. (The phrase AJ 113.20 'you who give the due reward to every deed' is a later interpolation).[343] I also reached the conclusion that AJ and Rev are not related when discussing the possible dependence of the AJ on Rev for its description of John's itinerary in Asia and his stay on Patmos (chapter 1). Both conclusions reinforce each other.

Overt references to Paul or to his letters are absent from the AJ.[344] In section B and C there is not even a trace of anything Pauline, while in section A some acquaintance with 2 Cor[345] (and other letters?[346]) seems

instances appear to be polemics between groups in the Johannine trajectory. See chapter 6.

[343] JK, 312 n. 2, correctly argue that it does not fit into the context and plainly contradicts AJ 81.9-12. The phrase states a general principle, whereas all other phrases in c.113 tell something personal about John. It invites comparison with several biblical passages, not only Mt 16:27 and Rom 2:6 (so JK, 312, and Karasszon, 'Quotations', 67-70) but also Prov 24:12 LXX, Ps 61: 13b LXX, Rev 2:23, and especially with Rev 22:12. The four words μισθός, ἔργον, ἀποδίδωμι and ἑκάστος are common to the AJ and Rev 22:12, though their order differs considerably.

[344] John calls himself apostle to the heathen in 112.1. Paul does the same in Rom 1:5; 11:13; Gal 2:8, but he uses different words in the contexts so that no textual relationship can be shown.

[345] 2 Cor seems to be alluded to thrice. 1) c.33 contains the phrase 'my confidence towards you' (ἡ τοσαύτη μου παρρησία πρὸς ὑμᾶς, 2-3), which resembles Paul's words πολλή μοι παρρησία πρὸς ὑμᾶς (2 Cor 7:4). παρρησία is a common word (seven times in the AJ) but the combination with πρὸς plus a human object is rare. 2) c.57 starts with a word-play on παρακαλέω, which echoes 2 Cor 7:6: ὁ παρακαλῶν τοὺς ταπεινοὺς παρεκάλεσεν ἡμᾶς ὁ θεὸς ... καὶ ἐν τῇ παρακλήσει ᾗ παρεκλήθη ἐφ' ὑμῖν... Word-play is absent from Paul, but he uses the verb παρακαλέω no less than four times within 30 words. The phrase ὁ παρακαλῶν τοὺς ταπεινοὺς is literally the same in Paul and the AJ. I further notice a similar accumulation of παρακαλέω earlier in the same letter (2 Cor 1:3-7). 3) The very rare word κατάλλαγμα (exchange, twice in 56.19-21) reminds of the use of καταλλαγή and cognates in 2 Cor 5:18-20. In view of the rareness of these words (cf. just Rom 5:11, 11:15), their occurrence here confirms the existence of the already postulated relation between 2 Cor and AJ. The conclusion is at hand that the AJ betrays knowledge of 2 Cor. Whereas the echoes in cc.33 and 56 are probably unconscious, c.57 would seem to be a conscious allusion to Paul, but its reason is by no means clear. Within the AJ the allusions do not seem to have a function. It is likely that knowledge of 2 Cor implies familiarity with all Pauline epistles, which circulated as a corpus early on.

[346] AJ 106.8-10 recalls 1 Cor 2:9, a very difficult verse in itself because scholars have not been able to identify the source from which Paul presumably quotes, and also of Isa 6:9-10 (Mt 13:14-15, Acts 28:26-27). It is unlikely that this is a direct citation from the book of Isaiah. Considering the wide circulation of these words which is documented by K. Berger, 'Zur Diskussion über die Herkunft von 1 Kor ii.9', *NTS* 24 (1978) 271-283, I conclude that

to be discernible, which however has no weight. These facts imply that the relation to Paul is neither friendly nor hostile: the AJ just neglects the person of Paul and his letters.[347]

Twice the AJ (the disputed c.57,[348] and 90.22) has the rare word ἀπείραστος; both times it refers to God or Christ. Jas 1:13 is the only other text in which the word refers to the deity. Nevertheless, the occurrence of the word ἀπείραστος both in Jas and the AJ seems to be accidental. An alternative view of the use of ἀπείραστος in AJ 90 focuses less on the word in isolation and more on its root πειραζ-. This explanation holds that the whole phrase μὴ πειράζειν τὸν ἀπείραστον polemises against the Synoptic accounts of the temptation of the Lord in which the root πειραζ- dominates.[349] If true, this is another indication of the author's familiarity with and inner distance from (the traditions behind) the Synoptic Gospels. In that case he bluntly denies the value of the story of the temptation because the Lord as a supernatural being cannot be tempted.

*7.3 Oral traditions*

In looking for parallels with the Synoptics, we found that c.22 and possibly c.34 quote one of Christ's authoritative words, which cannot with certainty be traced back to a gospel text. A similar distinctive piece of instruction features in 81.9-10: 'My son, we have not learnt to recompense evil with evil' (Οὐκ ἐμάθομεν, τέκνον, κακὸν ἀντὶ κακοῦ ἀποδοῦναι). These words also appear several times in the Jewish novel *Joseph and Aseneth* (23.9; 28.5,10,14; 29.3),[350] and in three different epistles that were incorporated in the NT (Rom 12:17, 1 Th 5:15, 1 Pe 3:9). A detailed study has demonstrated that 'The memory of Jesus' *explicit* denunciation of the ἀντὶ principle in Mt 5:38-39a (...) would have offered the incentive and criterion for the early church's frequent use of the Jewish saying ...', which

the intertextual relationships between these words are very complicated and that dependence on an oral tradition is by no means excluded. AJ 113.22-23, 'your stewardship (οἰκονομίαν) with which I was entrusted' (ἣν ἐπιστεύθην ὑπὸ σοῦ) recalls Paul's 'I am entrusted with a stewardship' (οἰκονομίαν πεπίστευμαι, 1 Cor 9:17), but this periphrasis for apostleship may have been part of the oral record. The age-limit of sixty years for the elderly women (30.5) conforms to 1 Tim 5:9, but it is probably a reference to a social convention rather than a direct parallel.

[347] *If* the APl was a model for the AJ, this absence is all the more remarkable, but it rather points the other way round.

[348] See p. 13 above. Text in JK, 373, trans. *ibid.*, 149. The present comparison with c.90 would suggest that cc.56-57 were written under the influence of c.90.

[349] Mk 1:13; Mt 4:1, 3, 7; Lk 4:2, 12, 13. So Hilgenfeld, 'Johannes', 26.

[350] I do not see any resemblances in the settings of the AJ and *Joseph and Aseneth*, *pace* Bolyki, 'Miracle stories', 30.

was 'a common proverb in the environment of the early church which she adapted to her own purposes'.[351] The verb 'to learn' (μανθάνω) often refers to the ecclesiastical tradition.[352] Only here it occurs in the AJ in a more of less related sense. As such, it indicates that the author is seldom dependent on traditions.[353]

The proverb has a positive function here. Its occurrence stands wholly apart from authoritative Scriptures. It differs from the saying in c.22 because it is not connected with Christ. It seems to be merely accidental that both phrases have also been preserved in books of the NT.

A notable characteristic of Jesus as he is represented in the AJ is his polymorphy, which will be discussed more fully in the next chapter. In the present chapter a look at the possible roots of this concept is in order. One such root would seem to be the (tradition behind the) longer ending of Mk. In this text, which probably circulated independently before it was included in Mk,[354] the words ἐν ἑτέρᾳ μορφῇ (16:12) attract our attention. Mk 16:12-13 is generally considered a summary of Lk 24:13-35.[355] The fact that the two followers of Jesus on the road to Emmaus did not recognise the Risen One is stated as 'after this he appeared in another form to two of them, as they were walking into the country.' However, Lk 24 does not deal with the Lord's outer appearance.[356] Although the author of the longer ending probably used the word ἑτέρᾳ with reference to verses 9-11,[357] as it stands it is open to diverse interpretations, including a docetic one.[358]

[351] J. Piper, *'Love your enemies'. Jesus' love command in the synoptic gospels and in the early Christian paraenesis*, Cambridge 1979, 53, 49.

[352] K.H. Rengstorf in *Theologisches Wörterbuch* IV, 414ff. See e.g. 1 Clem 21.8, Ignatius *Rom* 4.3, Ignatius *Magn* 10.1, *Barnabas* 9.9; 21.1, *EpistDiognetus* 4.6.

[353] The other occurrences of the verb are 91.7 (section B) and 97.12 (section C) for the teaching of Jesus to the disciples, and 74.7, 76.2, 80.4 and 86.5, all in the same story 63-86. The saying occurs also in Polycarpus, *Phil* 2.2.

[354] See the commentaries by Cranfield, 472; Pesch, 546; the date of the incorparation of this section into Mk is uncertain. The present discussion does not belong in the treatment of the gospels proper if this piece was not yet part of Mk when it influenced the AJ. It is however largely a compilation from, and thus dependent on, the Synoptics.

[355] But J. Hug, *La finale de l'Évangile de Marc*, Paris 1978, 65-67, argues that the text borrows from the Hellenistic motifs of metamorphoses and divine apparitions.

[356] The fact that Mary of Magdala (Jn 20:14-15) and the fishing disciples (Jn 21:4) fail to recognize Jesus is likewise left unexplained by the Fourth Evangelist.

[357] Hug, *Finale*, 62 with n. 3, lists advocates for this position and also for the alternative view which holds that the word refers to the way Jesus looked during his earthly ministry.

[358] Cf. Hug, *Finale*, 215, 218, and my 'Polymorphy', 115-116.

### 7.4 *The Epistula Apostolorum*

Only one more early Christian text demands our attention. AJ 93.10-13 relates that Christ left no traces when he walked, or rather glided, over the earth.[359] A statement to the contrary is found in *Epistula Apostolorum* 11 (22).[360] The Coptic version of the text raises the question whether Christ's feet touched the earth, the Ethiopic version text whether he left traces. However, it is impossible to prove that both writings are textually related. The context in which the matter occurs in the *Epistula* - an account of the resurrection - is rather different from that in the AJ. Had the *Epistula* been a direct reaction to the AJ,[361] it would surely have chosen another context for its statements, and would have had Christ address John instead of Andrew. A reverse order of influence, viz. that the AJ reacts against the *Epistula*, is also improbable, for in that case the AJ would quite possibly have responded to the belief that only spirits walk without leaving traces.

### 7.5 *Justin*

The list of Christological predicates in c.98 has a parallel in Justin's *Dialogue with Trypho* 61.1, in which the titles of the divine Logos are listed and given the same rhetorical structure as the list in the AJ. This parallel is remarkable because it concerns both the form and the contents of the two passages. It is not possible to make a case for the influence of one of the texts on the other, as a model common to both of them cannot be excluded. I will quote and discuss the contents of both lists in the next chapter, and deal with the implications for the origin of section C in chapter 6.

### 7.6 *Pagan literature*

The AJ never cites or quotes pagan literature.[362] In this respect this

[359] The idea is absent from C.W.M. Verhoeven, *Symboliek van de voet*, Assen 1957, who mentions the importance of footprints as evidence for religious claims and states: all over the world people point to the footprints of deities and heroes who have appeared on earth, 132-136.

[360] L. Bieler, *THEIOS ANER. Das Bild des 'göttlichen Menschen' in Spätantike und Frühchristentum*, Wien I 1935, II 1936, repr. Darmstadt 1967, 95, calls this ability 'a standing attribute of holiness', but there are no other places in which Christ's ability in this respect is discussed.

[361] As Weigandt, *Doketismus*, 120-121 thinks.

[362] Whether there are indeed no quotations from writings now lost will never be demonstrated with certainty. Plümacher, 'Paignion', 99-108, holds that the story cc.48-54 owes a lot to the tale of the beaver which castrates itself. He points out that self-castration also occurs in other second century texts that were influenced by Christian ideas. What he

writing differs remarkably from contemporary Greek literature and resembles the books of the NT. Yet we saw earlier that the AJ does use motifs from the ancient novels. In a small contribution published separately I have argued for an intertextual relation between the AJ and the novel *Callirhoe* by Chariton (dated between 100 BC and 100 AD).[363] A connection between these texts was first suggested by Junod and Kaestli, and I was able to adduce even more evidence for the relationship:[364]

*Callirhoe* 1.4.12 - 5.1 resembles AJ 48.7-8
*Callirhoe* 1.5.4-5 resembles AJ 51.10-11
*Callirhoe* 3.3.4 resembles AJ 43.1-2
*Callirhoe* 3.3.7 resembles AJ 20.14-19

In view of the lexical similarities, I suggest that these four cases constitute allusions of the AJ to *Callirhoe*. The internal evidence and the suggested dates of both writings justify the conclusion that the AJ is the recipient text in this relationship. The way in which the AJ makes use of *Callirhoe* is characteristic of the author's method. There is no reference to the architext, so that only the reader who happens to know it will notice the allusion or echo; those who miss it can still understand the phenotext.[365]

Several proposals concerning echoes of other novels are less convincing,[366] but there is an echo of the *Aitia* by the Hellenistic poet

seems to forget is that Mt twice contains the call rather to mutilate one's body than to sin (5:27-30; 18:8-9). In the present story the self-castration serves the same purpose of avoiding sin. This does not exclude that the actual wording of the story was influenced by tales, but Plümacher's dating of the texts is too confident, so that there is no proof for a discussion on encraticism in Alexandria.

[363] For the date of the novel see also Reardon, *Collected Novels*, 5, 17; Reardon, 'Chariton', in Schmeling, *Novel*, 309-335, esp. 312-317, 325, opting for ± 50 C.E; G.P. Goold in the Loeb edition, Cambridge MA/London 1995, 1-2; and Bremmer, 'The novel'.

[364] JK, 516-520; P.J. Lalleman, 'Classical Echoes (Callimachus, Chariton) in the *Acta Iohannis*?', *ZPE* 116 (1997) 66.

[365] It is more common for an author to mention the character or situation in the architext to whom/which he refers. Others, like Callimachus (on whom see below), composed texts so full of hidden echoes and allusions that their work cannot be understood unless the reader grasps them.

[366] 1. JK only once mention Achilles Tatius, viz. 517 n.1, where they call the similarity of AJ 21.12ff and 48.8-9 with *Leukippe and Clitophon* 7.14.5 'frappante'. (Achilles is now dated shortly after 170 AD, see Bremmer, 'The Novel'.) But the parallel is not convincing: AJ 21.12ff, which seems to draw on *Callirhoe* 3.3.7 (note the repeated σύ) lacks the interrogative form of *Leukippe and Clitophon*, whereas the brief 48.8-9 is not a complaint at all, but an obedient question that the Lord's servant asks.

2. Plümacher, 'Paignion', 75-79, points to resemblances between AJ 60-61 and a scene in Pseudo-Lucian's *The Ass*, but the similarities are less significant than he suggests. The word

Callimachus (3rd cnt. BC): AJ 113 seems to be based on the motif of an illness which three times hindered a planned marriage as it does in Callimachus' work. The fact that this motif occurs in the AJ at least suggests familiarity with pagan literature.

## 8 Summary and conclusions

Section A of the AJ is strongly influenced by the canonical Acts of the Apostles and resembles other Apocryphal Acts. But section B, part of the original AJ, displays hardly any influence from Acts, and section C none at all. Instead, sections B and C are related to the canonical gospels and, in some way, to the *Gospel of Peter*. The influence of the Fourth Gospel on sections B and C is even more important than that of the Synoptics. An ideological comparison between the Johannine literature and the AJ in order to determine some of the developments in the Johannine trajectory, which will be undertaken later in this study, will yield interesting results.

The similarities between the canonical Acts and section A are much greater than was previously thought. Similarities with other Apocryphal Acts are possibly due to the influence of the AJ and, in any case, underline shared generic features. The Gospels of Luke and John, Chariton's novel *Callirhoe*, and the *Aitia* of Callimachus also have left some traces in the text that we are studying.

Although he was influenced by the structure and vocabulary of books belonging to the nascent NT, the author of section A does not recognise them as authoritative. On the other hand, the way in which he treats oral traditions (cc.22, 81) suggests that he respects them as authority. In the relatively short section B the influence of Acts is replaced by the influence of the Gospels, which inform but never dictate the text. The Synoptic Gospels are never quoted explicitly and the number of textual allusions and echoes is small. The new gospel can - and is obviously intended to - be understood without knowledge of the biblical accounts of Jesus.

Section C has more allusions to and echoes of the Gospels (first of all John's, but also the Synoptics and Peter's) than the other parts of the text. This situation reflects the fact that its author consciously creates an alternative gospel. The overt contradiction of the Fourth Gospel evokes the

παίγνιον in AJ 60.3 functions more or less as a designation of genre in the way Plümacher describes, but in *The Ass* 47, 49 it is not a *terminus technicus*. The similarities do suggest a common background. Plümacher, 'Paignion', 97 n.124, also lists other alleged correspondences between the AJ and novels.

3. In chapter 2 I signalled that Apuleius' *Golden Ass* and the AJ have a similar structure.

struggle over the course of the Johannine movement and characterises the tone of the text. The author's polemic presupposes that his addressees have some knowledge of gospel traditions.

These conclusions confirm my earlier hypothesis that *qua* genre the non-Gnostic section B is a gospel-like text, so that from a generic point of view sections B and C belong together. The question if the AJ is polemical, which arose in chapter 2, can now be answered. Section A contains no polemics against other forms of Christianity, but section C interacts polemically with the Gospels, especially with the Fourth. This conclusion implies that the second author has considerably changed the character of the text.

The low number and the relative unimportance of the lexical relations suggest that the AJ is a remarkably autonomous writing. Those who contributed to it knew most of the books that were to be incorporated into the NT, but gave them no more than a marginal role in their own text. They felt no need for Scripture or tradition to underline their message. No doubt this has to do with the fact that they differ from much of the tradition. The first author was not unacquainted with the pagan literature of his days, but wrote for the general public that would not have appreciated references to other texts. In this respect the AJ (along with the other Apocryphal Acts) differs from the works of the Christian Apologists.

I close this chapter with some miscellaneous remarks that have a more general application and which may be developed in future research.

1. In contrast with earlier research, I demonstrated the influence of Acts on section A. The author has direct knowledge of Acts; there is no interaction from other Apocryphal Acts. Now Luke's Acts is often seen as a late addition to the sacred books of the church, although its origin is usually dated well within the first century. Vielhauer states that the first testimony to the existence of Acts is the *Epistula Apostolorum* (first half second century).[367] It has now become clear that the AJ, as well as APe and APl, witness its early circulation and use. Yet the AJ aims neither to replace Acts nor to be a sequel to it, but it is just a book about John.

2. The AJ is influenced by earlier writings and it affected many subsequent texts. Of the writings which certainly influenced the AJ, none is later than about 140 AD. The authors of the APl, the APe, the markedly later *Apocalypse of Peter* and the final form of the *Apocryphon of John* probably were familiar with our text. On the other hand, the AJ reflects a situation in which the Gospels and Acts have such a position in the Chris-

[367] E.g. Vielhauer, *Literatur,* 407. Wehnert, *Wir-Passagen*, 56-57 n.43, thinks that both Papias (dated by him ± 140) and Justin knew Acts.

tian community that these books exercise influence on a writing that has, as we will see below, a totally different theology. This state of affairs suggests that the AJ was written in the middle of the second century. It is not necessary to assume that much time passed between the composition of the first (sections A and B) and the second main part (C).

3. Junod and Kaestli argue that the author of the first main part of the AJ was a recently converted person. They base this conviction on their impression that the author was still largely stamped by his non-Christian background and that he had not completely understood all of the Christian faith.[368] This view must be rejected because the present research has demonstrated that the author is familiar with many Christian writings. Moreover, in the next chapter we will see that his Christology is far from naive. Our author knows enough of the Christian scriptures to select what suits him. The fact that the author's form of Christianity was later marginalised and hardly survived does not mean that it was based on an insufficient knowledge of the Christian faith.

4. Although it is often suggested that in the course of transmission and reading, 'biblical' phrases were added to ancient Christian writings, such additions only occur in cc.57 and 113.[369]

5. The author of section C saw John as the author of the Gospel that bears his name or as the beloved disciple who features in it and who best understood the Lord, or as both.

[368] JK, 686-687. E.g.: '... ce Dieu reste pour lui et son entourage une nouveauté encore mal connue! Il rend compte de sa foi sans s'apercevoir qu'il n'en a pas assimilé tous les éléments et qu'il en parle avec des mots et dans un esprit tout empreints de sa culture nourricière.'

[369] The diverse versions of cc.106-115 contain some more, cf. above n.332.

# CHAPTER 4: CHRISTOLOGY

Christology is the most important issue in the AJ. This is not only the case in the eyes of the modern reader, but also in those of the final author of the text, who added important parts (section C) to the gospel flashback (section B) in the novelistic biography of John. The addition deals virtually exclusively with John's teaching about Christ.

In focusing on the Christology of the AJ I take Christology in its broad sense: I will not merely deal with the person of Christ, but also with the concomitant concept(s) of redemption that appear(s) in the text. Besides, the consideration of Christ's person was and is always connected with the question of his relationship with God. As such, Christology and what later came to be the idea of the Trinity are mutually influential and they helped each other along in the process of theological development that occurred in the early church.[1]

First of all, the Christological thought in the second century will be briefly reviewed, in order to understand the peculiarities of this period and to focus better on the specific contribution of the AJ. When afterwards I turn to the AJ, my treatment is again based on the conviction that it is a composite text: section A and section B will be considered apart from section C. Although one may presume that the text as composed by the final author has a consistent Christology,[2] the question of the unity and diversity of the Christology of the AJ will be explicitly addressed after each of the respective sections have been discussed.

In the early days of Christianity the vocabulary of its worship was more advanced than the language of its treatises. It was in worship that Christ was first unequivocally proclaimed God.[3] We will investigate if this is also true of the AJ. Finally we will evaluate the position of the AJ within its age. It will become evident that our text takes an idiosyncratic position.

[1] In view of the fact that, as we will soon see, there is only one God Christ in the AJ, it would be true to the text's intentions to deal with all the activity of this one divine being. I will nevertheless limit the discussion to Christology and soteriology.

[2] Cf. Luttikhuizen, 'Gnostic reading', 123 n.10.

[3] A. Adam, *Lehrbuch der Dogmengeschichte I. Die Zeit der Alten Kirche*, Gütersloh 1965, 115-120.

## 1 The context

It was the all but universal conviction of second-century Christianity that Jesus Christ was both divine and human.[4] This belief was already expressed in the primitive formula 'Jesus is Lord'. The authors of the increasingly authoritative books of the New Testament were agreed that the Lord had appeared both as man and as God. The most influential formula in this respect is Paul's κατὰ σάρκα ... κατὰ πνεῦμα (Rom 1:3-4), and the church of the subsequent period generally built upon this belief.[5] It was not, however, until the latter part of the fourth century that the continuing controversies resulted in more exact formulations of the mystery of the person of Christ. Prior to that time, we should not expect the exactness of these later formulations and we may not use the later technical vocabulary in dealing with the earlier period.

The second century forms the bridge between the Jewish cradle of the church and the use of Greek-Hellenistic concepts by the Fathers and the Councils.[6] The general conviction was that, in Christ, God had become human and that Christ was somehow both human and divine. The main point at issue was the question how one should conceive that duality.[7] Melito of Sardes in his sermon *Peri Pascha* is fairly representative of the 'proto-orthodox' view in this period:

> In place of the lamb, God came, and in place of the sheep a man, and Christ in the man.
>
> Begotten as Son, carried along as a lamb, slaughtered as a sheep, burried as a man, he rose from the dead as God, being God and man in nature.
>
> The Lord put on man, and suffered for the one who suffered.[8]

The fact that God was incarnated in Christ is likewise beyond doubt for Ignatius, Irenaeus and Tertullian, to name some of the most important thinkers. Ignatius frequently calls the Lord both 'our God' and 'man' (e.g.

[4] Voorgang, *Passion*, has shown that most Gnostics are no exception to this rule.

[5] J.N.D. Kelly, *Early Christian Doctrines*, London ²1960, 138.

[6] J. Liébaert, *Christologie. Von der Apostolischen Zeit bis zum Konzil von Chalkedon (451)*, Freiburg/Basel/Wien 1965, 20.

[7] K.-H. Ohlig, *Fundamentalchristologie: im Spannungsfeld von Christentum und Kultur*, München 1986, 160-161.

[8] 'Αντὶ γὰρ τοῦ ἀμνοῦ θεὸς ἐγένετο καὶ ἀντὶ τοῦ προβάτου ἄνθρωπος, ἐν δὲ τῷ ἀνθρώπῳ Χριστός (5).
'Ως γὰρ υἱὸς τεχθείς, καὶ ὡς ἀμνὸς ἀχθείς,
καὶ ὡς πρόβατον σφαγείς, καὶ ὡς ἄνθρωπος ταφείς,
ἀνέστη ἐκ νεκρῶν ὡς θεός, φύσει θεὸς ὢν καὶ ἄνθρωπος (8).
Κύριος, ἐθδυσάμενος τὸν ἄνθρωπον, καὶ παθὼν διὰ τὸν πάσχοντα ... (100).

τοῦ τελείου ἀνθρώπου γενομένου, *Smyr* 4.2). His words sound modalistic when he states that God suffered (calling himself μιμητὴν τοῦ πάθους τοῦ Θεοῦ μου, *Rom* 6.3). Generally, Ignatius just states the paradox of the divine and the human aspects of Christ without attempting to resolve it.

It is evident that the view of Christian salvation influenced the ways that the person of Christ was conceived. Mere speculation had no place in our period. Thus Clement of Alexandria conceived of Christian salvation primarily as deification. His consequent view of the person of Christ has traits which, at least in our opinion, are docetic. Thus he denies that Christ ate and drank as ordinary people do (*Strom* 3.59; 6.71.2).

Within the main-stream church two concepts developed to explain exactly how the divine aspect had partaken of Jesus. We find the so-called Pneuma-Christology in the Apostolic Fathers Ignatius, Barnabas and Hermas. This view describes the divine aspect of the Lord, especially in his preexistence, in terms of the divine spirit. In the incarnated Christ, both the divine spirit and humanity were present side by side.[9] The clearest statement is 2 Clement 9.5: 'Christ, the Lord who saved us, who earlier was pneuma, became flesh and called us in this way.'[10] Otherwise Van de Kamp warns that Pneuma-Christology was not a coherent concept but consists merely in a series of tentative remarks.[11]

The other conception of the divine aspect of Jesus was the Logos-Christology, which originated at least partly under the influence of Philo. The divine Logos, who in the Old Testament period had manifested himself through prophets and others, had now entered to a much greater degree into one man. The best known champion of this explanation was Justin, who calls the Lord 'the Word of wisdom, who is himself this God, begotten of the Father of all things, and word and wisdom and power and glory of him who begot it.'[12] The Apologists used the Logos-Christology to show the relevance of Christianity in the fields of history, science and philosophy. Later Fathers judged that the concept too easily led to the subordination of Christ.

[9] Kelly, *Doctrines*, 142-145; G.C. van de Kamp, *Pneuma-christologie: een oud antwoord op een actuele vraag?*, Dissertation Amsterdam 1983, 1-63, who denies that Justin and Irenaeus had a Pneuma-Christology, 64-73.

[10] Χριστὸς ὁ κύριος ὁ σώσας ἡμᾶς, ὢν μὲν τὸ πρῶτον πνεῦμα ἐγένετο σάρξ καὶ οὕτως ἡμᾶς ἐκάλεσεν.

[11] Van de Kamp, *Pneuma-christologie*, 62, 92; cf. W.-D. Hauschild, *Lehrbuch der Kirchen- und Dogmengeschichte I: Alte Kirche und Mittelalter*, München/Gütersloh 1995, 8.

[12] *Dial* 61.3: ὁ Λόγος τῆς σοφίας, αὐτὸς ὢν οὗτος ὁ θεὸς ἀπὸ τοῦ πατρὸς τῶν ὅλων γεννηθεὶς καὶ λόγος καὶ σοφία καὶ δύναμις καὶ δόξα τοῦ γεννήσαντος ὑπάρχων.

Irenaeus, too, thought that the Logos, truly God (*Epideixis* 47), had assumed real flesh, exactly similar to the flesh that had to be saved.[13] According to him, we would not have been saved if Christ were not truly God and truly man (*AdvHaer* 4.6.7).[14] But he usually preferred the predicate 'Son' for Christ, and in his brief systematic treatise *Epideixis* uses mainly words from the Old Testament to describe Christ. This approach characterises his salvation-historical conception.

It was Tertullian who began, early in the third century, to use helpful concepts like *substantia* and *persona*.[15] See e.g. his *AdvPrax* 27 (about 213 AD):

> We see plainly the twofold state, which is not confounded but conjoined in one person, Jesus, God and man ... and the property of each nature is wholly preserved.[16]

Having looked at the proto-orthodox conceptions, it is also instructive to pay attention to some divergences from the main-line point of view. As was to be expected, these include on the one hand a limitation or denial of the divinity, and on the other hand a limitation or denial of the humanity of Christ. In part they originated out of the inability of the church to find a formula to resolve the paradox of the divine and the human in Christ.[17]

In Jewish Christian circles, an angel-Christology was found: the Messiah was regarded as the most important angel. Traces of it occur in Hermas.[18] The denial of the divine aspect of the Lord and the assertion that he had been a mere man (ψιλὸς ἄνθρωπος) are characteristic of the Ebionites, a Jewish-Christian group mainly known to us through those writers like Irenaeus and Tertullian who combatted it.[19] The Ebionites were motivated by the drive to protect biblical monotheism against the threat of ditheism. In a Semitic context, the idea developed that Jesus had been born as a man but had been been overshadowed by the power of God at his baptism, hence its name Dynamism.[20] In a Hellenistic context, on the other hand, the concern with monotheism often assumed the form of Adoptianism, which is the belief that God granted the exceptional man

[13] Kelly, *Doctrines*, 145-148.

[14] See further Weigandt, *Doketismus*, 126; Adam, *Dogmengeschichte*, 159-162.

[15] See the survey in E. Evans, *Tertullian's Treatise Against Praxeas*, London 1948, 38-75.

[16] *Videmus duplicem statum, non confusum sed coniunctum in una persona, Deum et hominem Iesum ... et adeo salua est utriusque proprietas substantiae.*

[17] Ohlig, *Fundamentalchristologie*, 162, 179.

[18] Kelly, *Doctrines*, 94-95; Hauschild, *Dogmengeschichte*, 8.

[19] Kelly, *Doctrines*, 139-140.

[20] Ohlig, *Fundamentalchristologie*, 169-170.

Jesus a unique, that is, a divine, position either at his baptism[21] or after his resurrection.[22] Equally motivated by monotheism, but more oriented towards the relationship between God and Christ than concerned with the person of Christ, was Modalism or Monarchianism,[23] the belief that in Christ none other than God himself had appeared. Later generations judged that this view leaves no room for the separate divine identity of Christ.[24]

The opposite position, characterised by a limited view of Christ's humanity, was labeled docetism. I will come back to docetism towards the end of the chapter. Suffice it here to say that there probably never was a specific group that bore the name Docetists, but that docetic tendencies can be found in several systems, including those of Marcion and of the Gnostics.[25] Often the human body of the Lord was regarded as a mere cover for the earthly activity of the Logos. Many Gnostics tended to separate two persons, the human Jesus and the divine Christ. This distinction has its 'Sitz im Leben' in theorising about the passion of the Lord. In order to attain a satisfactory explanation of the crucifixion, some Gnostic thinkers introduce the idea that the crucified figure was somebody else (Simon of Cyrene),[26] whereas others distinguish separate aspects of the person of Christ, the crucified one being called 'Jesus' and the impassible Lord 'Christ', 'Saviour' or 'Lord'.[27] This terminology generally indicates that an essential distinction is made between a suffering and a not suffering component within the divine envoy.

After this survey, what can we expect of the Christology of the AJ? First of all, no developed formulas unless the text is, after all, later than commonly assumed. In the earlier chapters it became evident that our text has nothing Jewish about it and is not bound by the authority of sacred texts. More positively, I called its theological tendency spiritualising and referred to the absence of reflection on incarnation.[28] What will a spiritualising Christology look like?

[21] Liébaert, *Christologie*, 20. So also Theodotus of Byzantium, cf. Kelly, *Doctrines*, 116.

[22] This conception was later current in Antiochene theology, cf. Ohlig, *Fundamentalchristologie*, 198-199.

[23] Cf. Hauschild, *Dogmengeschichte*, 13; Ohlig, *Fundamentalchristologie*, 170.

[24] On Monarchianism see Evans, *Against Praxeas*, 10-12; Th.L. Verhoeven, *Studiën over Tertullianus' Adversus Praxean*, Amsterdam 1948, 30-55; Kelly, *Doctrines*, 119-121.

[25] Kelly, *Doctrines*, 141-142.

[26] Basilides according to Irenaeus, *AdvHaer* 1.24.4; *Second Treatise of the Great Seth* (NHC VII.2) 56.11, cf. 55.30- 56.19.

[27] Voorgang, *Passion, passim.*

[28] Above pp. 35-38.

## 2 Section A

### *2.1 General observations*

The Christology of section A is characterised by its focus on the present. Except for things which Christ did for the characters in the narrative, we never hear anything about his deeds in the past.[29] One might object that a phrase like 'the mystery of the dispensation that has come to men, and why the Lord has so acted' (106.12-13) deals with past acts, but these words refer to events within the text, viz. the appearances told in the preceding section B. Likewise, John's prayer in c.77 seems to deal with the life and death of Christ for humanity: 'Oh, what greatness descended to servitude! O unspeakable freedom, which was enslaved by us! O inconceivable glory, which has come upon us! You have kept the grave from shame, and redeemed that man who contaminated himself with blood (etc.).' But Junod and Kaestli correctly state that the words only refer to the appearance of Christ in the form of a beautiful youth for the salvation of Drusiana.[30] The closest that we come to the idea of salvation history is in John's final prayer (c.112), especially when it is said that God (!) sent the apostles into the world and that he manifested himself through his apostles (lines 1-3). But even then the activity of God/Christ is seen only from the perspective of John.

If references to the life and mission of Christ in the past are absent, what does section A tell us about Christ? It first of all presents us with numerous timeless predicates such as 'caring and good' (33.8-9) and 'benign and not haughty, merciful and kind' (108.5-6). Christ is 'he whom every ruler fears, and every creature, power, abyss' (etc., 23.2-3), but the meaning of this and similar phrases never surpasses the horizon of the text. In the context of the destruction of the Artemision, the phrase 'my Jesus, the only God of truth'[31] is apparently synonymous with 'the only powerful God' and suggests that the author (unconsciously?) balances verity with effectiveness.

In the second place, section A highlights the help that Christ gives to John and the other characters. In particular, he heals the sick and raises the dead. He is an ever present helper 'who always consoles the downtrodden' (57.2, 58.10). Prayers such as those by Drusiana (c.82) and John (85, 113) are one long praise for what Christ had done *for them*.

I have mentioned above the fact that liturgical language is often

[29] In other words, the salvation historical meaning of Christ is absent from the AJ and its form of Christianity lacks the Christ-event. Cf. Sirker-Wicklaus, *Untersuchungen*, 118.

[30] JK, 278 n.1.

[31] Ἰησοῦ μου, ὁ τῆς ἀληθείας μόνος θεός (43.2-3, cf. 82.3).

different from the language used in other texts. The limited length and mixed composition of cc.106-115 enable us to look closely at differences in language of prayer and narrative in the AJ. The conclusion of this investigation is that no important distinction between these two types of discourse is visible, so that the general assumption about the Christian vocabulary is at least not true for the AJ. In the narrative, we only find the simple references κύριος and θεός. These also occur in the prayers and addresses, but in the prayers we also find 'Ιησοῦ (108.2), θεὲ 'Ιησοῦ Χριστὲ κύριε (108.8-9, cf. 112.14) and ὁ τῶν ὑπερουρανίων πατὴρ (112.15). The addresses give a similar picture with ὁ ἀγαθὸς ὑμῶν θεός (107.1) and θεὸς 'Ιησοῦς Χριστός (107.5). I conclude that the Christological vocabulary of the prayers, and to a certain extent that of all direct speech in the AJ, is more varied than that of the narratives, but that there is no significant difference from a theological point of view. I also suggest that the prayers of the AJ were not derived from actual worship, but originated with the author himself. After this general survey we will now deal in more detail with the most important items.

### *2.2 Titles*

The Christological titles are unevenly distributed throughout the AJ because the original author uses far fewer of them than the second author. Of the most important New Testament titles, section A contains only God, Christ and Lord. The three New Testament titles which Cullmann links with Christ's work on earth (prophet, servant and priest)[32] are conspicuously absent, as are Word and Son of God.[33] To this it must be added that Christ is used as a name, not as a title. The single name Jesus is not particularly frequent with eleven occurrences in section A alone; in combination with Christ it occurs slightly more often. In this respect the text is not noticeably different from other second-century texts.

Section A is characterised by long prayers[34] and the final story

[32] From the chapter-titles in O. Cullmann, *Die Christologie des Neuen Testaments*, Tübingen, [3]1963, a suitable list of NT titles can be drawn up:
Jesus' work on earth: prophet, suffering servant, high priest
Jesus' future work: Christ (Messiah), Son of man
Jesus' present work: Lord (Kyrios), Saviour
Jesus' preexistence: Word (Logos), Son of God, God.

[33] Other words and wordgroups which do not occur: ἀμνός, ἱερεύς (with reference to pagan priests 42.5; 46.3), λυτρόν, μονογενής, προφήτης (only as clearly secondary *v.l.* in 112.2-3), ὑπὲρ ὑμῶν/ πολλῶν, ὑψόω.

[34] 21.19-24; 22; 24.8-13; 41; 43.2-4; 51.6-12; 57.1-5; 75.3-8; 77; 79.8-20; 82 (the only one not said by John, but by Drusiana, a woman!); 85.

(cc.106-115) even consists in more than half of prayers.[35] In these prayers Christ is confessed as a medical doctor (22.5-6), master of all (22.8), king (22.12), God of truth (82.3), and a being with a πολυμόρφος ὄψις (85.6). In c.77 John praises Christ for what he is and it is interesting to see which words he uses. Only here and in 22.12 is the title 'king' used for Christ. The opening appellation is 'Lord Jesus Christ'; midway ὁ πατὴρ ὁ ἐλεήσας καὶ σπλαγχνισθεὶς occurs and towards the end ἅγιε 'Ιησοῦ, ὅτι σὺ μόνος θεὸς καὶ οὐχ ἕτερος. To him are ascribed εὐσπλαγχνία and μακροθυμία (line 4).

*2.3 Healing and saving*

The AJ portrays Christ primarily as healer and saviour. The meaning of the first of these predicates is not hard to grasp. Most of the stories of which this part of the AJ consists deal with some form of healing, especially when we take into account that the boundaries between sickness/healing and death/resurrection are vague (see below). In prayer John claims that Christ performs every acts of healing of which he is asked (51.9-10). Christ is a healer who heals without costs - mind the polemical tone directed against Asclepius - but who in exchange wants to receive the soul of those whom he cured (56.18-22, cf. 108.5). Miracles count as a very effective missionary tool of early Christianity, and the AJ fully underlines this point.[36]

But what does the text mean when it describes Christ as saviour?[37] The dead Cleopatra cries to Christ: 'I rise, master, save your Cleopatra',[38] but what that salvation means is not explicated in the context. Equally general is the use of σῴζω in 112.3-4. Remarkably, σῴζω in 22.18 is an act of John. The related word σωτηρία is sometimes synonymous with revivication (74.18; 77.2; 79.17) and in the other cases it has a rather general meaning (20.13; 53.2; 102.6). When on the brink of death John asks Jesus for σωτηρία (113.23-25), it is 'rest in him' that is requested.[39] I conclude that the σω-wordgroup is not uniquely connected with Christ and that it tells us little about the actual ideas concerning his work. Consequently, we must look beyond the mere words.

[35] ± 65 out of 124 lines; a further 35 lines constitute a farewell address, leaving 24 lines to narrate the action: prayers: c.108, 112-114; address: c.106-107; action: c.110-111, 115.

[36] Gallagher, 'Conversion', and the literature quoted there.

[37] The title σωτήρ occurs once - in a very general sense - in 108.7; the related σῴζω appears six times, two of which (23.8 and 67.3) are very general.

[38] 'Ανίσταμαι, δέσποτα· σῷζε τὴν σὴν Κλεοπάτραν (23.9).

[39] The fact that John still has to make a petition for it would not fit with the Gnostic certainty of salvation.

A good example in this respect is the story of Drusiana. After her death in despair Christ intervenes on her behalf in the form of a beautiful youth so that she is saved from a necrophiliac and can even be restored to life (70-80). The tale suggests that in the AJ salvation refers to the acts of Christ narrated in the text, the healing and resurrection of individuals. The other stories confirm this impression. Because stress falls on the spiritual effects of the healings, we may say that the salvation promised in the AJ is eminently spiritual.[40]

In so far as John partakes in the divine activities that make people well, he is also a saviour. This notion fits well with the fact that Asclepius was also called σωτήρ.

*2.4 Solidarity*

The Christ of the AJ is not immune to the influence of mankind. Somehow the actions and the fate of humanity are related to his fate. Cc.106-107 state clearly that Christ is with the believers wherever they are. The text stresses Christ's involvement in the world (106.15-17) and describes a kind of correlation: 'Let him rejoice along with us, because we behave well; let him be glad because we live in purity. Let him be refreshed because our behaviour is sober. Let him be unconcerned because we are temperate, let him be pleased because we live in fellowship' (etc., 107.5-10). The implication of this is that mankind can influence Christ either to the positive or to the negative.[41]

The ideas expressed here are uncommon in ancient Christianity.[42] They resemble some notions about the God of Israel mentioned in various places of the OT[43] and they have parallels in rabbinic traditions,[44] but

[40] Cf. Junod and Kaestli, 'Théologie', 137.

[41] But the Lord's dependence does not allow us to translate 85.9 (εὐχαριστοῦμέν σοι τῷ χρῄσαντι [φύσιν] φύσεως σῳζομένης) as 'We thank you that you needed a saved human nature', taking χρῄζω to mean 'need' (Schimmelpfeng, JK, Elliott, Klijn). Such a translation would be inconsistent with the rest of the text's Christology, which is dominated by notions of glory and strength. Therefore, the correct translation is 'We thank you that you desired a saving nature'. JK's reference (291 n.1) to APlTh 17 for confirmation is unwarranted: θεὸς ἀπροσδεής, χρῄζων τῆς τῶν ἀνθρώπων σωτηρίας supports the second sense. Papyrus Kellis 1 reads χωρίσαντι in stead of χρῄσαντι; the translation of the text reconstructed by Jenkins, 'Papyrus Kellis', 210, is: 'We give thanks to you, who have separated the nature which is perishing from the nature which is being saved.' This sounds more Manichaean than the original AJ.

[42] But see my discussion of section B, c.103 below.

[43] E.g. Isaiah 63:9a, where the qᵉre לו is considered the best reading by M.A. Beek, 'Das Mitleiden Gottes. Eine masoretische Interpretation von Jes. 63.9', in Beek, A.A. Kampman *et al.* (eds.), *Symbolae biblicae et mesopotamicae Francisco M.T. de Liagre Böhl dedicatae*,

differ greatly from Greek religion, since Greek gods never suffer. In the books of the NT the believers are said to follow and imitate Christ and indeed to share in his suffering (Col 1:24), but we never read that after his resurrection and ascension Christ *in the present* shares our sufferings. In the NT the suffering of Christ is nearly synonymous with his death on the cross, although he is always compassionate (Heb 2:18; 4:15). The solidarity of Christ with the believers as the AJ conceives it has just one parallel in early Christianity, viz. in the *Acts of the Christian martyrs of Lyons*, which states how 'Christ suffering in him [one of these martyrs] achieved great glory.'[45]

*2.5 Death and resurrection*

In section A words which refer to death are used exclusively with human beings as subjects;[46] the death of Christ is not mentioned in the text. Likewise, ἀνίστημι occurs no less than 35 times in section A[47] but never in the other parts of the AJ and *always* with reference to human beings. In exactly the same vein, ἐγείρω occurs only in section A and only with reference to human beings.[48] Thus the idea of resurrection is connected

Leiden 1973, 23-30, and by I. Fischer, *Wo ist Jahwe? Das Volksklagelied Jes 63,6 - 64,11 ...* , Stuttgart 1989, esp. 6-11, 131-141; cf. RSV 'In all their affliction he was afflicted'. LXX, on the other hand, follows the k<sup>e</sup>tib לא; this reading does not mention the suffering of God and is preferred by the majority of scholars, e.g. R.N. Whybray, *Isaiah 40-66* (NCB) ad loc. Modern translations are divided.

[44] Beek, *ibid.*

[45] ἐν ᾧ πάσχων Χριστὸς μεγάλας ἐπετέλει δόξας; H. Musurillo, *The Acts of the Christian martyrs*, Oxford 1972, 68-69; and A.A.R. Bastiaensen *et al.* (eds.), *Atti e passioni dei martiri*, n.p. 1987, 70 (= Eusebius *HE* V.1.23). But note that J. den Boeft, 'Δόξα in the Letter of the churches of Vienne and Lyons', in E.A. Livingstone (ed.), *Studia Patristica* XVIII.3, Kalamazoo/Leuven 1989, 111-118, stresses Christ's glory rather than his solidarity. The idea is absent from T. Baumeister, *Genese und Entfaltung der altkirchlichen Theologie des Martyriums*, Bern 1991, in which the index *s.v.* 'Jesus Christus im Martyrium gegenwärtig' only refers to passages that mention the presence of Christ, in contrast to a real correlation between the Lord and the believer.

[46] ἀποθνῄσκω (nine times); θνῄσκω (thirteen times); ἀποκτείνω (twice); νεκρός (twenty times; add *bis* to 29.19 in index JK); νεκρόω (twice); τελευτάω (twice); θανατόω (twice); θάνατος (eight times).

[47] Of the total of 43 occurrences, the meaning about 35 times is 'cease to be death', and about 8 times 'stand up' or something similar. The verb ἀνιστάω is used twice, once with reference to death. ἀνάστασις occurs four times.

[48] ζάω occurs in the exclamation ζῇ κύριος 'Ιησοῦς Χριστός (28.5-6) when John is surprised, and the appellation ἄνθρωπε τοῦ θεοῦ τοῦ ζῶντος concerns John (52.7-8). These phrases certainly do not link the resurrection-stories with Christ. The situation with

with humans but not with Christ, so that strictly speaking it is not part of the text's Christology. The resurrections are variously said to be performed by John, the Lord and God; these attributions are interchangeable. Here we have a confirmation of my above remarks about the absence of references to the life and death of Jesus.

The text's view of resurrection and indeed much more of its ideology are well encapsulated in John's words in 46.21-23: 'Our Lord is Jesus Christ, who will prove his power on the body of your relative by raising him.' This use of the concept of resurrection resembles that described by Tertullian:

> They [our adversaries] say that that which is commonly supposed to be death is not really so, - namely, the separation of body and soul: it is rather the ignorance of God, by reason of which man is dead to God, and is not less buried in error than he would be in the grave. Wherefore that also must be held to be the resurrection, when a man is reanimated by access to the truth, and having dispersed the death of ignorance, and being endowed with new life by God, has burst forth from the sepulchre of the old man, even as the Lord likened the scribes and Pharisees to 'whited sepulchres'. Whence it follows that they who have by faith attained to the resurrection, are with the Lord after they have put Him on in their baptism.[49]

The fact that in ancient times sickness and death were closer to each other than in our times is reflected in texts and religions. Hellenistic novels frequently play on the confusion that arises from apparent death.[50] Thus, in *Daphnis and Chloe* the fainted Daphnis is, 'with difficulty, brought back to life'.[51] The AJ resembles the attitude of the novels in that it hardly distinguishes between illness/healing and death/resurrection. In the resurrections which are John's primary miracles and which result in many conversions,[52] it is often unclear whether those helped were only ill, apparently dead or really deceased.

To give an example, resurrection is the key word in the first preserved story (cc.18-25). The simple idea of the illness of Cleopatra leads to the

ζωή, which only occurs in 47.11, is not much different.

[49] *De carnis resurrectione* 19, trans. P. Holmes, *Ante-Nicene Fathers* 15; also quoted by Sturhahn, *Christologie*, 48-49, and by Schneider, *Mystery*, 27; *idem*, 'Gnostic Transformation', 255 n.11.

[50] See Wesseling, *Leven, liefde en dood*, 73-119.

[51] μόλις δὲ ἔμβιος ... γενόμενος (2.30.1), trans. C. Gill, in Reardon, *Collected Novels*. See Wesseling, *Leven, liefde en dood*, 77.

[52] Gallagher, 'Conversion', 16-21; Schneider, *Mystery*, 24-26.

death or apparent death of both Cleopatra and Lycomedes, so that two resurrections can take place. These are followed by salvation because John stays with the couple in order to instruct them, that is, to strengthen their faith (c.25, cf. 44-45, 87).

The salvation of Callimachus is realised when, at the moment he is ready for it (76.35-36), a voice tells him that he must die in order to live (76.37). After having died and being resurrected the only thing he needs is teaching (76.39-40). The author designates this process as his σωτηρία (77.2). In 53.2 ἀνάστασις and σωτηρία are also closely connected and in 52 the resurrection is preparatory for the correct insight; cf. 47.10-14. The order of events is the same every time: after the body, the soul is saved.

I conclude that the first main part of the AJ is silent about the suffering, death and resurrection of Jesus, while at the same time paying much attention to human resurrection from death. Corporeal resurrection has no meaning of its own apart from its spiritual significance.[53] This is certainly a remarkable fact. The theme of resurrection, originally linked with Jesus, has come to lead its own life.[54]

The present conception can at least partly be explained as the result of a spiritualising reading of the Gospel of John.[55] In a way, this Gospel interprets the crucifixion of Jesus as a glorification and an elevation rather than as a humiliation (3:14, 8:28, 12:32, 34). This impression is increased by the notable absence of the Getsemane episode and of Jesus' cry in despair from the cross, as well as by the active role of Jesus himself in his arrest and trial. The concepts of life and death in the AJ and in the Gospel (3:3, 5:24) - as well as in 1 Jn (3:14) - resemble each other in that conversion is described in terms of resurrection. The Gospel expresses absolute certainty that one who has thus begun a new life will never die (Jn 6:48-51, 8:51, 10:27-28, 11:25-26).[56] Jesus claims that all who believe in him have already passed over from death into life. The connection of conversion, new birth and resurrection, first made in the Gospel of John, has become central in the AJ at the expense of other aspects of the Gospel's message.[57] In the AJ four of the eight miracle stories describe

[53] Sturhahn, *Christologie*, 47.

[54] In chapter 3 we saw that the story of the healing miracle in Acts 3 influenced the AJ; it is noteworthy that in the new text it has become a story about a resurrection (AJ 22).

[55] In chapter 3 I found no *literary* relationship between AJ 24 and 76 and Jn, *pace* Pervo, 'Trajectories'.

[56] Pétrement, *Dieu séparé*, 308.

[57] Pervo, 'Trajectories', correctly describes the *Tendenz* of the AJ to spiritualise the miracle and resurrection stories of Jn. I do not share his view of Jn, however, which resembles that of A. Loisy, *Le quatrième évangile*, Paris ²1921, esp. 347, 355, 505, 510.

resurrections; physical resurrection is just a first step (c.47) after which a spiritual life should follow.[58]

*2.6 The human response*

We just saw that the AJ tends towards an identification of salvation and resurrection.[59] In the process of salvation, resurrection is the divine side; on the human side conversion is its counterpart. Both the divine and the human aspects are necessary for the realisation of salvation. If conversion does not follow, all is lost. That is why Callimachus is saved but Fortunatus not. Cleopatra emphasizes her conversion when, at the moment of its completion, she says 'I rise, master; save your Cleopatra' (23.9, cf. 52.5).

Conversion means that one comes to trust Christ completely (36.10). The believers in the AJ have great faith and trust in Christ (30.12-13). In this sense salvation is clearly Christocentric.[60] But in accord with the text's synergetic conception of salvation, Christ plays no role in the preservation of the faith; the responsibility for that rests wholly on the believers themselves (67-69).[61] A major quality of the new life of the believers is the stability of their souls, a point eminently illustrated by Cleopatra.[62]

*2.7 Polymorphy: the beautiful lad*

When in 82.6 Christ is praised because he is polymorphous, the AJ confronts us with a word that is rather unusual in Christology and that is used here without any direct explanation of its meaning.[63] In the AJ not only Christ but also satan is called polymorphous (70).[64] These references to polymorphy function as a key to the episode in which they appear as well as to prepare for what is to follow in cc.87-93, where the author will develop its meaning.

The long story about Drusiana in which we find Christ and satan called polymorphous, narrates appearances of a beautiful young man (εὔμορφος νεανίσκος, 73.3 and 76.17), who is also called 'the beautiful

[58] Bolyki, 'Miracle stories', 32.

[59] Cf. Schneider, 'Gnostic Transformation', 242-243.

[60] Salvation is not connected with confession of sins or with an initiatory rite.

[61] The Lutheran Sirker-Wicklaus, *Untersuchungen*, 116, even states that the AJ brings the believer 'under the law'.

[62] This is brought out by Schneider, 'Gnostic Transformation', 243-245.

[63] For details, I once more refer to my 'Polymorphy'.

[64] The polymorphy of satan is a strong argument against those who, like Garcia, *Polymorphie*, want to make too much of Christ's polymorphy.

one' (ὁ καλός, 73.4,8; 74.11). We need to study this episode in more detail, especially since opinions are divided over whether behind this title, which is unique to the AJ, we have to see Christ or an angel.[65]

The word νεανίσκος is common in the AJ with reference both to Christ and to humans.[66] When we look at the use of καλός in our text, we see that John describes Christ in testimony nr. 1 (c.88.16-17) as ἑστῶτα ἄνδρα εὔμορφον καλὸν ἱλαροπρόσωπον. This identification suggests that the word will denote Christ also in cc.73 and 76. But in the present episode (76.31) Callimachus uses καλός with reference to John: '... in order to become beautiful like you, because otherwise it would be impossible to belong to God.'[67] This variety of usage means that the nouns do not help us much further.

There is a better key to the answer. When John sees the beautiful person, it is said that he hears a voice (ἀκούει φωνῆς λεγούσης αὐτῷ, 73.5) which answers a question that he poses. This circumscription of the speaker also occurs in 18.7 and 21.15, where it implies that Christ speaks to John. Thus the text itself suggests that the εὔμορφος νεανίσκος is Christ. This conclusion is confirmed by the parallels in section C of our text[68] as well as in the other AAA, in which a beautiful young man who appears for a while is always Christ in metamorphosis.[69]

But if it is Christ who appears in metamorphosis to John and his company, what are we to make of the fact that Callimachus claims that he saw an angel (76.16-22)? Rather than posing a problem, this apparent

[65] Christ: Peterson, 'Hamburger Papyrusfragment', 191-192; JK, 266-268 n.73.2, 274 n.1; Weigandt, *Doketismus*, 44. Angel: Hennecke, *Handbuch*, 516; Schneider, *Mystery*, 19, 40-42 with 42 n.1. The idea of Schimmelpfeng, 'Johannesakten', 516, that καλός should here be taken in an ethical sense does no justice to the parallel with εὔμορφος.

[66] Used of Christ: 87.3, 89.3; of anonymous human beings: 19.17, 56.6 and 86.7 in plural form and ten times in cc.47-53 in singular; of Callimachus in the present context: 71.3, 73.10, 75.6,8, 79.18.

[67] γενέσθαι με καλὸν [μὲν] ὡς σύ, ἐπεὶ δέ ἐστιν ἀδύνατον θεοῦ με εἶναι. JK tentatively suggest that we read καλοῦ instead of καλὸν, parallel to θεοῦ με εἶναι. In that case the word would refer to the beautiful youth ('... in order to belong to the beautiful one'). This conjecture is not impossible (the text is only preserved in one manuscript, viz. **O**; **R** and **Z** leave out several phrases), but even so the text does not clearly say who is meant by 'the beautiful one', Christ or an angel.

[68] See 98.4-6 ('... the Lord himself I beheld above the cross, not having a shape, but only a voice') and the use of φωνή in the Lord's self-description in 99.5 and 100.5. This parallel suggests that the author of cc.94-102, in as much as he was among the first readers of the AJ, uses 'the mere voice' to describe an appearance of Christ.

[69] APe 5, APl 7 [PH 3], AAnGr 32, ATh 27, 154-155, see also chapter 3 section 3, and Peterson, 'Hamburger Papyrusfragment', 191-192.

anomaly is fully understandable when we assume that we are dealing with a polymorphous appearance of Christ. The Lord appears to John and his followers in a different form than he does to others like Callimachus. In this case, he has assumed the forms of a youth and an angel at the same moment and is thus seen differently by different people.

*2.8 Christomonism*

At first sight there is no distinction between God, the Lord and Christ in the AJ. The words that denote godhead are used with apparent interchangeability for God and Christ in all stories, see e.g. 'God who does not desert us' next to 'Christ Jesus is always with you.'[70] This phenomenon deserves closer investigation.

The start of the prayer in c.82 is remarkable: Ὁ θεὸς τῶν αἰώνων Ἰησοῦς Χριστός, ὁ θεὸς τῆς ἀληθείας ... In cc.18-25 the deity is addressed in prayer as κύριε (20.3; 21.19), Χριστέ (22.5, 11) and Κύριε Ἰησοῦ (24.8), and spoken of as κύριος (21.9; 22.3; 25.10), Ἰησοῦς Χριστός (22.20) and θεός (19.13; 21.6; 23.16, 19; 24.18, 23). In the portrait-story of cc.26-29 we twice have κύριος Ἰησοῦς Χριστός (28.6; 29.17), further Ἰησοῦς (29.3) and θεός (26.11; 27.14, 15). Clear examples of this non-differentiation can also be found elsewhere. The prayer in c.77 starts with the appellation κύριε Ἰησοῦ Χριστέ (line 3), but in line 15 it uses ὁ πατὴρ, and in line 18 concludes with ἅγιε Ἰησοῦ, ὅτι σὺ μόνος θεὸς καὶ οὐχ ἕτερος. In the next chapter John says Δόξα τῷ θεῷ ἡμῶν, τέκνον, Χριστῷ Ἰησοῦ ... (78.2-3).[71] Here several manuscripts leave out the words Χριστῷ Ἰησοῦ, but these words are probably authentic. The election and sending out of the apostles is attributed to 'God' (112.1-2). Moreover, in the OT and NT it is God who raises the dead, but in the AJ we read ὁ κύριος ἡμῶν ἐστιν Ἰησοῦς Χριστός, ὅστις τὴν δύναμιν αὐτοῦ δείξει ἐν τῷ νεκρῷ σου συγγενεῖ ἀναστήσας αὐτόν (46.21-23).

After this survey, the reference to the Trinity in 57.8-9 comes unexpectedly. It can be nothing else than an interpolation.[72] The secondary character of the phrase as a whole is also evident in the reference to catechising and baptism, things mentioned nowhere else in the AJ, and in the fact that sections A and B do not contain any reference to

[70] τὸν θεὸν ... τὸν μὴ ἀπολιμπανόμενον ὑμῶν (58.7-8), Χριστὸς Ἰησοῦς σὺν ὑμῖν ἐστιν ἀεί (58.10).

[71] Cf. the reverse order of the words in 82.3 and 84.19.

[72] Cf. JK, 242 n.4.

the holy Spirit.[73]

The present study is not the first to signal that section A of the AJ knows no distinction between God, the Lord and Christ.[74] This phenomenon has been called 'Christomonism' or 'Unitarianism of the Second Person';[75] I accept the former term to designate it. The Christomonism of the AJ resembles the more familiar Modalism or Monarchianism introduced above, in that it recognizes only one divine person; but the two differ essentially in that Monarchians, like Noetus and Praxeas, affirm the Gospel teaching about the birth, suffering and death of Jesus, whereas Christomonism denies its validity.

The Christomonism of the AJ probably derives from a specific reading of statements in the Fourth Gospel,[76] such as Christ's claim that he and the Father are one, and that whoever sees him has seen the Father.[77] Praxeas read the Fourth Gospel in a similar way, so that Tertullian (*Adv Prax* 20-25) had to draw attention to the Gospel's frequent distinctions between Father and Son.

[73] The word πνεῦμα occurs eight times in the first main part of the AJ (thrice in section C). In 68.9 it means wind, and in 57.4 it denotes unclean spirits, as in the variant in 112.14-17. In 57.9 it is in the trinitarian interpolation. The word is used anthropologically in 115.4, in 82.1 (synonymous with ψυχή) and in 86.4, where John tells πνεῦμά τι ἐν ἐμοὶ ἐμαντεύσατο, πνεῦμά τι being the editor's transcription of the manuscript's πνι. This leaves us with one occurrence: in 46.8 we read concerning John 'he said, moved by the Spirit' (ἔφη ἐν τῷ πνεύματι). How to understand this? In the Stoa *spiritus* was used to denote divine substance. Van de Kamp, *Pneuma-christologie*, 36, 68-69, 79, 81 with n.37, has shown that in the Apostolic Fathers and other authors before the Councils πνεῦμα can simply refer to divine essence, belonging to the sphere of God. In view of his examples, it seems possible to understand ἐν τῷ πνεύματι in 46.8 as meaning 'under divine influence'. Cf. R. Cantalamessa, 'Méliton de Sardes. Une christologie antignostique du IIe siècle', *RSR* 37 (1963) 20.

[74] So already Photius, *Bibliotheca* cod. 114: καὶ φύρων ἅπαντα καὶ συγχέων καλεῖ αὐτὸν [sc. Χριστόν] καὶ Πατέρα καὶ Υἱόν. See also Zahn, 'Wanderungen', 205-208; Schmidt, *Petrusakten*, 90-91; Junod and Kaestli, 'Théologie', 138-139 (and in their later publications); Sirker-Wicklaus, *Untersuchungen*, 220-221; Schneider, *Mystery*, 57, 68, 163.

[75] By Schäferdiek, 'Herkunft', 266-267, resp. by Pervo, 'Trajectories', 61.

[76] Pervo, 'Trajectories', 62; Sirker-Wicklaus, *Untersuchungen*, 220.

[77] Jn 10:30; 17:11, cf. 10:38; 14:10-11, 20; 17:21, 23. Kaestli, 'Mystère', 38, points to Jn 12:28, 17:1.

## 3 Section B

### *3.1 General observations*

Section B, which consists of cc.87-93 and 103-105, is much briefer than the preceding one and extremely poor in Christological predicates. Christ is often just denoted by a third person singular verb or, when John is the subject, by αὐτόν. Next to θεός (cc.103 and 104 only), κύριος is the only title used. Nevertheless, these chapters are packed with Christology. More than section A, they discuss the correct view of the person of Christ.

The motif of solidarity which we already encountered in section A also finds clear expression in c.103, which not only states that Christ is with the believers wherever they are, but also that he suffers with them in their sufferings.[78] It is clear that these statements refer to the situation of Christ and his followers in the present, as do cc.107-108.[79] The Lord is in sympathy with those who know him, he is present with mankind in all kinds of situations.

This section stresses the non-human identity of Christ and ends by designating him as 'God unchangeable, God invincible, God higher than all authority, and all power' (etc., 104.2-3). Before he starts to recount his experiences with Christ, John says that he does so in order 'that you may see the glory that surrounds him who was and is both now and forever' (88.7-8).[80] This explanation implies that the δόξα of the Lord never changed. The author thus emphasises the divinity of Christ at the expense of his humanity. He displays a great interest in dehumanising Christ's being.

Insofar as the text's Christomonism is concerned, the identification God - Lord - Christ is less explicit in this section, but there is nothing to contradict it either. The evidence is limited since this section contains no prayers, which in cc.18-86 serve as major sources for the Christology. But 90.22 and 103.12 provide clear indications of the above identification. C.104 does not specify whether it concerns Christ or God, but as a continuation of c.103 it can only mean Christ, who is said to be elevated above all, eternal and immutable. We see again that the AJ identifies God and Christ in such a way that the divine aspect of Christ is given full attention while the human aspect is neglected or denied.

[78] ἅπασιν ἡμῖν συνὼν πάσχουσι συμπάσχει καὶ αὐτός. This is the only occurrence of συμπάσχω in the AJ.

[79] The word πάσχω appears in section A only with reference to humans. In 107.8 the words τοῖς παθήμασιν αὐτοῦ have been added secondarily to ἡδέσθω κοινονούντων ὑμῶν; πάθος does not occur in section A but only in sections B and C.

[80] ὅπως ἴδητε τὴν περὶ αὐτὸν δόξαν ἥτις ἦν καὶ ἔστιν καὶ νῦν καὶ εἰς ἀεί.

*3.2 Polymorphy*

The discussion of the polymorphy of Christ is concentrated in cc.87-93, which contain the twelve episodes concerning Christ, some of which we already discussed from another point of view in the last chapter.[81] But not all of these twelve short stories depict the Lord as polymorphous in the strict sense. On a closer look, the episodes can best be divided into four groups:

- nrs. 1, 2, 4, 7, 8 and 9 in which Christ's polymorphy is revealed through the ways in which he was seen;
- nrs. 5 and 10 in which Christ's polymorphy (lack of materiality) is revealed through the sense of touch;
- nrs. 3, 6 and 12 which tell what Christ looked like without suggesting polymorphy;
- nr. 11 which does not deal with Christ's outer appearance.

Nr. 1 narrates that at the same moment different people saw Christ as a man of several different ages. Nr. 2 amounts to the same and adds that the age difference manifested itself in terms of beard-growth. The main subject of these episodes is no longer the calling of disciples, as it is in the Gospels on which the episodes are based. Instead, the self-revelation of the Lord in his many forms is emphasised.[82] Nr. 4 differs from nrs. 1 and 2 in several ways. In this episode it is not Christ's age that is important; there are no other disciples involved; and this time Christ assumes forms that are physically impossible. The episode states that John saw that Christ's stature varied greatly from time to time. This contradicts Schneider's view that John, seeing older or bigger forms of the Lord than James, represents the mature believers.[83]

[81] For easy reference I give the chapters and lines of the episodes in JK:

| episode nr. | JK | episode nr. | JK |
|---|---|---|---|
| 1 | 88. 9-20 | 7 | 90. 4-22 |
| 2 | 89. 1- 7 | 8 | 91 |
| 3 | 89. 7- 8 | 9 | 92 |
| 4 | 89. 9-10 | 10 | 93. 1- 4 |
| 5 | 89.10-15 | 11 | 93. 4-10 |
| 6 | 90. 1- 4 | 12 | 93.10-13 |

[82] Cf. Beyschlag, *Überlieferung*, 100, goes, however, too far when he describes Christ in the *Apocryphon of John* as the 'überirdische Urbild der Menschheit überhaupt', the 'Urgestalt des Menschen'.

[83] Schneider, *Mystery*, 57-66, is convinced that John who sees the Lord as old represents the mature believers and James who sees him as young the immature ones. This is Christ adapting to the capacities of his public as in the *Gospel of Philip* and in Origen. Contrast JK, 471-472, 484: 'Ce thème [une vision adaptée à leur capacité, pjl] n'apparaît nulle part dans le discours de Jean.' Schneider, *Mystery*, 6, also says: 'And, with James and John

A doubling of the Lord occurs in nrs. 8 and 9. In the first situation John claims to understand the fact that other disciples see an old man who talks to the Lord; John thinks of 'his great grace and his unity which has many faces' (πολυπρόσωπον ἑνότητα, 91.6), a veritable key expression which implicates that the old man is a double of the Lord.[84] In nr. 9 only John is a witness to the revelation. This time there are two identical persons in dialogue.[85] Note that the AJ never makes John the twin of the Lord, as the ATh does with Thomas![86]

Nr. 7 is the longest of all episodes, drawing on the Synoptic story of the transfiguration as well as on the Johannine expression 'beloved disciple'. But the contents are far removed from the Gospel stories: John spies Christ and sees that he is naked, not human at all, and reaching into heaven. When John shouts from excitement, the Lord resumes his normal stature and reproaches him, pulling his beard so fiercely that it hurts for thirty days.

The closely similar nrs. 5 and 10 tell us what John felt when he touched the Lord. Nr. 5 states that his body was not always materially the same and that this secret was only revealed to John.[87] Nr. 10 goes a step further by adding that John came to know that sometimes the Lord was not material at all, which recalls the 'not a man at all' of nr. 7.[88] Though the change in corporeality is not described exactly, we get the impression that it happened under John's hands and thus nearly at one time. Therefore it can be regarded as a case of polymorphy.

To sum up, the polymorphy is not limited to Christ's stature, but also extends to other aspects of his being, such as his age and corporeality (materiality). Most polymorphous appearances are centred around a duality:

seeing progressively older manifestations of the Lord, the spirituality of both groups of Christians should be seen as maturing.' Judged from his point of view, episode nr. 4 exposes John's faith as an unstable one.

[84] *Pace* Schneider, *Mystery*, 65, who says that John himself is being indicated.

[85] Beyschlag, *Überlieferung*, 106, explains the double as an angel (Mt 18:10; Acts 12:13-15) and makes much of the fact that the episode happens during the night - which the text does not indicate.

[86] This is one more argument against Schneider's view, already mentioned in chapter 2 section 2.3, that in the AJ John is a more or less divine person. Also note the fact that John is not 'in total control' of his body (as Schneider, *Mystery*, 71, suggests), but suffers for thirty days (90.17-21)!

[87] There is a lacuna after episode nr. 5, indicated by the manuscript itself, see JK *ad loc.* Cartlidge, 'Transfigurations', 55, suggests that there originally stood an indication that Jesus' polymorphy extended to his sexuality. By way of proof, he refers to the *Apocryphon of John* in which Christ calls himself Father and Mother.

[88] ἄνθρωπος δὲ οὐδὲ ὅλως (90.10-11).

Christ appears in two forms. The number three is conspicuously absent from appearances in the AJ. I suggest that this characterises them as more ancient than e.g. APe 20-21 and the narrative frame of the *Apocryphon of John*, in which the appearing Lord assumes three different forms.[89]

*3.3 The other episodes*

All John's observations contribute to his conviction that Christ is non-human. Nr. 3 tells us that Christ never closed his eyes, thus suggesting a supernatural quality in the traditional Greek way.[90] Episode nr. 12 relates that the Lord left no traces when he walked, or rather hovered, over the earth. These episodes give a docetic view of Christ but not a polymorphous one.

Like nr. 7, nr. 6 resembles the NT transfiguration stories. Both are situated on a mountain where John can see that the Lord is not human; but nr. 6 is a case of metamorphosis rather than of polymorphy. Nr. 11 stands apart from the others; in clear contradiction to the post-Easter episodes Lk 24:41-42 and Jn 21:5-15, it relates that Christ did not eat.

The fact that John never tells how the Lord normally looked, contributes to the impression that he should not be considered a real human being.[91] He did not even have a semi-permanent mock body, but changed his appearance whenever he wished. This representation implies that his divine being can never adequately be expressed in a human form. In the eyes of our author, to believe that the Lord had a human body would amount to lessening his divinity. He rejects the immense paradox of the incarnation of the Logos (Jn 1). Lipsius aptly remarks:

> Es ist dies im Grunde dieselbe Vorstellung, welche auch die Katholiker von dem verklärten Leibe des Auferstandenen hegten, nur dass diese hier bereits auf die geschichtliche Erscheinung Christi übertragen ist.[92]

Consequently the message of the text is that Christ can only be known by spiritually enlightened eyes such as those of John, his great apostle, who now shares his knowledge with the readers of the AJ. The twelve episodes, which are packed in different and very engaging narrative forms, all essentially have this one message.

[89] See also my 'Polymorphy', 118.

[90] JK, 477.

[91] 'C'est qu'il n'y a pas d'aspect habituel puisque le Seigneur n'est pas un homme, mais le Dieu immuable', JK, 479.

[92] Lipsius, *Apostelgeschichten*, 522.

*3.4 Evaluation*

The episodes constitute a kind of response to questions arising in the minds of the believers upon hearing that Drusiana had seen a polymorphous appearance of the Lord. It is evident that these believers were weak in their faith (c.87).[93] John reacts by saying that, due to his supernatural glory, the Lord also tested the apostles. His appearances were such that they can hardly be conveyed by either spoken or written human words (88.1-8). But as the Lord himself has already initiated Drusiana, the time seems fit for John to share the mystery of the Lord with his other followers. I believe that the elaborateness of the introduction is meant as a careful preparation of the readers for the presentation of a new conception of Christ.[94] Again the text emphasises the insufficiency of human things: above it was the inadequacy of the human body to hold a divine being, now it is human language which is incapable of describing the Lord as he really is. Neither forms nor words are satisfactory. For that reason the text takes recourse to a multiplicity of forms and words.

In the last chapter we saw that the canonical Gospels are clearly in the background of some of these episodes. Their underlying presence suggests that the author consciously pictures an alternative to the Christ of these Gospels; in this sense section B is polemical. In contrast to the Gospel stories about the human being Jesus of Nazareth, the author places his new insight into the divine being of Christ. The fact that this idea receives so much emphasis suggests that the author is indeed well acquainted with the opposite view and possibly that the 'canonical' Christ is also well-known to the author's environment.

The aim of all of these episodes is to highlight that Christ was never in any way human. In this respect, the episodes which do not involve polymorphy do not differ from the others. They all stress the non-humanity of Christ; John sees that he is 'not at all a man' (90.10-11).[95]

*3.5 The relationship between sections A and B*

I conclude that, although they use different means, sections A and B contain the same conception of the divine: there is but one God, the Lord Christ, who revealed himself in an apparently human form to some but who never really lived on earth. Only enlightened eyes can know his true identity. Nevertheless he is not alien to the fate of humanity. In terms of their Christology there is no reason to distinguish between the sections.

[93] The testimony of Drusiana in c.87 is not included in the series of twelve testimonies but can be seen as a thematic introduction to it.

[94] Pervo, 'Trajectories', 58, stresses the pastoral intention of the section.

[95] Similarly Sturhahn, *Christologie*, 31-33.

## 4 Section C

### *4.1 Introduction*

Despite its relative brevity, section C has an intriguing and more complicated Christology and a richer theological vocabulary than the rest of the text. Our reading of the other sections raises questions about section C's Christomonism and its relationship to the concept of polymorphy. These questions are especially relevant when we realise that a majority of Gnostics distinguish between Jesus who was crucified and Christ who was not.[96] My treatment of this section includes the notion of ἄνθρωπος, which is allegedly connected with Christ.

On the lexical level, 'Christ' (98.9) and 'Jesus' (109.3) each occur only once.[97] The only other Christological title in this section, used both by John and by Christ himself, is 'the Lord'. The word God is relatively seldom; its three occurrences (96.17, 97.12, 98.6) are all self-references by the Lord Christ who is the main speaker in this section and who never refers to a deity beyond himself or to someone 'in heaven'. This fact coincides with the fact that all attention is focussed on the appearances and the revelatory words of 'the Lord'.

My discussion begins with the passages that form the key to the understanding of the whole section, viz. the lists of predicates in cc.98 and 109. Thereafter I will follow a trajectory in which I first deal with the names of the Lord, then with the forms of his appearance, and finally with his acts of salvation.

### *4.2 The polyonymy of Christ*

#### *4.2.1 The names and predicates of the Lord in cc.98 and 109*

As I said, the lists of Christological predicates which appear in 98.8-12 and 109.3-12 have a key role in the interpretation of the Christology of the whole section. Lists of Christ's predicates are frequently found in early Christian literature. Some of them are rooted in the Old Testament, but others mainly contain NT names and images. Roelof van den Broek argues that lists based on the NT are first found in the AJ, the APe and in Origen.[98] Most of the words in the lists in AJ 98 and 109 indeed derive from the four canonical Gospels and none clearly come from the Old Testament. It is worth looking at several parallel lists in order to help us

[96] Bauer, *Leben Jesu*, 238-239; Voorgang, *Passion, passim*.

[97] Cf. JK, 588-589, and chapter 1 above. The reader will remember that c.109 together with cc.94-102 forms my section C because it is Gnostic.

[98] Van den Broek, *Studies*, 238 n.12. He does not mention Melito, *Peri Pascha*, 9, 103, 105, and AJ 109. Typical OT lists are presented in Justin, *Dial* 34, 100, 126.

interpret the AJ.[99] First there is a remarkable enumeration of predicates for the Logos in Philo of Alexandria:

> ... Gods's First-born, the Word, who holds the eldership among the angels, their ruler as it were. He has many names for he is called 'the Beginning', and 'the Name of God', and 'His Word', and 'the Man after His image', and 'he that sees', 'Israel'.[100]

In Philo the word Logos is of course not associated with Christ as divine revelation, but that makes the parallels all the more intriguing. Notice that in this respect Philo makes use of the word polyonymous, a term to which I will return later.[101]

Another parallel to the lists in the AJ is APe 20, a long list which has eleven words in common with c.109. But the closest parallel to c.98 is a list of predicates of the Logos in Justin, *Dial* 61.1:

> God has begotten of Himself a certain rational Power. The Holy Spirit indicates this Power by various titles, sometimes the Glory of the Lord, at other times Son, or Wisdom, or Angel, or God, or Lord, or Word ...[102]

As we saw in the last chapter, this list manifests not only thematic but also formal parallels with c.98 because both lists are characterised by a repeated ποτὲ δὲ. The similarity is accentuated by the fact that c.98 mentions the predicate Logos at the head of the list. One of the things that the parallels make clear is that readers of the AJ may have known one or more of the

[99] Apart from the parallels mentioned in the main text, see ATh 80, Melito, Fragment 13, Ps.Clem. *Homily* 3.72, and *The Teachings of Silvanus* (NHC VII.4) 106.21-28; JK, 659-660. Sirker-Wicklaus, *Untersuchungen*, 122-127, includes the list in c.107 (a list that is more theo-logical than Christo-logical) in her explanation of cc.98 and 109, which opposes Junod and Kaestli's views.

[100] Philo, *De conf ling* 146 (ed. Colson and Whitaker, trans. slightly adapted): τὸν πρωτόγονον αὐτοῦ [sc. θεοῦ] λόγον, τὸν ἀγγέλων πρεσβύτατον, ὡς ἂν ἀρχάγγελον, πολυώνυμον ὑπάρχοντα· καὶ γὰρ ἀρχὴ καὶ ὄνομα θεοῦ καὶ λόγος καὶ ὁ κατ' εἰκόνα ἄνθρωπος καὶ ὁ ὁρῶν, 'Ισραήλ, προσαγορεύεται.

[101] πολυώνυμος occurs six times in Philo, e.g. it refers to Moses in *Mutat nom* 125, and to Wisdom in *Leg all* 2.43; cf. A.J.M. Wedderburn, 'Philo's "Heavenly Man"', *NT* 15 (1973) 301-326, esp. 320.

[102] ὁ θεὸς γεγέννηκε δύναμίν τινα ἐξ ἑαυτοῦ λογικήν, ἥτις καὶ δόξα κυρίου ὑπὸ τοῦ πνεύματος τοῦ ἁγίου καλεῖται, ποτὲ δὲ υἱός, ποτὲ δὲ σοφία, ποτὲ δὲ ἄγγελος, ποτὲ δὲ θεός, ποτὲ δὲ κύριος καὶ λόγος, ποτὲ δὲ ἀρχιστράτηγον ἑαυτὸν λέγει. *Iustini Martyris Dialogus cum Tryphone*, ed. M. Marcovich, Berlin/New York 1997; translation based on T.B. Falls, *The Works of Justin Martyr*, Washington D.C. 1948. This list has not so far been noticed in AJ studies; it is referred to by P. Hofrichter, 'Logoslehre und Gottesbild bei Apologeten, Modalisten und Gnostikern', in H.-J. Klauck (ed.), *Monotheismus und Christologie*, Freiburg 1992, 186-217, esp. 190-192, who argues for Philonic influence.

other lists of predicates. It is possible that the lists in the AJ consist to some extent of preexisting materials.

Let us now study the lists in the AJ in their contexts. In c.98 the predicates are said to apply to the cross of light and in c.109 to Jesus, but this difference is insignificant for the present treatment because, as we will see below, Christ and cross are closely connected here, the cross being an important revelation of the Lord. With 26 predicates the list in c.109 is the longer of the two. The list proper starts with the predicate Door (line 5) and continues with 'Resurrection, Way, Seed, Word, Grace, Faith,' etc. The preceding lines 3-5 are, in any case, the work of the present author, since they clearly express his theology and indicate his intentions for including this list. My interpretation of these textually complicated lines is based on the following reading:

> We glorify your name of Father, spoken by you;
> we glorify your name of Son, spoken by you.[103]

John praises Jesus for revealing to humanity that the predicates Father and Son apply to himself (cf. Jn 17:6, 26). Both names are presented as predicates of Christ, just as the following words in the list are. Consequently, Father, Son, and all the other predicates are here names given to the one divine revealer.[104]

The shorter list in c.98 runs: Logos, Mind,[105] Christ, Door, Way, Bread, Seed, Resurrection, Son, Father, Spirit, Life, Truth, Faith, Grace (98.7-12). The fact that so many Christological predicates are applied to the cross demonstrates that it is very closely associated with Christ, if not in some way a manifestation of him; I will return to this issue later in this chapter. The Lord expressly says that these names are given to the cross ὑπ' ἐμοῦ δι' ὑμᾶς (98.9). This statement again suggests that the revelation of the many names takes place for the sake of those addressed, whereas essentially the cross is one. In lines 12-13 Christ again suggests that the predicates are mere human words, which is a major depreciation of their value. Most predicates in this list and in the list in c.109 can be found in the NT as specifically Christological words, but others are not normally

[103] δοξάζομέν σου τὸ λεχθὲν ὑπὸ σοῦ πατρὸς ὄνομα· δοξάζομέν σου τὸ λεχθὲν ὑπὸ <σοῦ> υἱοῦ ὄνομα. The fourth σοῦ does not occur in any manuscript; it was proposed by Schimmelpfeng, 'Johannesakten', 539, and printed without brackets by JK. See JK, 300 n.1, and cf. 339 for an 'Orthodox' recension of the text.

[104] JK, 618 with n.5: 'Les noms qui y [cc.98 and 109] sont successivement employés renvoient tous à un seul et même être divin.' 'Jésus n'est donc pas un être distinct du Père, du Logos, de la Grâce, etc., mais il est lui-même, paradoxalement, le destinataire de la doxologie qu'il prononce.'

[105] Elliott here adds 'Jesus' with manuscript **C**, but the older witness to the text, the Acts of the Council of Nicea, does not have this.

associated with Christ, in particular Spirit and Father.

Two brief remarks must finally be made. First, as we saw above, Logos is given priority in this list; this order reminds us of Philo's and Justin's lists. Secondly, a notable absentee from both lists is ἄνθρωπος, a word that plays a central role in the rest of this section.

Both lists in the AJ contain the word Father as a predicate of Christ.[106] Second-century Christianity sometimes used Father as a title for Christ. We already saw this in section A (77.15; 112.15) and it also occurs in the *Epistula Apostolorum* 41 (Ethiopic) and in Melito, *Peri Pascha* 9.[107] The reverse also took place: the Pseudo-Clementine *Homily* 3.72.2, which in its present form must be later than the second century but which preserves older materials, uses some predicates to refer to the Father that are elsewhere applied to the Son.[108] But despite the superficial similarities the tendency of these texts differs considerably from what the AJ has to say. Melito, the *Epistula* and the *Homily* have a naivety of expression which clearly predates Tertullian's distinct formulations on the separate roles of Father and Son. These texts are simply not concerned with such doctrinal reflection, which anticipated the later decisions of the Councils.

The lists in section C of the AJ, on the other hand, are far from naive. On the contrary, they consciously blur all distinctions between Christ and the Father. They give expression to the conviction that whatever name is used for Christ also applies to the one God Christ. These lists thus share the view found in the earlier sections of the AJ that Christ and God must not be distinguished because Christ is God himself and accordingly not human. The individual predicates do not really inform about his real transcendent being.[109]

Section C employs a multitude of names and predicates, none of which is fully adequate because essentially the Lord is beyond human description. This observation goes hand in hand with another one: none of the predicates is clearly defined nor can they be defined. The author consciously mixes labels, titles and identities of the divine person. I

[106] In c.98, it is strictly speaking used as a predicate of the cross.

[107] See G. Racle, 'A propos du Christ-Père dans l'*Homélie pascale* de Méliton de Sardes', *RSR* 50 (1962) 400-408; R. Cantalamessa, 'Il Christo "Padre" negli scritti del II-III sec.', *Rivista di Storia e Letteratura Religiosa* 3 (1967) 1-27; V. Grossi, 'Il titolo "Padre" nell'antichità cristiana', *Augustinianum* 16 (1976) 237-269.

[108] Δέσποτα καὶ κύριε τῶν ὅλων, ὁ πατὴρ καὶ θεός (...) ὁ σωτήρ, τὸ τεῖχος, ἡ ζωή, ἡ ἐλπίς, ἡ καταφυγή, ἡ χαρά, ἡ προσδοκία, ἡ ἀνάπαυσις (ed. Rehm and Paschke). Of these, ζωή occurs also in AJ 98 and καταφυγή and ἀνάπαυσις in AJ 109.

[109] Luttikhuizen, 'Gnostic reading', 142-143, stresses the insufficiency of any name.

suggest that for the way in which our text describes Christ the term polyonymy be used. As we just saw, the notion of polyonymy occurs in Philo who uses it, among other things, for the Logos.

When we look at the use of predicates in the Fourth Gospel or in Justin, the meaning of this polyonymy becomes more clear. The fourth Evangelist and Justin both are conscious that a single title never exhausts what can be said of Christ, but in their opinion the predicates they use are nevertheless meaningful descriptions of the Lord. He *is* the good Shepherd, the way, the truth and the life, etc.[110] This feature is in marked contrast with our text, in which the lists are the expression of a conviction about the inadequacy of human language and resemble attitudes that we also met in section B: in principle it does not really matter which name is used to designate the Lord. Predicates applied to him lose their specific meanings and are taken up in the exalted praise of the trancendent deity.

An illustration of this effect of polyonymy can be seen in the predicate ἀνάστασις (98.10-11). Our author must have taken it from a previous Christian tradition, but in its new context it certainly does not refer to Easter events. It is, however, hard to ascertain what the word meant to the author. Possibly ἀνάστασις for him recalls the Gospel stories in which Christ resurrects several people, especially John 11, which includes a pregnant Christological saying in verse 25. Alternatively, we may connect it with the fact that Christ presently gives life to his followers, an idea that is more at home in section A than in C. We find that it is useless to look for the word's specific meaning because our author himself deliberately leaves it vague. Such is the case for all of these predicates: they contribute to the praise of the overarching divine presence.

It is important to stress that nothing in the lists of predicates is inherently Gnostic.[111] They do not correspond to any known list of pleromatic representations of Christ, whether Valentinian or other.[112] I would agree with Schmidt's suggestion that the author's decision to include these lists demonstrates that he adheres to a peculiar, probably early, form

[110] When taken together, the 'I am' sayings form a string of predicates of Jesus; within one context he is called both 'door' and 'shepherd' (Jn 10:11, 14), and 'way, truth and life' (14:6).

[111] The thesis of Lipsius, *Apostelakten*, 534, and JK, 618-619, that the lists have a specifically Gnostic background is unfounded. The speculations about the Name and names in the *Gospel of Philip* 11-13 (p.53.24-54.19), the *Excerpta ex Theodoto* 22.5-6, 26.1 and the *Tractatus Tripartitus* (cf. JK, 617-621, Schneider, *Mystery*, 94-95, and Luttikhuizen, 'Gnostic reading', 142) are different because they are theoretical discussions about the inadequacy of human language to describe the Lord. They are reflections on a meta-level of lists like these which stress the inadequacy of their terms.

[112] Lipsius, *Apostelakten*, 527.

of Gnosis. In Schmidt's opinion, which was later confirmed by the Nag Hammadi texts, Gnostic speculation tends to split up the divine and the heavenly beings into a cascade of entities. In more developed forms of Gnosis the concepts of polymorphy and polyonymy are not found;[113] they have been replaced by the distinction of separate aeons. It seems that in Gnostic thinking every predicate of God and Christ was eventually personified and came to be conceived as an aeon. In the AJ this tendency has not yet prevailed: Christ is still essentially a unity.[114]

### *4.2.2 The further use of divine names*

Because in the lists in cc.98 and 109 all predicates and titles apply to (the cross and to) Christ, it follows that the words Father, Son,[115] Logos and Spirit in these lists are used as predicates of the polyonymous Christ and do not refer to separate persons. We must now look at the other occurrences of the divine names in section C to see if this polyonymy appears everywhere in the section and if so, how it relates to the Christomonism of section A.

We first look at c.94, which confronts us with a seemingly trinitarian doxology. However, already Lipsius stated that it is hard to know whether this doxology addresses one or more divine beings.[116] Here follows the text in my own translation:

line 8 Glory be to you, Father! [...]
10 Glory be to you, Logos!
11 Glory be to you, Grace! (Amen)
12 Glory be to you, Spirit![117]
13 Glory be to you, Holy One!
14 Glory be to the Glory! (Amen)
15 We praise you, Father!
16 We give thanks to you, Light
17 in whom darkness does not abide!

Does the structure of this doxology help us to answer the question who is being praised here? At first sight, the distribution of the word 'amen' suggests that there is a plurality of objects of praise, which are grouped in

[113] On the relationship between polyonymy and polymorphy see below.
[114] Cf. Schmidt, *Petrusakten*, 126. This point is overlooked by Sturhahn, *Christologie*, 25-26.
[115] The use of the word υἱός in section C is limited to the lists.
[116] Lipsius, *Apostelgeschichten*, 527; Cantalamessa, 'Christo "Padre"', 10-11 also poses the question but his answer differs from mine.
[117] The text of c.94 appears in manuscript **C** and the Acta of the Council of Nicea; see chapter 1. Following the latter, Junod and Kaestli strike the word ἅγιον after πνεῦμα.

'triads'; it is indeed in this way that Junod and Kaestli present the text: Father, Logos and Grace form the first triad (lines 8-11). Spirit, Holy One and Glory constitute the second (12-14).[118] The Father and the Light-in-which-there-is-no-darkness (15-17) form a kind of 'dyad' that rounds off the praise. But the fact that there are not three complete triads is infelicitous. Moreover, it is clear that neither triad is exactly that of Father, Son and Spirit, though the first comes closer than the second. It would seem that a trinitarian form is not intended and that we have to regard this passage in another way.

I suggest that comparison with the polyonymy in the lists in cc.98 and 109 helps us to explain the present chapter: all predicates used here - Father, Grace, Word, Glory, Spirit - ultimately refer to one person.[119] This insight causes us to abandon not only the idea of triads but also that of separate divine persons. I conclude that c.94 is an eightfold glorification of the polyonymous Christ,[120] or a sixfold one (lines 8-14) with a kind of coda that repeats the word Father (lines 15-17). Thus Christ in fact asks the disciples to praise himself.

Another doxology that requires discussion is Δόξα σοι πάτερ, δόξα σοι λόγε, δόξα σοι πνεῦμα ἅγιον (96.21-23). Even more than c.94, the present formula seems to be trinitarian but this *prima facie* interpretation does not fit the present line of exegesis. As far as I can see, there are two possible explanations. The first is to consider not only ἅγιον, but the whole of 96.20-23 as an interpolation. This coincides with the fact that these lines fit oddly into the reconstruction of the original form of the hymn by D.I. Pallas.[121] They may have been added in a time when the doxology in c.94 was read in a trinitarian perspective and considered insufficient. It needed therefore some clarification (c.96). But in my opinion a second solution, the possibility that the author consciously uses

[118] S.G. Hall, 'Melito's Paschal Homily and the *Acts of John*', *JTS* 17 (1966) 95-98, esp. 97, rather suggests: 'The form is trinitarian, apparently constructed with one title for the Father, two for the Son, and three for the Spirit.' This alternative is correct in so far as it implies that 'Grace' refers to Christ.

[119] Cf. Zahn, 'Wanderungen', 205-206; Hennecke, *Handbuch*, 526; Sturhahn, *Christologie*, 33; JK, 646: 'En fait, tous les noms servent à célébrer un seul être divin, comme le montre clairement le parallèle avec les énumérations des ch. 98 et 109: 'Père', 'Logos' et 'Grâce' s'y retrouvent, appliqués à la Croix de lumière ou à Jésus.' M. Pulver, 'Jesu Reigen und Kreuzigung nach den Johannes-Akten', *Eranos-Jahrbuch* 9 (1942) 141-177, esp. 162-165, takes Grace and Spirit as deities belonging to other religions.

[120] This view accords with Schneider, *Mystery*, 163-164, who makes the additional argument that δόξῃ in the line δόξα σου τῇ δόξῃ refers to the metamorphoses of the Lord, just as in 88.7 and 93.1. If correct, this allusion connects section C with section B.

[121] Referred to in JK, 633.

an early trinitarian formula which does not reflect his own convictions, is more likely. This suggestion is supported by what follows in the text. The enigmatic words of Christ, 'As Logos I once for all deceived all things, and was not put to shame at all' (96.25),[122] suggest that, in the opinion of the author, Christological titles are without specific meaning and in fact just illusory. Christ can be the Logos or he cannot be it, because Logos is just one of the many predicates that can be applied to him. Consequently, one of the formulas that can be used to praise him is a trinitarian formula, one that can just as easily be exchanged for any other predicate or formula.[123] The God Christ is indeed polyonymous.[124]

There is one more phrase in which the predicate Father is used, viz. 100.11-12: 'Know that I am wholly with the Father, and the Father with me.' As we saw in the last chapter, this phrase is derived from the Fourth Gospel.[125] But removed from their original context, these words might suggest identification of God and Christ. It appears from the change of preposition (in Jn ἐν is used, in the AJ παρὰ) that our author has indeed taken them that way.[126]

The predicate Spirit occurs only three times in section C, once in the list of predicates in c.98 and twice in the doxological formulas that have just been discussed (94.12; 96.23). We can safely say that, for our author, the Spirit is none other than the God Christ himself.

[122] λόγῳ ἔπαιξα πάντα καὶ οὐκ ἐπῃσχύνθην ὅλως; this reading is established by JK, who explain it as 'pendant son séjour ici-bas, le Christ divin a dissimulé son être véritable et il a cru échappé à tous les outrages qu'on a pouvoir lui infliger' (655 n.13).

[123] E. Rose, *Die manichäische Christologie*, Wiesbaden 1979, 155-161, shows that the same is true for Manichaeism. Thus, the words could also be an addition made by Manichaeans.

[124] Lines 11-13 and 25 in c.96 show the influence of section B on the author of section C. The argument that what can be seen of the Lord is not his true being but a mere apparition (δόκησις) reflects the polymorphy of the earlier section. Notice that the song and the dance have not revealed the Lord's identity (*contra* the central thesis of Schneider, *Mystery*). John and the other Gnostics will come to know it later, cf. lines 14-15, viz. in the revelation on the Mount.

[125] Jn 10:38; 14:10-11; 17:21; cf. p. 116 above.

[126] Kaestli, 'Mystère', 45: 'un rappel de l'unité totale du Père et du Fils'. The only other occurrence of παρὰ with dative in section C is found just above (100.9). The text here is corrupt but suggests identity (... ὡς ἐγὼ παρ' ἐμαυτῷ). Such a use of παρὰ is fully in line with what we expect the text to say in 100.11-12. Sirker-Wicklaus, *Untersuchungen*, 220, thinks that, at face value, 100.11-12 contradicts the rest of the text but resolves the problem by stating 'Allerdings mutet dieser Satz wie ein Anhängsel an ...'

### *4.2.3 Christ as Logos*

Having dealt with the divine predicates in the strict sense, let us now look at the text's conception of Logos.[127] The question is similar to the one posed in the last paragraph, viz. does Logos designate a separate hypostasis, as it does in Justin and the other Apologists? We will also consider the possibility of more positively stating what the text means when it describes the Lord as Logos.

The occurrence of Logos in 96.6 recalls the language of the Gospel of John. Manuscript **C** has: 'To you I am the Logos, I was sent by the Father' (εἰμι σοι λόγος, ὑπὸ πατρὸς ἐστάλην).[128] This statement indicates that, in the eyes of mankind, Christ is an envoy from the Father, whereas nothing is said about his real being. Junod and Kaestli, following James, emend the text so that it reads εἰ μή instead of εἰμι. They connect the phrase with the preceding sentence and translate '(You would absolutely not be able to understand what you suffer) if I had not been sent to you as the Logos by the Father.' If this is correct, Christ distinguishes himself as Logos from the Father, who is implicitly a separate 'person'. But if we leave the text intact, σοι naturally qualifies εἰμι instead of ἐστάλην: 'To *you* I am the Logos.' This means that in reality Logos is just one of the forms which the God Christ can assume.[129] The author does not stress the unity of Christ and the Father, but neither does he contradict it.

The same c.96, the explanation of the meaning of the song and the dance of the Lord, has still more to say about the Logos. The concept of Logos appears at its beginning (lines 5-6) and end (24-25). Both these sentences make a true understanding of the revelation of the Lord dependent on the attainment of a proper insight into his appearance as Logos. Christ carries out his revelatory function as Logos. For the present day reader, this function of Logos recalls Philo and Justin as well as the Gospel according to John. Philo's use of the Logos-concept is notoriously complex[130] but turns around the function of the Logos as instrument of

[127] The occurrences of λόγος in sections A and B are Christologically insignificant. In cc.94-96 it occurs five times. Of these, 94.10 has already been dealt with, whereas 96.19 is not Christological.

[128] Actually the MS has ειμι, read εἰμι.

[129] This reminds us of Justin, *Dial* 61.1, quoted above.

[130] D.T. Runia, *Philo of Alexandria and the* Timaeus *of Plato*, Leiden 1986, 446-447; in relation to the NT, see C.A. Evans, *Word and Glory. On the Exegetical and Theological Background of John's Gospel*, Sheffield 1993, 100-114.

God's revelation par excellence.[131] In the words of David T. Runia:

> The Logos in Philo can be defined in the most general terms as that aspect or part of the divine that stands in relation to created reality. (...) The role of the Logos is thus intimately connected with the problem of the relation between God's transcendence and creatorship ... Through the doctrine of the Logos God can be said to be *immanent* in the universe ... without the affirmation of his transcendence being put at risk.[132]

The same holds true for the AJ if the idea of creation is replaced by that of suffering. In the authors referred to and in Melito the Logos represents the activity of God *ad extra*, his revelatory agent.[133]

In 99.1 the predicate Logos is used again, and in a similar dative as in 96.25: 'This is the cross which fastened all as Logos ...' Here we have an identification not of Christ and Logos but of cross and Logos. Not surprisingly some assume that the three predicates, Logos, cross and Christ, are synonymous;[134] I would say that we are dealing with a threefold polyonymous revelation of the Lord. Once again Logos functions as an agent of revelation.

Near the end of the section there is a passage that places all the emphasis on the Logos (101.12-14). It would seem that both the Logos and the cross are means of revelation.[135] The fact that Christ now asks John to understand him as Logos, once more implies that Logos acts as the mediator of revelation. This time Logos is qualified by eight words all connected with suffering, the last of which is death (θάνατος, 101.14). In giving this place to the Logos, the AJ echoes the prologue of the Fourth Gospel, identifying Christ and Logos, without however accepting the Gospel's ideas about the incarnation of the Logos.

In the meantime the present phrase (101.12-14) is the most explicit connection of Lord with suffering that is made in all the text. There would seem to be two aspects to this suffering, the Lord's descent from heaven

[131] E.g. *De sacr Abel et Caini* 8 (Colson and Whitaker): 'for that same Word, by which He made the universe, is that by which He draws the perfect man from things earthly to Himself' (τῷ αὐτῷ λόγῳ καὶ τὸ πᾶν ἐργαζόμενος καὶ τὸν τέλειον ἀπὸ τῶν περιγείων ἀνάγων ὡς ἑαυτόν).

[132] Runia, *Philo and the* Timaeus, 449-450.

[133] Melito, *Peri Pascha* 9, says that Christ is Logos in so far as he teaches. As Barrett, *John*, writes when he discusses the background of the Fourth Gospel: '... the term Logos is seen to describe God in the process of self-communication' (73); 'common Greek usage ... made λόγος a very convenient term for describing any kind of self-expression' (152).

[134] Cf. JK, 605 n.1; Schneider, *Mystery*, 116: 'The Lord identifies himself as the Cross of Light'; cf. 117.

[135] Justin, *Apol* 1.60, makes Plato say that the Logos stands crosswise in the universe.

and his incompleteness because his members are not at one (see below). In any case, the concept of death is completely spiritualised here.

It turns out that the Logos is a manifestation of the God Christ without a clear identity of its own and that it especially has a revelatory function. The use of the concept of Logos confirms that the idea of polyonymy is indeed a prominent element in our author's thinking. The divine revelation takes place in words rather than in actions. We will see below that these words are open to interpretation on more than one level.

I conclude that in his description of the polyonymous God Christ, the author of section C highlights the diversity of names given this God and downplays his unity. By playing with concepts and predicates, the author illustrates that the Christomonism which he found in the text (sections A and B) and on which he elaborated, is not very important for him. In this respect he differs from the author of sections A and B, although their positions are not very far apart.

### *4.2.4 Is there a distinction between Christ and Jesus?*

Having seen that our text uses many different words to designate the one Lord Christ, we must now pay attention to the absence of the common Gnostic distinction between Christ and Jesus discussed above. It is remarkable that such a distinction between Jesus and the divine Saviour, which can very well be observed in such a text as the Nag Hammadi *Apocalypse of Peter* (p.81.7-24), is absent from the AJ.[136]

But what about the pairs of contrasting pronouncements, one in the active form and one in the passive, in the song of the Lord in c.95?[137] As they stand, these sayings are (probably consciously) enigmatic. It is only Christ himself who dances and sings - the disciples are merely asked to answer (94.6) and join him (96.3, 8). Again, the word Grace (95.18) does not denote a separate character because it is a predicate of Christ.[138] And when the Lord refers back to the dance, he does so in the singular form, stating that he has revealed his suffering (101.2). Thus the structure of a part of the song (lines 2-17, 31-42) suggests that Christ is a two-sided figure, who possesses an active (redeeming) character and a passive (redeemed) one. In view of the context, the pronouncements may be understood in such a way that their first parts are spoken from the

[136] Cf. Schneider, *Mystery*, 100-101. For the *Apocalypse of Peter*, see also chapter 3 above.

[137] Luttikhuizen, 'Gnostic reading', 128-129, cautions against calling the song a hymn.

[138] Christ is called Grace in 94.11, 98.12, 109.7 (cf. Melito, *Peri Pascha*, 9, and Hall, 'Melito's Paschal Homily'). Hilgenfeld, 'Johannes', 31, suggests that Grace dances as syzygos of the Lord, but there are no indications that the author of our text knew the concept of syzygoi.

perspective of the heavenly Christ and their second parts from the perspective of the Lord, the divine revealer who partakes of human suffering.[139] Beyschlag suggests that this is a case of the polyonymy of the Lord,[140] but the absence of predicates makes the use of this word less felicitous.

We would expect that the description and explanation of the figure on the wooden cross (97.6-10) would use the distinction between Jesus and Christ, if the author knew any such distinction. The Lord who speaks to John distances himself from the figure on the cross (cf. 99.4-7) and emphatically states that his true passion does not involve the cross (101.6-11); these negations leave the identity of the one on the wooden cross unexplained.[141] The Lord does not even use a different predicate to distinguish himself from the crucified one, as he could easily have done. Our author does not avail himself here of the distinction between Christ and Jesus which could have helped him greatly. Does he not know it or does he reject it?

There is one text which constitutes a kind of parallel to this description of the crucifixion, viz. the *Letter of Peter to Philip* (NHC VIII.2) which, as we saw in chapter 3, also has intertextual parallels with the AJ:[142]

> Our illuminator, Jesus, [came] down and was crucified. And he bore a crown of thorns. And he put on a purple garment. And he was [crucified] on a tree and he was buried in a tomb. And he rose from the dead. My brothers, Jesus is a stranger to this suffering. But we are the ones who suffered through the transgression of the mother.[143]

Both the AJ and the *Letter of Peter to Philip* confront us with a Lord who is and is not crucified. The understanding of this paradox is left to the readers.

[139] Zahn, 'Wanderungen', 207: Jesus introduces himself as subject and as object of the Redemption; Sturhahn, *Christologie*, 35: 'Handelndes Subjekt ist die transzendente Erlösergottheit.' 'Von dem mythischen ἄνθρωπος aber, den Jesus ... darstellt, gelten die entgegengesetzten (zumeist passivischen) Aussagen'; similarly JK, 584: 'le Christ, à la fois envoyé du monde céleste et représentant de l'humanité spirituelle'; *ibid.*, 603: 'porte-parole de la "souffrance" des êtres pneumatiques'; reversal of the order in Luttikhuizen, 'Gnostic reading', 148: 'It would seem that in the first line the Lord speaks as 'Man' and in the second in his capacity as divine saviour.'

[140] Beyschlag, *Überlieferung*, 111.

[141] Hennecke, *Handbuch*, 532: 'Wie weit die Kreuzigung des Menschen Jesus noch als realer Vorgang gedacht ist, darüber hatte der Verf. kein Interesse eine Näherbestimmung zu treffen.' Cf. Luttikhuizen, 'Gnostic reading', 139.

[142] Luttikhuizen, 'Gnostic reading', 138-139, signals the same tension in several Gnostic texts; cf. Meyer, *Letter*, 156 with n.225. I would add that the AJ and the *Letter of Peter to Philip* do not resolve the tension.

[143] The *Letter of Peter to Philip*, 139.15-23 (ed. Sieber).

The best explanation of the identity of the figure on the cross in the AJ is to regard him as a manifestation of the polymorphous Christ. To ordinary believers the Lord appears to have been as crucified while the Gnostics know that he never was subject to this physical suffering.[144] In its use of the theme of polymorphy, this scene displays the considerable influence of the image of Christ in the Gospel-like stories of section B.

Another indication that, for our author, the Lord is polyonymous but essentially a single individual is the fact that the name Jesus occurs only once in this section (109.3), as I noted above. Moreover, a closer look at the text makes it evident that there are no other differentiations within the person of the Lord than those indicated by means of polyonymy and polymorphy, the concepts that serve to preserve his essential unity. We may conclude that the AJ contains a 'monophysitic' description of Christ, which makes it unique among Gnostic texts.[145] The AJ seems either to predate or to ignore developments in Gnostic Christology, which suggests that it represents a kind of proto-Gnosticism.

*4.3 The revelation of the cross*

With the discussion of the person on the wooden cross we have already passed from the realm of the polyonymous revelation of the Lord to that of his redemptive activity. I will first discuss the visible aspect of the Christological revelation, viz. the cross,[146] because this subject can form a bridge between the two topics of Christ's identity and his activity.

Three issues stand out in our discussion of the cross: how far can the cross be said to represent Christ himself, what is its separating and uniting

[144] Cf. H. Schlier, *Religionsgeschichtliche Untersuchungen zu den Ignatiusbriefen*, Giessen 1929, 102; Schneider, *Mystery*, 116 n.1: 'One can argue that there are places in this revelatory discourse where he does disassociate himself from this "man". However, when he does so, we have also noted an affirmation of his presence on the cross. The man on the cross should be identified as one of the various manifestations for the spiritually immature/orthodox Christians' (cf. 106, 194).

[145] The uniqueness of the AJ is highlighted by Weigandt, *Doketismus*, and illustrated by the fact that Voorgang, *Passion*, found no parallels.

[146] If we pose a question about the shape of the cross, we are confronted with the fact that until the fourth century Christians hardly ever depicted the holy cross, see H.J. van Schalkwijk, *Kruisen. Een studie over het gebruik van kruistekens in de ontwikkeling van het godsdienstig en maatschappelijk leven*, Hilversum 1989, 84-118 (= ch.4). But Luttikhuizen, 'Gnostic reading', 134-135, is no doubt correct in thinking that the cross is here conceived as having the shape of a capital T, not that of Plato's X; cf. Schneider, *Mystery*, 96; *contra* Bousset, 'Weltseele und Kreuz'. One wonders how the author of the APe, who depends on the AJ, conceives the cross on which Peter is suspended upside down; a T upside down will not stand.

function, and what does it mean that it is a cross of *light*?[147] The whole paragraph is prefaced by a brief discussion of polymorphy, whereas the redemptive function of the cross is dealt with in later paragraphs.

### *4.3.1 Polymorphy in c.97*

Above I stated that the identity of the figure on the wooden cross (c.97.5-10) is not revealed by the text itself and can best be explained with the help of the concept of polymorphy. If this explanation is accepted, we see that c.97 contains three visible appearances of Christ, one on the wooden cross, one in the cave and one above the cross of light. These three occur to different persons at the same moment and thus are polymorphous appearances. At the same time they stand for three levels of understanding.[148]

Contrary to section B, the other gospel-like part of the AJ, section C does not make much use of polymorphy. The main reason for this is that section C hardly describes visible appearances of the Lord and emphasises the fact that he has no outer form (σχῆμα, 98.4); cc.94-96 and 98-101 wholly concentrate on his words and predicates. It would seem that our author uses the notion of polymorphy in so far as his narrative runs parallel to the Gospels and, in that sense, forms a continuation of cc.88-93; as soon as he deviates from the gospel story, he refrains from describing visible appearances and prefers the use of polyonymy.

### *4.3.2 Christ and the cross*

The reader will have noticed that the above discussion implies that I consider the cross of light as one of the polymorphous manifestations of Christ, even the one aimed at the highest level of understanding. Is this a valid assumption? Initially it seems that Christ and the cross are separate entities because he is above it (98.3-4).[149] As we continue to read and come to the list of Christological predicates, we see that these predicates are applied to the cross (98.8-12). The author evidently thinks of this cross as a manifestation of the Lord. The cross of light - clearly distinguished from the wooden cross (cf. 99.3-5) - is referred to as Christ, Bread, Father, etc. It shares an important characteristic of the Lord, viz. it can be given many names; it is in other words polyonymous. The impression of its

[147] The word cross only occurs in AJ 98-100. Words for crucifying occur in 44.7 (figurative use) and 97.6,9.

[148] Cf. Schneider, *Mystery*, 161; *pace* JK, 601 n.2, 602-603, who assume two separate persons within Christ.

[149] αὐτὸν δὲ τὸν κύριον ἐπάνω τοῦ σταυροῦ ἑώρων σχῆμα μὴ ἔχοντα ἀλλά τινα φωνὴν μόνον (98.3-4).

identification with the Lord is strengthened when it is said that the cross also reveals itself as Logos (99.1).[150] In later Manichaeism the cross of light is in principle the same as the suffering Christ, although connected with several pantheistic ideas that are not yet found in the AJ.[151]

These observations cause us to return to the statement which claims that Christ is ἐπάνω the cross. A brief survey suggests that the preposition ἐπάνω can mean 'at the head of' or 'on top of' as well as 'above'.[152] If this is correct, we should choose the translation most fitting to the context, which is certainly 'on top of'.

Not only is the cross of light closely related to or a manifestation of Christ, it also represents the unity of the redeemed Gnostics. As c.100 explains, they will be united in this very cross. We will discuss this statement in more detail below.[153]

*4.3.3 The cross as Horos*

In the description of the cross of light much emphasis falls on stability and separation. The Lord explains that this cross is 'the marking off (διορισμός) of all things and the uplifting and foundation of those things that are fixed but had been unstable' (98.14-15).[154] The first lines of c.99 repeat the same idea in other words, again using a form of ὁρίζω.[155] The cross is fixed (πεπηγμένον, 98.1) and itself has affirmed (διαπηξάμενος) all things (99.1). The imagery suggests that by means of the horizontal bar of the cross, which separates the divine realm above from the world below, the universe is divided into two parts. Men are likewise divided into two

150 Schneider, *Mystery*, 91, 117; A. Böhlig, 'Zum Vorstellung vom Lichtkreuz in Gnostizismus und Manichäismus', in his *Gnosis und Synkretismus* I, Tübingen 1989, 135-163, who translates the preposition ἐπάνω as 'oben am' (145) and argues: 'Jesus selbst wird mit dem Kreuz identifiziert. Infolgedessen werden alle auf Jesus angewendeten Prädikate auf das Kreuz übertragen' (148).

151 Rose, *Manichäische Christologie*, 100.

152 'Above' finds support in Mt 2:9, 27:37; Justin, *Apol* 1.60.6. 'At the head of' is best in Jn 3:31, and more literally of the bedside in Lk 4:39. 'On top of' occurs in reference to a building in Mt 5:14; Josephus, *Bell* 5.165, 167, *Ant Jud* 3.132; Hermas *Sim* 9.3.1, 9.4.2); 'on' denotes riding or sitting in Mt 21:7, 28:2; Rev 6:8. A remarkable phrase occurs in Hermas *Sim* 9.21.1: τὰ ἐπάνω τῶν βοτανῶν χλωρά, 'with the top of the herbs green'.

153 Schneider, *Mystery*, 93: 'In chapter 98, it is Christ as the perfect man that John perceives in the Cross of Light. The luminous cross is where the spiritual body of Christ, the perfect man, is elevated. In chapter 100, the topic is Christ's body as the incorporation of the members of the elect.'

154 Philo, *De opif.* 35-37, uses the word ὅρος when describing the process of creation as strengthening and as separation between light (day) and dark (night).

155 JK, 663-664 n.1.

groups: those who stand around the cross, who have diverse forms (100.1) and who must be non-believers or non-Gnostics (98.2) and those who are part of the cross, who will have one form when salvation is attained (98.3, 100.2-3) and who must be the Gnostics.[156] The revelation of the cross of light envisages men who join the cross and are given salvation.

The functions of separating and fastening ascribed to the cross also occur in other second-century texts. Valentinianism knows an aeon Horos (Limit) or Stauros which separates and fastens the lower and higher spheres,[157] but this idea also occurs in non-Valentinian texts.[158] In some AAA the cross as Logos is the ordering principle of the universe.[159] I surmise that these parallels document a transfer of the originally Christological functions of separation and fastening first to the Logos and the cross and later to a separate entity, Horos.[160]

[156] J. Bolyki, '"Head Downwards": The Cross of Peter in the Lights of the Apocryphal Acts, of the New Testament and of the Society-transforming Claim of Early Christianity', in Bremmer, *Acts of Peter*, 111-122, 118, states that already in the theology of Paul the cross has a separating and a unifying function: it 'separates believers from non-believers, but it unites believers who come from different national and religious backgrounds.'

[157] *Excerpta ex Theodoto* 42.1: Ὁ Σταυρὸς τοῦ ἐν Πληρώματι Ὅρου σημεῖόν ἐστιν· χωρίζει γὰρ τοὺς ἀπίστους τῶν πιστῶν ὡς ἐκεῖνος τὸν κόσμον τοῦ Πληρώματος. Cf. *ibid.* 26.2, 35.1, Irenaeus, *AdvHaer* 1.3.5, Hippolytus, *Refutatio* 6.31.5-6.

[158] AAn Mart.pr. 14 (Prieur, *Acta Andreae*, 698): πέπηξαι γὰρ ἐν κόσμῳ ἵνα τὰ ἄστατα στηρίξῃς (cf. G.Q. Reijners, *The terminology of the holy cross in early Christian literature*, Nijmegen 1965, 209-210), and the second-century homily *In Pascha*: P. Nautin (ed.), *Homélies pascales I. Une homélie inspirée du traité sur la Paque d'Hippolyte*, Paris 1950, 51.9: Τοῦτο δένδρον οὐρανόμηκες ἀπὸ γῆς εἰς οὐρανοὺς ἀνέβαινεν, ἀθάνατον φυτὸν στηρίξας ἑαυτὸν ἐν μέσῳ οὐρανοῦ τε καὶ γῆς, ἕδρασμα τῶν ὅλων, στήριγμα τοῦ παντός ... ἀνθρωπίνης οὐσίας συνεκτικόν κτλ. The Homily was attributed to Hippolytus of Rome, but R. Cantalamessa, *L'omelia 'In s.Pascha' dello pseudo-Ippolito di Roma*, Milan 1967 (English conclusions 461ff.), has shown that it dates from the second century and is related to Melito's *Peri Pascha*. It has even been argued that *In Pascha* is the second book about Easter which Eusebius attributes to Melito: Β.Ψευτόγκα, Μελίτωνος Σάρδεων Τά περί τοῦ Πάσχα δύο, Thessaloniki 1971, noted in H. Drobner, '15 Jahre Forschung zu Melito von Sardes (1965-1980). Eine kritische Bibliographie', *VigChr* 36 (1982) 313-333.

[159] Viz. in the APe and the AAn, see Bolyki, 'Head Downwards', 116.

[160] Philo attributes a similar function to the Logos (*De fuga et inv.* 112) and to God's Power (*De conf ling* 9, 137).

### *4.3.4 The cross of light*

The fact that the AJ is the earliest surviving text to mention the cross *of light* has so far been given very little attention.[161] This neglect can partly be explained by the fact that this element plays only a minor role in the text. Contrary to what might be expected, our author never makes an *explicit* connection between the cross and the light which, according to Gnostic mythology, was scattered throughout humanity. We are left with the question if he already knew this concept. Is it correct to suppose that the cross of light is a transitory phase in the development of the idea of the light-world?

As far as we can see the cross of light is a creation of the AJ's author.[162] But he did not conceive of it out of nothing. Second-century Christianity commonly spoke about the cross in tropes, as we saw in the metaphors in Pseudo-Hippolytus' *In Pascha* 51. To give a few other examples, in the *Gospel of Peter* 39-42 on Easter morning a huge cross follows Christ from the grave and becomes a speaking character; and Ignatius, *Tral* 11.2, adopts the image of the tree of life when he speaks about the 'branches' of the cross.[163] In addition, elements of the NT can possibly be seen as leading up to it: the association of Christ with light in diverse books[164] and the tendency in Pauline and Johannine writings to transcend the wooden cross.[165] Finally, the language of the mysteries in which light plays a large role may also have influenced our author.[166]

The cross of light is a total reversal of the shameful cross of the canonical Gospels and of Paul. A certain tendency to see the cross in a more glorious light is already evident in the Fourth Gospel, but the AJ spoils the paradox maintained in the Gospel so that the divine glory of Christ completely swallows his humanity and death.

### *4.4 Suffering and salvation*

The author's view of suffering is primarily found in cc.96 and 101, in which πάθος is a key word. In the above discussion, suffering has already been mentioned several times. I will now put together what our text states about it but start with what it denies.

161 Böhlig, 'Lichtkreuz', is meager; cf. the criticism by JK, 657.

162 *Pace* E. Dinkler, *Das Apsismosaik von S.Apollinare in Classe*, Köln/Opladen 1964, 82-83, who considers the cross in the *Gospel of Peter* as a cross of light.

163 F.J. Dölger, 'Beiträge zur Geschichte des Kreuzzeichens 9', *JbAC* 10 (1967) 28.

164 Mt 17:2; Lk 2:32; Jn 1:4, 5, 9; 3:19; 8:12; 9:5; 12:35-36, 46; Rev 21:23-24; later texts in Peterson, 'Hamburger Papyrusfragment', 206 n.86.

165 1 Cor 1:18; Phil 3:18, Jn 3:14; 12:32-33.

166 E.g. Apuleius, *Golden Ass*, 11.23.

*4.4.1 The cross no suffering*

For our author the suffering of the Lord is not connected with his crucifixion. It is explicitly said that his suffering has nothing to do with what happens on the irrelevant and 'misleading' wooden cross (97.8-9): only in the opinion of the multitude down in Jerusalem which represents the non-Gnostic Christians is Christ crucified. It is nevertheless remarkable that the text never denies that there was a wooden cross, albeit only as the manifestation of the polymorphous Lord that appears to non-Gnostics.[167] C.101 is another effort to explain the paradoxical message that the Lord suffered in a way different from what the readers would think. The polemics against the description of Christ's death on the cross in the canonical Gospels is resumed and reaches its summit: '... those things that they say of me I did not endure, and the things that they do not say those I suffered' (9-11). At the end of the section, the synonyms 'symbolically and as a dispensation' (συμβολικῶς καὶ οἰκονομικῶς, 102.5-6) are one more expression of the polemics against the 'ecclesiastical' view of the life and death of Christ.[168] The Lord has attained σωτηρία for humanity, but not in the way the readers of the canonical Gospels would believe, viz. not on the cross.[169]

We are left with the question about the reality of the Lord's crucifixion. The author refers to the story of the crucifixion and rejects it, without suggesting who else was crucified if not Christ. Despite his own critical attitude towards the Gospels, the author assumes that his readers are familiar with them and feels obligated to polemise against them. In the new 'Gospel as revealed to John', the reference to the wooden cross is no more than a polemical rejection of other Christians' conviction.

Above we considered examples of how the cross was used in the tropes of second-century Christianity. Such tropes leave the importance of the wooden cross intact and intend to make its meaning evident. In this respect they differ sharply from the AJ which does not recognise the wooden cross as having any meaning.

*4.4.2 Human suffering*

Christ does not suffer on the cross - yet the text emphasises that he does suffer. This first happens in the phrase 'For yours is this passion of man which I am to suffer' (ὅτι σόν ἐστιν τοῦτο τὸ ἀνθρώπου πάθος ὃ μέλλω πάσχειν, 96.4). It is noteworthy that Christ's suffering is

[167] Cf. the words of Hennecke quoted in n.141 above.

[168] Zahn, 'Wanderungen', 204-205.

[169] *Pace* Pulver, 'Jesu Reigen', 153, who states that the death of Christ is a 'Vorbild, als Typos. Durch diesen Anschein wird dem Menschen gesagt: tua res agitur.'

immediately connected with man's, and it is to this representative quality that we first turn.

Human suffering is never explicitly defined in cc.97-102, but, in his dance, Christ gives a non-rational insight into it as he acts as the mouthpiece of mankind.[170] Suffering is man's restless errantry in darkness before the reception of the divine revelation.[171] Especially in 95.31-42 the Lord imitates human instability in order to confront mankind with its condition. He offers himself to humanity as a lamp, a mirror, a door and a way (95.43-50). Salvation means to recognise the Lord, to come to rest and to find stability in him (96.1-10).

From this perspective, the idea that mankind suffers because it lives in chaos and instability appears also in the description of the cross of light. Those who are (as yet) separate from it do not have only one form (98.2, 100.1). The stabilising work of the cross (99.1-3) creates a place of rest (99.7), but the one form will only be restored when men are lifted up (100.2-4). The description of suffering easily shades into that of salvation. To sum up, without proper knowledge of Christ mankind lacks stability and 'one form'. This view of human suffering is much more pessimistic than that in section A, where suffering merely pertains to the vicissitudes of life and where stability can be achieved by conversion leading to resurrection. Here existence as such is suffering.

I would therefore propose an emendation of the text in 98.16, a change that would involve reading a negation (μή) before the enumeration of the twelve chaotic elements in 98.16-19. These elements just cannot have a positive meaning for our author, nor can they be connected with the state of harmonious wisdom. According to my proposal, after it has been said that the cross is the ordering element of all and the harmonisation of wisdom, we read: 'When Wisdom is *not* in harmony, there are those on the right and those on the left, etc.' This correction has the concomitant advantage that it explains the repetition of the words Wisdom and harmony in two consecutive lines:

> But in truth, as known to itself and as spoken to us, it (the cross) is the marking off of all things and the uplifting and foundation of those things that are fixed but had been unstable, and the harmony of the wisdom. Yet when Wisdom is *not* in harmony, there are those on the right and those on the left, etc.

Thus the text argues that before salvation takes place, chaos reigns,

[170] See the observation of JK, 603, that Christ is the 'porte-parole de la "souffrance" des êtres pneumatiques', also quoted in n.139 above.
[171] Sturhahn, *Christologie*, 29.

whereas the stabilising effect of the cross results in harmony.[172] Read in this way, c.98 expresses the same view of suffering as cc.95-96, viz. that it is an all-encompassing lack of harmony.

*4.4.3 The true suffering of Christ*

The text never defines the suffering of the Lord,[173] but careful reading demonstrates that Christ's πάθος is a synonym for the whole of his revelatory existence as the Logos and the cross.[174] He has come to share man's instability and errantry (96.4-6). His appearance as the Logos means that he takes upon himself the suffering that is connected with all earthly existence (101.12-14). Specific qualities of the Lord's suffering are his descent from heaven and his incompleteness as a result of his members' not being unified. In the latter sense the suffering of the Lord *is* the suffering of man. The dispersion of the potential Gnostics causes him to suffer. He is at present somehow deficient and the unification of the Gnostics with him (100.3-4) also means his restoration. His task is to suffer with the people, in this way showing them their own salvation. This thought comes close to the words of Theodotus: συμπάθειν εἰς διόρθωσιν τοῦ παθόντος (*Excerpta* 30, cf. 31).[175] The song and dance of Christ express his suffering which is also their suffering. In the song and dance, or rather in Christ himself as a mirror (95.45-46), men see their real identity. They have no stability in the world because like the Lord, they are not at home here.

The Christ of this text is no less in need of salvation than man. Therefore his suffering must primarily bring about his own salvation. This priority is especially expressed by the phrase 'I want to be saved' (95.2). In the use of 'I want' (θέλω, 96.18) the personal necessity of the harmonisation of man with the Lord can also be heard.

172 I take the phrase to refer to the present state of the cosmos and man in it, not to cosmogony, in which the AJ has no interest.

173 Cf. JK, 605.

174 Schlier, *Untersuchungen*, 70-72. His remark on 163 n.1 that the use of the word πάθος in c.103 differs from that in cc.96 and 101 is a precursor of Junod and Kaestli's source criticism, in which cc.94-102 (my section C) are distinguished as the Gnostic parts of the text.

175 R. Cantalamessa, 'Les homélies pascales de Méliton des Sardes et du Pseudo-Hippolyte et les Extraits de Théodote', in *Epektasis. Mélanges Jean Daniélou*, Paris 1972, 263-271, esp. 263-265, shows that these words are combatted by Melito.

### *4.4.4 Salvation*

The understanding which flows from the song and dance and their explanation results in redemption. The onlookers of the dance and the readers of the text should come to regard themselves as subject to suffering in this world.[176] According to c.96, understanding of Christ's suffering is the door to humanity's self-understanding: his appearance (6) and example have a redemptive significance, for now mankind can see (1) in him as in a mirror that they are suffering, and this knowledge (19, 26) establishes a state of harmony with him (14-18). He is the way from suffering to bliss.[177] Another way to express this point is to say that men will be lifted up into the cross (see below).

The words 'not yet all' (οὐδέπω τὸ πᾶν, 100.3) imply that saving knowledge is eventually available for everybody. For the time being, the term kinsman (συγγενὴς, 101.6) is reserved for John who as a real Gnostic shares in the unification of the divine essence.

In the AJ salvation is not redemption from guilt, but the gift of knowledge and unification; Christ is the one who helps people to redeem themselves.[178] Clement of Alexandria's criticism that the Valentinians in fact think that they save themselves, applies with equal right to the AJ.[179]

### *4.4.5 The role of the cross of light*

What is the function of the cross-Logos in the process of salvation? We have a key to this problem in the fact that the cross-Logos is not only a revelation of Christ, but also incorporates all humans who have been saved.[180] Thus the cross has Christological and anthropological features. It denotes Christ's ordering and limiting function discussed above as well as the unification of humans when they enter the cross and regain 'one form'. In contrast, those who are outside the cross do not yet have the one form (98.2-3). When Gnostic Christians are united into the cross of light,

[176] Pulver, 'Jesu Reigen', 172-173, correctly argues that in the suffering of Christ the suffering of humanity is mirrored; left and right are shifted; God seemingly suffers and man suffers until he has been initiated, that is, divinised. (I would rather say that man is restored to his true self.) Cf. Schneider, *Mystery*, 184-185.

[177] Cf. Weigandt, *Doketismus*, 85, 150-151.

[178] Weigandt, *Doketismus*, 151.

[179] Clement, *Strom* 4.91.2-3.

[180] Schneider, *Mystery*, 112: '... the supernatural cross - the Logos - represents the collective identity of the elect.'

they regain their original status.[181]

C.100 concentrates on the future aspect of salvation which will take place when everyone will be gathered in the cross. The concept of ascension above the cross implies association and unification of Christ and men ('those in the cross', 100.2).[182] Redemption thus consists in imitating Christ (cf. 101.6). When mankind enters into the cross and is lifted above it just as Christ is above it, humanity assumes the one form (98.3-5, 100.4-7). Christ then will be as he was before and all suffering will be ended (96.14-15). To be sure, this elevation of mankind is still in the future because it awaits the unification of all members in the cross.

The way in which the text here speaks about Christians recalls the concept of particles of divine light fallen into the world, a conception well known as part of Gnostic mythology.[183] The fact that the Logos is identified with the cross of light also suggests a resemblance with the idea of the particles of the divine Logos that are spread over the world. A 'collection of members' (100.3-4) occurs in several other Gnostic texts[184] as well in two passages which are attributed to Melito and which are not obviously Gnostic.[185]

### *4.4.6 The meaning of 'man' (ἄνθρωπος)*

Several times the word ἄνθρωπος is used in connection with the theme of suffering and a closer look at this word will bring us to the heart of the text's concept of suffering and salvation. The key question is whether the

[181] These ideas probably owe much to Jn 11, 14-17 with their stress on the importance of being 'in Christ' and unity among the believers. Cf. Garcia, *Polymorphie*, 73, who remarks that in John's Gospel as in the AJ it is the cross which separates believers and non-believers, and that in Jn 17:5 it is Christ who preexists, not the believers. One might also compare 1 Cor 15:47-49.

[182] The same is expressed in *Excerpta ex Theodoto* 67.

[183] Luttikhuizen, 'Gnostic reading', 135-137.

[184] Cf. Irenaeus, *AdvHaer* 1.30.14; *Excerpta ex Theodoto* 22.3, where the human *pneumata* are the female counterparts of the angels (cf. Sagnard, *Gnose*, 557; *pace* JK, 606 n.2).

[185] The first is Fragment 13 (ed. Perler, 238): *vivificaret hominem et colligeret membra eius*. It would seem that *eius* here refers to *hominem* and not to Christ. This explanation is confirmed by Melito's *Peri Pascha* 55, which explains what he means: because of sin man desintegrated into his constituent parts (cf. *ibid.* 67), which must be restored by salvation through Christ. The other passage is Melito, New Fragment 2.4: (*Filius*) *natus est homo et resuscitavit perditum hominem, et collegit membra dispersa*. This text is preserved in Georgian, see M. Van Esbroeck, 'Nouveaux fragments de Méliton de Sardes dans une homélie géorgienne sur la croix', *AnBol* 90 (1972) 63-99, esp. 75, who regards them as fragments of the treatise *Peri Psyches* (99); English trans. in S.G. Hall (ed.), *Melito of Sardis,* On Pascha *and Fragments*, Oxford 1979, 87.

word refers to human beings only or also to Christ, and if so, how the latter use is connected with the former. Junod and Kaestli explain ἄνθρωπος primarily as a reference to mankind, but on the other hand they generally write Homme with a capital letter and include ἄνθρωπος among the Christological titles. They state: 'Au ch.98, c'est le Christ comme Homme parfait que Jean aperçoit dans la Croix de lumière' and 'La Croix de lumière est donc le lieu où est élevé le corps spirituel du Christ, l'Homme parfait, prémices de toute l'humanité pneumatique. Au ch.100, ce même corps du Christ, ce même Ἄνθρωπος est considéré sous son aspect collectif, ecclésiologique.'[186] This apparently ambiguous position will be tested below.

In the past scholars held that the AJ and many other early Christian texts should be read against the background of an hypothetical ἄνθρωπος myth,[187] but that idea has largely been abandoned,[188] not least because even Philo does not yet know an ἄνθρωπος myth.[189]

[186] JK, resp. 603 n.4, 588, 608, 609.

[187] E.g. R. Bultmann, 'Die Bedeutung der neuerschlossenen mandäischen und manichäischen Quellen für das Verständnis des Johannesevangeliums', *ZNW* 24 (1925) 100-146; Schlier, *Untersuchungen*, 6-8, 103-107, 162, 172-173 with n.3. In order to strengthen his case, Schlier adapts 76.35-36 (ἄνθρωπος θέλω γενέσθαι τῶν ἐπὶ Χριστὸν ἐλπιζόντων, I want to become a man of those who hope in Christ) to Ign *Rom* 6.2 (ἐκεῖ παραγενόμενος ἄνθρωπος ἔσομαι) by removing the words 'those who hope in Christ' from the text; Pulver, 'Jesu Reigen', *passim*; Sturhahn, *Christologie*, *passim* (who in n.35/1 distinguishes an earthly and a heavenly ἄνθρωπος); H.M. Schenke, *Der Gott 'Mensch' in der Gnosis*, Göttingen 1962, who on 14 argues that AJ 100 includes 'ein göttliches Wesen mit der Bezeichnung ἄνθρωπος', but on 103-105 explains c.100 as dealing with the descent of the primordial man - 'Urmensch', to be distinguished from Christ - whose divine aspects are not considered; more recently to a certain extent Sirker-Wicklaus, *Untersuchungen*, esp. 146, 148, 151.

[188] See C. Colpe, *Die Religionsgeschichtliche Schule. Darstellung und Kritik ihres Bildes vom gnostischen Erlösermythus*, Göttingen 1961; Yamauchi, *Pre-Christian Gnosticism*; and Pétrement, *Dieu séparé*, 147-181, who suggests that the complete myth occurs no earlier than in Manichaeism (148, 160, 165); with specific reference to John's Gospel see also G. van den Brink, 'Gnostische verlosser of geïncarneerde wijsheid?', *Soteria* 14.1 (1997) 14-25; JK, 603 n.4, likewise deny the existence of a myth of primeval man. Evans, *Word and Glory*, 18-20, provides good criteria for the reconstruction of a myth from later texts and the assumption of its existence at an earlier moment. He argues that this procedure is only valid if the following are present: external documentation, the exclusion of the possibility of contamination, suitable (geographic) provenance, and explanatory value.

[189] B.A. Pearson, 'Philo, Gnosis and the New Testament', in Logan and Wedderburn, *NT and Gnosis*, 73-89, esp. 77-80; *idem*, 'Philo and Gnosticism', *ANRW* II.21.1 (1983) 295-342; Wedderburn, 'Philo's "Heavenly Man"' (with reference especially to *De conf ling* 41,

Turning to the text, I first of all observe that ἄνθρωπος occurs with reference to mankind in 96.4 (clearly distinguished from Christ who is the speaker), in 97.11-12 (used parallel to 'disciple' and denoting John), and in c.102. The word is absent from the lists of Christological predicates in cc.98 and 109 as well as from c.94, which implies that it is not one of the regular designations of Christ.

There are two occurrences of ἄνθρωπος in c.109. The Messianic title Son of man is used in the list of Christological predicates without any indication of what the author means by it, so that we cannot regard its use as more than an echo of Gospel vocabulary. Secondly, John ends his prayer with the words: '... your greatness ... which is only visible to the pure, solely in the image of the man portrayed in you.' (... σου τὸ μέγεθος ... καθαροῖς δὲ θεωρητὸν μόνον ἐν τῷ μόνῳ σου ἀνθρώπῳ εἰκονιζόμενον, 109.15-17). Lipsius translates: '... indem sie allein in dem dir angehörigen Menschen abgebildet wird' and comments that in the ἄνθρωπος we have to do with the man who belongs to Christ, viz. the Gnostic.[190] I agree with this explanation of the text which implies that ἄνθρωπος refers to (Gnostic) man. But these words can easily been taken as calling Christ ἄνθρωπος.[191]

A more 'technical' use of ἄνθρωπος occurs in c.100, where we read about 'the nature of man' that 'shall be taken up'.[192] The phrase in which the word occurs parallels the following phrases, as is made clear in Elliott's translation:

62, 146); Runia, *Philo and the* Timaeus, esp. 248-249, 335, 467-475; T.H. Tobin, *The creation of man: Philo and the history of interpretation*, Washington 1983, 102-108, 132-134; Evans, *Word and Glory*, 104-105; (from another point of view) W.E. Helleman, 'Philo of Alexandria on deification and assimilation to God', *The Studia Philonica Annual* 2 (1990) 51-71; Holzhausen, *Mythos*. In Philo see e.g. his concept of two types of men in *Leg all* 1.31-32.

190 Lipsius, *Apostelgeschichten*, 533-534; cf. Hennecke, *Handbuch*, 539.

191 So Sturhahn, *Christologie*, 28, and JK, 303 n.7, cf. 609-610.

192 Junod and Kaestli, following Schlier, *Untersuchungen*, 97, emend: ἀνθρώπου φύσις κτλ. Manuscript **C** (see James, *Apocrypha anecdota*, 20; JK, 211) has: ὅταν δὲ ἀναλημφθῇ ἄνοι (= ἄνθρωποι) φύσις καὶ γένος προσχωροῦν ἐπ' ἐμὲ κτλ.; this reading is defended by Schneider, *Mystery*, 113-118 (one line accidentally absent after 114 line 1), but his translation 'human nature' would require ἀνθρωπίνη or ἀνθρωπική; one wonders if Schneider noticed the awkwardness of the Greek. Instead of the underlined word James in the *editio princeps* proposed: ἡ ἄνω φύσις κτλ., a reading motivated by the idea that one might expect something in antithesis to ἡ κατωτικὴ φύσις (line 1-2); see James, *Apocrypha anecdota*, 20: '*patet hic* τῇ κατωτικῇ φύσει *aliquid opponi; quid autem, nisi* ἡ ἄνω φύσις?' But not only is there a whole sentence in between the supposed antipodes, there is no proof that an antithesis is intended.

But when the nature of man (ἄνθρωπος) shall be taken up,
and the race which comes to me in obedience to my voice,
then he who now hears me shall be united with it.

Junod and Kaestli argue that the phrase 'the nature of man' is parallel to the phrase 'he who came down' in the sentence before ('That is because every member of him who came down has not yet been gathered together', 100.3-4), and that both phrases refer to the lack of a unified nature in the multitude.[193] But in my opinion the one 'who came down' is Christ, whereas we never read that mankind came down or originated in heaven. The word ἄνθρωπος here refers to the company of Gnostic Christians and does not directly designate the Saviour. But the position and meaning of the word ἄνθρωπος may well be deliberately ambiguous here: the author associates mankind and the Lord. The Lord came down in order to assemble humans who listen to him and to resurrect them in the cross through his intervention. Salvation ends the chaotic pluriformity of human existence and brings rest in the cross.

At the end of the revelation (101.14-16) ἄνθρωπος occurs twice: 'And so grasping man (ἄνθρωπον), I say: first think of (the) Logos, then you shall think of (the) Lord, and thirdly of the man (ἄνθρωπον) and what he has suffered.'[194] The first part of this phrase is hard to explain because of its brevity - several words may have been lost - and because of the many possible meanings of the verb χωρέω with which ἄνθρωπον is associated in this context.[195] In the preceding lines reference has been made to the Lord's revelation as the suffering Logos, which suggests that now the same Lord is designated as ἄνθρωπον, but this possibility cannot be more than a tentative conclusion.

Different interpretations of the meaning of the second part of the phrase, in which ἄνθρωπος stands in close connection with Logos and Lord, have been proposed.[196] The differences in opinion are caused by

[193] JK, 668.

[194] καὶ οὕτως χωρήσας ἄνθρωπον λέγω· τὸ μὲν οὖν πρῶτον λόγον νόησον, εἶτα κύριον νοήσεις, τὸν δὲ ἄνθρωπον τρίτον καὶ τὸ τί πέπονθεν.

[195] Taken as it stands, χωρήσας can either mean 'having made place' or 'finding room for', 'comprehending', 'containing' (cf. Mt 19:11, 12a.b; Ign *Tral* 5.1). James and Bonnet read χωρίσας ('separating off, distinguishing') which is possible in view of the similar pronunciation of the vocals. If the word requires emendation, the conjecture χορεύσας ('having danced', cf. 97.1) could also be considered because the context clearly demands a positive, confirmatory word.

[196] JK, 674, state: '... les trois appellations se rapportent chacune à un aspect de la personne du Sauveur qui s'est manifesté ici-bas.' This causes them to explain ἄνθρωπος thus: 'l'ensemble des hommes spirituels, que le Logos a assumé lorsqu'il s'est uni avec Jésus, "le Seigneur"' (675). They complicate the picture by adducing several three-part descriptions of

the ambiguity in the text, which is anything but accidental. On the one hand, the qualification 'what he has suffered' to ἄνθρωπον establishes a parallel with 96.4 which, as we saw, speaks about human suffering. As in c.96, the Lord explains that full understanding of his divine nature and his suffering will lead to insight into one's own suffering and to consequent salvation.[197] On the other hand, ἄνθρωπον is deliberately placed next to the Christological predicates Logos and Lord. Thus its use here comes close to qualifying mankind as the members of Christ because man and Christ suffer in the same way.[198] And that is at the same time the message of the text; the Lord and mankind suffer in the same way and are saved in the same way; they are able to leave the earth behind and then to unite. We see that in 101.14 and 101.16 ἄνθρωπον is used with deliberate ambiguity: it denotes humanity and is at the same time a Christological predicate. Consequently, the word signals the parallel fates of the Lord and men and points to the essential identity of the two. To understand this unity is to attain salvation.

We conclude that in the AJ ἄνθρωπος still primarily denotes mankind as earthly beings in need of salvation who must be united (the text never says reunited!) with Christ. The word is clearly not part of the stock of Christological titles which the author inherited from his predecessors. It highlights both the present (collective) identity of the saved and the future state of salvation. There is no outright identification of Christ and ἄνθρωπος, but the text assumes such a close connection between them that its readers are induced to employ the word ἄνθρωπος to denote Christ. As a result, the AJ takes an important step towards the incorporation of ἄνθρωπος into the developing Gnostic myth. The concepts of ἄνθρωπος and the cross go together in expressing the mystery of salvation, which lies in the identification of the saved humans with the divine.

### *4.5 Comparison with other Gnostic conceptions*

The reader will have noticed that the present interpretation makes less use of parallels to other Gnostic texts than most earlier interpretations,

Christ in the *Excerpta ex Theodoto*, none of which is a real parallel. Schneider, *Mystery*, 110-113, explains the three words as: the cross of light, the Lord as the one who danced, and the Lord as the man on the wooden cross; cf. his 'historic' interpretation of c.97 noted above.

[197] Notice that the verb νοέω is used, not γινώσκω. I take this as an indication that technical terms are not available.

[198] Luttikhuizen, 'Gnostic reading', 141-142: 'Here the aspect of the Lord as 'Man' rather serves to warrant his identity with the human light particles in the world.'

especially that of Junod and Kaestli. I have shown that section C has several features in common with other Gnostic texts, that it also shares elements with texts from the main church, and that important aspects are more or less unique to it. Let it be understood that the present exegesis is no effort to play down the Gnostic character of this section of the AJ, but an effort to bring out the peculiarity of its form of Gnosis as well as the fluency of boundaries between second-century Christians groups.

Voorgang has established that many Gnostic texts give little or no attention to the passion of Christ and that a complete story of the passion is nowhere to be found. For most Gnostic texts it cannot even be established if they were based on oral traditions or on the written Gospels.[199] Against this background, sections B and C of the AJ stand out as an exceptional example of a Gnostic gospel. Contrary to common Gnostic practice, section C not only never denies that the Lord suffered but also understands his passion as something beneficial to the Gnostics. If Voorgang is correct, it is the only known Gnostic text to do so.[200]

The question whether the AJ is a Valentinian text is hard to answer because no generally accepted definition of Valentinianism exists.[201] It is often regarded as a more 'Christian' form of Gnosis, having been influenced to a large extent by New Testament writings.[202] Given this evidently circular stipulation, the Christocentric AJ almost by definition belongs to Valentinianism.[203] In the AJ as well as in Valentinianism the Saviour is Jesus or Christ, and in both the Logos plays an important role. The fact that these features are absent from Sethianism confirms the usual labeling. On the other hand, there are clear differences between the AJ and Valentinianism. The AJ basically regards the Lord as one person manifested in several polymorphous and polyonymous ways, whereas Valentinianism normally distinguishes between Jesus and Christ or in

[199] Voorgang, *Passion*, 241, 250-251; out of 53 Nag Hammadi texts, only 22 mention the passion; just 8 have a discussion of it. Voorgang, 246-249, provides a list of elements of the passion traditions that appear in these texts.

[200] Voorgang, *Passion*, 258.

[201] M. Desjardins, 'The sources for Valentinian Gnosticism: a question of methodology', *VigChr* 40 (1986) 342-347, discusses the differences of opinion, signalling that the list of tractates from Nag Hammadi that are considered Valentinian differs almost from scholar to scholar.

[202] Sagnard, *Gnose*, 602: 'C'est un fait que les Valentiniens sont issus des chrétiens.' *Ibid.*, 604: 'Cet emploi constant de l'Écriture Sainte est un des caractères les plus saillants de la gnose *valentinienne*' (italics his).

[203] JK discuss the Valentinianism of the AJ on 589-593, 606, 612-614, 627-632 and generally stress the similarities. Cf. the comments of Schneider, *Mystery*, 105, 142-143, 205-206.

another way assumes a double Christ.[204] Another difference can be seen between the simple anthropology of the AJ which lacks any distinctions between pneumatics, psychics and hylics, and the ideas of the Valentinians in this respect. Again, the AJ lacks the common detailed discussions about pleroma and the aeons. In the AJ the very name Horos is absent, whereas in Valentinianism Christ and Horos are distinct aeons.[205] Though our author mentions a whole range of celestial elements (98.16-19), he never uses the word aeons.[206] As I argued above, the AJ has no interest in cosmogony. Even if we call the entities in 95.18-39 aeons, the cosmology at the background of the AJ is undeveloped.[207] It may be admitted that there are more Valentinian texts which do not spell out the complete myth, such as the *Letter to Flora* and the Fragments of Heracleon.[208] But to modern readers it is not even clear if the word 'wisdom' (*sophia*, AJ 96.19, 98.15, 16) should be spelled with a capital letter.[209] The ideas that Irenaeus ascribes to Valentinus (*AdvHaer* 1.11.1) are indeed much more involved than those of the AJ.[210]

Taking everything together, it is evident that the differences outweigh the similarities and that the AJ cannot be labeled Valentinian.[211] I agree with Schlier's suggestion that the AJ contains a pre-Valentinian form of Gnosis.[212] Or is it too bold to suggest that our section C fills the gap in our knowledge between the Valentinus of the testimonies discussed by

[204] So already Weigandt, *Doketismus*, 6-9.

[205] According to Irenaeus, Valentinus himself distinguished two Limits: *AdvHaer* 1.11.1: (Οὐαλεντῖνος) ὅρους τε δύο ὑπέθετο, ἕνα μὲν μεταξὺ τοῦ Βυθοῦ καὶ τοῦ λοιποῦ Πληρώματος, διορίζοντα τοὺς γεννητοὺς Αἰῶνας ἀπὸ τοῦ ἀγεννήτου πατρός, ἕτερον δὲ τὸν ἀφορίζοντα αὐτῶν τὴν μητέρα ἀπὸ τοῦ Πληρώματος.

[206] JK, 613-614, argue that 98.16-19 refer to the origin of the world. This interpretation challenges the Christological focus of the text because these lines should rather refer to the present or future activity of Christ.

[207] On the Gnostic background of 95.14-15 (νοῦς) and 35-36 (τὸ ἕν) see JK, 648 n.6, 649 n.11.

[208] JK, 628.

[209] Cf. JK, 653-654 n.11.

[210] Zahn, 'Wanderungen', esp. 215, attributes the AJ to a Valentinian and regards the absence of the myth as an adaptation for non-Gnostic readers; in view of the fierce polemics of the text this is unlikely.

[211] So also, with different motivation, Sirker-Wicklaus, *Untersuchungen*, 126. Schneider, 'Gnostic Transformation', 249-251, indicates both 'Sethian' and Valentinian elements.

[212] Schlier, *Unterschungen*, esp. 105, 107, 110.

Markschies and the mature Valentinus known to Irenaeus?[213]

*4.6 A note on the reception of the Acts of John*

Junod and Kaestli have written a separate book on the reception of the AJ in the period when the complete text is still traceable, i.e. until the ninth century.[214] Although the text's reception is not my subject, a supplementary remark regarding the σταυρὸς φωτοειδής is warranted.

In the second century, the cross of Christ was connected with the parousia (on the Mount of Olives), as a result of the idea that the sign of Christ's return mentioned in Mt 24:30a is no other than the cross. Evidence for this theologoumenon includes *Didache* 16.6, *Epistula Apostolorum* 16, the Ethiopic *Apocalypse of Peter* 1, and the *Apocalypse of Elijah*.[215] A further development is evident in the fourth-century writings of Cyril of Jerusalem, who assumes that the cross of the parousia is a cross *of light*. In one of his Catechetical Lectures he argues that φωτειδοῦς σταυροῦ σημεῖον προάγει τὸν βασιλέα.[216] It would be interesting to trace where this idea comes from and to see if the AJ was influential in its inception.

The person of Cyril is even more interesting because some time after his just mentioned Catechetical Lectures, on May 7th, 351 to be specific, an appearance of the cross of light was seen by the inhabitants of Jerusalem in the sky above the city. As an eyewitness to this event, the very same Cyril, then bishop of Jerusalem, writes:

> During these holy days of the holy Paschal season, on the Nones of May at about nine in the morning, a gigantic luminous cross was seen in the sky above holy Golgotha, extending as far as the holy Mount of

[213] This suggestion could find support in the central idea of Holzhausen, *Mythos*, esp. 151, 231, that Valentinus is an early Gnostic. There is a tendency among modern scholars to ascribe texts to Valentinus, but no suggestion has so far gained general approval; see Markschies, *Valentinus*, and the literature quoted there.

[214] Junod and Kaestli, *Histoire*.

[215] *Apocalypse of Elijah* (ed. Schrage) 32.4 = ed. Rosenstiehl 3.3. Dinkler, *Classe*, 95, 98, dates the AJ to the third century and states that in the AJ 'die ältere eschatologische Konzeption vom σταυρὸς φωτοειδής ... von einer kosmologischen Vorstellung verschlungen' is; 'Aber der eigentliche Sinn der die Parusie einleitenden Kreuzes-Epiphanie ist preisgegeben' (98). This view overlooks the fact that the second-century eschatological concepts never mention a cross *of light*.

[216] Cat. 15.22, ed. Reischl-Rupp, München 1848-1860, p.184, as quoted in Kretschmar, 'Festkalender', 190, trans. E.H. Gifford, New York 1894; Ph. Häuser, München 1922; L.P. McCauley and A.A. Stephenson, Washington D.C. 1970, which includes the Letter to Constantius (see below). The date given for the delivery of the catecheses varies but always lies before AD 351 (cf. Kretschmar, 175 n.30); however, A. Doval, 'The Date of Cyril of Jerusalem's Catecheses', *JTS* 48 (1997) 129-132 argues for AD 351.

Olives; not seen by one or two only, but clearly visible to the whole population of the city.[217]

We meet the cross of light again in the sixth-century mosaic of the return of Christ in the church S.Apollinare in Classe (Ravenna). The work displays a remarkable combination of three elements: the cross of light, the return of Christ and his transfiguration. Christ is represented by a cross of gold set off with jewels (*crux gemmata*) on which his head appears in a small medallion. The cross is on the Eastern wall of the church and appears to float in the air, a most certain indication that it represents the parousia. Is Erich Dinkler correct when this scholar who specialised in the interpretation of this mosaic argues that it was composed by somebody who knew the AJ?[218] The element of the Classe mosaic which is new in comparison with the writings of Cyril, viz. the connection between the transfiguration and the parousia, can already be found in the NT (2 Pe 2).[219] In the AJ there is indeed also some attention paid to the transfiguration (cc.90-91) as well as to the cross of light, but they are not directly connected. Moreover, it would be hard to find a reference to the parousia in the AJ. Therefore direct influence from the AJ on the Classe mosaic is not likely.

Other references to the cross of light occur in the *Acts of Philip* (3.12; appendix II.27, 32, 35).[220] It is also the sign which appears in Eusebius' account of the divine vision granted to the later emperor Constantine in 312.[221] Much later, in one of Macarius' homilies there is a reference to

[217] Ἐν γὰρ ταῖς ἁγίαις ἡμέραις ταύταις τῆς ἁγίας πεντηκοστῆς, νόνναις μαΐαις, περὶ τρίτην ὥραν, παμμεγέθης ὁ σταυρός, ἐκ φωτὸς κατεσκευασμένος, ἐν οὐρανῷ ὑπεράνω τοῦ ἁγίου Γολγοθᾶ μέχρι τοῦ ἁγίου Ὄρους τῶν ἐλαιῶν ἐκτεταμένος ἐφαίνετο· οὐχ ἑνὶ καὶ δευτέρῳ μόνον φανεὶς ἀλλὰ παντὶ τῷ τῆς πόλεως πλήθει φανερώτατα δειχθεὶς κτλ. E. Bihain, 'L'épître de Cyrille de Jérusalem à Constance sur la vision de la croix (BHG$^3$ 413)', *Byzantion* 43 (1973) 264-296, esp. 288. Trans. McCauley and Stephenson, 232. Cf. Kretschmar, 'Festkalender', 190-191. Cyril links this appearance with Mt 24:30 and the parousia.

[218] Dinkler, *Classe*, 95-98; cf. 77-105 for a complete analysis of the conceptual background of the mosaic; F.W. Deichmann, *Ravenna. Hauptstadt des spätantiken Abendlandes* I, Wiesbaden 1969, esp. 261-269.

[219] Dinkler, *Classe*, 88-89.

[220] = § 133, 138, 141 Bonnet; see Amsler, Bovon, Bouvier, *Actes de Philippe*, who think of an Asiatic origin (80).

[221] ἀμφὶ μεσημβρινὰς ἡλίου ὥρας, ἤδη τῆς ἡμέρας ἀποκλινούσης, αὐτοῖς ὀφθαλμοῖς ἰδεῖν ἔφη ἐν αὐτῷ οὐρανῷ ὑπερκείμενον τοῦ ἡλίου σταυροῦ τρόπαιον ἐκ φωτὸς συνιστάμενον, γραφήν τε αὐτῷ συνῆφθαι λέγουσαν· τούτῳ νίκα. Eusebius, *Vita Constantini* (ed. F. Winkelmann), Berlin 1975, § 28.2. For a critical discussion of this and other accounts of the vision see J.N. Bremmer, 'Het bekeringsvisioen van Constantijn de

the sign of the cross of light.[222]

## 5 Implications

In this final paragraph, we will first deal with the question about the AJ's relationship to docetic Christology, and then look at the differences and the agreements between the Gnostic and the non-Gnostic parts of our text, drawing together the results of the separate discussions of the two main parts. It is no longer necessary to distinguish between sections A and B. Finally, we sketch the position of the AJ within the Christology of the second century.

### *5.1 The Acts of John and docetism*

We have seen that polymorphy, polyonymy and Christomonism are important factors in the Christology of the AJ. These labels never occur in the Christological discussions of the Early Church or the modern period. We have seen above (par. 1.8) that Christonomism differs from Monarchianism or Modalism. In what follows I will investigate if the polymorphy and polyonymy of the AJ can be regarded as a form of docetism. On a closer look, however, the term docetism contains its own problems: there is no generally agreed definition of it. I will first give a brief survey of opinions about the issues involved, after which I will propose my own definition.[223]

#### *5.1.1 What is docetism?*

The obscurity enveloping the concept of docetism is at least partly caused by the fact that it is uncertain which groups or persons in the Early Church should be considered docetists. Unlike most labels used by the Fathers, the word itself is not derived from a personal name. It comes from the Greek verb δοκεῖν, which appears in the context of Christological contests as far back as Ignatius, who writes: 'But if ... he suffered only apparently - but it

Grote', in H.S. Benjamins *et al.* (eds.), *Evangelie en beschaving. FS Roldanus*, Zoetermeer 1995, 49-67, esp. 56-60.

[222] Hom. 8, ed. H. Dörries, E. Klostermann and M. Kroeger, Berlin 1964; Dutch in J.H. van de Bank, *Macarius en zijn invloed in de Nederlanden*, Dissertation Utrecht 1977, 140-141.

[223] There is still no published monograph on the subject, cf. M. Slusser, 'Docetism: A Historical Definition', *The Second Century* 1 (1981) 163-172, 163; and A.K.M. Adam, 'Docetism, Käsemann, and Christology. Why Historical Criticism Can't Protect Christological Orthodoxy', *SJT* 49 (1996) 391-410, esp. 392-399.

is they who exist only apparently - ... ' (*Tral* 10, cf. *Smyr* 2).[224] He defends the reality of the suffering of the Lord and suggests that those who deny it are themselves 'ghostlike'.[225]

As a designation for a group of people, the term 'docetists' is too rare to be helpful.[226] As far as our sources go, it occurs for the first time in a letter of bishop Serapion of Antioch (190-211 AD) with reference to people who read the *Gospel of Peter*.[227] The reference to docetists in Clement of Alexandria (*Strom* 7.108.2) does not really help to clarify the issue. Much more elaborate but very difficult to use is what Hippolytus writes (*Refutatio* 8.8-11). Modern scholars doubt whether he is correct in saying that a certain Gnostic group called themselves Docetists; in any case the group he describes has complicated ideas which are far removed from what is usually called docetism.[228]

The scarcity of ancient sources leaves the way open for modern scholars to define docetism. The definition of F.C. Baur is very broad and includes two concepts which would later be distinguished:

> The contention that the human appearance of Christ is mere illusion and has no objective reality. (...) Either objectivity is denied to the human in Christ, or at least the human is so separated from the divine that there is no personal unity between the two. The first is the purely docetistic view, since it holds that Christ was man only in appearance; but the second has at least this in common with genuine Docetism, that it declares the divine-human unity of the Savior to be mere appearance.[229]

In a later book Baur obscures the distinction by only mentioning the first concept (Jesus was not an ordinary man) without discussing the second one

[224] Εἰ δέ ... τὸ δοκεῖν πεπονθέναι αὐτόν, αὐτοὶ ὄντες τὸ δοκεῖν...

[225] Irenaeus also fiercely defends the flesh of the Lord: *Igitur qui dicunt eum putative manifestum, neque in carne natum neque vere hominem factum, adhuc sub veteri sunt damnatione* (...) *quod autem parebat (sc. caro), hoc et erat* (*AdvHaer* 3.18.7). But the context (3.17.1, 4) makes it clear that he aims at the Gnostics who distinguish between Christ and Jesus.

[226] Cf. N. Brox, '"Doketismus" - eine Problemanzeige', *ZKG* 95 (1984) 301-314, 304-305.

[227] Only part of Serapion's relevant letter has been preserved (Eusebius, *HE* VI.12.2-6). Equally vague is Irenaeus, *AdvHaer* 4.33.5; 5.1.2.

[228] Weigandt, *Doketismus*, 78-82, and many others.

[229] F.C. Baur, *Die christliche Gnosis oder die christliche Religions-Philosophie in ihrer geschichtlichen Entwicklung*, Tübingen 1835, 258-259, translated by Slusser, 'Docetism', 171. Hilgenfeld, 'Johannes', 49-50, likewise distinguishes between 'reinen Doketismus' with its 'Verflüchtigung des Lebens Jesu' and 'die dualistische Scheidung des Menschen Jesus und des göttlichen Christus'.

(the distinction between Christ and Jesus).[230] Subsequent scholars did not always distinguish the two concepts or introduced different distinctions, so docetism remained an umbrella term for different concepts; this lack of clarity has plagued research for a long time, as has Baur's assumption that docetism is a form of Gnosis.[231] J.G. Davies, for example, takes docetism as a broad term without defining it clearly; he fails to distinguish between Gnosis and docetism.[232]

Peter Weigandt's Heidelberg dissertation (1961) is an admirable attempt to clarify the subject. It is also the only monograph on docetism that we know. Although it was never published, quite a few scholars - like myself - are able to refer to it. It is all the more interesting for the present research because Weigandt sees the AJ as the classic docetic text.[233] Contrary to Baur and Davies, he gives a very limited definition of docetism as the idea that Christ's appearance on earth was only an illusion. God/Christ remains totally different from all earthly things.[234] Weigandt holds that docetism is only one of the ways in which Gnosticising Christianity resolves the tension between its basically a-historical religion and the faith in Jesus Christ as God's supreme revelation in history.[235]

As a result of his limited definition, Weigandt argues that many persons, like Valentinus, Basilides and the author of the *Gospel of Peter*, who are called docetists by Fathers of the church or by modern authors, do not deserve the label.[236] In his opinion, docetism is a movement of which the origins are obscure, limited in time and space, which becomes first

[230] F.C. Baur, *Das Christenthum und die christliche Kirche der ersten drei Jahrhunderte*, Tübingen ²1860, repr. Stuttgart/Bad Canstatt 1966, 228.

[231] Slusser, 'Docetism', 163-165. Harnack holds that the essence of Gnostic Christology is a dualistic doctrine of two natures, the separation of Jesus and Christ; see Koschorke, *Polemik*, 44 n.15.

[232] J.G. Davies, 'The Origins of Docetism', *Studia Patristica VI*, Berlin 1962, 13-35.

[233] Weigandt, *Doketismus*, 39. Van Kampen, *Apostelverhalen*, 285-286, calls all five AAA docetic and points to the role of the apostle as a mediator. Cf. *ibid.*, 109-110, for his view of the AJ.

[234] Weigandt, *Doketismus*, 21. Cf. Koschorke, *Polemik*, 26: '... da für den Doketismus eben dies kennzeichnend ist, dass zugunsten der *einen*, himmlischen Realität des Erlösers seine irdische Wirklichkeit als blosser "Schein" abqualifiziert bzw. geleugnet wird.'

[235] Weigandt, *Doketismus*, 20-23, cf. 4-19, who mentions as other solutions to this tension the conviction that the human being Jesus was uniquely endowed with Gnosis and the idea that the human body of Jesus was only a kind of *vehiculum* or coat for the divine Christ; the latter idea was rather common.

[236] Weigandt, *Doketismus*, 76-82. Markschies, *Valentinus*, 110-115, 353, obviously following Weigandt's definition, shows that Valentinus was not a docetist in this strict sense, as he recognised a human aspect in Christ.

visible when it is combatted by the Johannine writings and by Ignatius.[237] He argues that, as an imminently dangerous heresy, docetism was only shortlived, and geographically limited to Western Syria and Asia Minor, and probably included Marcion who migrated from Asia to Rome.[238] In his opinion it had already been reduced to a paper enemy by the times of Irenaeus and Tertullian, and it was only a pressing issue in Justin's younger years.[239] From Justin to Origen the polemics against it by the church are static and lacking in creativity.[240]

Weigandt's work has not found general approval and the discussions about the definition of docetism have not yet come to an end.[241] Although critical of Weigandt, Norbert Brox[242] takes over his insight that docetism and Gnosis cannot be identified.[243] He holds that the AJ is not docetic because he thinks that polymorphy is to be excluded from the definition of docetism and also because the emphasis in the AJ falls, he

[237] On Ignatius see chapter 6.

[238] Weigandt, *Doketismus*, 146.

[239] Weigandt, *Doketismus*, 107, 126, 131 n. 403, 133, 134. I think that in the second half of the second century the more sophisticated docetism of Cerinthus, who separated a human Jesus from Christ, took over and was combatted by Irenaeus who knows nothing of the AJ and its ideas; but this hypothesis cannot be demonstrated in this study.

[240] Weigandt, *Doketismus*, 145. Indeed, K.W. Tröger, 'Doketistische Christologie in Nag-Hammadi-Texten', *Kairos, neue Folge* 19 (1977), esp. 46-47, argues that no Nag Hammadi text fits Weigandts limited definition of docetism.

[241] His followers would include Voorgang, *Passion*, and U.B. Müller, *Die Menschwerdung des Gottessohnes. Früh-christliche Inkarnationsvorstellungen und die Anfänge des Doketismus*, Stuttgart 1990, esp. 99 n.236. Markschies, *Valentinus*, denies that Valentinus, who attributed a human aspect to Christ, had docetic ideas. But Slusser, 'Docetism', 168, states that 'Weigandt's "docetistic" Christologies are those which simply gloss over the problem of how the appearance of the Savior's life and death are effected.' An approach similar to Slusser's is K. Rudolph, '"Christlich" und "Christentum" in der Auseinandersetzung zwischen "Kirche" und "Gnosis"', in P. Bilde *et al.* (eds.), *Apocrypha Severini. FS Giversen*, Aarhus 1993, 192-214, esp. 202-208. J. McCant, 'The Gospel of Peter: Docetism Reconsidered', *NTS* 30 (1984) 258-273, does not define docetism.

[242] Brox, 'Doketismus', 308-309, 314, joins Baur and Slusser, and increases the terminological confusion when in a brief final paragraph he distinguishes two separate forms of docetism. See the critical comment by Müller, *Menschwerdung*, 99 n.236.

[243] Brox, 'Doketismus', 312-313. The differentiation between Gnosis and docetism is not found in M. Hengel, *Crucifixion*, London 1977, 15-21, but it occurs in Koschorke, *Polemik*, 164-165, who states that the Gnostic text *Melchisedek* (NHC IX.1) is anti-docetic, in Pétrement, *Dieu séparé*, 208, 308, and in B.A. Pearson, *Gnosticism, Judaism and Egyptian Christianity*, Minneapolis 1990, 183-193. This latter work argues that the texts in codex IX defend the reality of Jesus' flesh even more vigorously than Ignatius.

says, on the immutability of God/Christ.[244]

Both Baur's initial distinction and Weigandt seem to do justice to the factual evidence that there were two different conceptions among people commonly called 'docetists'. The first focuses on Christ's divine quality to such an extent that whatever human traits he seems to have had can only be considered as illusory. This conception implies that there never was a human being called Jesus.[245] The second conception recognises human qualities in the Saviour next to his divinity but keeps the two separate.[246] Only the first conception is docetic in the strict sense of the Greek word δοκεῖν, but it is not necessary to deny the label docetic to the second conception as long as we distinguish between the two.[247] I will now apply the above distinctions in my examination of the AJ.

*5.1.2 Are the Acts of John docetic?*

With regard to sections A and B, I can immediately leave the second type of docetic thinking out of consideration and seek to answer the question if the polymorphy and Christomonism of this part of the AJ are related to the first type of docetic thinking. In my opinion, they are indeed connected. The text presents only a divine Christ and emphatically denies his humanity.[248] In section C polyonymy largely takes the place of the polymorphy; this device is an effective way of denying that the Lord was really human when he made himself known on earth. The polemics against

[244] Brox, 'Doketismus', 309-311.

[245] Weigandt calls it 'monophysitic', but that label causes confusion with later Monophysitism which believes in one divine-human nature of Christ.

[246] I use the word 'quality' in a quasi-technical sense for lack of something better; the word 'nature' should be avoided. Weigandt calls this type of docetism 'dyophysitic'.

[247] The dualistic Christology of Gnosis which separates Christ and Jesus can go hand in hand with docetism in the broad form. The narrow form is by definition monistic. Rudolph, '"Christlich" und "Christentum"', 204, recognises only the dualistic form: 'Die mit "Doketismus" bezeichnete Auffassung ist nichts anderes als der Versuch, daran festzuhalten, dass der "Geist-Christus", also das eigentlich Erlösende, die göttliche Kraft als solche, nicht vom Tode getroffen werden konnte. Der "Geist-Christus" kann von dieser Denkposition gar nicht "leiden" oder gekreuzigt werden. "Fleisch" (σάρξ) oder "Leib" (σῶμα) ist daher nur seine Verkleidung, die sein eigentliches, erlösendes Wesen nicht berühren kann. Insofern ist die doketische Christologie eine Form der Zwei-Naturen- oder Pneumachristologie.' Notice that for Rudolph the stress falls on the fact that Christ cannot suffer, not on the divinity of Christ.

[248] The first part of the AJ illustrates the thesis that a docetic point of view is not necessarily also Gnostic. Marcion, a docetist according to my definition, was also not a Gnostic; cf. P. Head, 'The Foreign God and the Sudden Christ', *TynB* 44 (1993) 307-321, esp. 314.

an important part of the humanity of the Saviour, viz. his suffering on the cross, is very fierce in section C, which argues at length that the crucifixion of the Lord was not a real event. It does not deal with other events in Christ's life, but there is every reason to think that its author agreed with the author of section B to which he attached his own text. The non-humanity of Christ is less important in section C than in the other parts of the text because this section focuses on the explanation of Christ's suffering. The denial of Christ's humanity remains strong. The AJ in its final form suggests that the God Christ appears from heaven from time to time without really living an earthly life and of course without ever incarnating in a human body (96.6-7, 25-26; 97; 99.7-9; 100.11-12; 101). The AJ completely denies the humanity of Jesus as depicted in the canonical Gospels and only gives an account of a divine Saviour.[249]

Weigandt is therefore correct in seeing the AJ as docetic;[250] Pétrement's definition of docetists as those people who 'pour affirmer la divinité de Jésus-Christ, croyaient devoir nier son humanité', and her statement that 'le désir d'accentuer la divinité du Christ est la racine du docétisme' apply without reservation to the AJ.[251]

Nevertheless, Brox as well as Junod and Kaestli deny the docetic character of the AJ. It is necessary to consider their arguments, which in the case of Junod and Kaestli are much clearer than those of Brox. The prime reason why the two Swiss scholars do not want to regard the AJ as docetic is that the text does not deal with (the problems of) the incarnation and is situated outside the debate about the human nature of Christ.[252]

[249] In its complete denial of the reality of the body of Christ, the docetic Christology of the Manichaeans as described by Rose, *Manichäische Christologie*, 120-128, comes very close to that of the AJ.

[250] Cf. Sirker-Wicklaus, *Untersuchungen*, 104-105, 159-160; J. Helderman, 'Zum Doketismus und zur Inkarnation im Manichäismus', in A. Van Tongerloo and S. Giversen (eds.), *Manichaica selecta. FS Ries*, Leuven 1991, 101-125, 103-105. Liébaert, *Christologie*, 23, argues that the docetism of the AJ is a popular and not a systematic one.

[251] Pétrement, *Dieu séparé*, 61, 207, 208, 222, 389. She distinguishes, correctly in my opinion, between the followers of Paul and John who stressed Christ's divinity, and the Jewish Christians who tended to regard him as merely human. This excludes the likelihood that docetic thinking stems from Jewish Christianity, an idea found e.g. in Davies, 'Docetism', 14-16, 35; and Müller, *Menschwerdung*. Pétrement, 209-224, complicates the picture by distinguishing four different forms of docetism.

[252] JK, 493: 'Mais, en fait, l'apocryphe se situe au-delà du docétisme. Il ne combat même pas l'incarnation avec ses deux événements scandaleux: la passion et la naissance. Il s'abstient tout bonnement d'en parler. La difficulté n'est pas affrontée, elle est ignorée.' This view is related to their opinion that the AJ is not a polemical text but a quiet exposition of ideas; see JK, 686-687; 'Théologie', 141, 144; and E. Junod, 'Ce que l'étude

My first problem with this argument is that it tacitly reserves the word 'docetism' for positions that are explicitly polemical, a qualification that introduces a completely new factor. Again I would argue that, as we saw in chapter 3, if section A does not 'combat the incarnation', section B clearly does: it is a re-edition of Gospel stories from which the presentation of a human Jesus has been deleted and in which this humanity is even explicitly denied (90.10-11).[253] The familiarity of the author of sections A and B with the canonical Gospels means that when he is silent about the human quality of Christ, he implicitly denies it. Likewise, the explicit identification of Christ and God is an implicit statement of a docetic position if - as is the case here - it is not counterbalanced by statements regarding Jesus' humanity.

In the second place, Junod and Kaestli hold that the AJ contains a negative theology with special stress on the immutability of God.[254] Against this view I would argue that God's immutability hardly occurs as a theme in the AJ and that the AJ is in no way a bleak piece of speculation; attention rather is paid to the multifarious revelation of God. It is true that our text says many things about the God Christ in terms of his polymorphy (section B) and his polyonymy (section C). These forms of revelation indeed hide his essential being, but that does not make the label 'negative theology' very adequate.[255] The Lord of the AJ is neither unknown nor extremely remote, but worthy of praise and elated religious emotions.

Thirdly, I do not agree with Brox that polymorphy and docetism are mutually exclusive. In my opinion, polymorphy is a concrete narrative form given to docetic ideas.[256] The polymorphy and the Christomonism of sections A and B suggest that when the God Christ was seen on earth, he never had a human body but only appeared to be human. In fact Christ is completely divine. That is the essential tenet of docetic thinking.

des Actes apocryphes peut apporter à la connaissance du christianisme des premiers siècles', in *Rapport de gestion de la Société Suisse des Sciences Humaines 1980*, Berne 1981, II.24. Following in their footsteps, Prieur, *Acta Andreae*, 365 n.2, likewise denies that the AAn is docetic, using the same phrase 'au-delà du docétisme'.

253 Sirker-Wicklaus, *Untersuchungen*, 104, uses more dogmatic labels: '... unterstreicht mit jedem neuen Aspekt der Polymorphie das vere Deus, um das vere homo stillschweigend zu negieren. Psychologisch gesehen wird in dieser Weise geschickter vorgegangen als in einer argumentativen Auseinandersetzung.'

254 JK, 491-492.

255 One might even argue that, contrary to a negative theo-logy, a negative Christo-logy is either an internal contradiction or inherently docetic.

256 Cf. my 'Polymorphy', 108, and now Culpepper, *John*, 204-205.

*5.1.3 Conclusions*

Two conclusions may be drawn from the above. First with regard to the Johannine trajectory. The docetism of the AJ may have originated from a certain way of reading the Fourth Gospel. The famous Baur is among those who claim that the Gospel of John itself contains docetic elements.[257] In Jn 7:10 the evangelist suggests, Baur argues, e.g., that Jesus was not recognised because of his ability to change his appearance; in 8:59 Jesus could suddenly disappear ('ein doketisches Verschwinden').[258] The resurrection-appearances suggest that the holy Ghost, who came upon the disciples, is the spirit of Jesus. The resurrected Jesus has no firm footing on the earth.[259] According to Käsemann, the Johannine Jesus is a god striding over the earth, whose descent to earth meant no essential change.[260]

Most interpreters of the Gospel do not share the views of Baur and Käsemann,[261] while others would express themselves much more carefully.[262] The most we can say, in my opinion, is that the Gospel has no birth narratives and leaves readers room to deny the corporeality of Christ after Easter.[263] But one-sided interest in the divinity of Jesus has frequently lead to a docetic interpretation of the resurrection and even of his earthly life; the glorified Christ swallowed the earthly Jesus.[264] We

[257] F.C. Baur, *Kritische Untersuchungen über die kanonischen Evangelien*, Tübingen 1847, 233: 'Scheint doch schon jetzt das Fleisch, das er angenommen hat, nur wie eine leichte, immaterielle Hülle ihn zu umschweben'; cf. 233-234, 373.

[258] Baur, *Kritische Untersuchungen*, 286-291.

[259] Baur, *Kritische Untersuchungen*, 227-230.

[260] Käsemann, *Jesu letzter Wille*, 21-26, 29, 44-46, 51, 76, 98, following F.C. Baur, J. Wellhausen and E. Hirsch. For the expression 'über die Erde schreitende(r) Gott', Käsemann, 54, gives credit to J. Grill, *Untersuchungen über die Entstehung des vierten Evangeliums* I, 1902, 36. Käsemann's use of the term docetic (51-52, 83, 118, 124, 137) has been criticised by Adam, 'Docetism, Käsemann, and Christology'.

[261] Just one example: Weigandt, *Doketismus*, 102, argues that specific passages are rather anti-docetic, esp. 6:51b-58 and 20:24-29.

[262] Pétrement, *Dieu séparé*, 222, finds the root-tendency of docetism, unlimited stress on the divinity of Christ, already in the Fourth Gospel.

[263] Jn 20:14-15, 19; 21:1, 4, 12. For a rejection of the docetic approach to Jn, see M.M. Thompson, *The Humanity of Jesus in the Fourth Gospel*, Philadelphia 1988.

[264] Sirker-Wicklaus, *Untersuchungen*, 213: 'In den AJ ist der Doketismus Wirklichkeit geworden; die Linie, die der Evangelist Joh. zu zeichnen begonnen hat, ist konsequent ausgezogen.' One text that would not easily fit a docetic view of the resurrection, Jn 20:27, 'Put your finger here and see my hands; and put out your hand, and place it in my side; do not be faithless, but believing', was made harmless in AJ 90 by quoting only the last part of it.

will see in chapter 6 that the stress on the incarnation in 1 Jn and Ignatius is a reaction against interpretations of the Fourth Gospel by Johannine Christians such as the author of the AJ. It is equally perspicuous how some scholars who argue that the Gospel should be read as a docetic document, detect a direct line connecting it to the AJ.[265]

The second implication has to do with the origin of the AJ. The number of surviving texts that represent the first type of docetism is limited to one, viz. the AJ. Evidence for this type of docetic thinking has been found in the period from the end of the first century AD until about 150 AD, viz. among the adversaries combatted in the First Johannine Epistle, the adversaries of Ignatius, and in Cerdo and Marcion. After the middle of the second century, Weigandt argues, the fear of docetism lived on but its *viva vox* had disappeared.[266] This reconstruction of the history of docetism coincides with the view that the form of Gnosis which embraced the first type of docetic thinking is more primitive than the Gnostic conception of the Lord's duality. When the latter position became popular, the former disappeared.[267]

If the above is correct, it means that the ideas contained in the AJ were current from the end of the first century to about the middle of the second century. Thus the natural time span for the origin of our text lies within that period. It is surprising that Weigandt himself did not come to this conclusion but stuck to the traditional date of the AJ, i.e. later in the second century.

[265] Pervo, 'Trajectories', 56 n.54: 'E. KAESEMANN (*Jesu letzter Wille nach Johannes 17*, Tübingen 1967²) has demonstrated how the Fourth Gospel *could* be read. The *AcJn* reveal that some *did* so read it'; Sirker-Wicklaus, *Untersuchungen*, 213: 'In den AJ ist der Doketismus Wirklichkeit geworden; die Linie, die der Evangelist Joh. zu zeichnen begonnen hat, ist konsequent ausgezogen'; Garcia, *Polymorphie*, 26-27: 'La religion des AJ apparaît comme une forme de Christianisme éminemment spiritualisé, de type pagano-chrétien et de tendance docète et pré-gnostique.'

[266] Weigandt, *Doketismus*, 39, 100.

[267] Voorgang, *Passion*, 11, 242, 255, who finds docetism in Marcion (in Irenaeus, *AdvHaer* 1.27), in the Simonic and Basilidean Gnosis (also as described in *AdvHaer* 1.23-24) and in *2 LogSeth* (NHC VII.2).

*5.2 Further comparison*

The Christologies of both major parts of the AJ have more in common than just their docetic character, although the fact that they are the only surviving witnesses to the same type of docetism is worth being repeated here.

Another important point in common is that to a certain extent the non-Gnostic and the Gnostic parts of the text make use of the same device, viz. polymorphy. It may be recalled that no other text describes the Lord before the resurrection as polymorphous.[268] The motif of the polymorphy of the Lord works as a 'trait d'union' in the AJ.[269] It is the leading idea behind the original part of the gospel flashback (cc.87-93, section B) and also plays a role in the stories of section A; in section C it recurs in the appearance of the Lord in c.97. For the rest the author of section C prefers the use of polyonymy, which may be considered an even more sophisticated device.

This brings us to the importance which both parts of the text attach to the unity of the divine person. Section A explicitly identifies Father/God and Son/Christ/Logos. Sections B and C each in their own way implicitly support this identification, so that the AJ as a whole is Christomonistic. A difference in interest between the authors is evident in that section C apparently plays with the strong emphasis on this element in the first part of the text by using many different titles for Christ and even playing with trinitarian formulas.

Both authors of the text are familiar with more than one of the Gospels, among which in any case the one attributed to John, but they prefer to give their own interpretation of the person of Christ and of his saving revelation.

Both parts of the text regard instability as a negative characteristic of human life which can be solved only by divine salvation, although, as we have seen, the precise way in which this happens may vary widely.

Yet there are also considerable differences between section A and B on the one hand and C on the other. To mention the most important, the suffering and the cross of Christ are never mentioned in the first main part, which wholly focuses on the present of the believers. Whereas the author of that part of the text avoids all references to death and resurrection, the Gnostic author of the second part presents the traditional views on that subject and contradicts them with full force.

Again, both main parts have clearly different concepts of salvation. In contrast to the emphasis on spiritual resurrection and good works in the

[268] See my 'Polymorphy'.

[269] Cf. Pervo, 'Becomes Christian', in Schmeling, *Novel*, 698.

first main part, the second part emphasises Christ's suffering as a mirror of mankind's, and man's knowledge of Christ's passion as the saving revelation. The concept of salvation in section A is a-historical in character and in fact does not involve Christ. It sometimes appears as if John has taken the place of the Lord. But not so in section C. This section looks like an effort by one who has read sections A and B to integrate Christ into that concept, which led to a radical change, a kind of re-historising that occurs to the detriment of John. The emerging concepts of suffering and salvation can be summarised: Christ appears as the cross of light and as the Logos in order to bring mankind the knowledge that enables them to unite in that cross and finally to return to the divine realm. Understanding sets them free.

In the AJ we are dealing with two spiritualising theologians who, each in their own way, try to cope with the Christian message and with the emerging books of the New Testament. Because both present us with docetic Christology and make use of the concept of polymorphy, the final text nevertheless gives a unified impression.[270] It appears that the non-Gnostic part could well be read in the context of a Gnostic concept of salvation.[271] I would suggest that the present reading of the AJ affords us insight into the development of the spiritualising form of the Johannine Christology and soteriology as it developed along a trajectory leading from the Fourth Gospel to Gnosis.

*5.3 The Acts of John in context*

The above analysis clearly shows that the AJ occupies a place at one extreme on the spectrum of second-century Christological views. Its concept of salvation is Gnostic: it can do perfectly well without an incarnate God because it presupposes that salvation consists of the revelation of redemptive knowledge. But the AJ's denial of the humanity of Christ is more radical than that of other Gnostic texts. Even the author of the non-Gnostic first part completely ignores the cross, whereas the author of the second part makes references to the wooden cross, which are no more than polemics against the Gospel stories. The cross, as he himself sees it, is beyond history.

In the AJ we find nothing of the second-century attempts, however

[270] Their positions contrast remarkably with the ideas of the author of the APe, who never denies the historic reality of Christ and of the cross, even when meditating on the meaning and cosmic functions of that cross. Cf. Bolyki, 'Head Downwards', 113.

[271] Cf. Schneider, 'Gnostic Transformation', 247, who suggests that the first main part of the AJ left its original readers with many questions that are only answered in section C; in my opinion sections A and B formed a complete text in themselves.

feeble in the eyes of later generations, to maintain a balance between the divine and the human qualities of the Lord. A one-sided perspective is given, in which the humanity of Christ is denied altogether and he is placed entirely in the realm of God. Other movements that downplay the human element in Christ, like Modalism, never denied that he was at least partly human. The Christomonism of the AJ is, as far as we can see, unparalleled. No wonder that later generations found the AJ a docetic, and therefore, unacceptable text.

# CHAPTER 5: ASCETICISM

Several times in the preceding chapters we touched upon the ascetic features of the AJ. It is time now to give more detailed attention to them. By means of a study of the text's attitude towards asceticism, the present chapter intends to offer a clearer picture of the position of the AJ among the other AAA and within second-century Christianity as a whole. It is commonly assumed that the AJ and the other AAA originated in a strongly ascetic environment and that they are very much characterised by their asceticism.[1] The most important proponent of this thesis, Peterson, directly links nearly all the AAA with the formative period of the supposed sect of the Encratites. Moreover, basing himself upon a rather uncritical selection of Irenaeus' and Epiphanius' statements about the Encratites,[2] he associates the AAA and their encraticism with Jewish Christianity.[3] I will

[1] Söder, *Apokryphen Apostelgeschichten*, 116-117; E. Peterson, 'Einige Beobachtungen zu den Anfängen der christlichen Askese', in his *Frühkirche*, 209-220; J. Gribomont, 'Askese IV. Neues Testament und Alte Kirche', *TRE* 4 (1979) 204-225, 210-211, who suggests that the message of the apostles in the AAA can be summarised as one of abstinence, whereas the texts contain hardly any other ideas; K.S. Frank, *Grundzüge der Geschichte des christlichen Mönchtums*, Darmstadt 1979, 9; M. Van Uytfanghe, 'Encratisme en verborgen erotiek in de apocriefe "apostelromans". Omtrent de christelijke problematisering van de sexualiteit', *Handelingen van de Koninklijke Zuidnederlandse Maatschappij voor Taal- en Letterkunde en Geschiedenis* 45 (1991) 175-194; A. Cameron, *Christianity and the Rhetoric of Empire. The Development of Christian Discourse*, Berkeley 1991, 115-119, 175; and Hauschild, *Dogmengeschichte*, 266.

[2] Irenaeus, *AdvHaer* 1.28.1; Epiphanius, *Panarion*, 30.2.6, 30.16.6, 47.1.5. Two comments: 1. Irenaeus places the origin of the Encratites *after* Marcion so that Peterson's dating (before 138) is too early. 2. Irenaeus normally calls a sect after its founder; in this case he probably does not have in mind a separate group with a name of its own but rather one of the tendencies among the Gnostics (opposed to the licentious Gnostics in 1.28.2). I therefore suggest that we follow Y. Tissot, 'Encratisme et Actes apocryphes', in Bovon, *Actes apocryphes*, 109-119, and write encratites in Irenaeus with a lower-case letter.

[3] Peterson, 'Anfängen der Askese', 211-213, cf. 207-208. Cf. the positive comments of G. Quispel, 'The Study of Encratism: A Historical Survey', in U. Bianchi (ed.), *La tradizione dell'enkrateia. Motivazioni ontologiche e protologiche*, Rome 1985, 35-81, esp. 80-81. Despite Peterson and G. Kretschmar, 'Zur Frage nach dem Ursprung frühchristlicher Askese', orig. in *ZTK* 61 (1964) 27-67, now in K.S. Frank (ed.), *Askese und Mönchtum in der alten Kirche*, Darmstadt 1975, 129-180, there are not enough indications that Jewish Christianity had a specific attitude towards asceticism; cf. Pétrement, *Dieu séparé*, 641; Lohse, *Askese*, 94-95, 101. Much of Peterson's view seems to have been taken over by P. Nagel, *Die Motivierung der Askese in der alten Kirche und der Ursprung des Mönchtums*, Berlin 1966, who occasionally notes (39): 'Bis zum Ausgang des 2. Jahrhunderts beherrschten die enkratitischen Tendenzen der apokryphen Apostelliteratur nach Formen

nonetheless take the ideas of Peterson seriously, because sexual abstinence is undoubtedly an important theme in some of the AAA and because, as we have seen, the AJ is characterised by a certain dualism.

We begin by briefly surveying the forms of asceticism among both pagans and early Christians and the motivations for their practices. Because the AJ dates from the second century, this overview will not exceed the first two centuries of our era, although it will include Clement of Alexandria who died after 202 and who did much to combat what he saw as overly encratic tendencies in historical and contemporary Christianity (esp. *Strom* 3). I will also discuss Tertullian and take him to be representative of the largely second-century Montanism. After this historical summary, we will study the two main parts of the AJ successively and ask where they are to be situated in the emerging historical patterns.

A good proposal for the translation of the word ἄσκησις that maintains its multiple connotations is 'training in denial'.[4] A study of early Christian asceticism cannot limit itself to sexual denial, although for many contemporary readers that is the most fascinating (and irritating) aspect of asceticism. An ascetic point of view could also involve a declining attitude towards (some kinds of) food, especially meat and wine, towards property, as well as towards living in a (comfortable) house and having (comfortable) clothes.

## 1 Asceticism: its pagan and Christian forms

### *1.1 The general climate in the first two centuries*

The Christians were not the only group in the early period of the Roman Empire that tended to be ascetic: in pagan society a similar trend was visible. Stoic philosophers propagated a lifestyle of abstinence from luxury,[5] whereas several forms of religion promised salvation by way of an ascetic effort. Thus the mystery cult of Attis and Kybele laid value on the renunciation of food and sexual activity as preparatory acts for initiation, and entry into its priesthood involved self-castration. The mystery cult of Eleusis propagated fasting and sexual continence as means

und Motiven die frühchristliche Exegese.'

[4] D. Clay, 'Lucian of Samosata', *ANRW* II.36.5 (1992) 3412, as quoted in J.A. Francis, *Subversive Virtue. Asceticism and Authority in the Second-Century Pagan World*, University Park PA 1995, xvii n.6.

[5] W. Deming, *Paul on marriage and celibacy. The Hellenistic background of 1 Corinthians 7*, Cambridge 1995, 76-89; Frank, *Grundzüge*, 3-7.

of attaining not sanctity (ἁγνεία) but salvation (σωτηρία). The cult of Iṣis probably laid more stress on sexual abstinence than the other cults, but we are handicapped by the fact that a large part of what we know about it comes from Christian authors.[6] As far as we know, most mystery religions contained some elements of asceticism, but they mainly limited the necessary abstinence to the period before initiation and/or before major events.[7] Abstinence thus seems to function as a way of achieving (temporary) ritual purity. In pagan cults, lifelong sexual asceticism is virtually absent except, of course, for the castrated priests.

Among the motivations for this practice there is, first of all, the Greek dichotomy between body and soul which often developed into a contempt of the body and an associated desire to set the soul free to commune with the divine. Later Stoicism implied a strong drive towards freedom from bonds, including those of the body.[8] A second motivation, that of *secundum naturam vivere*, emphasises the leading role of the mind and the need to subject the body to the powers of reason. A third stimulating factor is the idea that in certain cults gods grant salvation only to those who are fully devoted and who show this self-effacing attitude in their lives. Not all was done out of pious motives; one could also gain great prestige by means of an exemplary lifestyle.[9]

In view of the evidence it might be argued that in order to be regarded as serious by the larger public, a religion or philosophy needed an ascetic component.[10] Groups like the Neo-Pythagoreans and other ascetic communities constituted a more general cultural phenomenon, which gave expression to the same psychological impulses.

But not everybody was enthusiastic about the flood of pagan and Christian asceticism. Both the pagan upper class and the leaders of emerging Orthodoxy regarded rigorous asceticism as deviant behaviour.[11] Educated people like Plutarch, Epictetus and Clement of Alexandria disapproved.[12] A serious lifestyle was greatly valued, but radical asceticism was seen as a threat to culture and society and as such hardly

[6] B. Lohse, *Askese und Mönchtum in der Antike und in der alten Kirche*, München/Wien 1969, 36-38.

[7] W. Burkert, *Ancient mystery cults*, Cambridge MA/London 1987, 107-108, 169 n.118.

[8] Frank, *Grundzüge*, 5-6. A different picture emerges from Deming, *Paul on marriage*, 106-107.

[9] E.R. Dodds, *Pagan and Christian in an Age of Anxiety. Some Aspects of Religious Experience from Marcus Aurelius to Constantine*, Cambridge 1965, 31-32, 33 n.4.

[10] Cf. Frank, *Grundzüge*, 7.

[11] Francis, *Subversive Virtue*, 175, 183 n.1, 188-189.

[12] Dodds, *Age of Anxiety*, 35; on Clement see Francis, *Subversive Virtue*, 176-178.

tolerable. Stoic philosophers emphasised the moral obligation of marrying and educating children.[13] James Francis argues that ascetic leaders, who combined the roles of prophet, miracle worker and charismatic leader in one person, were 'authorities in their own right' and as such dangerous for vested interests.[14]

Not all forms of asceticism were, however, equally revolutionary. Although the famous emperor Marcus Aurelius was a convinced Stoic, he favoured a largely cerebral asceticism which actually supported and justified the status quo in the empire: 'Rather than reflecting any sort of radicalism, asceticism - in Aurelius' Stoic sense - was a vehicle for conforming to traditional standards of moral behaviour. For those who would not conform, Aurelius' philosophy also provided a justification for persecution.'[15] Persons who would not adapt to current values and whose ascetic lifestyles made them objectionable, such as Peregrinus, were ostracised - in the case of Peregrinus by Lucian's book against him, in the case of Christ by the vigorous attack of Celsus.[16] As a conservative, Celsus stresses current class distinctions and brings Christians into disrepute because of their low social status.[17]

*1.2 Christian asceticism*

It is this climate into which Christianity entered.[18] Because neither Jesus nor the earliest Christians nor the second-century church introduced practices not already widely known, the external practices involved in Christian asceticism were not distinct.[19] Consequently, to pagan eyes at least, Christian asceticism in the first and second centuries did not differ essentially from other forms of asceticism. But internally Christianity was by no means unanimous in the lifestyle it prescribed or propagated, so that in the first two centuries of its existence it displayed enormous diversity. The traditions about John the Baptist, Jesus and the earliest Christian writings contained several divergent elements which did not decisively

[13] Deming, *Paul on marriage*, 87, 91.

[14] Francis, *Subversive Virtue*, xiii-xv, 81; quotation from 2.

[15] Francis, *Subversive Virtue*, 50-51, cf. 21-52 and the analysis of the evolution of Stoicism from a revolutionary idea to a conformist philosophy, 2-6.

[16] Francis, *Subversive Virtue*, 53-81 (Peregrinus), 131-179 (Celsus *adversus* Christianity). He observes that Celsus is the first to attack not only the Christians but the moral character of Christ himself (139).

[17] Francis, *Subversive Virtue*, 151-162. I will come back to Francis' opinion that Celsus specifically criticises the form of Christianity represented by the ascetic AAA.

[18] Cf. K. Heussi, *Der Ursprung des Mönchtums*, Tübingen 1936, repr. Aalen 1981, 13-15. Niederwimmer, *Askese*, nowhere pays attention to the Umwelt.

[19] Nagel, *Motivierung*, 2.

point in one direction.[20] Although the New Testament is not the subject of the present investigation, it may be remarked that as a reflection of the situation in the first century, it is a veritable quarry of divergent elements. Next to sayings that recommend certain degrees of asceticism, there are texts which give Christians considerable freedom to develop other lifestyles. Preoccupation with the world to come co-exists with prescriptions about how to live in this world. To give some examples, the New Testament suggests that John the Baptist was not married and in so doing promoted an ascetic lifestyle (Mk 1:6; Lk 1:15, 3:11, 7:33); at the same time, the fact that he defended the sanctity of marriage was also not neglected (Mk 6:18). Again, despite what people have made him say, a case could be made to demonstrate that Paul was far less radical than the communities in Corinth to which he wrote.[21] But the same Paul did use the antithesis 'flesh and spirit', and time and again he emphasised the Lord's imminent return as an incentive for the believers to maintain a Christian lifestyle; such notions were picked up and used in diverse ways by his later readers. Moreover, the first readers of his letters also discovered teaching on the subject where we do not see it. Texts that in modern opinion are not related to an ascetic way of life were read as commentaries on it, like the Lord's words on the two or three believers who gather in his name (Mt 18:20).[22]

Of the first-century churches, Paul faced believers in Corinth who opted for more freedom than he himself thought wise, and who were even visiting prostitutes (1 Cor 6:15-20). There were others in the same church who advocated the cessation of all sexual activity (7:1).[23] In Colossae rival teachers had apparently burdened the church with all kinds of rules that Paul deemed unnecessary and indeed harmful. Col 2:16-23 denies the relevance of regulations regarding food and (other) ascetic practices under the new dispensation. For the present purpose it is not necessary to be specific about the exact ideas and motivations of those targeted by Paul; suffice it to say that Paul was confronted by people who advocated a stricter attitude than he did and whose legalism he found it necessary to

[20] P. Brown, *The Body and Society*, New York 1988, ch. 1 and 2. A good brief summary of the NT is Van Uytfanghe, 'Encratisme', 179-180. Elaborate treatment of the Synoptics, 1 Cor 7 and Eph 5 occurs in Niederwimmer, *Askese und Mysterium*, 12-157, who stresses the unsettled character of primitive Christianity.

[21] On 1 Corinth 7, see Deming, *Paul on marriage*, 108-225.

[22] Clement, *Strom* 3.68-70.

[23] See now D. Wenham, 'Whatever Went Wrong in Corinth?', *Expository Times* 108 (1996-'97) 137-141, esp. 140, on the 'remarkable division of the Corinthians into sexual ascetics and sexual libertines'.

denounce.

The First Epistle to Timothy likewise refers to ascetic practices - such as prohibition of marriage and of certain forms of food (4:3-5) - that go beyond those which Timothy should recommend to believers. The author emphatically defends the legitimacy and even necessity of marriage and childbearing (2:9-15; 3:2, 12; 5:14), and recommends the drinking of wine (5:23). On the other hand he curtails immoderate riches (6:9-10).[24]

The second century witnessed an even greater diversity than the first. The Jewish heritage of the church involved a basic acceptance of the created world as good, yet Christianity increasingly came under the influence of the general culture and philosophy in which ascetic tendencies were prominent. The Christian who collected the so-called *Sentences of Sextus* could draw from pagan, especially Pythagorean, sources to compose a very popular set of maxims in which sexual abstinence is required. Moreover, these *Sentences* are among the few Christian texts to discuss not just sexual but also other forms of continence.[25]

It is important to signal that asceticism not only occurred among Gnostics or other groups that were suspect in the eyes of the adherents of emerging mainstream Christianity; within the latter group we find at least as many reports of ascetic behaviour.[26] I will quote some testimonies, indicating motives for ascetic behaviour that are evident in the sources. The survey of these motives is not meant to suggest that in actual life they were mutually exclusive or neatly distinguished. On the contrary, it is only natural that in individual authors we find combinations of several incentives and that one writing may, on analysis, display several motives. The survey does not pretend to be exhaustive but just aims to illustrate the diversity.

In Rome, Hermas calls for decency but not for virginity[27] and Justin, *Apol* 1.29, accentuates the good behaviour of Christians by saying that they either marry only to have children or decline marriage and live continently. This passage suggests that in the eyes of Justin both options had equal

[24] In none of the letters (Cor, Col, 1 Tim) do we have any clean indication that Gnostics were the adversaries.

[25] H. Chadwick, *The Sentences of Sextus. A contribution to the history of Early Christian Ethics*, Cambridge 1959; about their disputed Christian origin see 112-116 and about their asceticism 99-102; cf. also Van den Broek, *Studies in Gnosticism*, 260-261.

[26] Surveys of the second century in Tissot, 'Encratisme', 109-113; Lohse, *Askese*, 131-159; Plümacher, 'Apostelakten', 46-48; Gribomont, 'Askese', 209-213; with reference to Alexandria, Van den Broek, *Studies in Gnosticism*, 185.

[27] *Mand* 4 (29), 8 (38), 12 (45).

value. The same equivalence of marriage and virginity occurs in Ignatius, *Polyc* 5.2, and in 1 Clem 38.2. But *Didache* 6.2 probably has sexual continence in mind when it exhorts: 'If you are able to bear the whole yoke of the Lord, you will be perfect. But if you are not able, do what you can.'[28] These words point to a preference for abstinence rather than to a balanced position in which both options are equal.

Also in Hermas, as well as previously in the Epistle of James and later in Clement of Alexandria, we find the conviction that Christians are strangers on earth, who should therefore renounce luxury in order to live with the poor and to assist them.[29]

A very strong motive for ascetic behaviour is the imitation of Jesus Christ and of his first followers. Thus Tertullian, *De monogamia* 8.5-6, assumes that none of the apostles was married. In itself the idea of 'Nachfolge' can be very broad, but in practice it was usually an incentive for an ascetic lifestyle.[30] This motive finds eloquent expression in the (admittedly early third century) Pseudo-Clementine letters *De virginitate* (1.6-7): Christ was born from a virgin; 'if you want to be a Christian, then become like him in every respect.'[31]

Another but not unrelated motivation is derived from the ascetic elements of the Gospel teaching itself, more particularly from its call for believers to become eunuchs for the sake of the Kingdom of God (Mt 19:12). When Justin Martyr, *Apol* 1.15, gives some examples from the teaching of Christ, he starts with his words on man-wife relationships, including Mt 19:12. Justin, *Apol* 1.29, also tells the story of a boy in Alexandria who wanted a surgeon to make him an eunuch; when the request was refused, he nevertheless resolved to live single. Justin himself apparently approves of the idea. Bishop Melito of Sardes received the title 'eunuch'; it is possible that this happened because he had physically made

28 J.B. Lightfoot and J.R. Farmer, *The Apostolic Fathers*, second ed. revised by M.W. Holmes (Grand Rapids 1989), Leicester 1990, 152.

29 Jas 2:5-7, 5:1-3; Hermas, *Sim* 1; Clement, *Strom* 3.101, 7.44, 72; see Nagel, *Motivierung*, 75-79; J. Roldanus, 'Tweeërlei burgerschap van de christen', *Kerk en Theologie* 36 (1985) 265-283, esp. 272.

30 Kretschmar, 'Askese', 157-179; Frank, *Grundzüge*, 14-15; Nagel, *Motivierung*, 5-19. G.G. Stroumsa, 'Ascèse et gnose: aux origines de la spiritualité monastique', *RT* 81 (1981) 557-576, repr. in *idem*, *Savoir et salut*, Paris 1992, 145-162, esp. 155, argues that this incentive is not found among Gnostics.

31 My translation following H. Duensing, 'Die dem Klemens von Rom zugeschriebenen Briefe über die Jungfräulichkeit', *ZKG* 63 (1950-51) 166-188; cf. A. Harnack, 'Die pseudoclementinischen Briefe de virginitate und die Entstehung des Mönchtums' (1891), in Frank, *Askese und Mönchtum*, 37-68; Kretschmar, 'Ursprung', 136-139, 174-175; Lohse, *Askese*, 154-158.

himself a eunuch.[32]

The desire to make oneself available for service in the Kingdom corresponds with the Cynical idea that philosophy on the one hand and marriage and children on the other are mutually exclusive because the latter involve heavy wordly responsibilities.[33] Among Christians, this belief sometimes assumed a radical-eschatological form, in which ascetics hoped to force the coming of the Kingdom by their continence.[34] This hope found expression in the wide-spread *agraphon* that the Kingdom (or: the end) will come when male and female have become one, i.e. when sexuality will no longer exist.[35] It is significant that the Gnostic Theodotus (*Excerpta* 67.2-3) did not support the encratic interpretation of this *agraphon*, which means that he did not reject marriage.

The hope to receive heavenly wages forms another incentive to live a continent life. Athenagoras who, like Justin, argues that marriage and virginity are equally valid options for Christians, intimates that believers who live in abstinence do so in the hope of becoming closer to God.[36] He adds that Christian marriage is without sinful lust, that it has procreation as its goal and that it cannot be broken. It is evident that this Apologist has to defend his fellow-Christians against diverse kinds of slander regarding alleged disbehaviour. In the same way the other Apologists are at pains to point out the acceptability of Christian moral behaviour to their upper class readers.[37]

Even more than the former ones, wage incentives led to a distinction between ordinary believers and a specific group of ascetics who perform *opera supererogatoria*.[38] Tertullian was among the first to develop the idea of commandments for all and additional regulations which only some could obey.[39] In this respect, we may also mention the notion of substitution. This idea did not exist from the beginning but when the division between ordinary believers and ascetics was well defined, the

[32] Eusebius, *HE* V.24.5; cf. Lohse, *Askese*, 152.

[33] Deming, *Paul on marriage*, 77.

[34] Nagel, *Motivierung*, 48-55, esp. 49, 53, argues that this radicalism was inspired by the influence of Gnostics, but Niederwimmer, *Askese*, 178-179 with n.55, disagrees.

[35] 2 Clement 12.2-5; the *Gospel of the Egyptians* as quoted in Clement of Alexandria, *Strom* 3.9; *ExcTheodoto* 21.3; *Gospel of Thomas*, 22, 106, 114; *Gospel of Philip* 68.22-24; cf. Niederwimmer, *Askese*, 177-179.

[36] *Supplication* 33: ἐλπίδι τοῦ μᾶλλον συνέσεσθαι τῷ θεῷ; cf. Lohse, *Askese*, 143.

[37] Deming, *Paul on marriage*, 100-101, demonstrates that Stoicism underlies the idea that procreation is the sole purpose of marriage; cf. *Epistle to Diognetus* 5.4-6 and Minucius Felix, *Octavius* 31.5.

[38] Nagel, *Motivierung*, 62-69.

[39] *Ad uxorem* 2.1; cf. Lohse, *Askese*, 160.

latter group argued that they performed vicariously for the whole of the church.[40] In their liminality the ascetics formed one pole of the Christian community at large.[41] The themes of assisting the poor and of being rewarded occur together in *De virginitate* 1.12.6: 'Those who are thus will receive good wages from God, because they serve the brothers with the gifts the Lord gave them.'[42]

The eschatological expectation of Early Christianity in general provided another rationale for asceticism.[43] Next to 1 Cor 7, Lk 20:34-36 played a large role in the propagation of this view.[44] Clement urges his adversaries, who claim to have reached the state of resurrection, to demonstrate the consistency of their attitude by refusing to eat and to drink (*Strom* 3.48, cf. 12-21). A representative of eschatological Christianity in the second century is Montanism, which became relatively well-known because early in the third century Tertullian joined the movement and became its eloquent advocate.[45] Its line of reasoning implied the suggestion that the Church could become mature in that particular period of history by means of more severe ascetic practices than had existed previously, of which fasting was not the least important.[46]

Closely related to the eschatological drive is the desire to anticipate the heavenly existence, and that based itself on Christ's statement that marriage will not exist in heaven (Mk 12:25 par.). Persons who are attracted by these words often wished to live like the prophets of old, like angels, or like divine beings.[47]

Also literally present in the later canonised Scriptures is the related idea that the church is the bride of Christ (esp. Eph 5:22-33). This belief is developed in *2 Clement* 14 into the notion of a pre-existent, spiritual church. Others in Early Christianity extended it to each individual member of the community and on that basis either regulated or prevented (ATh 14)

[40] E. Troeltsch, 'Askese' in Frank, *Askese und Mönchtum*, 69-90, esp. 84, 89-90. This motivation is not discussed by Nagel, *Motivierung*.

[41] Stroumsa, 'Ascèse et gnose', 161.

[42] After Duensing, 'Briefe über die Jungfräulichkeit'.

[43] Nagel, *Motivierung*, 20-34.

[44] T.H.C. van Eijk, 'Marriage and virginity, death and immortality', in *Epektasis. Mélanges Jean Daniélou*, Paris 1972, 209-235, esp. 214-215, 220, 235, who is one-sided when on his last page he states without qualification that 'Christian ascetism is eschatologically motivated.'

[45] Heussi, *Mönchtum*, 34-35; Nagel, *Motivierung*, 21-25.

[46] Lohse, *Askese*, 168 n.3, 145-146.

[47] Nagel, *Motivierung*, 34-48.

marriage.[48]

A dualistic ontology lies at the basis of several forms of early Christianity and of the later Manichaeism.[49] An early representative of this attitude, the Gnostic Saturninus, rejected marriage and childbirth as practices governed by the devil, and moreover forbade the eating of flesh.[50] The same attitude is ascribed to Marcion, who not only forbade marriage but also objected against eating more than was strictly necessary.[51] Marcion and his movement propagated a very strict asceticism, involving complete renunciation of marriage and sexuality so that there was no procreation of believers along natural lines.[52] As Clement, *Strom* 3.12, puts it: 'They do not wish to fill the world made by the Creator-God'; he malignantly adds that they nonetheless 'use the food made by the Creator and breathe his air'. With regard to the 'Entweltlichung und Entkörperung' of the Marcionites, it has been said: 'Die so leben sind Übermenschen geworden.'[53] Tertullian, *De praescr haer* 30, 33, tells us that Marcion's disciple Apelles gave up continence. As with the other aspects of his teaching, the church condemned Marcion's ethics; but his influence was keenly felt for a prolonged period because his followers spread throughout the empire.[54] It is to Marcion and his adherents that authors like Irenaeus and Clement were essentially reacting.

Clement of Alexandria himself was among those guided by another type of dualism. He elevates the Christian life far above the ordinary created life.[55] As God is without passion, so the Christian Gnostic - Clement is proud to use the term - can arrive at the exalted state of ἀπάθεια in this life (*Strom* 7.15-21). Inner freedom is much more important for the believer than the observation of specific rules. Marriage is meant to be beyond desire and to lead to childbirth, after which a couple can live without sexual relationship (*Strom* 3.95, 108). The Gnostic should

[48] This idea is prominent in Niederwimmer, *Askese*, 58-63, 134-157, 186-198, but absent from Nagel, *Motivierung*.

[49] G. Sfameni Gasparro, *Enkrateia e antropologia. Le motivazioni protologiche della continenza e della verginità nel cristianesimo dei primi secoli e nello gnosticismo*, Rome 1984, 367; cf. Frank, *Grundzüge*, 8-9.

[50] Irenaeus, *AdvHaer* 1.24.2.

[51] Irenaeus, *AdvHaer* 1.28.1; cf. Lohse, *Askese*, 136-138.

[52] A. Harnack, *Marcion: das Evangelium vom fremden Gott*, Leipzig 1921, who comments (186-187): '... eine weltflüchtigere und schwerere Lebensordnung und -führung hat keine christliche Gemeinschaft vorgeschrieben als die Marcionitische.' Cf. Heussi, *Mönchtum*, 31, who refers to the second ed. (1924) of Harnack's book.

[53] Harnack, *Marcion*, 188.

[54] Justin, *Apology* 1.26; 1.58; cf. Head, 'Foreign God', 310.

[55] On Clement: Heussi, *Mönchtum*, 40-44; Lohse, *Askese und Mönchtum*, 162-168.

be able to refrain from wine and meat. Clement argues that Gnosis is the rational death that delivers the soul from the body (*Strom* 7.71), and he goes on:

> There is then one alone who is free from desire to begin with, viz., the Lord, who is the lover of men, who for our sakes became man; but all that are eager to be assimilated to the stamp given by him, strive to become free from desire by training. For he who has felt desire and has gained the mastery over himself, like the widow also, becomes virgin again through chastity. ... so the gnostic gets spiritual life and is saved.[56]

The differences between Clement and pagan philosophic asceticism are minimal.[57]

The protological position argues that marriage was not part of God's original creation. This view is not primarily dualistic but monotheist, and consists in a longing to return to paradisiac conditions, i.e. the situation before the intrusion of sexuality. It finds expression in the conviction that marriage is either a concession of God to control the damage resulting from sin's entry into the world or even itself the primal sin.[58] Clement, *Strom* 3.104, intimates that those who think in this way, argue that marriage is the knowledge resulting from eating the forbidden fruit. Nagel correctly observes that this view often implies that man can save himself by practicing asceticism.[59]

The idea of marriage as the primal sin occurs in Julius Cassian,[60] in the *Gospel of Thomas*, in the ATh and the AAnGr 37.[61] The *Gospel of the Egyptians*, in so far as we know it through Clement of Alexandria, was

[56] *Strom* 7.72, trans. J.B. Mayor, in J.E.L. Oulton and H. Chadwick, *Alexandrian Christianity. Selected Translations of Clement and Origen with Introductions and Notes*, London 1954.

[57] Lohse, *Askese und Mönchtum*, 165-166; Deming, *Paul on marriage*, 102-103.

[58] Sfameni Gasparro, *Enkrateia e antropologia*; *eadem*, 'L'Epistula Titi discipuli Pauli de dispositione sanctimonii e la tradizione dell'enkrateia', *ANRW* II.25.6 (1988) 4551-4664, esp. 4554-4559; Nagel, *Motivierung*, 55-62; U. Bianchi, 'Encratismo, acosmismo, diteismo come criteri di analisi storico-religiosa degli apocrifi', *Augustinianum* 23 (1983) 309-317.

[59] Nagel, *Motivierung*, 58-59, 62: 'Dabei gilt nicht mehr gegenüber dem Neuen Testament die Menschwerdung Christi als Heilstat Gottes, sondern die aus Gottes Heilsplan stammende Askese als Instrumentum satisfactionis für den Urfall des Menschen.'

[60] As referred to by Clement of Alexandria, *Strom* 3.91.

[61] Andrew to Maximilla (AAnGr 37, trans. Elliott): 'I rightly see in you Eve repenting and in me Adam converting. For what she suffered through ignorance, you - whose soul I seek - must now redress through conversion.' 'You healed her deficiency by not experiencing the same passions, and I have perfected Adam's imperfection by fleeing to God for refuge.'

also a representative of this radical asceticism.[62] Irenaeus, *AdvHaer* 1.28.1, shows no understanding for those who reject marriage on the basis of the protological motives because, in his opinion, they contradict God's express purpose in creating man and woman. Clement is no less fierce:

> If birth is something evil, let the blasphemers say that the Lord who shared in birth was born in evil, and that the virgin gave birth to him in evil. Woe to these wicked fellows! They blaspheme against the will of God and the mystery of creation in speaking evil of birth (*Strom* 3.102).

Irenaeus alleges that Tatian, a leader of the church in Syria, was a pupil of Justin and one of the first to propagate sexual continence (*AdvHaer* 1.28.1). Clement (*Strom* 3.79-93) combats Tatian and Julius Cassian for the very same reason, intimating that Tatian forbade not only marriage but also meat and wine (3.85). Both Fathers defend the lawfulness of a Christian marriage. The preserved writing of Tatian, the *Oratio ad Graecos*, does not contain ascetic traits. But both the unanimous ancient testimony and the preserved fragments of the Diatessaron point to ascetic tendencies in Tatian's thinking.[63] In (parts of) the church in Syria, the absolute continence of all believers was indeed a primary requirement throughout much of its history. Consequently, the promise to live as a virgin was a requirement for baptism. This strictness was later relaxed, giving way to a division of believers into two classes, the true ascetics and the ordinary members.[64] It is likely that the roots of this rigorous asceticism, which is typical of the Syrian churches, are not specifically Christian but must be sought in the general cultural climate of Syria.[65] In general Lohse's thesis, that Christian asceticism was at its strongest in areas with strong pagan asceticism, would seem to be true.[66]

The concept of the Spirit-filled ascetic does not seem to occur during the period being studied, but it may be mentioned for the sake of clarity. It assumes that there is either a direct line from the earliest charismatic

[62] Schneemelcher, *NA* I$^5$, 174-179; Elliott, *Apocryphal NT*, 16-19.

[63] Tatian, *Oratio ad Graecos and fragments*, ed. and trans. M. Whittaker, Oxford 1982; F. Bolgiani, 'Tatian', in A. Di Bernardino (ed.), *Encyclopedia of Early Christianity* 2, Cambridge 1992, 815; W.L. Petersen, *Tatian's Diatessaron. Its creation, dissemination, significance, and history in scholarship*, Leiden 1994, 67-72 (biography), 76-83 (encratism).

[64] On Syria see Kretschmar, 'Ursprung', 132-146, 177; Niederwimmer, *Askese*, 180-183.

[65] H.J.W. Drijvers, 'Apocryphal literature in the cultural milieu of Osrhoëne', *Apocrypha* 1 (1990) 231-247, esp. 241, repr. in his *History and Religion in Late Antique Syria*, Aldershot 1994, III; likewise Lohse, *Askese*, 158-159, cf. 152-154; different Niederwimmer, *Askese*, 185, 196-197, but cf. 182.

[66] Lohse, *Askese*, 159.

prophets and teachers to the later wandering ascetic monks, or that asceticism was practised with a view of receiving the divine Spirit.[67]

In addition to theological arguments, sociological factors also contributed to the rise of the asceticism. Frank suggests that in the Orthodox church women had hardly any other chances to gain status than by remaining virgins.[68] Asceticism was a way to escape male domination and possibly the perils of childbirth. Bremmer discusses the tendency in the early Empire to promote more intimate relationships within upper-class marriages, which put many women under such strain that they opted out of marriage and preferred virginity. For such persons, Christian asceticism was a welcome option.[69]

This survey makes evident that the attitudes towards asceticism ranged from outright rejection by Irenaeus to its institution as a prequisite for baptism in Syria. In terms of its asceticism, Early Christianity was a very colourful movement with many internal and external tensions. It is evident that Christian communities everywhere had to deal with the questions raised by the subject and that many debates were held, not only in the period being studied here but also in later centuries. Consequently, if we will find below that the AJ and the other AAA propagate some kind of sexual asceticism, that fact does not in itself place them outside what was acceptable in the second century.

*1.3 Specific Gnostic and Jewish points of view?*

It is hard to discern any specific contribution to Christian asceticism that can be identified with the Gnostic movement. In their attitude[70] towards sexuality, the Gnostics were as diverse as the other Christian groups and they were hardly more friendly towards women.[71] Above I have already referred to the encratic position of Saturninus; but the Gnostic Justin vigorously defended not just the legitimacy but even the necessity of marriage.[72] Again, according to Clement of Alexandria, Theodotus as well

[67] Nagel, *Motivierung*, 69-75.

[68] Frank, *Grundzüge*, 11; cf. Hauschild, *Lehrbuch*, 268.

[69] J.N. Bremmer, 'Why did Early Christianity attract Upper-class Women?', in A.A.R. Bastiaensen *et al.* (eds.), *Fructus centesimus. FS Bartelink*, Steenbrugge 1989, 37-47, esp. 44-46.

[70] See the opening phrases of Clement of Alexandria, *Strom* 3. Lohse, *Askese*, 133-141, is still valid.

[71] Some examples in P. McKechnie, '"Women's Religion" and Second-Century Christianity', *JEH* 47 (1996) 409-431, esp. 415.

[72] Van den Broek, *Studies in Gnosticism*, 139, quoting R.M. Grant, *Gnosticism and Early Christianity*, New York/London ²1966, 22-24.

as the Valentinians were not opposed to marriage, sex and childbearing;[73] the allegedly Valentinian *Gospel of Philip* has much to say on spiritual marriage ('the mystery of the bridal chamber') but avoids pronouncements about ordinary marriage.[74] Irenaeus accuses some Gnostics of very lax morality and reports that others completely rejected marriage.[75]

It would seem that sexuality is about the only issue involved in asceticism that explicitly concerned the Gnostics. On the subject of food, clothing or material possessions, they are remarkably silent. Stroumsa argues that this silence has to do with the root conviction of the Gnosis which, in his opinion, is a hatred against the God of the Old Testament and his creation, more specifically procreation, and with its implicit lack of interest in morality.[76]

The available sources likewise do not support the connection of Jewish Christian sects with asceticism.[77] This was only to be expected in view of the fact that Judaism as such is generally not ascetic in attitude, except when fasting is concerned.[78] The Therapeutae described by Philo in *De vita contemplativa,* as well as the Essenes who were divided over the question of marriage, are exceptions to this rule.[79] And yet it is remarkable that while Philo reports that women as well as men were part of the community of the Therapeutae, that they abstained from food during

[73] *Strom* 3.1.1; *ExcTheodoto* 67.2-3. See G. Quispel, 'The original doctrine of Valentinus the Gnostic', *VigChr* 50 (1996) 327-352, esp. 334-336; Van Eijk, 'Marriage', 219; *pace* Niederwimmer, *Askese*, 213 n.72.

[74] E.H. Pagels, 'The "Mystery of Marriage" in the *Gospel of Philip* Revisited', in B.A. Pearson (ed.), *The Future of Early Christianity. FS Köster*, Minneapolis 1991, 442-454.

[75] *AdvHaer* 1.6.1-4 and 1.24.2, resp.

[76] Stroumsa, 'Ascèse et gnose', 150-152. Stroumsa never mentions that Valentinus and others allowed marriage. Niederwimmer, *Askese*, 198-207, likewise stresses the primarily negative motivation of Gnostic behaviour, whether libertine or strict.

[77] The collection of testimonies by A.F.J. Klijn and G.J. Reinink, *Patristic Evidence for Jewish-Christian Sects*, Leiden 1973, is most eloquent in its silence. It gives evidence that Jewish Christians propagated marriage (Eusebius, *HE* III.28.5; Epiphanius, *Panarion*, 19.1.7; 30.2.6; 30.18.2-3) but abstained from meat (Epiphanius, *Panarion*, 30.15.3; 53.1.4). Notice that with Epiphanius we are in the late fourth century and that he is less trustworthy than earlier authors. As I suggested in n.2 above, there is little evidence that those called encratites by Irenaeus and Epiphanius formed a separate group of Christians.

[78] The words of Proverbs 18:22 are representative: 'He who finds a wife finds a good thing, and obtains favour from the Lord.' Cf. for a later period G.F. Moore, *Judaism in the first centuries of the Christian era* II, Cambridge MA 1927, repr. 1970, 263-270.

[79] Moore, *Judaism*, 264; M. Simon, 'L'ascétisme dans les sectes juives', in Bianchi, *Tradizione dell'enkrateia*, 393-426, who concludes that both groups were clearly distinct, marginal to Judaism and probably unrelated to Christian asceticism.

certain periods, and that the women were mainly elderly virgins,[80] he never says that they were opposed to marriage as such.[81]

## 2 Asceticism in the Acts of John

As in the earlier chapters, it is vitally important to let the AJ speak for itself and not to include it *a priori* in a corpus of AAA.[82] At the risk of strengthening the common view that asceticism is nothing but sexual abstinence, I begin with a treatment of the attitudes towards women and sexuality contained in the AJ, a topic about which it has rather much to say. Several other issues can be dealt with in a single paragraph.

### *2.1 Women and sexuality*

The first preserved story of the AJ (cc.18-25) contains no word about the nature of the marital relationship of the couple that is central in it, Lycomedes and Cleopatra. Although they both convert to Christ, nothing is said about a change in or an end to their marital life. John even commands Lycomedes to 'receive his wife' (21.5) which does not suggest abstinence. The conclusion that this part of the AJ does not teach an ascetic lifestyle is certainly valid.

It has been argued that the ethical recommendations in c.29 imply complete sexual renunciation.[83] The episode in which these exhortations occur does not lead us to expect far-reaching statements about asceticism because John's message does not focus on it. In fact there is only one phrase that requires discussion: the list of tropes indicating the beneficial effects of 'spiritual painting' ends with τὰ ὑπογάστριά σου ἐκκόπτων (29.14). In Greek literature the word ὑπογάστριά (things of the lower belly) generally indicates the abdomen; it is only in Philo that the term probably refers to sexual pleasures.[84] In view of these facts, it seems that

80 Presence of women: *Contempl* 32, 69, 87-88; diet *ibid.* 34-37; virgins *ibid.* 68.

81 Deming, *Paul on marriage*, 96, solves the matter by assuming that the Therapeutae fulfilled their civic duties (i.e., married and reared children) before they devoted themselves completely to φιλοσοφεῖν.

82 The corpus-approach is found in Van Uytfanghe, 'Encratisme', 180-181, and in Frank, *Grundzüge*, 9, who severely misrepresents the AJ: 'Besonders folgenreich war, dass eine christliche Erbauungsliteratur vom späten 2.Jh. an - bes. die sog. apokryphen Apostelakten - sich weithin unter dem Einfluss der häretischen Propaganda stellte. Darin wurde Jesus von Nazareth selbst zur asketischen Gestalt, ebenso seine Apostel, deren Verkündigung vielfach auf den Appell zum entschieden asketischen Leben zusammenschrumpfte.'

83 Sirker-Wicklaus, *Untersuchungen*, 177-178.

84 E.g. *Opif.* 158 (τοὺς ὑπογαστρίους οἴστρους); *Mos.* I.28, II.23.

Junod and Kaestli's translation 'ampute tes organes sexuels' is too specific and that Elliott's 'mutilates your abdomen' is preferable. John combats passions in general because they are dangerous for the spiritual life, and he does not preach complete abstinence.

Cc.30-36 focus on the Ephesian women and especially on the widows among them. John pronounces a speech that is not theological but ethical in content. He condemns adultery and divorce (c.35), but not marriage or sexuality as such, so that it seems that he defends rather than attacks decent marriages.[85] The audience is not instructed on the subject of abstinence, and the (admittedly editorial) final sentence of the story tells that all women were healed without preconditions. If the author had a specific message about ascetic behaviour for his readers, he fails to even allude to it. This silence is a strong indication that the AJ does not preach abstinence.[86]

Cc.37-47 contain nothing concerning our subject, but cc.48-54 deal with a young person who first commits adultery and then castrates himself. The episode discusses the questions posed by the fact that both Christians and pagans propagated complete asceticism, and that some cults indeed required self-castration, as we have already seen above.[87] It would seem that it is one of the lifestyle issues that new converts to Christianity might face. The sexual activity of the man in the first part of the story (cc.49-50) is regarded as adultery just because the woman whom he loves is married to somebody else; John condemns the adulterous act but not marriage as such. The intermediate chapters 51-52 report the resurrection of the boy's father and the conversion of father and son.

Here the story could have reached a happy end, but in c.53 the boy suddenly cuts off his masculine organs and throws them in the face of the woman. His accompanying words are: 'On your account I became a parricide and should also become a murderer both of you two and myself. Here is the cause of all.'[88] Instead of 'on your account' one would expect

[85] *Pace* JK, 463, whose statement about the remark on children in c.34 and its apparent aversion to procreation is unfounded.

[86] *Pace* Plümacher, 'Apostelakten', 44.

[87] E.g. Kybele, cf. n.6 above. Philostratus, *Vita Apollonii* 1.33, 36, discusses the merit of making eunuchs. See now D.F. Caner, 'The Practice of Prohibition of Self-Castration in Early Christianity', *VigChr* 51 (1997) 396-415.

[88] Plümacher, 'Paignion', 99-101, has to argue that the wife is the enemy of the boy in order to prove his thesis that the AJ depends on the folklore tale of the beaver which castrates itself when hunted, but admits (101) that both stories hardly fit together. *Idem*, 102-108, explains this episode against the background of a hypothetical situation in Alexandria at the end of the second century. In chapter 6 I will show that this reconstruction is untenable.

'because of these (organs)'. As the text stands, the boy blames both the woman and his own desires. John fiercely condemns this self-castration as an act inspired by satan (54.2-5) and argues that not the body but the spirit must be clipped. This pronouncement is a clear guideline for the readers: chastity is important because passions are a threat to the soul, yet the right form of chastity is not essentially different from that of such philosophically minded people as the Stoics. Chastity is a completely spiritualised attitude.[89]

For those who read the AJ in translation, cc.60-61 seem irrelevant in a discussion of the text's views on asceticism. This short episode is designated as a 'paignion', a humorous piece (60.3), and Plümacher argues: 'die Anekdote selbst besitzt keinerlei tieferen Sinn.'[90] But several elements of the paignion, some of them brought to light by Plümacher's own research, suggest that this episode is more than a funny intermezzo. The first indication of its underlying seriousness is that three of the four manuscripts contain puns on the word louse (κόρις): in 60.10 instead of the expected κόρεις (lice, so **O**) manuscript **M** uses the plural of the word 'girl' (κόραι), and manuscripts **R** and **Z** have the female plural form κόριδες.[91] Thus 60.7-8 can be taken to suggest that female beings disturbed John at night. In lines 10-11 the animals are addressed as girls who should stay away from the bed of the apostle.

In the second place, the genre of the episode reminds us of the 'paraklausithyron', the poem of the lover who has been barred from the house and has to spend the night on the doorstep.[92] Both elements suggest that John cannot bear female company in bed and that by means of this funny story the author of our text intends to stress the importance of the continence of the apostle. Lastly, we can refer to the admonition at the end of the episode, which encourages the readers to listen even better to the commandments of God than the animals did. The proper behaviour of a Christian is here, as it is frequently in the text, represented by the word ἡσυχάζω,[93] which does not denote complete asceticism but rather a conscious and moderate way of life.

The long episode in cc.63-86 throws a particular light on the author and his occupation with sexuality. He does not even shrink from describing

[89] Cf. Plümacher, 'Paignion', 92-96. There is no exact parallel in extant Stoic literature.

[90] Plümacher, 'Paignion', 79.

[91] Bovon in *Actes apocryphes*, 154; JK, 246 n.1, 540; Plümacher, 'Paignion', 83, who argues for the originality of the reading of **M**.

[92] Plümacher, 'Paignion', 84-85.

[93] Cf. 54.12, 66.3, 75.9, 79.12.

an attempted necrophilia.[94] Initially, 63.5-6 explicitly inform us that Drusiana and Andronicus had stopped having sexual intercourse out of reverence for God (διὰ θεοσέβειαν).[95] This abstinence was undertaken on her initiative, and at first he threatened to kill her on account of it, but eventually he was won over to her viewpoint. All these things are in marked contrast to the relationship of Cleopatra and Lycomedes that we discussed above.[96] Abstinence, however, is not presented as something that is binding to all but rather as a matter of individual decision.[97] Drusiana and her husband are exemplary believers but the text never forces other believers to follow their example and to renounce marriage. The message of John in this episode can be summarised as 'contempt of the temporary' (70.2-3). The statement is highly spiritual, but hardly implies a specific rejection of marriage or even of sexual intercourse within marrital relationships.[98]

There is more to the story. John says that 'the beauty of a body can only be judged when it completely undressed' (69.5-6). This is not the kind of thought we would expect to be mentioned by a propagandist of virginity![99] Again, the role of Drusiana is so ambiguous that it is impossible to regard her as an example for the readers. She occupies an important position in that she is willing to face martyrdom for the sake of her chastity. Moreover, she raises her former enemy from the dead (cc.64, 81-84), but ironically this Fortunatus turns out to be wholly unrepentant, so that his resurrection does not increase her prestige. Her role would have been much more important if she had resurrected the good character Callimachus, but that resurrection is performed by John prior to her own revivication (cc.78-80). To conclude, cc.63-86 cannot be regarded as a plea for asceticism.[100]

Of the rest of the text, only c.113 has anything to do with marriage and celibacy, but something important indeed. John tells how in the past, apparently in Galilee, the Lord kept him from marrying despite his repeated attempts to do so. Some scholars take this episode to teach that

[94] Vielhauer, *Literatur*, 707: 'Das erotisch-asketische Element ... enthüllt mit seiner Extravaganz die Askese als Erotik mit negativem Vorzeichen.'

[95] G. Bertram in *TDNT*, *s.v.*, argues that θεοσέβεια is not a specifically Christian motive.

[96] Unlike Drusiana, Cleopatra does not appear in the Manichaean Psalms (ed. Allberry).

[97] The motivation of Drusiana as referred to in 63.9-10 by the anonymous speaker suggests that he shares her condemnation of sexual intercourse.

[98] Having children is included among the ordinary problems humans face (68.5), and its inclusion there shows that the author does not live in an abstinent community.

[99] The occurrence of ἔρως as sinful lust in the catalogue of vices 68.5-8 is again no outright condemnation of all sexuality.

[100] *Pace* Sirker-Wicklaus, *Untersuchungen*, 182, 234.

sexuality as such is wrong, suggesting that John functions as a model for all believers.[101] But those who take this view overlook the Lord's explicit statement in lines 6-7: 'John, if you were not mine, I would have let you marry.' These words make it crystal clear that the AJ teaches not abstinence for everyone but just celibacy for some.[102] As an apostle, John must be completely dedicated in his service of the Lord. He does more than just imitate Christ.[103] This motive is of Cynic-Stoic origin; it especially reminds us of Epictetus and resembles the strictly personal standpoint of Paul in 1 Cor 7:7.[104]

Taken as a whole, the attitude towards women reflected in the text is neither specifically feminist nor misogynist. Unlike what we see in the pagan novels, the noted beauty of one of the female characters is a marginal aspect rather than the central feature.[105] Unlike Thecla, Maximilla and Migdonia in some other AAA, there are no women in the AJ who experience a spiritual love for the apostle.

The absence of an absolute condemnation of sexuality confirms the essential correctness of Van Kampen's view that it is interest in the soul which motivates our author. The way to salvation presented in the AJ is through spiritual resurrection and through the care of one's soul, and not the result of any specific lifestyle. Sexuality might indeed keep people from this spiritual life and, as such, it is one of the possible threats to the soul, but that does not make it wrong in itself.[106] The conviction of our author differs fundamentally from the maxim in APlTh 12, which states

[101] E.g. G. Sfameni Gasparro, 'Gli Atti apocrifi degli Apostoli e la tradizione dell'enkrateia', *Augustinianum* 23 (1983) 287-307, esp. 299, who especially mentions lines 12-14 which speak of impure folly and bitter death, and directly links these words to sexuality.

[102] Cf. JK, 576-577. Cf. also the fact that in many pagan cults only the priests or prophets were abstinent, cf. Lohse, *Askese*, 29.

[103] *Pace* Nagel, *Motivierung*, 8, who lists AJ 113 under the motif of imitation of Christ, and who includes ATh, in which abstinence is compulsory for all believers, under the same motif.

[104] Epictetus (about 50-135 AD), with whom no other points of contact exist; Deming, *Paul on marriage*, 83-89.

[105] Cleopatra is beautiful (c.20) but only in the (words and) eyes of her own husband. The introduction of Drusiana into the narrative has been lost, but cc.63-86 never discusses her appearance, leaving the necrophiliacs motive for raping her in the dark. Even when she stands exposed nearly naked (c.80) there is no word about how she looks. Likewise, nothing is said about the looks of the anonymous woman who attracted the young man (cc.48, 53-54).

[106] Van Kampen, *Apostelverhalen*, 110-114.

that only those who live in abstinence will be resurrected.

It has become evident that sexual asceticism is a theme which features in some - but by far not all! - of the many stories, sermons and prayers in the AJ.[107] The prohibition of marriage and sexuality is strictly limited to John alone and motivated by the fact that Christ needs him. As such, it distinguishes the apostle(s) from most other believers. There is no evidence for the existence of a specific class of clergy in the group in which the AJ originated.

*2.2 Asceticism censored?*

It is necessary once more to examine the hypothesis that parts of the original AJ were subject to censorship[108] and to deal specifically with the suggestion that the pseudonymous *Epistula Titi discipuli Pauli* preserves authentic fragments from the early AJ.[109] If these three alleged fragments of the AJ, all of which propagate continence, are indeed genuine, the character of the AJ must be considered in a completely different light. One thing is beyond dispute: the author of the *Epistula Titi* was not a forger; he must have found the words he cites in his copy of the AJ. But the question is whether he had the AJ in the second-century version that we consider more or less identical with the original. To put it in other words, did the AJ originally recommend complete abstinence and were the relevant passages removed at some later date, or do the extremely ascetic passages derive from a later redaction? Given the text's transmission history, both views are possible.

As to the internal evidence of the 'quotations', the first one derives from c.113, whereas the second and the third are not found in the present text.[110] In contrast with Junod and Kaestli's text, in the first fragment the

[107] Cf. Van Kampen, *Apostelverhalen*, 110; Tissot, 'Encratisme', 117. An exception is c.29. *Pace* Vielhauer, *Literatur*, 707, who argues 'Das erotisch-asketische Element dominiert.'

[108] In chapter 1, I have argued that there is insufficient evidence to support a hypothesis of doctrinal censorship.

[109] Ed. D. De Bruyne, 'Epistula Titi Discipuli Pauli, de Dispositione Sanctimonii', *RevBen* 37 (1925) 47-63; now also in *PLS* 2; trans. A. de Santos Otero in *NA*[5], 50-70 (without line-numbers); studies: C. Schmidt, 'Studien zu den alten Petrusakten', *ZKG* 43 (1924) 321-348; A. Harnack, 'Der apokryphe Brief des Paulusschülers Titus "De dispositione Sanctimonii"', *Sitzungsberichte der Preus. Akademie der Wissenschaften, Phil.-hist. Klasse* 17 (1925) 180-213; A. de Santos Otero, 'Der Apokryphe Titusbrief', *ZKG* 74 (1963) 1-14; JK, 136-145, with the relevant passages in Latin and French; Sfameni Gasparro, 'Epistula Titi'. This *Epistula* is strongly encratitic because it completely rejects marriage.

[110] The fact that the first fragment stems from the very end of the AJ does not imply that later fragments, if authentic, had their place after c.113, for the *Epistula* does not observe the order of its sources.

important word 'for yourself' (ἑαυτῷ, 113.1) is absent. This absence qualifies the virginity of John as being 'for the Lord' and thus implicitly limited to him, not a prerequisite for all Christians. But in view of the bad Latin of the text of the *Epistula* and the further freedom in the transmission of the text, we cannot draw firm conclusions from this omission. The interpretation of c.113 has been discussed above.

In the second fragment the deacon Byrrhus, who belongs to the cast of the original AJ, appears. But we also have the phrase 'in the last days' (*in novissimis temporibus*), which reflects a perspective on history foreign to the original AJ. The motivation for ascetic behaviour here is unclear. The demons who speak at the same time announce their defeat and express confidence in their strength.[111] It seems that sexuality is connected with demonic activity. This motive is not found in the original AJ.

The third and longest fragment is introduced by the information that John went to a wedding in order to prevent its taking place. Twice John addresses his audience as 'little children' (*filioli*), an expression which occurs frequently in the AJ and that gives the fragment an air of authenticity.[112] But this impression fades away because at the end there is again an eschatological expression, 'expecting Christ from heaven', which stands in acute tension with the theology of the early AJ. Christ is even regarded as the bridegroom of the believers, a conception which also sounds much more 'Catholic' than the early AJ does. Some items in the long list of negative characteristics of marriage, like *experimentum serpentis*, *nativitatis fructum sordidum* and *materiae conversatio*, remind us of the protologically motivated condemnation of marriage (discussed above), which is not otherwise found in the AJ. The authenticity of this episode is even more doubtful because of the fact that it has important parallels: one of the other quotations in the *Epistula Titi* is a similar story in which the apostle Andrew is the main character and which has no counterpart in the remains of the AAn. In the earliest versions of the AAA, an incident about a wedding only occurs in the ATh 4-16. It would therefore seem that a narrative motif has secondarily been transferred from one text, the ATh, to others.

From the internal evidence I conclude that the second and third of the alleged quotations in the *Epistula Titi* cannot have been part of the original AJ because they do not comply with the very consistent theological tendency of the rest of the AJ.[113] This conclusion contradicts the

[111] JK, 142.

[112] AJ 27.5, 28.2,6-7, 46.19, 47.5, 54.9, 78.2, 81.10,18, 111.4.

[113] *Pace* Sfameni Gasparro, 'Epistula Titi', 4633-4636, who hesitates about the second and accepts the third fragment as authentic.

suggestion that the AJ was a victim of doctrinal censorship. The passages cited in the *Epistula Titi* must have been introduced into the AJ at some later moment.

We may even be able to discover in what circles the interpolations were made. It is probable that the author of the *Epistula Titi* received his copy of the AJ from the Manichaeans.[114] Although the authorship and geographical origin of the *Epistula* are disputed, all hypotheses about its authorship allow the possibility that Manichaeans were the source of the text of the AAA used by the *Epistula Titi*.[115] It is significant that the Manichaeans are often alleged to have written or changed the AAA, e.g. by Filastrius of Brescia.[116] We have already come upon weighty evidence that suggests considerable Manichaean reworking of the AJ.[117] It is therefore likely that the Manichaeans added the strongly ascetic passages to their version of the AJ, bringing it in line with the APl and the ATh, both of which we will study below.

*2.3 Further aspects of asceticism*

As for nutrition, the AJ does not teach abstinence.[118] The only significant reference to food occurs in the evidence that the eucharist is celebrated only with bread.[119] Ascetic groups of Christians likewise just used bread, or bread and water instead of wine (see e.g. APe 2); but we may legitimately ask if our author is conscious of the fact that his form of the eucharist has this ascetical quality.

With respect to property and riches, the AJ does not have a particular

[114] This is argued by Santos Otero, 'Apokryphe Titusbrief', 8-9, but had been denied by Harnack, 'Apokryphe Brief', 207.

[115] 1) Harnack's now traditional view ('Apokryphe Brief', 205-209, cf. JK, 138, and Junod and Kaestli, *Histoire*, 87-102) assumes that the *Epistula* stems from Priscillianist circles; see the sceptical reaction of H. Chadwick, *Priscillian of Avila. The occult and the charismatic in the early church*, Oxford 1976, 109-110. The Priscillianists, a fourth/fifth-century sect in Spain, used the AJ and other apocrypha but the form in which they had the text has not been reconstructed. 2) Santos Otero, 'Apokryphe Titusbrief', 10-11, argues that the *Epistula Titi* was written in the fifth century by someone within the mainline Spanish church, in which the AAA were in use even in the services. 3) Sfameni Gasparro, 'Epistula Titi', 4652-4655, suggests an origin in Africa towards 400; cf. now Bremmer, 'The Novel'.

[116] Filastrius 88 (CSEL 38.48); cf. Chadwick, *Priscillian*, 24, 119-120.

[117] Papyrus Kellis 1 and Augustine. The latter had a version that differed from what we consider the original. See chapter 1.

[118] *Pace* Bauer, *Leben Jesu*, 322, and R. McL.Wilson, 'Alimentary and sexual encratism in the Nag Hammadi tractates', in Bianchi, *Tradizione dell'enkrateia*, 317-332, esp. 322-323, who argue that AJ 93 presents the ideal of ascetic abstinence and poverty.

[119] Cf. Roldanus, 'Eucharistie', 79-82.

message. Riches (c.19) and power (cc.31, 56, 73) are mentioned without condemnation. In c.59 John leaves money to the believers, which he apparently possessed himself - at least we are not told how he got it! John's sermon against the rich (cc.34-36) has an ascetic element, but the emphasis falls on the positive counterpart of the prohibitions, viz. on the care of the soul that is made possible by these ascetic practices.[120]

Finally we come to the subject of wandering. It might be argued that John is depicted as a man who travels very much, but two observations modify this view. In so far as John is a wandering missionary, this presentation is no doubt influenced by the Book of Acts and by oral traditions about how apostles lived and worked. A closer look at the text reveals that John soon settles down in Ephesos and raises no objections about living in a house. It requires other people, from Miletus and Smyrna, to almost force him to go on a missionary tour (37.1-2; 55). The situation reflected in the AJ differs considerably from that in *Didache* 11, in which wandering apostles are allowed only short stays in any house and in which prophets play a major role. The AJ limits the title of apostle to John and does not mention any prophets. In sum, nothing suggests that the AJ has its background in a tradition of wandering preachers.[121] If these wandering ascetics were a common feature in Syria and Palestine, the AJ originated in a different environment.

All in all the author adopts moderate positions and cannot be regarded as a propagandist for strict asceticism. Amid the very broad spectrum of attitudes within second-century Christianity as well as among the pagan views described above, the AJ does not stand out. In the course of our survey, we have already come upon the deep motivation behind the concrete advice given by the author: the care for the soul.[122] If it is well

[120] In this respect the text from the Irish *Liber Flavus* in which John changes hay into gold is much more explicit. See JK, 114-115, 130-132; and J.-D. Kaestli, 'Fiction littéraire et réalité sociale: Que peut-on savoir de la place des femmes dans le milieu de production des Actes apocryphes des Apôtres?', *Apocrypha - le champ des Apocryphes* 1 (1990) 279-302, esp. 301-302.

[121] *Pace* Sirker-Wicklaus, *Untersuchungen*, 240-241, who even argues that 'die Menschen dieser [die AJ tragende] Gemeinschaft nicht anders gelebt haben als die fiktive Apostelgestalt und ihre ebenso fiktive Anhängerschar: als Wanderasketen.' Would she also argue that Theophilus (Acts 1:1) and his circle were tentmakers like Paul?

[122] It is insufficient to repeat the old view that the AJ is Gnostic and therefore opposed to sexual relations, expressed by Lipsius, *Apostelgeschichten*, 519, and by Sturhahn, *Christologie*, 94. But neither can we follow Sirker-Wicklaus, *Untersuchungen*, 234-235, in postulating a connection between the docetism of the AJ and its ascetic point of view; she overlooks the fact that ascetic viewpoints also occur among Christians with different Christologies.

with your soul, the AJ never disturbs you with ascetic principles. The dualism of soul and body that characterises the AJ receives a specific Christian colouring only with respect to the apostle himself, who must remain a virgin in order to serve Christ.

*2.4 The position of section C and the redaction of the early Acts of John*
The survey of what the Gnostic part of the AJ has to say about asceticism can be brief. In cc.94-102 and 109, no attention is paid to any elements of an ascetic lifestyle that we discussed above. In fact, this state of affairs was only to be expected because of the brevity of this text and because of the strong focus on the person and work of the Lord. Nevertheless, the situation implies that the author of this part of the text complied with what he found in the first main part and saw no reason to change or extend its message. For the author himself, salvation is not connected with a certain lifestyle but with insight, as it also is for the author of the first main part of the text. The interest of both authors lies with matters of Christology and salvation, not with asceticism.

A few details may yet be noted. C.95.8-9 refers to being born and bringing about other births without the explicit qualification that such acts are meant spiritually. That the gnostic author interpolated c.109 into the story of John's final eucharist suggests that he ratified its celebration with bread alone. Thus the AJ provides evidence for my view that the difference between non-Gnostic and Gnostic attitudes towards asceticism was rather small. In other words, Gnosticism was no more or less ascetic than any other type of second-century Christianity.

## 3 The asceticism of the Apocryphal Acts

*3.1 The other Apocryphal Acts*
At the outset it can be said that sexual asceticism is the only prominent form of asceticism in the AAA and that the other forms hardly deserve attention. The sexual asceticism in some of these texts is much more pervasive than it is in the AJ. Its importance is already evident at the level of the narrative: Andrew, Paul, Peter and Thomas are all martyred for their ascetic message and the consequent break-up of marriages. But the recurrence of that theme does not mean that there are no differences among these four AAA.

As we have seen above, marriage is the primal sin in the AAn. Nevertheless stress falls on the spiritual dimension of relationships rather than on abstention from sexuality as such.[123] In the ATh, which originated in Syria, the message of sexual renunciation is about the only message Thomas proclaims. The ATh does not (yet) know a division between true ascetics and ordinary believers, so that it must belong to the strict period of the Syrian church.[124] As to other forms of asceticism, Thomas omits the request for the daily bread from the Lord's Prayer (144). The APl also pays much attention to sexual asceticism, although it is not so prominent a theme here as in the ATh.[125] I have shown elsewhere that in most parts of these Acts chastity is a prerequisite for the resurrection.[126] Drijvers argues that the baptised lion is a symbol of encraticism.[127] In the Acts of Thecla continence is the most important theme and sexual intercourse is completely rejected,[128] though in view of the presence of married couples it would seem that marriage itself is not under attack.[129]

The APe differs from the texts just discussed and is more on the side of the AJ in so far as abstinence is not so central an issue in it. Chastity is propagated in the separately transmitted stories of Peter's own daughter and the gardener's daughter, and it is again important when the author needs a pretext for the execution of the apostle.[130] It would seem that the

[123] Van Kampen, *Apostelverhalen*, 141-158.

[124] Peterson, 'Hamburger Papyrusfragment', 187, assumes that the rigorous ATh is earlier than the APl which in his opinion testifies to a weakening of regulations. But modern research has shown that the APl must precede the ATh and that it has nothing to do with Syria.

[125] See now P.W. Dunn, 'Women's Liberation, the *Acts of Paul*, and Other Apocryphal Acts of the Apostles. A Review of Some Recent Interpretations', *Apocrypha* 4 (1993) 245-261.

[126] P.J. Lalleman, 'The resurrection in the Acts of Paul', in Bremmer, *Acts of Paul*, 126-141, esp. 132-133.

[127] H.J.W. Drijvers, 'Der getaufte Löwe und die Theologie der Acta Pauli', in P. Nagel (ed.), *Carl-Schmidt-Kolloquium 1988*, Halle 1990, 181-189 (repr. in his *History and Religion in Late Antique Syria*, Aldershot 1994), 188: 'Der redende und getaufte Löwe in den Acta Pauli hat eine ganz spezifische Bedeutung und stellt in ganz kondensierter Form die Theologie von Enthaltsamkeit und ewigem Leben dar. Er hat einen klar erkennbaren Symbolwert (...).'

[128] See also Dodds, *Age of Anxiety*, 32; Van Eijk, 'Marriage', 212-214.

[129] Bauckham, 'Sequel', 123-124.

[130] In c.5 Christ appears to Peter and the recently baptised Theon in the form of a young man. Peterson, 'Hamburger Papyrusfragment', 194-196, regards this vision as an allusion to Adam in his young, i.e. innocent and virginal state before the fall; but this view is rather far-fetched.

text is not consistent in this respect.[131] The attitude of the APe towards possessions also deserves attention. It represents a Christian form of patronage, making Christ the patron of his followers and the apostle the channel through whom the benefits flow. Although the APe is not immediately socially disruptive, this principle of patronage can finally undermine the whole social and political system.[132] The present survey underlines my previous conclusion that the AJ and the APe have close connections,[133] whereas the distance of the AJ from the APl, AAn and ATh is much greater.

*3.2 The Apocryphal Acts within early Christianity*

In previous scholarship the ascetic quality of the AAA has been credited with widely different causes. On the one hand Kurt Niederwimmer regards it as a relic of first-century enthusiasm which was discarded in the development towards the catholisation of the church. In his opinion, this process of catholisation took place in the second and third centuries and involved the separation between the specific class of those living as virgins and the mass of believers who were no longer subjected to this requirement.[134] On the other side of the spectrum Peterson gives the AAA a very important role in the development of second-century Christianity because, as we saw above, he makes them nearly solely responsible for the rise of Christian asceticism.

Niederwimmer's reconstruction of first-century Christianity can hardly be correct. He overaccentuates its enthusiastic aspects because he

[131] One can suppose 1. that only the lost first part was encratic (so Vielhauer, *Literatur*, 697-698); 2. that a strong encratic tendency in the original text was eradicated from the Latin version (*Actus Vercellenses*); 3. or that the encratic tendency was a secondary addition to the APe (so Van Kampen, *Apostelverhalen*, 64).

[132] R.F. Stoops, Jr., 'Patronage in the *Acts of Peter*', *Semeia* 38 (1986) 91-100; *idem*, 'Christ as Patron in the *Acts of Peter*', *Semeia* 56 (1992) 143-157; J.B. Perkins, 'The Social World of the *Acts of Peter*', in J. Tatum (ed.), *The Search for the Ancient Novel*, Baltimore/London 1994, 296-307.

[133] Lalleman, 'Acts of John and Acts of Peter'. A major difference is that the AJ focuses on individuals whereas the APe is community oriented.

[134] Niederwimmer, *Askese*, 176-186; '... ein später Reflex jener ursprünglichen enthusiastischen Weltabkehr und Sexualabkehr, durch das Umschlagen in blosse Weltverneinung gesteigert bis zum Sexualhass. Träger dieser Literatur sind Schichten am Rande der Grosskirche, am Rande der kirchlichen Organisation und der kirchlichen Theologie' (184); 'Der Enkratismus der Akten erklärt sich mithin letztlich aus einer anachronistischen *Resistenz gegenüber dem Katholisierungsprozess*' (186; italics original). For the dating of the AAA, Niederwimmer would seem to follow Schneemeelcher in *NA*[3]; notice the assumption of a corpus.

misrepresents Paul and neglects the Johannine churches. Conversely, he underestimates the power of the ascetic tendencies in the second century, such as I described in the beginning of the present chapter.

But Peterson c.s. (see note 1 above) ascribe rather too much influence to the AAA. My description of second-century asceticism in the beginning of this chapter demonstrates that it was widespread and, to a certain extent, accepted among pagans and Christians alike. There is simply no proof that the AAA, which are hard to date exactly, played a key role in its origin. After all, of the numerous and diverse motivations for ascetic behaviour which we discovered, the AAA only contain a few.

The truth about the AAA lies somewhere in the middle, and their role in the history of asceticism was probably quite modest. They reflect the ascetic aspect of Christian life and thinking rather than instigate it; they are a mirror, not a motor. The diverse AAA mirror second-century Christianity even to the extent that they represent clearly divergent points of view. Some of them are representative of the strongly ascetic form of Christianity attacked by Celsus[135] and these Acts may have promoted asceticism by their rather unbalanced statements, but we should be careful not to give them to much credit.

The AJ would probably have been more acceptable to Celsus than the more ascetic among the AAA. This supposition holds for the non-Gnostic first part of the AJ no less than for the Gnostic addition, which as we saw above makes few original contributions to the ideas about a redeemed lifestyle. It would seem that Francis, who follows what he labels as Stevan Davies' 'masterly analysis of the social world of the Apocryphal Acts of the Apostles',[136] fails to appreciate the essentially spiritual character of the religious and ethical views of the AJ, which pose no threat at all to vested interests because they only call for an inward transformation. In so far as the AJ is concerned, the criticism of Christianity's potential for social destabilisation by people like Celsus could refer to the rather emancipated position that women such as Drusiana could occupy.[137]

[135] Francis, *Subversive Virtue*, 166-174.

[136] Francis, *Subversive Virtue*, 172, referrring to Davies, *Widows*. Francis distances himself from Davies' hypothesis of female authorship. Other points on which I disagree with Francis include: 1. He considers AJ 14, 16, and fragments preserved in the *Epistula Titi* as integral parts of the text (34, 44, 47). 2. He holds that the communities of the AAA saw themselves as brides of Christ (121-122). 3. The AAA do not describe roaming preachers nor mirror situations in which there is an ecclesiastical hierarchy (Francis, 173, 175). 4. The statement (173) that in the AAA the apostles 'condemn not only wealth, but even ownership (A.Jn. 16, ed. James), and urge the giving up of not only homes and possessions, but fathers, mothers, and children (A.Th.6.61)' needs no comment.

[137] See above; cf. Francis, *Subversive Virtue*, 174.

Does the last sentence mean that the AJ reflects historical or at least 'possible' situations? Virginia Burrus argues that the stories in the AAA about chaste women reflect the historical reality of defiant Christian women, and that the story of Drusiana in the AJ must therefore be taken as a historically 'true' event.[138] She argues for a factual basis by suggesting that, since the women's stories cannot be derived from the ancient novels, they must be historically true. The argument is clearly a *non sequitur*.[139] Bremmer, who assumes that the AAA are directed at upper-class women and that asceticism made Christianity attractive for this group, nevertheless argues that only a few of them could afford to remain unmarried for a prolonged period.[140] The case of Drusiana may thus be 'true to life' but not representative for all believers.

*3.3 Conclusion*

The AJ is not characterised by a specific attitude towards asceticism that would enable us to be more specific about its origin. It did not originate with severe Encratites nor can it have given rise to such a movement within early Christianity. Claims that the AJ can be pinned down in time or place on the basis of its ascetic attitude should be avoided. As might have been expected, the Gnostic part of our text adds nothing to the asceticism that is already apparent in the preceding parts.

[138] V. Burrus, 'Chastity as Autonomy: Women in the Stories of the Apocryphal Acts', *Semeia* 38 (1986) 101-117.

[139] Burrus, 'Chastity', 106-107, cf. J.-D. Kaestli, 'Response', *Semeia* 38 (1986) 119-131.

[140] Bremmer, 'Upper-class women', 40, 44.

# CHAPTER 6: HISTORICAL QUESTIONS

So far we have examined the structure and the realm of thought of the AJ. Now, at the end of our study, we are going to address the historical questions of authorship, date and place. We will also pay attention to the historical value of what the text tells us about the apostle John, the position of the AJ as a witness to the reception of the Johannine Gospel and its position within the historical development of the Johannine movement. We will begin by addressing the latter issues since, as we will see, our answers to them have implications for the other issues.

## 1 The Johannine trajectory

### *1.1 Introduction*

In chapter 3, pp. 110-112 above, I made some remarks - to which the reader may wish again to refer - about the previous research on the relationship between the Gospel of John and the AJ. I adopted the word 'trajectory' to denote a theological tradition which is visible on the literary as well as the socio-historical level. I expressed the expectation that, contrary to what is sometimes assumed, study of the Johannine trajectory is a promising new approach to the second century and more specifically to its dark first half.[1] It is this topic that will now be taken up again. Consequently, the question to be addressed in this section is what the AJ contributes to our knowledge of the alleged Johannine trajectory.

There is no external evidence of a Johannine community in the second century. The internal evidence of the 'Johannine' texts is all we have.[2] The present investigation of the AJ has not yet yielded indications for the existence of a clearly defined Johannine group. On the one hand, this lack

[1] Contrast C.K. Barrett, *The Gospel according to St.John*, London ²1978, 62: '... to trace its (sc. the Fourth Gospel's) influence upon the thought of the first half of the second century is easy, for it had none.'

[2] In fact the situation is the same for the first century. Hengel, *Johanneische Frage*, esp. 97-99, 221-222, 248-252, 325, states that we know of only one head of the Johannine school, the Elder John, and that already in Ignatius and Polycarp no trace of the school remains. Indeed, the existence of a Johannine community has recently been questioned by J.A.T. Robinson, *The Priority of John*, London 1985, 28-32, and denied by W. Schmithals, *Johannesevangelium und Johannesbriefe. Forschungsgeschichte und Analyse*, Berlin/New York 1992, 208-214, 429. On the other hand, R.A. Culpepper, *The Johannine School. An Evaluation of the Johannine-School Hypothesis based on an Investigation of the Nature of Ancient Schools*, Dissertation Duke University 1974, esp. iii, 54-60, 414, merely claims that there was a Johannine community and then sets out to find out whether this community can be called a school.

of evidence is due to the fact that the AJ neither reflects tangible features of the communities in which the two main parts originated, nor preserves historically reliable reminiscences of the person of John.[3] On the other hand, it has become evident that the AJ did not originate in a secluded Johannine sect, for its familiarity with the Fourth Gospel does not hamper its knowledge of other Gospels. The absence of evidence for a Johannine community in the AJ is most remarkable: if anywhere, then it is in the AJ that one would expect to find evidence for its existence in the second century. After all, this text has John as its main character.

### *1.2 The adversaries in 1 and 2 John*

#### *1.2.1 Introduction*

Let us turn to the Johannine Epistles in order to get a better picture of the position of the AJ on the Johannine trajectory. Our specific question is whether the adversaries combatted in 1 Jn have things in common with the circles in which the AJ originated.[4] As far as I am aware, this question is a new one.[5] I do realise that one must be careful with pronouncements about the identity of the adversaries mentioned in the Epistles because there is no external evidence about them (except possibly the AJ!) and because the Epistles are quite vague about what exactly they condemn.[6] The question is nonetheless a legitimate one.

An important clue to the identity of the adversaries is provided by 1 Jn 2:18-19: 'They [the so-called antichrists] went out from us, but they were not of us; for if they had been of us, they would have continued with us.' These words imply that the community or communities addressed have gone through something of a schism. The adversaries are not just outsiders, but were formerly part of the Johannine community and, therefore, co-

[3] Cf. p. 40 above.

[4] Like most present-day scholars I assume that there is only one group of adversaries in 1 Jn; cf. K. Wengst, *Häresie und Orthodoxie im Spiegel des ersten Johannesbriefes*, Gütersloh 1976, 11 n.2; R.E. Brown, *The Epistles of John* (AB), Garden City 1982, 50; J. Painter, 'The "Opponents" in 1 John', *NTS* 32 (1986) 48-71; H.-J. Klauck, *Der erste Johannesbrief*, Zürich/Neukirchen-Vluyn 1991, 35.

[5] The AJ is conspicuously absent from R.E. Brown, *The Community of the Beloved Disciple*, New York 1979. But cf. the loose remark of Crossan, *Four Other Gospels*, 35: '... just as the Pastoral Epistles redeemed Paul from such as the Acts of Paul and the Johannine Epistles redeemed John from such as the Acts of John.' With the majority of scholars I assume that the Epistles are later than Jn; *pace* Hengel, *Johanneische Frage*, 156, 162.

[6] J.M. Lieu, 'Authority to become children of God. A Study of 1 John', *NT* 23 (1981) 210-228, warns against taking the polemics as the main objective of the author of the Epistle. She argues that the author's interest is with his readers, not with those who have left the community.

recipients of the Gospel of John. In fact, the adversaries may well have claimed that they were (also) a Johannine community or even the true Johannine Christians.

The main polemics of 1 Jn and 2 Jn concerns Christology.[7] Since we already know the importance of the Christology of the AJ, it is interesting to see if the Christology of the adversaries in the Epistles can be identified with that of the community in which the AJ was written. In view of the results of chapter 4, the question is more specifically whether the adversaries have a Christology which recognises only one - viz. divine - quality in Christ or whether both divine and human elements are thought to co-exist in him.[8] It will become evident that the relevant texts (2 Jn 7; 1 Jn 1:1-4, 2:22-23, 4:2-3, 5:6-8) clearly support the former position.

*1.2.2 Exegesis of 1 and 2 John*

The second Epistle gives us the best indications about what the adversaries believed. In 2 Jn 7 the adversaries are said to deny that Jesus Christ was ever physically present on earth: 'For many deceivers have gone out into the world, men who will not acknowledge the coming of Jesus Christ in the flesh.'[9] The right view of the person and work of Christ is under debate. The coming of Christ is the undisputed core of the Christian faith for both parties; the question under discussion is, *how* he came (or will come). The author stresses the flesh (σάρξ), the real humanity of Christ. The adversaries denied the σάρξ, the human embodiment of Christ. They taught that he had never possessed a fleshly body or any body at all.[10]

Emphasis is placed on the reality of Jesus' life on earth right at the beginning of the first Epistle (1 Jn 1:1-4). The author claims that he has

[7] See esp. Wengst, *Häresie,* 15.

[8] Most exegetes (see Brown, *Epistles*, 65 n.149) think that the Epistles combat a Christology which distinguishes between the human being Jesus and the divine Christ; this Christology is often associated with the early heretic Cerinthus. Hengel, *Johanneische Frage*, 170-181, a priori defines the adversary (Cerinthus) and then reads the Epistle in this light. A monograph on Cerinthus is urgently needed. Until then, see esp. Klijn and Reinink, *Patristic Evidence*, 3-19 (introduction), 102-105, 110-125 (main patristic texts); Pétrement, *Dieu séparé*, 409-430; O. Skarsaune, *The Proof from Prophecy*, Leiden 1987, 407-409.

[9] πλάνοι ... οἱ μὴ ὁμολογοῦντες Ἰησοῦν Χριστὸν ἐρχόμενον ἐν σαρκί.

[10] If the present participle ἐρχόμενον is taken as a future, stress falls primarily on the fact that, at the second coming, Christ is still incarnate. This change does not alter the intent of the pronouncement, i.e. to stress the corporeal being of Christ, cf. Hengel, *Johanneische Frage*, 182-185. G. Strecker, *Die Johannesbriefe*, Göttingen 1989, 333-337, takes the participle as a future.

with all his senses experienced the revelation of the word of life.[11] Though the name Jesus is not used, the reference is certainly to more than hearing the preaching of the gospel: what was 'felt with hands' and 'seen with eyes' is the life of Christ.[12] The author uses past tenses for past events and present tenses for the present of the readers and himself. He implies, in this way, that he was an eyewitness to the life of Christ.[13]

The following interpretation of 1 Jn 5:6a differs from that of most interpreters.[14] The verse runs: 'This is the one who came by (or: through) water and blood, Jesus Christ; not only in water, but in water and blood.'[15] The author suggests that his adversaries held that Jesus had come only in water and replies that in reality he had come in both water and blood. Both views require explanation, especially as to what is meant by water and by blood.

The standard exegesis relates the water to Jesus' baptism, but there are two objections to this view. First, the Gospel and the Epistles do not explicitly mention the baptism of Jesus; in the case of the Gospel this is a deliberate omission.[16] Second, if we interpret the author's statement that Christ came through water and blood as a reference to the importance of Jesus' baptism, the author would seem to accept the docetic position that Christ had not been the incarnate son from the beginning, but only from

[11] Weigandt, *Doketismus*, 104, refers to what Origen, *Contra Celsum*, 7.34 says: the reality of a person was ascertained by hearing, seeing and touching.

[12] Cf. Hengel, *Johanneische Frage*, 157-158, 265; Adam, 'Docetism, Käsemann and Christology', 395-396. The prologue to Jn also delays the use of the name Jesus.

[13] This interpretation resembles that of R. Schnackenburg, *Die Johannesbriefe*, Freiburg, 2nd impr. 1963, 49-58, and Strecker, *Johannesbriefe*, 59-62; *contra* J.M. Lieu, *The theology of the Johannine Epistles*, Cambridge 1991, 75, 78, who says that the Epistle does not pay much attention to the life of Jesus, because she reads 1:1-4 in a different way (24). This prologue is understandable as an attack on the docetists; it would not be effective in combatting a Cerinthian type of Christology, which did not deny the reality of Jesus, cf. B.D. Ehrman, '1 Joh 4 3 and the Orthodox Corruption of Scripture', *ZNW* 79 (1988), 221-243, 239.

[14] But see G. Richter, 'Blut und Wasser aus der durchbohrten Seite Jesu (Joh 19,34b)', *MTZ* 21 (1970) 1-21; B. Witherington III, 'The waters of birth: John 3.5 and 1 John 5.6-8', *NTS* 35 (1989) 155-160.

[15] οὗτός ἐστιν ὁ ἐλθὼν δι' ὕδατος καὶ αἵματος, Ἰησοῦς Χριστός, οὐκ ἐν τῷ ὕδατι μόνον ἀλλ' ἐν τῷ ὕδατι καὶ ἐν τῷ αἵματι.

[16] Ehrman, '1 Joh 4 3', 238-239. *Contra* U.B. Müller, *Die Menschwerdung des Gottessohnes. Frühchristliche Inkarnationsvorstellungen und die Anfänge des Doketismus*, Stuttgart 1990, 92-93.

his baptism.[17] It is preferable to interprete the water as referring to the very beginning of Christ's life; as such it can be a circumlocution of birth[18] or of that which causes birth, the male seed.[19] In both cases the reference to water emphasizes the factuality of Christ's birth. This approach is in harmony with the likely meaning of the verb 'to come', which in this Epistle refers to a definite entrance or beginning (2:18; 4:2b; 4:3b).

The blood is commonly taken as a reference to the violent death of Christ. In that case, belief in his 'coming in water (only)' would amount to a denial of his death. But the most natural reading of 'to come in water and blood' is that the two nouns refer to the same event.[20] Can the element of blood also be connected with the beginning of the life of Christ? This meaning certainly fits better with the phrases 'to come "through" or "in" blood', which cannot refer to the manner of Christ's death because the prepositions (διά, ἐν) cannot be taken to refer to the crucifixion.[21] The meaning of the word blood in our verse should be connected with its use in Jn 1:13 ('... who have not been born out of blood or out of the will of flesh ...') and in 19:34 ('... and immediately blood and water come out', viz. of the side of Jesus), in which it represents the corporeal-human side of existence. I conclude that blood has a physiological sense here, and that in combination with ἔρχομαι it refers to the beginning of life.

Blood and water were the elements of which a human body was allegedly composed.[22] This explanation matches best with Jn 19:34, for whatever the sacramental allusions in that verse, the words water and blood must primarily be taken in their literal-physical sense: the Jesus who died

[17] Cf. Richter, 'Blut und Wasser', 5.

[18] Witherington, 'Waters of birth', who refers to Prov 5:15-18 and Cant 4:12-15 as well as to extra-biblical sources.

[19] H. Odeberg, *The Fourth Gospel. Interpreted in its relation to contemporaneous religious currents in Palestine and the Hellenistic-Oriental world*, Uppsala/Stockholm 1929, 48-71, esp. 49-55, gives rabbinic parallels, and states (49) that 'the ὕδωρ is that which in the spiritual process corresponds to the semen in the sarcical process.'

[20] Richter, 'Blut und Wasser', 5; Brown, *Epistles*, 573.

[21] The translation 'to go' for ἔρχομαι does not fit well with the proposition 'in', so that I prefer 'to come'.

[22] E. Schweizer, 'Das johanneische Zeugnis vom Herrenmahl', *EvTheol* 8 (1952-53) 341-363, esp. 350-353, referring to *LevR* 15 (115c) and to Greek sources; Richter, 'Blut und Wasser', 14-16.

on the cross had a body, and so his death was real.[23]

This interpretation of Jn 19:34 is confirmed by an unexpected source, viz. the author of AJ 101. In his denial of the reality of Christ's body and of the passion, he intimates that Jn 19:34 was taken literally by those whose interpretation he combats, for he writes: (ἀκούεις) αἷμα ἐξ ἐμοῦ ῥεῦσαν καὶ οὐκ ἔρευσεν ('blood flowed from me, yet it did not flow'). These words demonstrate that he knew or supposed that the flowing of the blood and the water in the Gospel of John were literally meant. The AJ deletes the element blood from the pair water and blood found in the Gospel, thus suggesting that 'Christ came in water only'.[24] This is exactly the otherwise unattested thought of the Johannine adversaries! These adversaries, whose beliefs are expressed in the AJ, held that Christ had only apparently or not at all been human.[25]

We conclude that to come in both water and blood in 1 Jn 5:6 means 'to consist from the beginning of water and blood, to have a real human body.' In the opinion of the author, Christ did not just appear to be born, but he was really born. Conversely, the adversaries are those who deny the human aspect of Christ.

Earlier in the Epistle we read: (4:2b) πᾶν πνεῦμα ὃ ὁμολογεῖ Ἰησοῦν Χριστὸν ἐν σαρκὶ ἐληλυθότα ἐκ τοῦ θεοῦ ἐστιν, (3a) πᾶν πνεῦμα ὃ μὴ ὁμολογεῖ τὸν Ἰησοῦν[26] ἐκ τοῦ θεοῦ οὐκ ἔστιν. Verse 3a has an oft-disputed and very intriguing variant reading: second-century witnesses have λύει instead of μὴ ὁμολογεῖ.[27] This reading is discussed and

[23] R.W. Paschal, Jr., 'Sacramental symbolism and physical imagery in the Gospel of John', *TynB* 32 (1981) 151-176, esp. 172-173, excludes Jn 19:34 from passages with sacramental symbolism and wants to take blood and water literally here. Cf. also Richter, 'Blut und Wasser', 20; R.E. Brown, *The Gospel According to John* I, New York 1966, 946-952; Schweizer, 'Johanneische Zeugnis', 349-350.

[24] Richter, 'Blut und Wasser', 17: 'Warum polemisieren die doketischen Johannesakten nur gegen das Herausfliessen von Blut, nicht von Wasser? Weil sie gegen das Herausfliessen von Wasser nichts einzuwenden haben! Das Herausfliessen von Wasser allein beweist für sie, dass der Christus nur einen Scheinleib hatte, dass er nur "im Wasser" und nicht "im Blut" gekommen ist.'

[25] Richter, 'Blut und Wasser', 10-11, argues that the Mandaeans conceived of the Redeemer as having an apparent body of mere water. Wengst, *Häresie*, 19-20, disputes the value of this parallel, but he does not react to the parallel in the AJ.

[26] sc. ἐν σαρκὶ ἐληλυθότα.

[27] (The Latin translations of) Irenaeus, Origen and perhaps Clement of Alexandria. Of the Greek MSS, only one from the tenth century has λύει.

convincingly exposed as a corruption by Bart Ehrman.[28] The affirmative statement does not say *that* Jesus came in the flesh, but the aim of the words is clear: in accordance with 1:1-4 the stress is on the way in which Christ came, viz. ἐν σαρκὶ. I conclude that the 'antichrists' (3b) denied the reality of Jesus' flesh.[29] The perfect form ἐληλυθότα can best be understood by comparison with 1:1-4 and 1:5, which illustrate the author's use of this tense in describing the lasting impact of the coming of Jesus. The author wants his readers to continue confessing their faith in the incarnation.[30] As members of a Johannine community, acquainted with the Fourth Gospel, the adversaries laid extreme stress on its high Christology.

In 1 Jn 2:22 we are confronted with persons who are called antichrists because they 'deny that Jesus is the Christ' and 'deny the Father and the Son', which means a denial of the central belief in Johannine Christianity, Jn 20:31.[31] Everything here indicates that the author places a great deal of importance on the defense of this core belief. The denial that Jesus is the Christ has been read as an indication that the adversaries separated the man

[28] Ehrman, '1 Joh 4 3', passim. The subtitle of the essay, 'Orthodox Corruption of Scripture', is misleading, for one of its first statements is that the disputed reading entered into *no* extant Greek manuscript. Ehrman shows that in fact we are not dealing with a textual variant but with an interpretative paraphrase, found in many Fathers side by side (!) with the original reading (242). Cf. M. de Jonge, *De brieven van Johannes*, Nijkerk 1968, 186. Those who prefer this reading are divided over its exact meaning. When taken as 'destroy' Jesus, it means more or less the same as 'not to confess'; but the meaning 'separate Jesus from God' would fit better in the second-century Christological thinking.

[29] Cf. De Jonge, *Brieven,* 117-124, 183-184.

[30] Brown, *Epistles*, 75, 492-494, 504-505, who argues that 'Jesus Christ come in the flesh' is the object of 'negates' and 'confesses'. He considers 4:2-3 as the key verses in support of his view that the adversaries negated the importance of Jesus, and states: 'This text gives little support to those scholars who have assumed that the secessionists denied that there was a real incarnation.' But in defending this position he can only refer back to his own introductory remarks. He is unable to grant that some of the first readers of the Fourth Gospel could develop a docetic Christology (76). Ehrman, '1 Joh 4 3', uses italics in his reply to Brown: 'The author of 1 John does not simply assert that it is *important* that Christ died, but rather that it is important *that* he died.' Brown's position is developed by M.C. de Boer, 'The Death of Jesus Christ and His Coming in the Flesh', *NT* 33 (1991) 326-346. My failure to agree with De Boer rests mainly on his very pregnant explanation of ἐληλυθότα.

[31] U.B. Müller, *Die Geschichte der Christologie in der johanneischen Gemeinde*, Stuttgart 1975, 53-61, makes the confession a *baptismal* confession, but his evidence comes from outside the Johannine tradition.

Jesus from the divine being Christ[32] but that view brings our verse into disharmony with the rest of the Epistle, which gives no indication of any such separation. Schnackenburg correctly argues that Christ here means saviour, σωτήρ (cf. 4:14-15), and is closely connected with the word Son in vss.22b-23.[33] Vs.23, a parallel to vs.22, suggests that the adversaries 'denied the Son'. It is difficult to imagine Christians who do not believe in Christ at all, so these words probably mean that they identified Father and Son so closely that the author saw the separate existence of Christ endangered. Thus these verses again refute those who deny Christ's individuality and his abiding significance for the salvation of mankind.[34] As Brown comments (*ad loc.*), they denied the full humanity of Christ and 'could have arisen from a (one-sided) reading of the GJohn and/or the Johannine tradition.' We see that the Epistles combat a form of docetism which ignores or denies the human quality of Christ.[35]

*1.2.3 Conclusions about the Johannine Epistles*
In addition to the common conviction that the Epistles show how the readers of the Fourth Gospel quarrel over the correct interpretation of its Christology, I have argued that the adversaries who are criticised in the Epistles have the same Christology as the author of the first part of the AJ. Thus the opposing parties in the Christological conflict within the Johannine tradition come to word in the texts under consideration: the one group in 1 Jn and the other in the AJ.[36] Consequently, we have first hand access to the opinions of both groups resulting from the bifurcation of the recipients of the Gospel of John.

This conclusion has important implications for both the date and the area of origin of the AJ. The most important characteristic of the AJ, its docetic Christology, must have been common when First John was written, i.e. before the end of the first century AD. As for the place where it was

[32] So e.g. Wengst, *Häresie*, 17; Müller, *Menschwerdung*, 85; and Klauck, *Johannesbrief*, 162, who refers to 4:2 for justification.

[33] Schnackenburg, *Johannesbriefe*, 18-19.

[34] Müller, *Christologie*, 61, paraphrases the verse: 'Lügner ist, wer leugnet, dass Jesus ist der Gottessohn, *der am Kreuz sein Heilswerk vollbracht hat*'. Cf. De Jonge, *Brieven*, 118-119.

[35] This Christology is not necessarily Gnostic; see Brox, 'Doketismus', 312-313; Klauck, *Johannesbrief*, 39-40; W.S. Vorster, 'Heterodoxy in I John', *Neotestamentica* 9 (1975) 87-97, who remarks (96) that 'scholars tend to label anything which is different from the 'normal' as *gnostic.*' *Contra* e.g. Schackenburg (16, also right at the start), Richter, 'Blut und Wasser', *passim*, and Wengst, *Häresie*, 38.

[36] Painter, 'Opponents', argues that the adversaries of 1 Jn were from a pagan background, whereas the Johannine community was originally Jewish.

written, it is increasingly being accepted that the three Epistles originated in Asia.[37] The fact that the Christology of the AJ is combatted in writings that derive from Asia makes it probable that the AJ was itself also written in Asia.

*1.3 Ignatius and his adversaries*

We now look at the letters of Ignatius because he also had to cope with persons teaching a Christology that differed from his own, and because at least some of them were also docetists.[38] The identity of his adversaries is disputed because we only have his own allusions to them, and his references are rather unspecified. An important methodological step forward is the recent realisation that Ignatius does not, in all his letters, combat the same persons or ideas, so that in this respect we must consider each letter on its own.[39] Another important, although not generally accepted, assumption is that Ignatius addresses actual problems in the churches to which he writes and that he does not project the situation in his own town Antioch onto these diverse churches.[40] On the basis of these presuppositions, the Christology of some of the adversaries of Ignatius becomes apparent.

In writing to Philadelphia and Magnesia the captive bishop battles Judaism, whereas in the Letters to the Smyrneans and the Trallians Ignatius indeed combats docetism.[41] For this reason, I will focus on these last two

[37] The first witnesses to know them are Papias and Polycarp. Cf. Hengel, *Johanneische Frage*, 99, 113.

[38] Strecker, *Johannesbriefe*, 136-137, mentions Ignatius and AJ in close connection.

[39] C. Trevett, *A study of Ignatius of Antioch in Syria and Asia*, Lewiston NY 1992, 99, 150-152; J.L. Sumney, 'Those Who "Ignorantly Deny Him": The Opponents of Ignatius of Antioch', *JECS* 1 (1993) 345-365. *Contra* e.g. Müller, *Menschwerdung*, 109 and the whole tendency of 106-122; W. Bauer, *Die Briefe des Ignatius von Antiochia und der Polykarpbrief*, 2nd ed. by H. Paulsen, Tübingen 1985, 64; and A.F.J. Klijn, *Apostolische Vaders* I, Kampen 1981, 56-61. For a survey of earlier opinions, see C. Trevett, 'Prophecy and Anti-Episcopal Activity: A Third Error Combatted by Ignatius', *JEH* 34 (1983) 1-18, esp. 14.

[40] J. Moffatt, 'An approach to Ignatius', *HTR* 29 (1936) 1-38, 141-5; Klijn, *Apostolische Vaders* I, 20; Trevett, *Study of Ignatius*, 75-76. *Pace* V. Corwin, *St.Ignatius and Christianity in Antioch*, New Haven 1960, 25-29; and Weigandt, *Doketismus*, 102-103, n.315, 117, who thinks that Ignatius combats docetism in his native Antioch (not in Asia!) and therefore concludes that Antioch was the centre of docetism. He even surmises that the Fourth Gospel originated in Antioch.

[41] Weigandt, *Doketismus*, 109-111; Müller, *Christologie*, 63-65, who advocates a different position in *Menschwerdung*, 108-109, 115; Ehrman, '1 Joh 4 3', 237-240; Brown, *Epistles*, 58; Strecker, *Johannesbriefe*, 135-136; Trevett, *Study of Ignatius*, esp. 97-98, 176. Sumney,

letters. To be exact, in both letters he states that docetism does not occur among the local believers (*Tral* 8; *Smyr* 2, 4.1), but he nevertheless warns against it. The docetism reflected in *Smyr* and *Tral* does not accept that Christ had human qualities because it denies the humanity and the suffering of Jesus Christ.[42] In *Tral* Ignatius writes:

> (9.1) ... Jesus Christ, who was of the family of David, and of Mary, who was truly born (ἀληθῶς ἐγεννήθη), both ate and drank, was truly persecuted (ἀληθῶς ἐδιώχθη) under Pontius Pilate, was truly crucified and died (ἀληθῶς ἐσταυρώθη καὶ ἀπέθανεν) ...
> (10.1) But if, as some affirm who are without God, - that is, are unbelievers - his suffering was only a semblance (τὸ δοκεῖν πεπονθέναι αὐτόν) - but it is they who are only a semblance (αὐτοὶ ὄντες τὸ δοκεῖν) - ...

In *Smyr* he also stresses the reality of Christ's birth, baptism and death:

> (2.1) ... he truly suffered even as he also truly raised himself,[43] not as some unbelievers say, that his passion was merely in semblance (τὸ δοκεῖν πεπονθέναι αὐτόν) - but it is they who are merely in semblance - and even according to their opinions it shall happen to them, and they shall be without bodies (ἀσωμάτοις) and phantasmal.
> (3.1) For I know and believe that he was in the flesh even after the resurrection.

Later on he labels the denial that Jesus bore flesh (μὴ ὁμολογῶν αὐτὸν σαρκοφόρον, 5.2) as a blasphemy. Notice that the word docetism is derived from Ignatius's use of the verb δοκεῖν. Nothing suggests that the docetists to which he refers were Gnostics.[44] Ignatius is probably dealing with the same form of docetism that is combatted in 1 and 2 Jn, and advocated by the AJ. He lays special stress on the suffering of Christ at the expense of the rest of his life because he himself faces martyrdom. Our conclusions support those who argue that Ignatius is closely connected with the Johannine trajectory,[45] and we also suggest that the AJ likewise represents part of that trajectory, albeit a group opposed to Ignatius and the

'Opponents', only analyses *Smyr*, *Phil* and *Magn*, and concludes that *Smyr* attacks docetism and *Phil* a form of Judaism, whereas *Magn* has no specific opponents.

42 C.P. Hammond Bammel, 'Ignatian Problems', *JTS* 33 (1982) 62-97, esp. 86, and Pétrement, *Dieu séparé*, 437, argue that Ignatius in several letters combats both forms of docetism.

43 Brown, *Community*, 156-157 overlooks this Johannine expression (cf. Jn 10:17-18).

44 Sumney, 'Opponents', 353; Trevett, *Study of Ignatius*, 155-169, does not clearly distinguish docetism from Gnosis.

45 E.g. Bammel, 'Ignatian problems', 87-88; Trevett, *Study of Ignatius*, 197-198; Hengel, *Johanneische Frage*, 69-70.

Johannine Epistles. The AJ, the Johannine Epistles and Ignatius all testify to a fatal division among the readers of the Fourth Gospel.

*1.4 The trajectory*

In chapter 2 we saw that the author of the Gnostic part of the AJ used the outline of the Gospel of John for the composition of his own 'gospel'. In chapter 3 I concluded that both parts of the AJ stand in a close intertextual and conceptual relationship with the Fourth Gospel.[46] The second main part of the AJ (section C) is especially involved in a critical dialogue with the Fourth Gospel, to which it owes much. At the time of the writing of section C, the Gospel is being claimed by people who interpret it in a way that differs radically from the one in which the author of this section reads it. This author even has to contradict the text of the Gospel in order to convey his spiritualising interpretation of it.

Thus the thesis of earlier scholars, that the AJ is part of the Johannine trajectory, was confirmed in so far as there is a conceptual line connecting the Gospel to both parts of the AJ. In the future it would be better, however, to avoid using the word trajectory in the singular: there are two divergent courses of the trajectory, viz. to the Johannine Epistles on the 'right' hand and to the AJ on the 'left'. The AJ can be situated on the road from the Fourth Gospel to a form of Gnosticism,[47] as it gives voice to groups such as those combatted in the Johannine Epistles and by Ignatius in his Letters to the Smyrnaeans and the Trallians. The second, Gnostic part of the AJ gives us a view of the fate of this ultra-Johannine group at a later moment in its history: it has become so radical that it contradicts the very contents of the Gospel which had been at the root of its existence. The AJ may have originated at the same time as the Johannine and Ignatian Epistles, or later, in case the AJ's spiritualising type of Christology survived.

Because there was interaction between both trajectories and also with several other Christian writings, we cannot maintain a strict definition of the Johannine community as a sect with only Johannine texts at its disposal; at least, the group behind the AJ does not conform to this definition. The AJ should therefore make us aware that such a definition is not likely to reflect historical reality.[48] Because of the individual character of the text, the AJ does not allow us to assert that the readers of the Fourth

[46] Both parts of the AJ, although not securely dated so far, are among the oldest texts to cite the Fourth Gospel.

[47] For this development see W.A. Meeks, 'The Man from Heaven in Johannine Sectarianism', *JBL* 91 (1972) 44-72, esp. 45-46, 72.

[48] Cf. Hengel, *Johanneische Frage*, 134, 160, 164-165.

Gospel formed a distinct Johannine community.

This result leaves us with the question why the apostle John was selected as the book's main character. I would suggest that it was because his name was bound up with the Fourth Gospel, the conceptual basis on which both authors of the AJ are building.

## 2 The place of origin

### *2.1 Introduction*

The AJ testifies to the existence of Johannine trajectories and to the reception of the NT books (esp. Acts) in the second century, and it contributes to the task of discovering the origins of a Gnostic form of Christianity. Because early Christianity was characterised by much travel and interaction, and by the common use of Greek, the value of knowing the place of origin of our text can not be determined *a priori*, but it could increase our knowledge of second-century Christianity. My quest will primarily deal with the original text (sections A and B). I will first discuss the current theories and then make my own suggestion.

### *2.2 Egypt*

Junod and Kaestli have argued that sections A and B of the AJ are of Egyptian origin. They base this conviction on a general impression: 'Le climat spirituel du texte, ses thèmes, son vocabulaire présentent des affinités avec des éléments des oeuvres de Clément et d'Origène ainsi qu'avec les traités hermétiques.'[49] Afterwards they develop this impression into six concrete points.[50] In fact, none of these points is convincing:

1. Christ is pictured (mainly in cc.88-93) as polymorphous.[51] Junod and Kaestli's evaluation of this fact has strongly been influenced by Weigandt, who holds that the idea of the polymorphy of Christ originated in the polymorphy of the Egyptian sun god and was first taken over by the *Apocryphon of John*. In Weigandt's opinion, this text was written in Egypt in the first half of the second century and read in Asia before 150. The *Apocryphon* was known to the Asiatic author of the AJ and via the AJ the

[49] JK, 692, with note referring to passages in their commentary.

[50] JK, 692-694; they repeat only the numbers 1, 3 and 5 in their *ANRW* article 'Dossier', 4354. Schäferdiek, *NA*[5], 154, does not react to points 2 and 6. For the whole, cf. Sirker-Wicklaus, *Untersuchungen*, 238-239. Culpepper, *John*, 188, finds the case 'strong but not conclusive'.

[51] Jones, 'Orientations', 499-500, considers this to be the most important argument.

theme entered the other AAA.[52]

Contrary to Weigandt, Junod and Kaestli do not say that the AJ was influenced by the *Apocryphon*; they rather think that the AJ itself is a product of Egypt. In my essay on polymorphy, however, I concluded that there is no evidence that the idea of the polymorphy of Christ originated in Egypt.[53]

2. Egypt is generally regarded as the birthplace of the ancient novel, Junod and Kaestli argue. They add that by the second century AD the novel had become generally known. But the hypothesis that the novel originated in Egypt hardly has recent support.[54] Below (section 2.4) I will come back to the relationship with one specific novel discussed in chapter 3.

3. Clement of Alexandria uses the same tradition about John found in the AJ in which John discovered that the Lord had no real body. Junod and Kaestli believe that Clement's *Adumbrationes in 1 Jn 1:1* and AJ 93.1-4 derive from a common source.[55] Again they expose the weakness of their argument by admitting that Clement had travelled a great deal.[56] The resemblance of the ideas in the two texts is striking - though I think it more likely that Clement knew the AJ than that they shared a common source - but this similarity proves nothing about the origin of the AJ. Moreover, traditions parallel to and possibly derived from the AJ are also found in Melito and Tertullian. In my view, all these facts just testify to the fact that the AJ found many readers and soon had a wide circulation.[57]

4. The spiritualism of the AJ resembles that of Clement and Origen; Junod and Kaestli give no specific passages for this point. In my opinion the spiritualism is not specifically Egyptian and best explained by seeing the

[52] Weigandt, *Doketismus*, 40, 50-53, 83, 120.

[53] Lalleman, 'Polymorphy'.

[54] Schmeling, *Novel*, shows that the scholar who suggested an Egyptian origin of the genre, J.W.B. Barns, hardly has adherents nowadays; see esp. C. Ruiz-Montero, 'The rise of the Greek novel', 29-85 (71-75!) and S. Stephens, 'Fragments of lost novels', 655-683 (665-666, 681). Cf. S.A. Stephens and J.J. Winkler, *Ancient Greek Novels. The Fragments*, Princeton N.J. 1995, 12-18. The one recent supporter of the Egyptian origin is I. Rutherford, 'Kalasaris and Setne Khamwas: A Greek Novel and some Egyptian Models', *ZPE* 117 (1997) 203-209, who, however, merely shows that Heliodorus' *Aithiopika* was influenced by Egyptian models.

[55] See note 112.

[56] Clement had indeed travelled much before settling in Alexandria and at least heard teachers from Greece, Italy, Assyria and Palestine; see C.W. Griggs, *Early Egyptian Christianity*, Leiden 1990, 56-57; and A. Méhat, 'Clemens von Alexandrien', *TRE* 8 (1981) 101-113, esp. 101.

[57] On Melito see Van Unnik, 'Dance of Jesus'.

AJ as one of the Johannine trajectories.[58]
5. The AJ contains the rare word δικρόσσιον (71.1-2; 74.3; 80.3; 111.12) which denotes a piece of clothes, probably an undershirt. Until recently, in all extant Greek literature the word δικρόσσιον was found only in the AJ and once (in plural) in the *Periplus maris Erythraei*, an anonymous text about trade in the region of the Red Sea dating from the middle of the first century AD.[59] Junod and Kaestli conclude that δικρόσσιον is a specifically Egyptian piece of clothing: 'Ce mot mystérieux est assurément un indice précieux pour l'établissement de la location de notre texte.'[60] The Coptic translation of AJ 106-115 shows this conclusion to be incorrect. Its use of a periphrasis in order to render δικρόσσιον instead of only one word, makes an Egyptian origin of the clothing improbable: evidently, the Egyptian language had no single word for it.[61]

In 1986 a third text with the word δικρόσ(σ)ων was published. In this Ptolemaic text the δίκροσσος/-ον is an expensive type of garment that costs between 20 and 50 days' wages, since a certain Egyptian Harpedones receives 'the price for five garments, in silver 26 drachmes'.[62] The editors

[58] Schäferdiek, *NA*$^{5}$, 154, says that the parallels with Clement result from the openness of the Alexandrinian eclecticism.

[59] L. Casson (ed.), *Periplus maris Erythraei*, Princeton 1989, § 6:

| Προχωρεῖ δὲ εἰς τοὺς τόπους | In this area there is a market |
|---|---|
| τούτους ἱμάτια βαρβαρικὰ | for: articles of clothing for |
| ἄγναφα τὰ ἐν Αἰγύπτῳ | the Barbaroi, unused, the kind |
| γινόμενα, 'Αρσινοΐτικαὶ | produced in Egypt; wraps from |
| στολαὶ καὶ ἀβόλλαι | Arsinoe; colored *abollai* |
| νόθοι χρωμάτινοι καὶ λέντια | of printed fabric; linens; |
| καὶ δικρόσσια | double-fringed items; |
| καὶ λιθίας ὑαλῆς | numerous types of |
| πλείονα γένη κτλ. | glass stones (etc.) |

Note Casson's hesitant translation 'items'. Later in the same chapter the list includes οἶνος Λαδικηνὸς καὶ 'Ιταλικὸς (wine from Laodicea and Italy), which is just one of the many indications in the text that not all listed items are Egyptian.

[60] JK, 694.

[61] Coptic text (JK, 391) and translation of AJ 111:

| ntof de nefaheratf ereouštên | And he arose wearing only a |
|---|---|
| nhboos hiôôf mauaas | cloth of linen which had |
| esjitôte epsa snau, | two fringes, |
| auo afperš nefcij ebol | and he spread out his hands |
| afšlêl nteihe efjô mmos je | and prayed thus, saying... |

The one word δικρόσσιον is rendered by 'štên nhboos esjitôte epsa snau'. Cf. Schäferdiek, *NA*$^{5}$, 154.

[62] τειμὴν δικρόσων ἀργ[υρίου] [δραχμὰς] κς.

comment: 'Zwischen Diminutivum (δικρόσσιον) und Positivum (δίκροσσος/-ον) gibt es wahrscheinlich keinen Bedeutungsunterschied.'[63] For the present research the new papyrus does not offer much help. In view of the relative abundance of Egyptian every day texts in comparison with the scarcity of material from other regions, and of the fact that the object in question was an item of international trade, we conclude that the mentioning of the δικρόσσιον in connection with Egypt in no way excludes that it was known in other areas as well.[64] The origin of the AJ cannot be discovered from this term.

6. In c.71 a serpent kills the bad Fortunatus but not the good Callimachus. According to Junod and Kaestli, this attitude conforms to an Egyptian tradition concerning the behaviour of holy snakes.[65] This argument is not decisive since Callimachus behaves no better than Fortunatus who is killed by the snake. Moreover, the Greek religion also knows the snake as the protector of tombs.[66]

I conclude that none of the points mentioned by Junod and Kaestli carries enough weight to prove an Egyptian origin of the AJ. The same must be said regarding the additional evidence brought forward by Plümacher, who uses the position of Junod and Kaestli as his point of departure. He argues that c.53, the story of the self-castration, is derived from a tale about the beaver by Aesopus and Phaedrus. In its present form as a part of the AJ it contributes, so Plümacher says, to polemic about self-castration in Alexandria. In chapter 5 we have already seen that the alleged relationship with the tale about the beaver is not particularly striking. Furthermore, Plümacher argues that the theme of self-castration also occurs in Justin, *Apology* 1.15, the *Sentences of Sextus* and the *Physiologus*. He holds that these texts derive from the same context as the AJ.[67] But he is overconfident about our knowledge of the origin of the other two texts: the

[63] W.H.M. Liesker and A.M. Tromp, 'Zwei Ptolemäische Papyri aus der Wiener Papyrussammlung', *ZPE* 66 (1986) 79-82. The papyrus is P.Vindob. Gr. 12942. It is still not exactly clear what kind of clothing it is. In the AJ the δικρόσσιον is the last garment of the dead, an undercloth. But the papyrus implies that a δικρόσ(σ)ος is expensive. This suggests a difference between the positive ('uppercloth'?) and the diminutive ('undercloth'?).

[64] *Pace* Bremmer, 'Women', 55-56.

[65] Aelian, *On the characteristics of animals* (Περὶ ζῴων ἰδιότητος) 10.31, ed. A.F. Scholfield, Cambridge MA/London 1971, says that the Egyptians believe in a kind of viper 'which does not touch virtuous people but kills evildoers'.

[66] E. Küster, *Die Schlange in der griechischen Kunst und Religion*, Giessen 1913, 62-72; cf. Sturhahn, *Christologie*, 46 n.2. Plinius, *Hist Nat* XVI.234 mentions a place in Italy with a cave '*in quo manes eius (sc. Scipio Africanus) custodire draco traditur*'.

[67] Plümacher, 'Paignion', 99-108. The parallel with Justin was discussed in chapter 5.

*Sentences of Sextus* has no assured date.[68] And even if there was a 'debate about the admissibility of self-castration at the time of writing of the AJ', as he states,[69] the fact that Justin Martyr can refer to it demonstrates that it had become known outside Egypt. Consequently, it cannot be used to determine where the AJ was written.[70]

*2.3 Syria*

Another current hypothesis is that the AJ originated in Syria. In 1964 Schäferdiek suggested a Syrian origin for cc.87-105, keeping Asia Minor as the location where the main part of the AJ was written.[71] In his 1983 essay 'Herkunft und Interesse der alten Johannesakten' he argues for Eastern Syria as the place of origin for *all* of the AJ. His first argument is based on the resemblance of the AJ with the ATh; when dealing with the date of the AJ I have already argued that this resemblance is not very significant. Secondly, he argues that the *Sitz im Leben* of our text is a branch of the Johannine community, but since modern research into the origin of the Fourth Gospel points to Asia Minor, it no longer is an argument in favour of Syria.[72] Schäferdiek also thinks that the use of the AJ in the Manichean Psalmbook points to Syria, but in my opinion enough time passed between the composition of the AJ and the redaction of the Manichean Psalms to allow for the spread of the AJ.[73] Finally Schäferdiek suggests that the AJ may originally have been written in Syriac, but this hypothesis is not supported by the extant manuscripts in this language, which only contain cc.106-115 and display clear signs of being a transla-

[68]For the *Physiologus*, Egypt in the second half of the second century is now rather certain, see K. Alpers, 'Physiologus', *TRE* 26 (1996) 596-602, esp. 598.

[69] Plümacher, 'Paignion', 106.

[70] Bremmer, 'Women', 56, presents another argument in favour of Egypt, the allegedly Egyptian phrase μόνος σύ (AJ 51.11). But this phrase also occurs elsewhere, e.g. in APe 39 and in the OT (e.g. Ex 3:14, cf. Vouaux, *Actes de Pierre*, 457 n.3).

[71] He was not the first to propose Syria: Dobschütz, 'Roman', 91, 98, 103-104, used genre as a criterion for determining the origin of the AAA and as, in his view, the ancient novel came from Syria, so the AAA had to come from that area too. An extra argument was based on the work's Gnosticism: in his opinion this kind of Christianity also came from Syria, and he viewed all the AAA as Gnostic. I will come back to Schäferdiek's view when I discuss section C below.

[72] Schäferdiek, 'Herkunft', 267; but see Hengel, *Johanneische Frage*, 75, 99, 290-291; U. Schnelle, *Einleitung in das Neue Testament*, Göttingen 1994; Culpepper, *John*, who hardly even mentions Syria; and S. van Tilborg, *Reading John in Ephesus*, Leiden 1996.

[73] Schäferdiek, 'Herkunft', 248f, 255. Allberry, *Manichean Psalm-Book* II, xx, dates the Coptic corpus of collected Psalms ± 340, which means that there was a 150 to 200 year gap between the AJ and it.

tion of a Greek original, as Schäferdiek himself admits.[74]

Sirker-Wicklaus is led by two dubious presuppositions, viz. that the AJ originated in a wandering community and that it dates from the third century. These assumptions lead her to think of the Syrian-Palestinian area, where Orthodoxy allegedly gained control later than in Asia Minor and where the Johannine community lived, as the AJ's place of origin.[75]

*2.4 Older arguments for and against Asia Minor*

Having seen that neither Egypt nor Syria has much to recommend it as the place of origin for the AJ, we come to the possibility that Asia was the place of origin. In fact this view means a return to an original 19th-century hypothesis. Although some of the arguments that were advanced in the past are rather weak, the suggestion receives important confirmation from recent studies.[76] For Junod and Kaestli the strongest argument in favour of Asia is the probable Asiatic origin of the novelists Chariton and Xenophon.[77] We may add that in chapter 3 we saw that the AJ are indeed familiar with Chariton's *Callirhoe*. Moreover, several scholars have recently highlighted the Asiatic origin of this novel so that we have one more argument to link the AJ with Asia.[78]

Of the arguments that have been brought forward against Asia, most have to do with the (lack of a proper) description of Ephesos in the text.

[74] Schäferdiek, 'Herkunft'; cf. *NA*[5], 150.

[75] Sirker-Wicklaus, *Untersuchungen*, 199, 237-241. Note that she speaks of 'einen kirchengeschichtlichen Anachronismus' (241).

[76] Traditional arguments for Asia Minor include: 1) the fact that the book's action is situated in and around Ephesos; 2) the fact that the Johannine writings in the NT originated in Asia; 3) the view of Photius, discussed on p. 67 above, that the author of the AJ (and the other AAA) was Leukios Charinos who lived in Asia; cf. Zahn, *Acta Johannis*, cxliv, cxlviii; Schmidt, *Petrusakten*, 27-77; 4) Zahn's assumption, *Apostel und Apostelschüler*, 15, 209, that the AJ was read among the Montanists and the Quartodecimans in Asia; 5) arguments based on the text's theology; this view finds no support in the present study; 6) identification of the Ephesian person Bourros in the letters of Ignatius (*Eph* 2.1; *Phil* 11.2; *Smyr* 12.1) with the Ephesian character Byrrhus or Beros of the AJ (30, 61, 110; for the different spellings cf. JK, 306 n.3), see Zahn, *Acta Johannis*, cliii, and Lightfoot, *Apostolic Fathers* II.1, 366. Both names are indeed rare (P.M. Fraser and E. Matthews, *A Lexicon of Greek Personal Names*, Vol I Oxford 1987; Vol II Oxford 1994, has one Βῆρος [2nd century AD, = CIG 5181, in Vol. I] and one Βοῦρρος [2nd century AD, Vol. II]), but the spellings differ too much to think of one person.

[77] JK, 691.

[78] D.J. Edwards, 'Defining the Web of Power in Asia Minor. The Novelist Chariton and his City Aphrodisias', *JAAR* 62 (1994) 699-718; E. Bowie, 'The ancient readers of the Greek novels', in Schmeling, *Novel*, 90; B.P. Reardon, 'Chariton', in *idem*, 309-335.

As the place of origin for the AJ, this city seems to be disqualified because of the story of the destruction of the temple of Artemis in cc.38-42; scholars think that nobody who knew the city and the mighty temple could invent this story before the actual fall of the sanctuary;[79] the famous temple was sacked, though not destroyed, in 262.[80] Junod and Kaestli hold that this is just one example of the author's lack of knowledge of the geography of Asia in general and of the Artemision in particular.[81] But while it is indeed unlikely that in the second century an Ephesian would write a text narrating the destruction of the famous temple, a person from another part of Asia would have less scruples about doing so.

The similarities between the AJ and the ideas of the Gnostic Theodotus, signalled in chapter 4, need not exclude Asia because the Asians Melito and the anonymous homelist *In Pascha* were also familiar with Theodotus.[82] If Theodotus did not himself live in Asia, his work was at least known there independently from Clement of Alexandria.[83]

*2.5 Recent more valid arguments for Asia Minor*

Recent research enables us to present a number of arguments in favour of Asia as the place of origin for the AJ. Our strongest argument involves the AJ's link to the Johannine trajectory. The renewed recognition of the connection between the Gospel of John and Asia as well as the link established above between the AJ and the Johannine Epistles and Ignatius' letters make it probable that the AJ also comes from Asia. In addition, I will discuss the position of the women in the community of believers, the vindication of the author's knowledge of both Ephesos and the Asian legal system, and the similarities between the AJ and some texts that are definitely Asiatic.[84]

It is common knowledge that women played a greater public role in the cities of Asia Minor than in other parts of the Roman Empire. It is here

[79] Hennecke, *Handbuch*, 174, who opts for the inland area of Asia Minor as place of origin. In *NA*$^3$, Schäferdiek tentatively kept this position for the uninterpolated text.

[80] G.H.R. Horsley, 'The Inscriptions of Ephesos and the New Testament', *NT* 34 (1992) 105-168, esp. 108. The Artemision was plundered by the Goths in the sixth decade of the third century, lost importance in the years thereafter and was deserted in the beginning of the fifth century. For the date (262, 263, or 268/9), cf. Schäferdiek, 'Herkunft', 257 n.39.

[81] JK, 500-503, 690-691. See our discussion on pp. 263-264 below.

[82] See T. Halton, 'Valentinian Echoes in Melito, *Peri Pascha*?', *JTS* 20 (1969) 535-538; Cantalamessa, 'Méliton, Pseudo-Hippolyte et Théodote'.

[83] Cantalamessa, 'Méliton, Pseudo-Hippolyte et Théodote', 270.

[84] These arguments involve facts that others have developed but that have not been applied to the AJ.

that women could be leaders of synagogues.[85] This evidence fits well with the position of women in the AJ as we described it in chapter 5, viz. a position that is relatively prominent without being deviant.[86]

A specific group of women to which the AJ pays much attention are older women, especially widows. Although the relevant story (cc.30-36) is regrettably truncated, it is evident that it focused on the fate of women in society and in the Christian community. This attention matches with the fact that around the same time Ignatius pays special attention to widows in his Letters both to the church and to the bishop of Smyrna.[87]

The contention that the author of the AJ was not acquainted with Ephesos has recently been contradicted by Engelmann.[88] He argues that the descriptions of the festival that shine through the polemics in 43.6-12 testify to knowledge of the city of Ephesos and its religion. The essential historical correctness of the background to c.38 can even be vindicated in three cases. An inscription confirms that the Ephesians wore white at the festival of Artemis.[89] Secondly, the name of the festival, γενέθλιος ἡμέρα (38.1, cf. 43.10), fits with the belief that Artemis had been born in the city.[90] Third and most important is Engelmann's explanation of John's 'going up' to the Artemision. This expression in the AJ was a major problem because the famous temple was not situated on a hill but on the flat country inland from the city. Having John go up, as the AJ seems to

[85] Though ἀρχισυνάγωγος could be a mere honorary title, cf. T. Rajak and D. Noy, '*Archisynagogoi*: Office, Title and Social Status in the Greco-Roman Synagogue', *Journal of Roman Studies* 83 (1993) 75-93.

[86] See P.R. Trebilco, *Jewish Communities in Asia Minor*, Cambridge 1991, 104-113, 124-126 with n.113; R. van Bremen, *The Limits of Participation. Women and Civic Life in the Greek East in the Hellenistic and Roman Periods*, Amsterdam 1996; Bremmer, 'Magic', 58; for Ephesos, Van Tilborg, *Reading John*, 154-164.

[87] *Smyr* 6.2, 13; *Polyc* 4; Trevett, *Study of Ignatius*, 112 n.65, suggests that an order of widows was developing in Smyrna.

[88] H. Engelmann, 'Ephesos und die Johannesakten', *ZPE* 103 (1994) 297-302, who admits (300) that this knowledge need not have been more than literary knowledge. He also argues that a 'first governor' of Ephesos occurs on inscriptions, so that 31.7 makes perfect sense when we move the comma from after στρατηγός to before it and read: 'A certain Andronicus, first governor ...' To the inscriptions, add IEph 232, 645, 724, 892; a γραμματεύς πρῶτος features in IEph 3058, 3071. Generally, πρῶτος τῶν... is a title from Southern Anatolia.

[89] IEph 907; cf. IEph 27 l.442, also printed in G.M. Rogers, *The Sacred Identity of Ephesos. Foundation Myths of a Roman City*, London/New York 1991, Appendix 1.

[90] See Rogers, *Sacred Identity*, esp. 2, 145-147, 150-151. The inscription on which Rogers bases his research (IEph 27) uses γενέσιος.

do, would be a definite proof of ignorance of the local situation.[91] Yet the prefix ἀνα in 'John went (ἀνῄει) to the temple' (38.3) can also be translated as 'upstream'; the composite verb thus means 'go inland' or 'go up-stream' instead of 'go uphill'.[92] In this way the alleged difficulty is removed. I would add one more observation: I see the author's knowledge of the fact that the Artemision was situated in a low, humid area reflected with some humour in John's remark that it is he who will place the believers on a firm rock (45.9). The author of the AJ was not unfamiliar with the Artemision.

Thus the author's knowledge of Ephesos would seem to be accurate, an observation that leaves us with the (im)probability that an Ephesian author would write about the destruction of the Artemision before the year 263. Consequently, the author may either be an Ephesian or somebody from the wider region of Asia.

In a recent essay Plümacher argues that the traditional rivalry between Ephesos and Smyrna sheds light on the disputes about the duration of the stay of John in his respective residences (AJ 37, 45, 55, 58).[93] He states that the author of the AJ depicts John as an impeccable leader preferable to the Roman provincial governors who annually toured the central cities of the province to administer justice, according to the so-called assize (*conventus*) system.[94] Details of the route of John's Asiatic tour probably imitate those of the governors, which covered 13 or 14 cities.[95]

[91] JK, 501.

[92] Engelmann does not mention the second occurrence of ἀν- in ἀνῆλθον (39.9) and the counterpart καταβαίνοντος (44.4). He gives no strictly Ephesian parallel nor does he discuss the possibility of interpreting ἀν- as up-stream (and κατα- as down-stream); to me this meaning is suggested by ancient reports that a river flowed along the temple, see W. Alzinger, *Die Stadt des siebenten Weltwunders. Die Wiederentdeckung von Ephesos*, Wien 1962, 10-11. Engelmann's arguments suffice to counter W.M. Gessel, 'Die Johannestradition auf dem Ayasoluk im Lichte der apokryphen Johannesakten', in R. Schulz and M. Jörg (eds.), *Lingua restituta orientalis. Fs Assfalg*, Wiesbaden 1990, 108-113. The AJ is admittedly vague about the exact place of John's burial, but it is not *ipso facto* wrong.

[93] Plümacher, 'Missionsreise'. He maintains his earlier view that the AJ stems from Egypt, but his argument that one did not need to live in Asia to know about these matters (264 n.12) is weak: for the author of the AJ this rivalry was not just some fact, but a matter of importance. On the rivalry between Ephesos and Smyrna, see now E. Collas-Heddeland, 'Le culte impérial dans la compétition des titres sous le haut-empire', *Revue des études grecs* 108 (1995) 410-429.

[94] Plümacher, 'Missionsreise', 276-278; cf. G.P. Burton, 'Proconsuls, assizes and the administration of justice under the Empire', *JRS* 65 (1975) 92-106; A.D. Macro, 'The cities of Asia Minor under the Roman Imperium', *ANRW* II.7.2 (1980) 658-697, esp. 670-671.

[95] Plümacher, 'Missionsreise', 271; cf. Bremmer, 'Women', 39 n.6.

It is possible to draw even more conclusions from the evidence advanced by Plümacher than he himself does.[96] Not only does the AJ portray John's behaviour in a better light than that of the highest political authority, in cc.37, 45, 55 and 58 the text also attacks the claim that John was exclusively Ephesian. This polemical view is best explained if we assume that the author lived in a rival city of Ephesos. As we will see below, the author was bound by the common assumption that John's main residence and place of burial were Ephesos, but the thematic discussion of the apostle's stay in diverse cities indicates a desire to connect the apostle with the rest of Asia. This claim indicates a polemical attack on Ephesos. The same attitude also explains why the author, writing before 263, does not shrink from having John destroy the Artemision: he is not proud of Ephesos at all!

Two indications specifically point to Smyrna as the author's city of residence.[97] Within the text itself there is the so far unnoticed fact that John receives a better welcome in Smyrna than in Ephesos. Careful reading demonstrates that on his arrival in the area around Ephesos, John is neither invited nor welcomed by brothers from that city (cc.18-19). This behaviour stands in stark contrast with that of the Smyrneans: envoys from Smyrna come all the way down to Ephesos to invite John to their city (55.2), and as soon as he arrives the whole population gathers to meet him (56.2). This description is the more remarkable in view of the traditional rivalry between Ephesos and Smyrna.

The second Smyrnean affinity of the AJ is constituted by the newly discovered *Fragments on Polycarp*. The AJ and the *Fragments* have the following traits in common:

1. the virginity of John (AJ 113)
2. a certain anti-Judaism (AJ 94.2)
3. the charge of magic (AJ 31)
4. use of the word 'canons' for John's teaching (AJ 57)

Of these, especially the last trait is remarkable.[98]

[96] Plümacher does not discuss the origin of the text and apparently still supports the Egypt hypothesis, despite the fact, mentioned by him (270 with n.40), that the legal system in Egypt was different from that in Asia and all other provinces in that there were permanent courts. As a result, an Egyptian audience was not likely to understand the allusions to the assize system.

[97] See also the discussion of cc.30-36 just above.

[98] Weidmann, *Polycarp*. For 1. see 100-102, for 2. see 140-144, for 3. see 147-154, for 4. see 124-125. Ephesos has yielded extremely little Jewish material of any kind: Horsley, 'Inscriptions', 121-127; cf. G. Mussies, 'Pagans, Jews, and Christians at Ephesus', in P.W. van der Horst and G. Mussies, *Studies on the Hellenistic Background of the New Testament*, Utrecht 1990, 177-194, esp. 187-188.

Finally, the rather close relationship between the AJ and the APl, which we discussed in chapter 3, supports the case for an Asiatic origin of the AJ as the APl quite certainly originated in Asia Minor. The same holds for the fact that the AJ influenced the APe. Taking everything together, an Asiatic origin of the first part of the AJ is relatively certain. Minor arguments point to Smyrna as the best candidate for that honour.

*2.6 The origin of section C*

Section C contains two elements that may give us a clue about its origin, viz. in 97.5 the occurrence of τῷ ἀρουβάτῳ and, in line 7, the reference to a cave in the Mount of Olives. The expression τῷ ἀρουβάτῳ does not occur in any other Greek text and its meaning must be construed from the context.[99] The first editor of manuscript **C**, which contains this part of the text, James, proposed to read σταυροῦ βάτῳ as a correction of the difficult but not impossible reading which occurs in the other textual witness, the manuscripts of the Acts of the second Council of Nicea. We should, however, leave the word as it is. It must be the Greek transcription of the Aramaic/Syriac ʻarubhta: evening, sunset, preparation, Friday.[100] What are we to make of the occurrence of this word? It suggests that the author used a source in which he came upon this expression, which for some reason he preferred to leave untranslated. The source might have been a separately circulating story or a longer text, even a passion narrative or a gospel. The use of τῷ ἀρουβάτῳ hardly points to a Syriac original of the AJ. Had the text originally been written in Syriac, then the person who translated it into Greek had no reason to leave this word without translation.

The other clue contained in c.97 is not so much the fact that the revelation to John takes place on a mountain - this is a well-known motif especially in Gnostic texts - but the fact that the text specifically states that it occurs in a cave on the Mount of Olives. Local Jerusalem traditions regarding the existence of such a cave are attested by the *Vita Constantini* of Eusebius,[101] and the early pilgrim Egeria refers to a church on this

[99] Search in Pandora Greek Thesaurus, August 1997.

[100] James, *Apocrypha anecdota*, xxiii-xxiv; A. Hilgenfeld (Review of James, *Apocrypha anecdota*), *Zeitschrift für wissenschaftliche Theologie* 40 (1897) 467-471; R.H. Connolly, 'The Diatessaron in the Syriac Acts of John', *JTS* 8 (1907) 571-581, esp. 578-580; Schäferdiek, *NA*$^3$, 143; JK, 364, 631-632.

[101] Eusebius, *Vita Constantini* 3.43.3, ed Winkelmann (GCS), Berlin 1975: τῆς εἰς οὐρανοὺς πορείας τοῦ τῶν ὅλων σωτῆρος ἐπὶ τοῦ τῶν ἐλαιῶν ὄρους ... ἐπεὶ κἀνταῦθα λόγος ἀληθὴς κατέχει ἐν αὐτῷ ἄντρῳ τοὺς αὐτοῦ θιασώτας μυεῖν τὰς ἀπορρήτους τελετὰς τὸν τῶν ὅλων σωτῆρα.

spot.[102] There must have been a cave on the Mount of Olives to which Christians attached a special significance. The reference in our text probably depends on some knowledge of these local circumstances,[103] or, more likely, of a written Palestinian tradition.

We saw earlier that, whereas section C as a whole seems to be a literary creation by its author, c.97 draws on traditions about the earthly Jesus contained in some of the canonical Gospels. It is therefore likely that our author had another written source than the Gospels, a source written in Aramaic or Syriac which contained the two elements we are discussing, the expression τῷ ἀρουβάτῳ and the reference to the cave. This source may have been a lost gospel.[104] It is exactly this use of sources that prevents a conclusion regarding the place of origin of the text.

There are indications that section C has affinities with Asiatic material, viz. with the work of Melito of Sardes and the anonymous homilist of *In Pascha*. In the discussion of the christological titles in chapter 4, I already referred to Melito, especially in connection with the use of the words Father and Logos and with the 'collection of members' (AJ 100.3-4); I also incorporated *In Pascha* in the explanation of the role of the cross.[105]

Moreover, the homiletic style of the song in cc.94-96 with its alternation of rhythmical and non-rhythmical passages resembles that of Melito.[106] Especially remarkable are the similarities between the antitheses in Melito, *Peri Pascha* 80 and AJ 95. A final point of comparison is the fact that Melito speaks of dancing in the context of the Passover-meal in a way comparable to the AJ.[107] Notice that nearly all alleged parallels between Melito and the AJ pertain to section C of the

[102] *Itinerarium* (CCSL 175) 30.3-31.1, quoted by P. Devos, 'Appendice: Égérie n'a pas connu d'église de l'Ascension', *AnBol* 87 (1969) 208: ... *Eleona, id est in monte Oliveti, ubi est spelunca illa, in qua docebat Dominus* (cf. 35.2, 39.3, 43.6. 49.3).

[103] So K. Schmaltz, 'Die drei "mystischen" Christushöhlen der Geburt, der Jüngerweihe und des Grabes', *Zeitschrift des Deutschen Palästina-Vereins* 42 (1919) 132-165, esp. 151-152, and Kretschmar, 'Festkalender', 184-185.

[104] Hilgenfeld, 'Johannes', 470; Connolly, 'Syriac Acts of John', 580.

[105] Cf. also Cantalamessa, *L'omelia 'In s.Pascha'*, 125, 134, 463.

[106] M. Brioso, 'Sobre el "Tanzhymnus" de *Acta Ioannis* 94-6', *Emerita* 40, Madrid 1970, 31-45, referred to by JK, 637.

[107] Van Unnik, 'Dance of Jesus', 4. On pp. 63-64 above, I qualified Van Unnik's suggestion that the author of the AJ 'did not invent it [sc. the dance] himself, but derived it from existing practice' by arguing that our text is an original composition: the practice may have been taken over from others, but the wording of the AJ is original.

AJ.[108] Although we have scant evidence for the origin of section C, what evidence there is points to Asia Minor, the location for the writing of the first main part of the text.

## 3 The date

The first explicit reference to the AJ is in Eusebius (*HE* III.25.6, early fourth century). Current opinions about the date of its origin range from before 138 to after 262 AD. The early date is proposed by Peterson, who connects the ATh, AAn and AJ with the supposed sect of the Encratites.[109] On the other extreme we find those who attach much weight to the fact that the AJ narrates how John destroys the Artemision in Ephesos.[110] This argument loses much of its weight if, as I have argued above, the AJ did not originate in Ephesos.

Zahn originally dated the AJ about 130. When he later changed his mind in favour of 160-170, he remained convinced that the Muratorian Canon and Clement of Alexandria were familiar with the AJ.[111] Indeed, older scholars generally considered Clement of Alexandria's *Adumbrationes* (± 200) as *terminus ante quem*, but nowadays it is argued that Clement does not refer to the AJ at all. Clement says that there are traditions according to which John touched the Lord but felt no solid body. This remark clearly resembles AJ 93 but the word 'traditions' leaves open the possibility of oral traditions and is no proof of any literary influence.[112] A similar case is the reference of Tertullian to (the apostle?)

[108] Cf. Hall, 'Melito's Paschal Homily', 97, who suggests a common Johannine tradition. Melito is a notable anti-docetic author, cf. Cantalamessa, 'Méliton de Sardes', 14-16.

[109] Peterson, 'Anfängen der Askese', 211.

[110] Plümacher, 'Apostelakten', 19; Engelmann, 'Ephesos', 301.

[111] Zahn, *Acta Joannis*, cxliv-cxlv, cxlviii, excluding from this dating the passage about the destruction of the Ephesian temple (cxiv); *idem*, *Geschichte des Kanons* II, 861-864; *idem*, *Apostel und Apostelschüler*, 16-17, 201-204; *idem*, 'Wanderungen', 192, 198, 201; cf. *idem*, *Acta Joannis*, cxl-cxliv.

[112] *Adumbrationes*, in *Clemens Alexandrinus III: Fragmente*, ed. O. Stählin, Leipzig 1909, Berlin ²1970 (ed. L. Früchtel and U. Treu), 210: *Fertur ergo in traditionibus, quoniam Iohannes ipsum corpus quod erat extrinsecus tangens, manum suam in profunda misisse et ei duritiam carnis nullo modo reluctatam esse, sed locum manui praebuisse discipuli* ('There are traditions that when John touched that body that was outward, he extended his hand in depths, and that the solidity of the flesh in no way hindered it but rather gave way to the hand of the disciple.'). See Zahn, *Acta Joannis*, cxl-cxli; James, *Apocrypha anecdota*, x; Hilgenfeld, 'Johannes', 27, 41; *NA*³, 126; Junod and Kaestli, *Histoire*, 13-16.

John as *Johannes aliqui Christi spado*.[113] Is it likely that Tertullian, who knew the APl, was informed about the contents of AJ 113, or did he know of some oral tradition? After all, Tertullian also knows the story of John's oil martyrium that we find in *Virtutes Johannis* 1 but not in the AJ.[114]

Most present-day scholars adhere to the date proposed by Lipsius, the second half of the second century,[115] but Schäferdiek argues for a date in the third century on two grounds. He alleges that there are important parallels between the AJ and the ATh.[116] In chapters 3 and 5, however, I have argued that AJ and ATh have different origins. One more argument for this conviction deserves to be mentioned here. The AJ differs from the ATh in the attitude towards Scripture in that the ATh often quotes NT writings and regards them as authoritative, whereas the AJ works from a radically different point of view.

Schäferdiek also states that the AJ depends on a fully developed tradition about the activities of the apostle John in Ephesos, a tradition that he regards as late second century because, in his opinion, the earliest important witnesses to it (esp. Irenaeus) date from that period.[117] The argument of dependence on an Ephesos tradition is also used by Junod and Kaestli, who likewise date the text with reference to the rise of Johannine traditions; but in their case it results in an earlier date, viz. after 150 AD.[118] Is this line of argument valid?

[113] Tertullian, *De monogamia* 17.1: 'A noted voluntary celibate of Christ's'; see Zahn, *Acta Joannis*, ciii; Culpepper, *John*, 140 with nn. 9-10.

[114] Tertullian, *Praescr Haer* 36.3. Cf. Hengel, *Johanneische Frage*, 116-117; Culpepper, *John*, 139-140.

[115] Lipsius, *Apostelgeschichten* I, 31, 515. Cf. the thesis of Van Unnik, 'Dance of Jesus', that bishop Melito of Sardes and the author of the AJ were contemporaries and lived in the same area.

[116] Schäferdiek, 'Herkunft', 249-255. The ATh is generally dated in the third century, see Elliott, *Apocryphal NT*, 442; Klijn, *Acts of Thomas*, 26.

[117] Schäferdiek, *NA*[3], 143; 'Herkunft', 263. According to Schäferdiek's pupil Sirker-Wicklaus, *Untersuchungen*, 130, 241, the miracle stories in the AJ derive from the third or even fourth century; she opts for a date after 200 AD and calls the AJ 'einen kirchengeschichtlichen Anachronismus' in a time of Catholicising tendencies. In this respect she follows Niederwimmer, *Askese*, esp. 186. But Niederwimmer, who calls AJ 29 'Nachwirkung der jüdischen Tradition, die die "Augenlust" verurteilt' (166 n.19), is not reliable here.

[118] JK, 695. Although Junod and Kaestli regard section C as an interpolation, they pay remarkably little attention to the time of origin of this part of the text, only stating (700) that the uninterpolated AJ and the interpolation are roughly contemporary and were joined at an early moment, in any case before 300. In 'Le dossier', 4342-4343, they are hardly more precise.

The author of the first main part of our text situates its events in and around Ephesos, but his limited knowledge of the city makes it unlikely that he is personally familiar with the city. The fact that he is not an Ephesian himself suggests that he is not the first to link John with that city; he rather *presupposes* a tradition concerning the activity of John in and around Ephesos. This being so, the *terminus a quo* for the writing of the AJ is indeed formed by the existence of a tradition that John the apostle lived and died in Ephesos.[119]

But this recognition does not mean that the dates suggested by Schäferdiek (after 200) or by Junod and Kaestli (between 150 and 200) are convincing. Hengel persuasively argues that the Fourth Gospel originally bore the name of John, became known from about 100 AD and originated in or near Ephesos.[120] Thus the traditions that connect John with Ephesos go back to the very beginning of the second century. The AJ, building on these traditions, can have been written at any moment after that time.

Taking everything together, in the course of the present study we found the following indications for the date of the AJ:

* The AJ postdates the Johannine Epistles and Ignatius by not too much time.
* The *terminus a quo* is the fact that the first author of the AJ already draws on the Synoptic tradition, the Fourth Gospel and Acts (chapter 3).[121]

The *terminus ante quem* has several elements:

* The AJ never refers to texts written after 140 AD.
* In its final form the AJ influenced the APe, the final form of the *Apocryphon of John*, and probably the *Apocalypse of Peter* (chapter 3).
* The AJ shows a pre-Valentinian fase in the development towards Gnosticism.[122]
* The AJ has a docetic Christology of the kind that was current from the end of the first until the middle of the second century, especially among those combatted in 1 Jn and by Ignatius. It is never found afterwards.[123]

These indications lead us to propose a date in the second quarter of the second century for the redaction of the final text.

[119] JK, 695: 'L'unique raison qui nous retienne de faire remonter la datation des *AJ* dans les premières décennies du IIe siècle est sa dépendance à l'égard de traditions fixant l'activité de Jean en Asie Mineure et sa mort à Éphèse.' Cf. Junod, 'Créations romanesques'.

[120] Hengel, *Johanneische Frage*, 21-25, 204-209.

[121] Siegert, 'Analyses rhétoriques', 249-250, argues that the AJ is written in a developed ecclesiastical style, but he gives no date.

[122] See pp. 200-202 above.

[123] See pp. 212-213 and 255 above.

# EPILOGUE

At the end of this study a few retrospective and forward-looking remarks are in order. First of all, the AJ, as it has been reconstructed from the various manuscripts, is clearly a consistent unity in diversity. We can distinguish the contributions of two authors, the second of whom created a two-stage initiation into an eminently spiritual form of Christianity. The two-stage form is not without parallels in contemporary texts. In order to recover this form, chapters 87-105 were restored to the position assigned to them prior to 1964. This restructuring vindicates the insight of the first generation of scholars who discussed the text inclusive of cc.87-105.

It was already known that cc.94-102 of the AJ were written by someone other than the author of the rest of the text. This second author aimed at expanding the existing "gospel" (cc.87-93, 103-105) by adding a revelation (cc.94-102) which contains a more explicit Christology and more polemics against other texts. Whereas the first part aimed at readers without much knowledge of Christianity, the second part forms an introduction into its deeper levels, and is meant for those who have absorbed the initial teachings. The second author may have been somebody who had recently left his ecclesiastical home to start a new community and wished to give this new group its own spiritual gospel.

The present study concludes that the Acts of the Apostles exercised considerable influence on the AJ. Taken together with the recent claim that the APl was also written by an author who consciously interacted with Luke's Acts, this fact has two important ramifications. First, it means a considerable addition to the history of the reception of Acts in the second century. The book was influential at a much earlier moment than has so far been assumed. Secondly, the discussion of the genre of the Apocryphal Acts has to take into account the influence both of Acts of the Apostles and of the ancient novels. Consequently, I argued that the Apocryphal Acts should be regarded as novelistic biographies of apostles. The AJ is unique in the fact that within the narrative frame of a biography it contains not only prayers, miracle stories, etc., but also John's gospel-like flashback.

Another distinctive mark of the AJ is its position in the Johannine trajectory. This applies not only to the Gnostic part of our text, as was previously suggested, but also to the non-Gnostic first part. I presented arguments for the thesis that a conflict over the identity of Christ divided the readers of the Fourth Gospel into a group which adhered to the proto-orthodox Christology as it is found in the Johannine Epistles and Ignatius, and a spiritualising group to which we owe the AJ.

In the present study much attention was devoted to the theological concepts of the text. Junod and Kaestli argue that the first main part of the AJ has a consistent theology and this view has been confirmed by studies of its Christology and its attitude towards asceticism. In opposition to

Junod and Kaestli, it was argued that the Christology should be regarded as docetic because it denies the humanity of Jesus Christ in order to lay exclusive stress on his divinity. It is remarkable that an author who knows both the Synoptic tradition and the Fourth Gospel has sketched a picture of Christ that is so radically different from that of the Gospels. Because of its exceptional Christology and concomitant concept of salvation, the ultimate establishment of the orthodox church which condemned and combatted deviant views inevitably had to lead to the marginalisation of the AJ.

In the Gnostic part of the text (cc.94-102, 109), no knowledge of earlier Gnostic writings or of an elaborate Gnostic mythology could be established. I therefore suggest that this piece of text belongs to a very early phase in the development of Gnosis.

As remarkable as the Christology of our text is, its attitudes towards marriage and sexuality are rather commonplace. The oft-heard allegations that in this respect the Apocryphal Acts as a group share a common stance are contradicted by the considerable diversity among these five books that comes to light.

In view of the AJ's consistent ideology it is likely that any now lost pieces of the text displayed just the same ideas. In other words, the present state of research forms a basis for evaluating whether a particular fragment belongs to the original AJ or to a later redaction. Of course, this conclusion does not imply that it has become superfluous for scholars to deal with the lacunae in the reconstructed text. It is not unlikely that in the future new manuscripts of the AJ, either in Greek or in translation, will be found. The continuing archaeological work in the Dakleh oasis, which already resulted in the finding of Papyrus Kellis 1, might yet bear fruit in this respect. It may also be hoped that one day new techniques will enable us to read the now illegible parts of manuscript **H**, which preserves a somewhat longer version of the AJ than the other manuscripts. A stylistic analysis can be undertaken only when the text has been further reconstructed.

We found no knowledge of traditions concerning a historical person called John, nor traces of the existence of a secluded Johannine sect in the second century. Although both parts of the AJ have a typically Johannine ideology, they are witness to an open interaction with other texts and other groups of Christians. The context in which this process took place was Asia Minor, the area of origin of the other Johannine writings and of the Ignatian Letters. The most likely date for the writing of the AJ is earlier than is generally supposed, viz. the second quarter of the second century.

Future research into the still unclear origins of Gnosticism can profit from the discovery of the trajectory which leads from a certain way of reading the Gospel of John, via a spiritualising form of Johannine Christianity, to the incipient form of Gnosis in the last-written part of the AJ. The existence of this trajectory suggests that scholars holding that Gnosticism owes more to Christianity than vice versa may be close to the truth. More research in this area may prove very fruitful.

Future research on the AJ itself could aim at shedding more light on the early transmission and translation of the text, in particular on the lost Latin translation. Until now, it is unclear how Augustine could quote from the gnostic part of our text without realising its true nature. Were cc.87-105 transmitted separately in Latin, or did they already circulate in Greek apart from the rest of the text? What was the role of the Manichaeans in the transmission of the AJ? Were they responsible for considerable abbreviations of the text? In this area, research has only just begun.

Now that the AJ is firmly anchored in second-century Asia Minor, more detailed comparisons with contemporary texts can be undertaken. First of all, the long awaited publication of new editions of the APl and the APe will open the road for more exact comparisons of the three closely related Apocryphal Acts. The suggestions, made in chapter 4, regarding the development of the concept of the Logos should be verified and developed further; the remarkable parallel with Justin, viz. the common use of lists of Christological predicates in which Logos is prominent, deserves special attention. Students of the Johannine writings and the Johannine community, and very specifically future commentators of 1 Jn, can no longer afford to ignore the AJ. The same applies to new studies of second-century Christology and of docetism, as well as to studies of Gnostic teachers like Theodotus and the legendary Cerinthus.

# BIBLIOGRAPHY

Adam, A., *Lehrbuch der Dogmengeschichte I. Die Zeit der Alten Kirche*, Gütersloh 1965.

Adam, A.K.M., 'Docetism, Käsemann, and Christology. Why Historical Criticism Can't Protect Christological Orthodoxy', *Scottish Journal of Theology* 49 (1996) 391-410.

Alexander, P.J., *The Patriarch Nicephorus of Constantinople*, Oxford 1958.

Alexander, P.S., '"The Parting of the Ways" from the Perspective of Rabbinic Judaism', in J.D.G. Dunn (ed.), *Jews and Christians. The Parting of the Ways A.D. 70 to 135* (WUNT 66), Tübingen 1992, 1-25.

Allberry, C.R.C. (ed.), *A Manichaean Psalm-Book* II, Stuttgart 1938.

Altaner, B., and A. Stuiber, *Patrologie*, Freiburg/Basel/Wien [8]1978.

Alzinger, W., *Die Stadt des siebenten Weltwunders. Die Wiederentdeckung von Ephesos*, Wien 1962.

Amsler, F., F. Bovon, B. Bouvier, *Actes de l'apôtre Philippe* (Collection de poche de l'AELAC 8), n.p. [Turnhout] 1996.

Anderson, G., *Ancient fiction. The novel in the Graeco-Roman world*, London 1984.

Ascough, R.S., 'Narrative Technique and Generic Designation: Crowd Scenes in Luke-Acts and in Chariton', *Catholic Biblical Quarterly* 58 (1996) 69-81.

Aune, D.E., *The New Testament in Its Literary Environment* (Library of Early Christianity 8), Philadelphia 1987.

Bastiaens, J.C., *Interpretaties van Jesaja 53. Een intertextueel onderzoek naar de lijdende Knecht in Jes 53 (MT/LXX) en in Lk 22:14-38, Hand 3:12-16, Hand 4:23-31 en Hand 8:26-40*, Dissertation Tilburg 1993.

Bastiaensen, A.A.R., *et al.* (eds.), *Atti e passioni dei martiri*, n.p. 1987.

Bauckham, R.J., 'The *Acts of Paul* as a Sequel to Acts', in B.W. Winter and A.D. Clarke (eds.), *The Book of Acts in Its Ancient Literary Setting*, Grand Rapids/Carlisle 1993, 105-152.

Bauer, J.B., 'Die Korruptel *Acta Johannis* 52', *VigChr* 44 (1990) 295-297.

Bauer, W., *Das Leben Jesu im Zeitalter der neutestamentlichen Apokryphen*, Tübingen 1909.

--, *Die Briefe des Ignatius von Antiochia und der Polykarpbrief*, 2nd ed. by H. Paulsen (HNT 18), Tübingen 1985.

--, *Griechisch-Deutsches Wörterbuch zu den Schriften des Neuen Testaments und der frühchristlichen Literatur*, 6th ed. by K. and B. Aland, Berlin/New York 1988.

Baur, F.C., *Kritische Untersuchungen über die kanonischen Evangelien*, Tübingen 1847.

Benoît, A., *et al.*, *Biblia Patristica. Index des citations et allusions bibliques dans la littérature patristique, I: Des origines à Clément d'Alexandrie et Tertullien*, Paris 1975.

Bergholz, Th., *Der Aufbau des lukanischen Doppelwerkes. Untersuchungen zum formalliterarischen Charakter von Lukas-Evangelium und Apostelgeschichte*, Frankfurt 1995.

Bethge, H.-G., *Der Brief des Petrus an Philippus. Ein neutestamentliches Apokryphon aus dem Funde von Nag Hammadi (NHC VIII.2)* (TU 141), Berlin 1997.

Beyschlag, K., *Die verborgene Überlieferung von Christus* (Siebenstern Taschenbuch 136), München/Hamburg 1969.

Blumenthal, M., *Formen und Motive in den apokryphen Apostelgeschichten* (TU 48.1), Leipzig 1933.

Böhlig, A., 'Zum Vorstellung vom Lichtkreuz in Gnostizismus und Manichäismus', in his *Gnosis und Synkretismus* I (WUNT 47), Tübingen 1989, 135-163, esp. 144-153.

Boer, M.C. de, 'The Death of Jesus Christ and His Coming in the Flesh', *Novum Testamentum* 33 (1991) 326-346.

--, *Johannine Perspectives on the Death of Jesus* (Contributions to Biblical Exegesis and Theology 17), Kampen 1996.

Bolyki, J., 'Miracle stories in the Acts of John', in Bremmer, *Acts of John*, 15-35.

--, '"Head Downwards": The Cross of Peter in the Lights of the Apocryphal Acts, of the New Testament and of the Society-transforming Claim of Early Christianity', in Bremmer, *Acts of Peter*, 111-122.

Bonnet, M., *Acta Apostolorum Apocrypha* II.1, Leipzig 1898, repr. Hildesheim 1959.

Bousset, W., 'Platons Weltseele und das Kreuz Christi', *ZNW* 14 (1913) 273-285.

Bovon, F., 'Miracles, magie et guérison dans les Actes apocryphes des apôtres', *JECS* 3 (1995) 245-259.

Bovon, F., *et al.*, *Les Actes apocryphes des apôtres*, Genève 1981.

Braun, F.-M., *Jean le Théologien et son Évangile dans l'église ancienne*, Paris 1959.

Bremmer, J.N., 'Why did Early Christianity attract Upper-class Women?', in A.A.R. Bastiaensen *et al.* (eds.), *Fructus centesimus. FS Bartelink*, Steenbrugge 1989, 37-47.

--, 'Pauper or Patroness: the widow in the early Christian Church', in J.N. Bremmer and L.P. van den Bosch (eds.), *Between Poverty and the Pyre. Moments in the History of Widowhood*, London 1995, 31-57.

--, 'Het bekeringsvisioen van Constantijn de Grote', in H.S. Benjamins *et al.* (eds.), *Evangelie en beschaving. FS Roldanus*, Zoetermeer 1995, 49-67.

--, 'Women in the Apocryphal Acts of John', in *idem* (ed.), *The Apocryphal Acts of John* (Studies on the Apocryphal Acts of the

Apostles 1), Kampen 1995, 37-56.
--, 'Magic, martyrdom and women's liberation in the Acts of Paul and Thecla', in *idem* (ed.), *The Apocryphal Acts of Paul and Thecla* (Studies on the Apocryphal Acts of the Apostles 2), Kampen 1996, 36-59.
--, 'Aspects of the Acts of Peter: Women, Magic, Place and Date', in *idem* (ed.), *The Apocryphal Acts of Peter: Magic, Miracles and Gnosticism* (Studies on the Apocryphal Acts of the Apostles 3), Leuven 1998, 1-20.
--, 'The Novel and the Apocryphal Acts: place, time and readership', forthcoming in H. Hofmann and M. Zimmerman (eds.), *Groningen Colloquia on the Novel* 9, Groningen 1998.
Broek, R. van den, 'The present state of gnostic studies', *VigChr* 37 (1983) 47-71.
--, 'Hermes en zijn gemeente te Alexandrië', in G. Quispel (ed.), *De Hermetische Gnosis in de loop der eeuwen*, Baarn 1992, 9-26.
--, *Studies in Gnosticism and Alexandrian Christianity* (NHMS 39), Leiden 1996.
Brown, P., *The Body and Society*, New York 1988.
Brown, R.E., *The Gospel According to John* (2 vols., AB), New York 1966.
--, *The Community of the Beloved Disciple*, New York 1979.
--, *The Johannine Epistles* (AB), New York 1982.
Brox, N., '"Doketismus" - eine Problemanzeige', *Zeitschrift für Kirchengeschichte* 95 (1984) 301-314.
Bruce, F.F., 'St. John at Ephesus', *Bulletin of the John Rylands Library* 60 (1977) 339-361.
Burkert, W., *Ancient mystery cults*, Cambridge MA/London 1987.
Burrus, V., *Chastity as Autonomy. Women in the Stories of the Apocryphal Acts* (Studies in Women and Religion 23), Lewiston/Queenston 1987.
--, 'Chastity as Autonomy: Women in the Stories of the Apocryphal Acts', *Semeia* 38 (1986) 101-117.
Burton, G.P., 'Proconsuls, assizes and the administration of justice under the Empire', *Journal of Roman Studies* 65 (1975) 92-106.
Cameron, A., *Christianity and the Rhetoric of Empire. The Development of Christian Discourse*, Berkeley 1991.
Cantalamessa, R., 'Méliton de Sardes. Une christologie anti-gnostique du IIe siècle', *Revue des Sciences religieuses* 37 (1963) 1-26.
--, *L'omelia 'In s.Pascha' dello Pseudo-Ippolito di Roma. Richerche sulla teologia dell' Asia Minore nella seconda metà del II secolo*, Milano 1967.
--, 'Il Christo 'Padre' negli scritti del II-III sec.', *Rivista di Storia e Letteratura Religiosa* 3 (1967) 1-27.

--, 'Les homélies pascales de Méliton des Sardes et du Pseudo-Hippolyte et les Extraits de Théodote', in *Epektasis. Mélanges Jean Daniélou*, Paris 1972, 263-271.

Cartlidge, D.R., 'Transfigurations of Metamorphosis Traditions in the Acts of John, Thomas, and Peter', *Semeia* 38 (1986) 53-66.

--, 'Evangelist Leaves Wife, Clings to Christ: An Illustration in the Admont "Anselm" and Its Relevance to a Reconstruction of the *Acta Ioannis*', in E.H. Lovering (ed.), *Society of Biblical Literature 1994 Seminar Papers*, Atlanta 1994, 376-389.

Casson, L. (ed.), *Periplus maris Erythraei*, Princeton 1989.

Chadwick, H., *The Sentences of Sextus. A contribution to the history of Early Christian Ethics*, Cambridge 1959.

--, *Priscillian of Avila. The occult and the charismatic in the early church*, Oxford 1976.

Chariton, *Le roman de Chairéas et Callirhoé*, ed. G. Molinié, Paris 1979.

--, *Callirhoe*, ed. G.P. Goold (Loeb 481), Cambridge MA/London 1995.

Childs, B.S., *The New Testament as Canon: An Introduction*, London 1984.

Claes, P., *De mot zit in de mythe*, Leuven 1981.

--, *Echo's echo's. De kunst van de allusie*, Amsterdam 1988.

Clemens Alexandrinus, ed. O. Stählin (GCS 17). Vol. I: *Protrepticus, Paedagogus*, Berlin $^{3}$1972; Vol. II: *Stromata* I-VI, Berlin $^{3}$1960; III: *Fragmente*, Leipzig 1909, Berlin $^{2}$1970 (ed. L. Früchtel and U. Treu).

Colpe, C., *Die Religionsgeschichtliche Schule. Darstellung und Kritik ihres Bildes vom gnostischen Erlösermythus* (FRLANT 78), Göttingen 1961.

--, 'Zur Leib-Christi-Vorstellung im Epheserbrief', in W. Eltester (ed.), *Judentum - Urchristentum - Kirche. FS Jeremias*, Berlin 1964, 172-186.

Connolly, R.H., 'The original language of the Syriac Acts of John', *Journal of Theological Studies* 8 (1907) 249-261.

--, 'The Diatessaron in the Syriac Acts of John', *Journal of Theological Studies* 8 (1907) 571-581.

Copenhaver, B.P, *Hermetica. The Greek* Corpus Hermeticum *and the Latin* Asclepius *in a new English translation, with notes and introduction*, Cambridge 1992.

Corsaro, F., *Le ΠΡΑΞΕΙΣ di Giovanni*, Catania 1968.

Corssen, P., *Monarchianische Prologe zu den vier Evangelien. Ein Beitrag zur Geschichte des Kanons* (TU 15), Leipzig 1896.

Corwin, V., *St.Ignatius and Christianity in Antioch*, New Haven 1960.

Crossan, J.D., *Four Other Gospels*, Minneapolis 1985.

--, *The Cross That Spoke. The Origins of the Passion Narrative*, San Francisco 1988.

Cullmann, O., *Die Christologie des Neuen Testaments*, Tübingen $^{3}$1963.

--, *Der johanneische Kreis. Zum Ursprung des Johannesevangeliums,* Tübingen 1975.

Culpepper, R.A., *The Johannine School. An Evaluation of the Johannine-School Hypothesis based on an Investigation of the Nature of Ancient Schools*, Dissertation Duke University 1974.

--, *John, the Son of Zebedee. The Life of a Legend*, Columbia SC 1994.

Davies, J.G., 'The Origins of Docetism', *Studia Patristica VI* (TU 81), Berlin 1962, 13-35.

Davies, S.L., *The Revolt of the Widows. The Social World of the Apocryphal Acts*, Ph.D. Dissertation Temple University 1978.

Deming, W., *Paul on marriage and celibacy. The Hellenistic background of 1 Corinthians 7* (SNTS MS 83), Cambridge 1995.

Denker, J., *Die theologiegeschichtliche Stellung des Petrusevangeliums. Ein Beitrag zur Frühgeschichte des Doketismus*, Bern/Frankfurt 1975.

Dewey, A.J., 'The Hymn in the *Acts of John*: Dance as Hermeneutic', *Semeia* 38 (1986) 67-80.

Dinkler, E., *Das Apsismosaik von S.Apollinare in Classe*, Köln/Opladen 1964.

Dobschütz, E. von, 'Der Roman in der altchristlichen Literatur', *Deutsche Rundschau* 111 (1902) 87-106.

Dodds, E.R., *Pagan and Christian in an Age of Anxiety. Some Aspects of Religious Experience from Marcus Aurelius to Constantine*, Cambridge 1965.

Dölger, F.J., 'Beiträge zur Geschichte des Kreuzzeichens 9', *Jahrbuch für Antike und Christentum* 10 (1967) 1-29.

Drijvers, H.J.W., 'Der getaufte Löwe und die Theologie der Acta Pauli', in P. Nagel (ed.), *Carl-Schmidt-Kolloquium 1988*, Halle 1990, 181-189, repr in his *History and Religion in Late Antique Syria*, Aldershot 1994, X.

--, 'Apocryphal literature in the cultural milieu of Osrhoëne', *Apocrypha* 1 (1990) 231-247, repr in his *History and Religion in Late Antique Syria*, Aldershot 1994, III.

Dunn, P.W., 'Women's Liberation, the *Acts of Paul*, and Other Apocryphal Acts of the Apostles. A Review of Some Recent Interpretations', *Apocrypha* 4 (1993) 245-261.

Egger, B., 'Looking at Chariton's *Callirhoe*', in Morgan and Stoneman (eds.), *Greek Fiction*, 31-48.

Ehrman, B.D., '1 Joh 4 3 and the Orthodox Corruption of Scripture', *ZNW* 79 (1988) 221-243.

Eijk, T.H.C. van, 'Marriage and virginity, death and immortality', in *Epektasis. Mélanges Jean Daniélou*, Paris 1972, 209-235.

Elliott, J.K. (ed.), *The Apocryphal New Testament*, Oxford 1993.

--, 'The Apocryphal Acts', *Expository Times* 105 (1993-'94) 71-77.

Engelmann, H., 'Ephesos und die Johannesakten', *ZPE* 103 (1994) 297-302.

Epiphanius of Salamis, *Panarion* Book I, trans. F. Williams, Leiden/New York 1987.

Erbetta, M., *Gli Apocrifi del Nuovo Testamento, Vol.II: Atti e Leggende*, Casale Monferrato 1966 (1978).

Eusebius, *Kirchengeschichte*. Kleine Ausgabe, ed. E. Schwartz, Leipzig $^{5}$1955.

--, *Über das Leben des Kaisers Konstantin*, ed. F. Winkelmann (GCS), Berlin 1975.

Evans, C.A., *Word and Glory. On the Exegetical and Theological Background of John's Gospel* (JSNT Sup 89), Sheffield 1993.

Evans, E., *Tertullian's Treatise Against Praxeas*, London 1948.

Fabricius, J.A., *Codex Apocryphus Novi Testamenti*, Hamburg, I, II 1703 ($^{2}$1719), III 1719.

Festugière, A.-J., *La révélation d'Hermès Trismégiste IV. Le dieu inconnu et la gnose*, Paris 1954.

--, *Les Actes Apocryphes de Jean et de Thomas. Traduction française et notes critiques* (Cahiers d'Orientalisme 6), Genève 1983.

Findlay, A.F., *Byways in Early Christian Literature. Studies in the Uncanonical Gospels and Acts. The Kerr Lectures ... 1920-21*, Edinburgh 1923.

Fischer, J.A. (ed.), *Die Apostolischen Väter*, München 1956.

Fossum, J.E., 'Jewish-Christian Christology and Jewish Mysticism', *VigChr* 37 (1983) 260-287.

--, *The Image of the Invisible God. Essays on the influence of Jewish Mysticism on Early Christology* (NTOA 30), Freiburg CH/Göttingen 1995.

Francis, J.A., *Subversive Virtue. Asceticism and Authority in the Second-Century Pagan World*, University Park PA 1995.

Frank, K.S., *Grundzüge der Geschichte des christlichen Mönchtums*, Darmstadt 1979.

Fraser, P.M., and E. Matthews, *A Lexicon of Greek Personal Names*, Vol I: The Aegean Islands - Cyprus - Cyrenaica, Oxford 1987; Vol II: Attica, Oxford 1994.

Funk, W.-P., *Die zweite Apokalypse des Jakobus aus Nag-Hammadi-Codex V* (TU 119), Berlin 1976.

Gärtner, B., *The Theology of the Gospel of Thomas*, London 1961.

Gallagher, E.V., 'Conversion and Salvation in the Apocryphal Acts of the Apostles', *The Second Century* 8 (1991) 13-29.

Garcia-Iberg, H., *Polymorphie du Christ dans la tradition johannique gnostique* (mémoire de D.E.A., École pratique des hautes études Paris, V[e] section, 1993-'94).

Gardner, I., 'The Manichaean Community at Kellis', in P. Mirecki and J. BeDuhn (eds.), *Emerging from Darkness. Studies in the Recovery of Manichaean Sources* (NHMS 43), Leiden 1997, 161-175.

Gardner, I., and K. Worp, 'Leaves from a Manichaean Codex', *ZPE* 117 (1997) 139-155.

Gessel, W.M., 'Die Johannestradition auf dem Ayasoluk im Lichte der apokryphen Johannesakten', in R. Schulz and M. Jörg (eds.), *Lingua restituta orientalis. FS Assfalg*, Wiesbaden 1990, 108-113.

Giversen, S, 'Hermetic Communities', in J.P. Sorensen (ed.), *Rethinking Religion. Studies in the Hellenistic Process*, Copenhagen 1989, 49-53.

Grese, W.C., *Corpus Hermeticum XIII and Early Christian Literature* (Studia ad corpus hellenisticum novi testamenti v), Leiden 1979.

Gribomont, J., 'Askese IV. Neues Testament und Alte Kirche', *Theologische Realenzyklopädie* 4 (1979) 204-225.

Griggs, C.W., *Early Egyptian Christianity* (Coptic Studies 2), Leiden 1990.

Groag, E., and A. Stein, *Prosopographia Imperii Romani saec I.II.III* pars I, Berlin/Leipzig $^{2}$1933.

Grossi, V., 'Il titolo cristologico "Padre" nell'antichità cristiana', *Augustinianum* 16 (1976) 237-269.

--, 'La Pasqua quartodecimana e il significato della croce nel II secolo', *Augustinianum* 16 (1976) 557-571.

Hägg, T., *The Novel in Antiquity*, Oxford 1983.

Hainthaler, Th., 'Doketismus', *Lexikon für Theologie und Kirche*$^{3}$ 3 (1995) 301-302.

Hall, S.G., 'Melito's Paschal Homily and the *Acts of John*', *Journal of Theological Studies* 17 (1966) 95-98.

Hamman, A., '"*Sitz im Leben*" des actes apocryphes du Nouveau Testament', *Studia Patristica* VIII (TU 93), Berlin 1966, 62-69.

Hammond Bammel, C.P., 'Ignatian Problems', *Journal of Theological Studies* 33 (1982) 62-97.

Harnack, A., 'Die pseudoclementinischen Briefe de virginitate und die Entstehung des Mönchtums' (1891), in K.S. Frank (ed.), *Askese und Mönchtum in der alten Kirche* (Wege der Forschung 409), Darmstadt 1975, 37-68.

--, *Marcion: das Evangelium vom fremden Gott* (TU 45), Leipzig 1921.

--, 'Der apokryphe Brief des Paulusschülers Titus "De dispositione Sanctimonii"', *Sitzungsberichte der Preus. Akademie der Wissenschaften, Phil.-hist. Klasse* 17 (1925) 180-213.

Harrison, S.J., 'Apuleius' *Metamorphoses*', in Schmeling, *Novel*, 491-516.

Hauschild, W.-D., *Lehrbuch der Kirchen- und Dogmengeschichte I: Alte Kirche und Mittelalter*, München/Gütersloh 1995.

Havelaar, H.W., *The Coptic Apocalypse of Peter (Nag Hammadi Codex VII,3). A Study of Generic, Intertextual and Christological Questions*, typescript Dissertation Groningen 1993.

Hays, R.B., *Echoes of Scripture in the Letters of Paul*, New Haven/London 1989.

Head, P., 'On the Christology of the Gospel of Peter', *VigChr* 46 (1992) 209-224.

--, 'The Foreign God and the Sudden Christ: Theology and Christology in Marcion's Gospel Redaction', *TynB* 44 (1993) 307-321.

Heine, R., 'Picaresque novel versus allegory', in B.L. Hijmans Jr and R.Th. van der Paardt (eds.), *Aspects of Apuleius' Golden Ass*, Groningen 1978, 25-42.

Helderman, J., 'Zum Doketismus und zur Inkarnation im Manichäismus', in A. Van Tongerloo and S. Giversen (eds.), *Manichaica selecta. FS Ries*, Leuven 1991, 101-125.

Hemer, C.J., *The Book of Acts in the Setting of Hellenistic History*, ed. C.H. Gempf (WUNT 49), Tübingen 1989.

Hengel, M., *Crucifixion*, London 1977.

--, *Zur urchristlichen Geschichtsschreibung*, Stuttgart 1979.

--, *Die johanneische Frage* (WUNT 67), Tübingen 1993.

Hennecke, E., 'Johannesakten', in *idem* (ed.), *Handbuch zu den Neutestamentlichen Apokryphen*, Tübingen 1904, 494-543.

--, (ed.), *Neutestamentliche Apokryphen*, Tübingen ²1924.

Hermas, *The Shepherd*, ed. and trans. K. Lake (The Apostolic Fathers II, Loeb), London/Cambridge MA 1913, repr. 1950.

Hermas, *Der Hirt*, ed. M. Whittaker (GCS, Die apostolischen Väter I), Berlin 1956.

Heussi, K., *Der Ursprung des Mönchtums*, Tübingen 1936, repr. Aalen 1981.

Hilgenfeld, A., Review of James, *Apocrypha anecdota*, *Zeitschrift für wissenschaftliche Theologie* 40 (1897) 467-471.

--, 'Der gnostische und der kanonische Johannes über das Leben Jesu', *Zeitschrift für wissenschaftliche Theologie* 43 (1900) 1-61.

Hilhorst, A., review of H.W. Hollander and M. de Jonge, *The Testaments of the Twelve Patriarchs* (Leiden 1985), in *Journal for the Study of Judaism* 17 (1986) 252-255.

Hills, J.V., 'The Acts of the Apostles in the *Acts of Paul*', in E.H. Lovering (ed.), *Society of Biblical Literature 1994 Seminar Papers,* Atlanta 1994, 24-54.

Hippolytus, *Refutatio omnium haeresium*, ed. M. Marcovich (Patristische Texte und Studien 25), Berlin/New York 1986.

Hofrichter, P., 'Logoslehre und Gottesbild bei Apologeten, Modalisten und Gnostikern', in H.-J. Klauck (ed.), *Monotheismus und Christologie*, Freiburg 1992, 186-217.

Holzhausen, J., *Der 'Mythos vom Menschen' im hellenistischen Ägypten. Eine Studie zum 'Poimandres' (= CH I), zu Valentin und dem gnostischen Mythos* (Theophaneia 33), Bodenheim 1994.
Hope, C.A., 'The Archaeological Context of the Discovery of Leaves from a Manichaean Codex', *ZPE* 117 (1997) 156-161.
Horbury, W., 'The Christian use and the Jewish origins of the Wisdom of Solomon', in J. Day, R.P. Gordon and H.G.M. Williamson (eds.), *Wisdom in ancient Israel*, Cambridge 1995, 182-196.
Horsley, G.H.R., 'The Inscriptions of Ephesos and the New Testament', *Novum Testamentum* 34 (1992) 105-168.
Horst, P.W. van der, 'Het onderzoek van de vroege Joodse mystiek na Scholem', *Nederlands Theologisch Tijdschrift* 44 (1990) 121-138.
--, 'The Birkat ha-minim in Recent Research', *Expository Times* 105 (1993-'94) 363-368.
Hug, J., *La finale de l'Évangile de Marc*, Paris 1978.
Ignatius, *Epistles*, ed. K. Lake (The Apostolic Fathers I, Loeb), London/Cambridge MA (1912) 1952.
Irenaeus von Lyon, *Epideixis - Adversus haereses I*, ed. N. Brox (Fontes Christiani 8/1), Freiburg/Basel usw. 1993; *Adversus haereses III* (FChr 8/3) 1995.
Irénée de Lyon, *Contre les hérésies*, ed. and trans. A. Rousseau and L. Doutreleau (SC), Paris, Book I (SC 263-264) 1979; II (293-294) 1982; III (210-211) 1974; IV (100, with Ch. Mercier and B. Hemmerdinger) 1965; V (152-153, with Ch. Mercier) 1969.
*Iustini Martyris Dialogus cum Tryphone*, ed. M. Marcovich, Berlin/New York 1997.
Jacobson, H., *The* Exagoge *of Ezekiel*, Cambridge 1983.
James, M.R., *Apocrypha Anecdota. Second Series* (Texts and Studies 5.1), Cambridge 1897, repr. Nendeln/Liechtenstein 1967.
Janssens, Y., 'L'Évangile selon Philippe', *Le Muséon* 81 (1968) 79-133.
Jenkins, G., 'Papyrus I from Kellis. A Greek text with affinities to the Acts of John', in Bremmer, *Acts of John*, 197-216.
Johnson, S.E., 'Parallels between the letters of Ignatius and the Johannine Epistles', in E.W. Conrad and E.G. Newing (eds.), *Perspectives on Language and Text. FS Andersen*, Winona Lake Ind. 1987, 327-338.
Jones, F.S., 'Principal Orientations on the Relations between the Apocryphal Acts', in E.H. Lovering (ed.), *Society of Biblical Literature 1993 Seminar Papers*, Atlanta 1993, 485-505.
Jonge, M. de, *De brieven van Johannes* (PNT), Nijkerk 1968.
Junod, E., 'Actes apocryphes et hérésie: le jugement de Photius', in Bovon, *Actes apocryphes*, 11-24.
--, 'Les vies de philosophes et les actes apocryphes des apôtres poursuivent-ils un dessein similaire?', in Bovon, *Actes apocryphes*,

209-219.

--, 'Ce que l'étude des Actes apocryphes peut apporter à la connaissance du christianisme des premiers siècles: le cas des Actes de Jean', in *Rapport de gestion de la Société Suisse des Sciences Humaines 1980*, Berne 1981, II.19-26.

--, 'Créations romanesques et traditions ecclésiastiques dans les Actes apocryphes des Apôtres. L'alternative fiction romanesque - vérité historique: une impasse', *Augustinianum* 23 (1983) 271-285.

Junod, E., and J.-D. Kaestli, 'Les traits caractéristiques de la théologie des "Actes de Jean"', *Revue de Théologie et de Philosophie* 26 (1976) 125-145.

--, *L'histoire des Actes apocryphes des apôtres du IIIe au IXe siècle: le cas des Actes de Jean* (Cahiers de la Revue de Théologie et de Philosophie 7), Genève/Lausanne/Neuchâtel 1982.

--, *Acta Iohannis*, Tomus 1: Praefatio - Textus; Tomus 2: Textus alii - commentarius - indices (CCSA 1-2), Turnhout 1983.

--, 'Le dossier des "Actes de Jean"', in W. Haase (ed.), *Aufstieg und Niedergang der Römischen Welt* II.25.6, Berlin/New York 1988, 4293-4362.

--, 'Actes de Jean', in F. Bovon and P. Geoltrain (eds.), *Écrits apocryphes chrétiens* 1 (Pleiades), Paris 1997, 973-1037.

Käsemann, E., *Jesu letzter Wille nach Johannes 17*, Tübingen ²1967 [ET *The Testament of Jesus*, London 1968].

Kaestli, J.-D., 'Valentinisme italien et valentinisme oriental: leurs divergences à propos de la nature du corps de Jésus', in B. Layton (ed.), *The Rediscovery of Gnosticism* I, Leiden 1980, 391-403.

--, 'Les scènes d'attribution des champs de mission et de départ de l'apôtre dans les actes apocryphes', in Bovon, *Actes apocryphes*, 249-264.

--, 'Le rôle des textes bibliques dans la genèse et le développement des légendes apocryphes: le cas du sort final de l'apôtre Jean', *Augustinianum* 23 (1983) 319-336.

--, 'Response' [to A.J. Dewey], *Semeia* 38 (1986) 81-88.

--, 'Response' [to V. Burrus], *Semeia* 38 (1986) 119-131.

--, 'Le mystère de la croix de lumière et le Johannisme. Actes de Jean ch. 94-102', *Foi et vie 86 (Cahier biblique 26)* 1987, 35-46.

--, 'Fiction littéraire et réalité sociale: Que peut-on savoir de la place des femmes dans le milieu de production des Actes apocryphes des Apôtres?', *Apocrypha - le champ des Apocryphes* 1 (1990) 279-302.

--, 'Remarques sur le rapport du quatrième evangile avec la gnose et sa réception au IIe siècle', in *idem et al.* (eds.), *La communauté johannique et son histoire. La trajectoire de l'évangile de Jean aux deux premiers siècles*, Genève 1990, 351-356.

--, 'Le rapport entre les deux Vies latines de l'apôtre Jean. A propos d'un récent article de K.Schäferdiek', *Apocrypha* 3 (1992) 111-123.

Kamp, G.C. van de, *Pneuma-christologie: een oud antwoord op een actuele vraag?*, Dissertation Amsterdam 1983.

Kampen, L. van, *Apostelverhalen. Doel en compositie van de oudste apokriefe Handelingen der apostelen*, Dissertation Utrecht 1990.

Kany, R., 'Der lukanische Bericht von Tod und Auferstehung Jesu aus der Sicht eines hellenistischen Romanlesers', *Novum Testamentum* 28 (1986) 75-90.

Karasszon, I., 'Old Testament quotations in the Acts of Andrew and John', in Bremmer, *Acts of John*, 57-71.

Kelly, J.N.D., *Early Christian Doctrines*, London [2]1960.

Klauck, H.-J., *Der erste Johannesbrief* (EKK), Zürich/Neukirchen-Vluyn 1991.

Klijn, A.F.J., *The Acts of Thomas* (SupNT 5), Leiden 1962.

--, *Apostolische Vaders* I, Kampen 1981; II, Kampen 1983.

--, (ed.), *Apokriefen van het Nieuwe Testament II*, Kampen 1985.

Klijn, A.F.J., and G.J. Reinink, *Patristic Evidence for Jewish-Christian Sects* (SupNT 36), Leiden 1973.

Köster, H, *Einführung in das Neue Testament*, Berlin/New York 1980.

--, 'Les discours d'adieu de l'évangile de Jean: leur trajectoire au premier et au deuxième siècle', in Kaestli *et al.*, *Communauté johannique*, 269-280.

Köster, H. and J.M. Robinson, *Entwicklungslinien durch die Welt frühen Christentums*, Tübingen 1971.

Kortekaas, G.A.A., *Historia Apollonii regis Tyri. Prolegomena, text edition (...)*, Dissertation Groningen 1984.

Koschorke, K., 'Eine gnostische Pfingstpredigt', *Zeitschrift für Theologie und Kirche* 74 (1977) 323-343.

--, *Die Polemik der Gnostiker gegen das kirchliche Christentum* (NHS 12), Leiden 1978.

--, 'Eine neugefundene gnostische Gemeindeordnung. Zum Thema Geist und Amt im frühen Christentum', *Zeitschrift für Theologie und Kirche* 76 (1979) 30-60.

Koskienniemi, E., *Apollonios von Tyana in der neutestamentlichen Exegese* (WUNT 2.61), Tübingen 1994.

Kretschmar, G., 'Festkalender und Memorialstätten Jerusalems in altkirchlicher Zeit', *Zeitschrift des Deutschen Palästina-Vereins* 87 (1971) 167-205.

--, 'Zur Frage nach dem Ursprung frühchristlicher Askese', orig. in *ZTK* 61 (1964) 27-67, now in K.S. Frank (ed.), *Askese und Mönchtum in der alten Kirche* (Wege der Forschung 409), Darmstadt 1975, 129-180.

Lalleman, P.J., 'Polymorphy of Christ', in Bremmer, *Acts of John*, 97-118.
--, 'The resurrection in the Acts of Paul', in Bremmer, *Acts of Paul and Thecla*, 126-141.
--, 'Classical Echoes (Callimachus, Chariton) in the *Acta Iohannis*?', *ZPE* 116 (1997) 66.
--, 'Healing by a mere touch as a Christian concept', *TynB* 48 (1997) 355-361.
--, 'The relationship between the Acts of John and the Acts of Peter', in Bremmer, *Acts of Peter*, 161-177.
--, 'The sources of the Apocryphal Acts of the Apostles or what Richard Pervo did not tell you', in H. Hofmann and M. Zimmerman (eds.), *Groningen Colloquia on the Novel 9*, Groningen 1998.
Lambrecht, J., 'Paul's Farewell-Address at Miletus (Acts 20, 17-38)', in J. Kremer (ed.), *Les Actes des Apôtres. Traditions, rédaction, théologie* (BETL 48), Gembloux/Leuven 1979, 307-337.
Larcher, C., *Études sur le Livre de la Sagesse*, Paris 1969.
--, *Le Livre de la Sagesse ou la Sagesse de Salomon I*, Paris 1983.
Layton, B., *The Gnostic Scriptures. A New Translation with Annotations and Introductions*, Garden City NY 1987.
--, *Nag Hammadi Codex II,2-7* Vol. I (NHS 20), Leiden/New York 1989.
--, 'Prolegomena to the Study of Ancient Gnosticism', in L.M. White and O.L. Yarbrough (eds.), *The Social World of the First Christians. FS Meeks*, Minneapolis 1995, 334-350.
Liébaert, J., *Christologie. Von der Apostolischen Zeit bis zum Konzil von Chalkedon (451)* (Handbuch der Dogmengeschichte III.1a), Freiburg/Basel/Wien 1965.
Liesker, W.H.M. and A.M. Tromp, 'Zwei Ptolemäische Papyri aus der Wiener Papyrussammlung', *ZPE* 66 (1986) 79-82.
Lieu, J.M., 'Authority to become children of God'. A Study of 1 John', *Novum Testamentum* 23 (1981) 210-228.
--, *The theology of the Johannine Epistles* (New Testament Theology), Cambridge 1991.
Lightfoot, J.B., *The Apostolic Fathers II: S.Ignatius, S.Polycarp* (3 vols.), London/New York $^{2}$1889, repr. Hildesheim/New York 1973.
Lightfoot, J.B., and J.R. Farmer, *The Apostolic Fathers*, second ed. revised by M.W. Holmes (Grand Rapids 1989), Leicester 1990.
Lipsius, R.A., *Die apokryphen Apostelgeschichten und Apostellegenden. Ein Beitrag zur altchristlichen Literaturgeschichte*, I Braunschweig 1883; II.1 Braunschweig 1887.
Loewenich, W. von, *Das Johannes-Verständnis im zweiten Jahrhundert* (BZNW 13), Giessen 1932.
Logan, A.H.B., 'John and the Gnostics: The Significance of the Apocryphon of John for the Debate about the Origins of the Johannine

Literature', *Journal for the Study of the New Testament* 43 (1991) 41-69.

--, *Gnostic Truth and Christian Heresy. A Study in the History of Gnosticism*, Edinburgh 1996.

Lohse, B., *Askese und Mönchtum in der Antike und in der alten Kirche*, München/Wien 1969.

Loisy, A., *Le quatrième Évangile (deuxième édition) - les Épitres dites de Jean*, Paris 1921.

Luttikhuizen, G.P., *The Revelation of Elchasai*, Tübingen 1985.

--, *Gnostische geschriften* I, Kampen 1986.

--, 'The Jewish Factor in the Development of the Gnostic Myth of Origins: Some Observations', in T. Baarda *et al.* (eds.), *Text and Testimony. FS Klijn*, Kampen 1988, 152-161.

--, 'The evaluation of the teaching of Jesus in Christian Gnostic revelation dialogues', *Novum Testamentum* 30 (1988) 158-168.

--, 'A gnostic reading of the Acts of John', in Bremmer, *Acts of John*, 119-152.

--, 'Johannine Vocabulary and the Thought Structure of Gnostic Mythological Texts', in H. Preissler and H. Seiwert (eds.), *Gnosisforschung und Religionsgeschichte. FS Rudolph*, Marburg 1994, 175-181.

--, 'The thought pattern of Gnostic mythologizers and their use of Biblical traditions', in J.D. Turner and A. McGuire (eds.), *The Nag Hammadi Library after fifty years* (NHMS 44), Leiden 1997, 89-101.

McCant, J.W., 'The Gospel of Peter: Docetism Reconsidered', *New Testament Studies* 30 (1984) 258-273.

MacDonald, D.R. (ed.), *The Acts of Andrew and The Acts of Andrew and Matthias in the City of the Cannibals*, Atlanta GA 1990.

--, '*The Acts of Paul* and *The Acts of John*: Which Came First?', in E.H. Lovering (ed.), *Society of Biblical Literature 1993 Seminar Papers*, Atlanta 1993, 506-510.

--, '*The Acts of Peter* and *The Acts of John*: Which Came First?', *ibid.*, 623-626.

--, MacDonald, D.R., *Christianizing Homer: The* Odyssey, *Plato, and* the Acts of Andrew, New York/Oxford 1994.

McKechnie, P., '"Women's Religion" and Second-Century Christianity', *Journal of Ecclesiastical History* 47 (1996) 409-431.

Macro, A.D., 'The cities of Asia Minor under the Roman Imperium', *Aufstieg und Niedergang der Römischen Welt* II.7.2 (1980) 658-697.

Mara, M.G., *Évangile de Pierre* (SC 201), Paris 1973.

Markschies, C., *Valentinus Gnosticus?* (WUNT 65), Tübingen 1992.

--, 'Valentinian Gnosticism: Toward the anatomy of a school', in J.D. Turner and A. McGuire (eds.), *The Nag Hammadi Library after fifty years* (NHMS 44), Leiden 1997, 401-438.

Maurer, C., *Ignatius von Antiochien und das Johannesevangelium*, Zürich 1949.

Mayer, G., *Index Philoneus*, Berlin/New York 1974.

Meeks, W.A., 'The Man from Heaven in Johannine Sectarianism', *Journal of Biblical Literature* 91 (1972) 44-72.

Méhat, A., 'Clemens von Alexandrien', *Theologische Realenzyklopädie* 8 (1981) 101-113.

Méliton de Sardes, *Sur la Pâque et fragments*, ed. O. Perler (SC 123), Paris 1966.

Meliton von Sardes, *Vom Passa. Die älteste christliche Osterpredigt*, ed. J. Blank, Freiburg 1963.

Melito of Sardis, *On Pascha* and Fragments, ed. S.G. Hall, Oxford 1979.

Miller, R.H., 'Liturgical Materials in the Acts of John', in E.A. Livingstone (ed.), *Studia Patristica* XIII, Berlin 1975, 375-381.

Moffatt, J., 'An approach to Ignatius', *Harvard Theological Review* 29 (1936) 1-38.

Molland, E., 'The Heretics Combatted by Ignatius of Antioch', *Journal of Ecclesiastical History* 5 (1954) 1-6, repr. in *Opuscula Patristica*, Oslo 1970, 17-23.

Moore, G.F., *Judaism in the first centuries of the Christian era* II, Cambridge MA 1927, repr. 1970.

Moraldi, L., *Apocrifi del nuovo testamento* II, Torino 1971.

Morgan, J.R., and R. Stoneman (eds.), *Greek Fiction. The Greek novel in context*, London/New York 1994.

Müller, U.B., *Die Geschichte der Christologie in der johanneischen Gemeinde* (SBS 77), Stuttgart 1975.

--, *Die Menschwerdung des Gottessohnes. Frühchristliche Inkarnationsvorstellungen und die Anfänge des Doketismus* (SBS 140), Stuttgart 1990.

Mussies, G., 'Pagans, Jews, and Christians at Ephesus', in P.W. van der Horst and G. Mussies, *Studies on the Hellenistic Background of the New Testament*, Utrecht 1990, 177-194.

Musurillo, H., *The Acts of the Christian martyrs*, Oxford 1972.

Nagel, P., *Die Motivierung der Askese in der alten Kirche und der Ursprung des Mönchtums* (TU 95), Berlin 1966.

--, 'Die apokryphen Apostelakten des 2. und 3. Jahrhunderts in der manichäischen Literatur', in K.W. Tröger (ed.), *Gnosis und Neues Testament*, Gütersloh 1973, 149-182.

Nautin, P. (ed.), *Homélies pascales I. Une homélie inspirée du traité sur la Paque d'Hippolyte* (SC 27), Paris 1950 [= anonymi, *In Pascha*].

Niederwimmer, K., *Askese und Mysterium. Über Ehe, Ehescheidung und Eheverzicht in den Anfängen des christlichen Glaubens* (FRLANT 113), Göttingen 1975.

Nock, A.D., and A.-J. Festugière, *Corpus Hermeticum* II, Paris 1960.
Norden, E., *Agnostos theos. Untersuchungen zur Formengeschichte religiöser Rede*, Leipzig/Berlin 1913.
Ohlig, K.-H., *Fundamentalchristologie: im Spannungsfeld von Christentum und Kultur*, München 1986.
Painter, J., 'The 'Opponents' in 1 John', *New Testament Studies* 32 (1986) 48-71.
--, *The Quest for the Messiah. The History, Literature and Theology of the Johannine Community*, Edinburgh 1991.
Palmer, D.W., 'Acts and the Historical Monograph', *TynB* 43 (1992) 373-388.
--, 'Acts and the Ancient Historical Monograph', in B.W. Winter and A.D. Clarke (eds.), *The Book of Acts in Its Ancient Literary Setting*, Grand Rapids/Carlisle 1993, 1-29.
Patte, D., *Early Jewish Hermeneutic in Palestine* (SBL Dissertation Series 22), Missoula Mo 1975.
Paulien, J., *Allusions, Exegetical Method, and the Interpretation of Revelation 8:7-12*, Dissertation Andrews University 1987.
Pearson, B.A., *Gnosticism, Judaism, and Egyptian Christianity* (Studies in Antiquity and Christianity 5), Minneapolis 1990.
Perkins, J.B., 'The *Acts of Peter* as Intertext: Response to Dennis MacDonald', in E.H. Lovering (ed.), *Society of Biblical Literature 1993 Seminar Papers*, Atlanta 1993, 627-633.
--, 'The Social World of the *Acts of Peter*', in J. Tatum (ed.), *The Search for the Ancient Novel*, Baltimore/London 1994, 296-307.
Perkins, P., *The Gnostic Dialogue. The Early Church and the Crisis of Gnosticism*, New York 1980.
Pervo, R.I., *Profit with Delight. The Literary Genre of the Acts of the Apostles*, Philadelphia 1987.
--, 'Johannine Trajectories in the *Acts of John*', *Apocrypha - le champ des Apocryphes* 3 (1992) 47-68.
--, 'Early Christian Fiction', in Morgan and Stoneman, *Greek Fiction*, 239-254.
--, 'The ancient novel becomes Christian', in Schmeling, *Novel*, 685-711.
Pervo, R.I., and M.C. Parsons, *Rethinking the Unity of Luke and Acts*, Minneapolis 1993.
Petersen, W.L., *Tatian's Diatessaron. Its creation, dissemination, significance, and history in scholarship* (Sup VigChr 25), Leiden 1994.
Peterson, E., *Frühkirche, Judentum und Gnosis. Studien und Untersuchungen*, Rom/Freiburg/Wien 1959.
Pétrement, S., *Le Dieu séparé. Les origines du gnosticisme*, Paris 1984; ET *A Separate God*, London 1991.

Plümacher, E., 'Apokryphe Apostelakten', in *Paulys Realencyclopädie der classischen Altertumswissenschaft*, Supplementband XV, 1978, 11-70.
--, 'Die Apostelgeschichte als historische Monographie', in J. Kremer (ed.), *Les Actes des Apôtres. Traditions, rédaction, théologie* (BETL 48), Gembloux/Leuven 1979, 457-466.
--, 'Paignion und Biberfabel', *Apocrypha - le champ des Apocryphes* 3 (1992) 69-109.
--, 'Apostolische Missionsreise und statthalterliche Assisetour', *ZNW* 85 (1994) 259-278.
Praeder, S.M., 'Luke-Acts and the Ancient Novel', in K.H. Richards (ed.), *Society of Biblical Literature 1981 Seminar Papers*, Chico Ca. 1981, 269-292.
--, 'The Problem of First Person Narration in Acts', *Novum Testamentum* 29 (1987) 193-218.
Prieur, J.-M., *Acta Andreae* (CCSA 5-6), Turnhout 1989.
Pulver, M., 'Jesu Reigen und Kreuzigung nach den Johannes-Akten', *Eranos-Jahrbuch* 9 (1942) 141-177.
Quispel, G., 'Judaism, Judaic Christianity and Gnosis', in A.H.B. Logan and A.J.M. Wedderburn (eds.), *The New Testament and Gnosis. FS Wilson*, Edinburgh 1983, 46-68.
--, Review of J.Holzhausen, *Der 'Mythos vom Menschen*, *VigChr* 48 (1994) 300-307.
--, 'The original doctrine of Valentinus the Gnostic', *VigChr* 50 (1996) 327-352.
Racle, G., 'A propos du Christ-Père dans l'*Homélie pascale* de Méliton de Sardes', *Recherches de science religieuse* 50 (1962) 400-408.
Reardon, B.P. (ed.), *Collected ancient Greek novels*, Berkeley/Los Angeles/London 1989.
Richter, G., 'Blut und Wasser aus der durchbohrten Seite Jesu (Joh 19,34b)', *Münchener Theologische Zeitschrift* 21 (1970) 1-21.
Riessler, P., *Altjüdisches Schrifttum ausserhalb der Bibel*, Augsburg 1928.
Robert, L. (ed.), *Le martyre de Pionios prêtre de Smyrne*, Washington D.C. 1994.
Robinson, J.A.T., *The Priority of John*, ed. J.F. Coakley, London 1985.
Robinson, J.M., see H.Köster.
-- (ed.), *The Nag Hammadi Library in English*, Leiden/San Francisco [3]1988.
Röhl, W.G., *Die Rezeption des Johannesevangeliums in christlich-gnostischen Schriften aus Nag Hammadi* (Europäische Hochschulschriften XXIII/428), Frankfurt usw. 1991.
Rogers, G.M., *The Sacred Identity of Ephesos. Foundation Myths of a Roman City*, London/New York 1991.

Roldanus, J., 'Tweeërlei burgerschap van de christen', *Kerk en Theologie* 36 (1985) 265-283.
--, 'Die Eucharistie in den Johannesakten', in Bremmer, *Acts of John*, 72-96.
Rose, E., *Die manichäische Christologie*, Wiesbaden 1979.
Runia, D.T., *Philo of Alexandria and the* Timaeus *of Plato*, Leiden 1986.
Rutherford, I., 'Kalasaris and Setne Khamwas: A Greek Novel and some Egyptian Models', *ZPE* 117 (1997) 203-209.
Sagnard, F.-M.-M., *La gnose valentinienne et le témoignage de Saint Irénée*, Paris 1947.
Sandy, G.N., 'Book 11: Ballast or anchor?', in B.L. Hijmans Jr and R.Th. van der Paardt (eds.), *Aspects of Apuleius' Golden Ass*, Groningen 1978, 123-140.
Santos Otero, A. de, 'Der Apokryphe Titusbrief', *Zeitschrift für Kirchengeschichte* 74 (1963) 1-14.
Sbordone, F. (ed.), *Physiologus*, Roma 1936, repr. Hildesheim/ New York 1976.
Scarpat, G., *Libro della Sapienza I*, Brescia 1989.
Schäferdiek, K., 'Johannesakten', in W. Schneemelcher (ed.), *Neutestamentliche Apokryphen* II, Tübingen [3]1964, 125-176.
--, 'Herkunft und Interesse der alten Johannesakten', *ZNW* 74 (1983) 247-267.
--, 'Die "Passio Iohannis" des Melito von Laodikeia und die "Virtutes Iohannis"', *Analecta Bollandiana* 103 (1985) 367-382.
--, 'Die Leukios Charinos zugeschriebene manichäische Sammlung apokrypher Apostelgeschichten', and 'Johannesakten', in W. Schneemelcher (ed.), *Neutestamentliche Apokryphen* II, Tübingen [5]1989, 81-93, 138-190.
--, 'Johannes, Apostel u. Evangelist, 7. Apokryphe Schriften', *Lexikon für Theologie und Kirche*[3] 5 (1996) 869-870.
--, 'Johannes-Akten', *Realencyclopädie für Antike und Christentum* Lief. 139-140 (1997) 564-595.
Schelkle, K.H., *Die Petrusbriefe - der Judasbrief* (Herders Theologischer Kommentar), Freiburg [2]1964.
Schenke, H.-M., *Der Gott 'Mensch' in der Gnosis. Ein religionsgeschichtlicher Beitrag zur Diskussion über die paulinische Anschauung von der Kirche als Leib Christi*, Göttingen 1962.
Schimmelpfeng, G., 'Johannesakten', in E. Hennecke (ed.), *Handbuch zu den Neutestamentlichen Apokryphen*, Tübingen 1904, 492-543.
Schlier, H., *Religionsgeschichtliche Untersuchungen zu den Ignatiusbriefen* (BZNW 8), Giessen 1929.
Schmaltz, K., 'Die drei "mystischen" Christushöhlen der Geburt, der Jüngerweihe und des Grabes', *Zeitschrift des Deutschen Palästina-*

*Vereins* 42 (1919) 132-165.

Schmeling, G. (ed.), *The novel in the ancient world*, Leiden/New York/Köln 1996.

Schmidt, C., *Die alten Petrusakten im Zusammenhang der apokryphen Apostellitteratur untersucht. Nebst einem neuentdeckten Fragment* (TU 24), Leipzig 1903.

--, *Acta Pauli aus der heidelberger koptischen Papyrushandschrift Nr.1*, vol.1 Leipzig 1904, 2nd ed. 1905, repr. Hildesheim 1965; vol.2 (plates) Leipzig 1904, repr. Hildesheim 1965.

--, *Gespräche Jesu mit seinen Jüngern nach der Auferstehung* (TU 43), Leipzig 1919 (= Text with commentary of *Epistula Apostolorum*).

Schneemelcher, W., 'Apostelgeschichten des 2. und 3. Jahrhunderts. Einleitung', in *idem* (ed.), *Neutestamentliche Apokryphen* II, Tübingen [5]1989, 71-81 [abbr.: *NA*[5]].

--, and J.-M. Prieur, 'Andreasakten. Einleitung', in *NA*[5], 93-108.

Schneider, P.G., *The Mystery of the Acts of John. An Interpretation of the Hymn and the Dance in the Light of the Acts' Theology* (Distinguished Dissertations Series 10), San Francisco 1991.

--, '"A Perfect Fit": The Major Interpolation in the Acts of John', in E.H. Lovering (ed.), *Society of Biblical Literature 1991 Seminar Papers*, Atlanta 1991, 518-532.

--, 'The *Acts of John*: The Gnostic Transformation of a Christian Community', in W.E. Helleman (ed.), *Hellenization Revisited: Shaping a Christian Response within the Greco-Roman World*, Lanham MD 1994, 241-269.

Schnelle, U., *Antidoketische Christologie im Johannesevangelium* (FRLANT 144), Göttingen 1987.

Scholes, R., and R. Kellogg, *The Nature of Narrative*, New York 1966.

Schweizer, E., 'Das johanneische Zeugnis vom Herrenmahl', *Evangelische Theologie* 8 (1952-53) 341-363, repr. in his *Neotestamentica*, Zürich/Stuttgart 1963.

Scott, A.B., 'Churches or Books? Sethian Social Organization', *JECS* 3 (1995) 109-122.

Sheeley, S.M., *Narrative Asides in Luke-Acts* (JSNT Sup 72), Sheffield 1992.

Siegert, F., 'Analyses rhétoriques et stylistiques portant sur les *Actes de Jean* et les *Actes de Thomas*', *Apocrypha* 8 (1997) 231-250.

Sirker-Wicklaus, G., *Untersuchungen zu den Johannes-Akten. Untersuchungen zur Struktur, zur theologischen Tendenz und zum kirchengeschichtlichen Hintergrund der Acta Johannis* (Dissertation Bonn), Witterschlick/Bonn 1988.

Skarsaune, O., *The Proof from Prophecy* (SupNT 56), Leiden 1987.

Slusser, M., 'Docetism: A Historical Definition', *The Second Century* 1 (1981) 163-172.

Söder, R., *Die apokryphen Apostelgeschichten und die romanhafte Literatur der Antike* (Dissertation Würzburg 1929), Stuttgart 1932.

Soemers OSB, P., *Athanasius, die Vita Antonii und die Bibel* (2 vols.), Vaals/Frankfurt am Main 1989.

Speyer, W., 'Religiöse Pseudepigraphie und literarische Fälschung im Altertum', *Jahrbuch für Antike und Christentum* 8/9 (1965/66) 88-125, repr. in N. Brox (ed.), *Pseudepigraphie in der heidnischen und jüdisch-christlichen Antike*, Darmstadt 1977, 195-263.

Stephens, S.A., and J.J. Winkler, *Ancient Greek Novels. The Fragments*, Princeton N.J. 1995.

Sterling, G.E., *Historiography and Self-definition. Josephos, Luke-Acts and Apologetic Historiography*, Leiden 1992.

Stibbe, M.W.G., 'The Elusive Christ. A New Reading of the Fourth Gospel', *Journal for the Study of the New Testament* 44 (1991) 19-37, repr. in *idem*, *John's Gospel* (New Testament Readings), London 1994.

Stillman, M.K., 'The Gospel of Peter. A case for oral-only dependence?', *Ephemerides Theologicae Lovanienses* 73 (1997) 114-120.

Stroumsa, G.G., 'Ascèse et gnose: aux origines de la spiritualité monastique', *Revue Thomiste* 81 (1981) 557-576, repr. in *idem*, *Savoir et salut*, Paris 1992, 145-162.

Sturhahn, C.L., *Die Christologie der ältesten apokryphen Apostelakten. Ein Beitrag zur Frühgeschichte des altkirchlichen Dogmas*, typescript Dissertation Göttingen 1952.

Sumney, J.L., 'Those who "Ignorantly Deny Him": The Opponents of Ignatius of Antioch', *JECS* 1 (1993) 345-365.

Swain, S., 'Dio and Lucian', in Morgan and Stoneman, *Greek Fiction*, 166-180.

Tatian, *Oratio ad Graecos and fragments*, ed. and trans. M. Whittaker, Oxford 1982.

Tatum, J. (ed.), *The Search for the Ancient Novel*, Baltimore/ London 1994.

[Theodotos] *Clément d'Alexandrie, Extraits de Théodote*, ed. and trans. F. Sagnard (SC 23), Paris 1970.

Thompson, M.M., *The Humanity of Jesus in the Fourth Gospel*, Philadelphia 1988.

Thornton, C.-J., *Der Zeuge des Zeugen. Lukas als Historiker der Paulusreisen* (WUNT 56), Tübingen 1991.

Tilborg, S. van, *Reading John in Ephesus* (SupNT 83), Leiden 1996.

Tissot, Y., 'Encratisme et Actes apocryphes', in Bovon, *Actes apocryphes*, 109-119.

Trebilco, P.R., *Jewish Communities in Asia Minor* (SNTS MS 69),

Cambridge 1991.

Trevett, C., 'Prophecy and Anti-Episcopal Activity: A Third Error Combatted by Ignatius', *Journal of Ecclesiastical History* 34 (1983) 1-18.

--, *A study of Ignatius of Antioch in Syria and Asia*, Lewiston NY 1992.

Tröger, K.W., *Mysterienglaube und Gnosis in Corpus Hermeticum XIII* (TU 110), Berlin 1971.

--, 'Doketistische Christologie in Nag-Hammadi-Texten', *Kairos, neue Folge* 19 (1977) 45-52.

Unnik, W.C. van, 'Johannesakten', *Die Religion in Geschichte und Gegenwart* ³III, Tübingen 1959, Sp.821-822.

--, 'A Note on the Dance of Jesus in the "Acts of John"', *VigChr* 18 (1964) 1-5, repr. in *Sparsa Collecta. The Collected Essays of W.C. van Unnik* III (SupNT 31), Leiden 1983, 144-147.

--, 'Luke's Second Book and the Rules of Hellenistic Historiography', in J. Kremer (ed.), *Les Actes des Apôtres. Traditions, rédaction, théologie* (BETL 48), Gembloux/Leuven 1979, 37-60.

--, 'Les idées des gnostiques concernant l'église', in his *Sparsa Collecta* III, 285-296.

Uytfanghe, M. Van, 'Encratisme en verborgen erotiek in de apocriefe 'apostelromans'. Omtrent de christelijke problematisering van de sexualiteit', *Handelingen van de Koninklijke Zuidnederlandse Maatschappij voor Taal- en Letterkunde en Geschiedenis* 45 (1991) 175-194.

Vaganay, L., *l'Évangile de Pierre*, Paris 1930.

Vetters, H., D. Knibbe *et al.*, *Die Inschriften von Ephesos* I-VIII (Die Inschriften der griechischen Städten Kleinasiens 11-17), Bonn 1979-1984.

Vielhauer, Ph., *Geschichte der urchristlichen Literatur. Einleitung in das Neue Testament, die Apokryphen und die Apostolischen Väter*, Berlin/New York 1975.

Voorgang, D., *Die Passion Jesu und Christi in der Gnosis* (Europäische Hochschulschriften XXIII/432), Frankfurt 1991.

Vorster, W.S., 'Heterodoxy in I John', *Neotestamentica* 9 (1975) 87-97.

Wehnert, J., *Die Wir-Passagen der Apostelgeschichte: ein lukanisches Stilmittel aus jüdischer Tradition* (Göttinger Theologische Arbeiten 40), Göttingen 1989.

Weidmann, F.W., *The Martyrdom of Polycarp, Bishop of Smyrna in early Christian literature: A Re-evaluation in light of previously unpublished Coptic fragments*, Dissertation Yale University 1993.

--, 'Intertextuality and Intent: John and the Apostolic Mission in the Harris Fragment on Polycarp', in E.H. Lovering (ed.), *Society of Biblical Literature 1995 Seminar Papers*, Atlanta 1995, 394-398.

Weigandt, P., *Der Doketismus im Urchristentum und in der theologischen Entwicklung des zweiten Jahrhunderts*, typescript Dissertation Heidelberg 1961.

Wengst, K., *Häresie und Orthodoxie im Spiegel des ersten Johannesbriefes*, Gütersloh 1976.

Wenham, D., 'Whatever Went Wrong in Corinth?', *Expository Times* 108 (1996-'97) 137-141.

Wesseling, B., *Leven, liefde en dood: Zelfmoord, vermeende dood, huwelijk en dood: motieven in antieke romans*, Dissertation Groningen 1993.

Wikenhauser, A., 'Doppelträume', *Biblica* 29 (1948) 100-111.

Wiles, M.F., *The Spiritual Gospel. The Interpretation of the Fourth Gospel in the Early Church*, Cambridge 1960.

Williams, J.A., *Biblical Interpretation in the Gnostic Gospel of Truth from Nag Hammadi* (SBL Dissertation Series 79), Atlanta 1988.

Wilson, R.McL., *The Gospel of Philip*, New York/Evanston 1962.

Wisse, F., 'Stalking those elusive Sethians' (563-576) and 'Discussion' (578-587), in B. Layton (ed.), *The Rediscovery of Gnosticism* II, Leiden 1981.

Witherington III, B., 'The waters of birth: John 3.5 and 1 John 5.6-8', *New Testament Studies* (1989) 155-160.

Yamauchi, E.M., *Pre-Christian Gnosticism. A Survey of the Proposed Evidences*, Grand Rapids 1973.

--, 'The Crucifixion and Docetic Christology', *Concordia Theological Quarterly* 46 (1982) 1-20.

--, 'Pre-Christian Gnosticism, the New Testament and Nag Hammadi in recent debate', *Themelios* 10 (1984) 22-27.

--, 'Gnosticism and Early Christianity', in W.E. Helleman (ed.), *Hellenization Revisited: Shaping a Christian Response within the Greco-Roman World*, Lanham MD 1994, 29-61 (with a Response by M. Desjardins, 63-67).

--, 'The Issue of Pre-Christian Gnosticism Reviewed in the Light of the Nag Hammadi Texts', in J.D. Turner and A. McGuire (eds.), *The Nag Hammadi Library after fifty years* (NHMS 44), Leiden 1997, 72-88.

Zahn, Th., *Acta Joannis unter Benutzung von C.v.Tischendorf's Nachlass bearbeitet*, Erlangen 1880, repr. Hildesheim 1975.

--, *Geschichte des Neutestamentlichen Kanons* I, Erlangen 1888; II, Erlangen/Leipzig 1890-1892.

--, *Das Evangelium des Petrus*, Erlangen/Leipzig 1893.

--, 'Die Wanderungen des Apostels Johannes', *Neue Kirchliche Zeitschrift* 10 (1899) 191-218.

--, *Apostel und Apostelschüler in der Provinz Asien* (Forschungen zur Geschichte des neutestamentlichen Kanons und der altkirchlichen Literatur, VI.i), Leipzig 1900.

# INDICES

Numbers in bold type indicate the main discussions

## 1 *Acts of John* and related texts

2 *Bible*

## 3 Names and subjects